twentieth-century theologians

One needs to be a lunatic to become a Christian, the nineteenth century Danish philosopher Søren Kierkegaard once observed. Had he lived in the twentieth century he might have discerned even more of an obstacle to faith. For during the last century the human condition changed more rapidly than during any previous era, taking that condition far away from the historical circumstances in which Christianity was born. In his new book Philip Kennedy explores the ways Christian theologians of the twentieth century tried to live a productive religious life in a world overtaken by massive upheaval and innovation. There is a need for a sensitive new textbook that reassesses modern theologians in the light of contemporary concerns and scepticism about religion. This book meets that requirement. It will have strong appeal to undergraduate students seeking a clearly written, objective and non-partisan survey of the whole field; to agnostics interested in the impact that major theological ideas have made on culture and society during the last century; and to general readers, whatever their views on faith and belief, interested in the 'great minds' who have given shape to some of the most profound and far-reaching thinking of our times.

PHILIP KENNEDY teaches theology in the University of Oxford, where he is a Senior Research Fellow at Mansfield College. He is the author of two volumes on Edward Schillebeeckx (1993), and of *A Modern Introduction to Theology: New Questions for Old Beliefs* (2006) and *Christianity: An Introduction* (forthcoming, 2011), both published by I.B. Tauris.

'This stunning book will prove an invaluable resource for professional theologians, students and general readers interested in the makers of twentieth-century theology. The author's in-depth treatment of a range of historical contexts, and his penetrating analysis of key figures ranging from Adolf von Harnack to the writings of indigenous Rainbow Spirit Elders, are simply breathtaking. Kennedy's many insights into the contributions of people as diverse and different as Karl Rahner and Mercy Amba Oduyoye are rooted in a sweeping panorama of twentieth-century theologians that will enlighten, inform and delight.' – *Maryanne Confoy, President, United Faculty of Theology, Melbourne, and Visiting Professor of Pastoral Theology, Boston College*

'Philip Kennedy writes with the impressive authority that comes with years of engagement as a Christian theologian and also with the clarity of an experienced teacher of undergraduates. There are several texts available which cover twentieth-century theology, but what is unique and arresting about Kennedy's highly readable book is that the exponents of modern theology whom he discusses are placed firmly and illuminatingly in the context of the turbulent history of the last century. This is a novel, satisfyingly multi-layered and exciting take on the whole story, and it is one that should prove highly attractive to students and general readers alike.' – *Fergus Kerr, OP, Honorary Fellow, School of Divinity, University of Edinburgh, and author of* Twentieth-Century Catholic Theologians: From Neoscholasticism to Nuptial Mysticism

'This is a great book. It provides a wonderfully clear introduction to some 21 Christian theologians, from a wide variety of backgrounds, explaining their ideas but also their lives: the setting in which their thought developed. More importantly, it sets their theologies against the history of the twentieth century: a time of untold riches and grinding poverty, of technological marvels and terrible violence. For Philip Kennedy the measure of theology is the extent to which it challenges injustice. This is also the challenge that his book poses to its readers: what is the point of theology if it doesn't want to change the world?' – *Gerard Loughlin, Professor of Theology and Religion, Durham University*

'*Twentieth-Century Theologians* is a tremendous achievement - colossal in stature, subtle in intellectual grasp and enviable in its scope. The volume packs a number of important surprises (not least the contribution made to twentieth-century theology by women like Evelyn Underhill and Dorothy Day), and does so with a pedagogical sensitivity and a linguistic lucidity that we all have to admire. It also negotiates the difficult task of covering the field without prejudice, drawing on the best and the most influential thinking from all denominational traditions. Philip Kennedy has pulled something off here that is as original as it is fresh, exciting and unpredictable: a first-rate textbook for students and for university teachers alike.' – *Graham Ward, Professor of Contextual Theology and Head of the School of Arts, Histories and Cultures, University of Manchester*

twentieth-century theologians

a new introduction to modern christian thought

PHILIP KENNEDY

I.B. TAURIS

LONDON · NEW YORK

Published in 2010 by I.B.Tauris & Co Ltd
6 Salem Road, London W2 4BU
175 Fifth Avenue, New York NY 10010
www.ibtauris.com

Distributed in the United States and Canada exclusively by Palgrave Macmillan,
175 Fifth Avenue, New York NY 10010

ISBN: 978 1 84511 955 3 (HB)
ISBN: 978 1 84511 956 0 (PB)

A full CIP record for this book is available from the British Library
A full CIP record is available from the Library of Congress

Library of Congress Catalog Card Number: available

Designed and Typeset by 4word Ltd, Bristol, UK
Printed and bound in India by Thomson Press India Ltd

table of contents

preamble

Now that the twentieth century has ended, the task of interpreting it can begin. This book depicts it with an eye to some of its theologians.

A theologian is someone who tries to talk about God – always without success. Deities, if such there be, are not perceptible in human experience. That is why they elude conceptual description. Whether there is one God or several Gods cannot be ascertained with certainty by human intelligence. It is not even clear to what or to whom the noun 'God' refers, or whether it designates a reality in or beyond the world. Because God is not a locatable, quantifiable thing in the world, there is no observable homology between God and humankind. That did not prevent theologians throughout the twentieth century from discussing God at length in multiple publications. Many of them posited that there is only one God who has revealed Godself to human beings. They *postulated* that God has been manifested to people, but were unable *to demonstrate* as much rationally. Most of them presumed to know that there are three persons in God, on the basis of an assumption that this is the way God has been revealed to people.

The term 'theologian' is broadly and inclusively understood in these pages. A theologian is anyone who communicates about God in the medium of human language. Since music, movement, cinema, poetry and verbal discourse are all forms of linguistic communication, a poet or musician has the potential, together with actors, farmers and professorial academics, to convey ideas about God. An atheist or agnostic may also be an adroit theologian. Some atheists of the past, like Ludwig Feuerbach (1804–72), were driven to explore the concept of God, and they did so in highly intelligent ways.

Theology is the product of human processes of reason, living-in-the-world, imagination, reading, ruminating, writing and speaking. It is always a stammering because the object of its discourse, God, is ungraspable, atemporal, indecipherable and extraphenomenal. In the words of the Bible, 'No one has ever seen God' (1 Jn 4: 12a). The struggle which theologians encounter when attempting tentatively to discourse about God is evident in the language many of them employ. The terms of their language referring to God frequently denote more of themselves than of God, when God is designated as 'He', 'Him', 'Father' and 'Lord', who wills, loves, commands and punishes.

This book does not debate whether or not there is a God. Instead, it draws attention to the ways an array of decidedly disparate theologians in utterly dissimilar historical contexts of the twentieth century attempted to elaborate who or what God might be. The variety of twentieth-century approaches to discussing God is astoundingly multiplex.

At various points, the following text is interspersed with bordered areas that either explain theological and philosophical terms frequently used by theologians, or provide historical information that is relevant to theologians being discussed.

> **godself**   The word 'Godself' is a neologism in English, and an awkward one at that. An advantage of using it in referring to God, rather than 'himself', 'herself' or 'itself', is that it does not connote or denote human gender in God. It acts as a linguistic signal to remind people that God is not any kind of thing they could possibly depict with words.

The opening chapter of the book describes some of the more starkly prominent features of the twentieth century. It concludes that despite manifold and marvellous human achievements throughout the century, the period was nonetheless a wilderness. It was a baneful wasteland overly devoid of compassion, love, generosity and justice. By the end of the twentieth century the human population had reached about 6 billion, or 6,000 million individuals. It had more than doubled since 1950 alone.[1] Never before had it been so enormous. Nor had it been so technologically skilled and scientifically accomplished. At the same time, never previously were such vast populations of human beings daily deprived of food, water, sanitation, education, medicine, shelter, and access to aid and information. In 1997, about 1.5 billion people were not expected to reach the age of 60; 840 million people suffered from malnutrition; 880 million had no access to health services; 850 million were illiterate; 1.3 billion lived on less than US$1 a day; 340 million women were not expected to survive until the age of 40; and 2.6 billion people were without access to basic sanitation.[2] The world in 1997 did not look manifestly saved, despite 2,000 years of Christian declarations that God had graciously redeemed it through the crucifixion of Jesus Christ.

Whatever else it may have been, the twentieth century was clearly a barren terrain of corpses, often civilian bodies, killed by armies and precision-guided bombs in a ceaseless series of blood-letting struggles. There was more military conflict during the twentieth century than in any earlier era. Attempts to bleach meaning, point and purpose out of such large-scale destruction for people of the twentieth century often fell to philosophers and theologians, with little if any demonstrable success.

The thread tying the different chapters of this book together is not a survey of theologians' philosophical backgrounds, educational achievements or denominational allegiances. The glue binding the pages is an attention to poverty, violence and warfare, the misery these inflicted on hundreds of millions of unsung faces in the twentieth century, and the ways theologians spoke about God in an age of unrelieved human suffering.

The book is written for any interested inquirer. It does not assume that its readers are religiously committed, in a Christian or any other guise. The theologians it deals with come from the five continents of the globe. They all worked from a Christian tradition, although not exclusively so, and some renounced the religious allegiances of their youth. Many of the human and intellectual struggles of these theologians are shared by devotees of all religions.

The text is structured in a simple chronological way. After an introductory chapter, it focuses on theologians working at the beginning of the twentieth century, and then progresses to discussing theologians working in the successive decades of the century.

It is arguable that to read the entire Bible is to chart a gradual historical awareness on the part of its writers that God is not violent, and indeed abhors human aggression.[3] Similarly, studying theologians of the twentieth century, it soon becomes apparent that by the latter half of that era, more and more Christian theologians realized that human poverty and deprivation, often consequences of greed and war, ought to be of uppermost concern for them. This is so for two reasons. First, modern historical studies have confirmed that Jesus Christ was not a champion of empires and wealth. And second, contemporary biblical studies illuminate a progressive development detectable in the Bible from traditions that revel in divine violence, to those that abjure it.

The Bible is a hotchpotch of inconsistent ideas. The Book of Exodus declares: 'The LORD is a warrior; the LORD is his name. Pharaoh's chariots and his army he cast into the sea; his picked officers were sunk in the Red Sea' (Ex 15: 3–4). A very different and less belligerent note is sounded later in the Bible, when God is quoted in the Book of Hosea: 'I will break bow and sword and weapon of war and sweep them off the earth, so that all living creatures may lie down without fear' (Hos 2: 18). It could plausibly be asserted that the ancient Israelites were among the first people known to humanity gradually 'to regard a nation's reliance upon force as evil'.[4]

theology's acutest problem

When people turn to discussing theology and theologians today, a good way of discerning what they think of such matters is to pose a single question in different forms: what is theology's greatest current problem? How is it to straddle its largest hurdle? What is its most daunting dilemma? Answers would be varied, but could include at least the following 20 rejoinders:

- the steady rise of atheism since the First World War;
- the decline of membership in Christian churches;
- the unintelligibility to many people of biblical and traditional theological terminology;
- the social marginalization of theology in the West;
- secularization;
- the de-Christianization of Europe;
- competition from sport and the pursuit of pleasure and leisure;
- the lure of consumer capitalism;
- a perceived incompatibility of traditional doctrines with contemporary sciences, coupled with new forms of demonstrated knowledge that discredit traditional religious world-views;
- the corrosive activity, real or illusory, of dissenting theologians in academies and ecclesiastical communities;
- the exclusion of women from theological discussion and leadership;
- a loss of trust in the Bible's truthfulness and attempts to revive it;
- the alleged indifference of young people to theological pursuits;
- the failure of Christian leaders boldly to entertain new ideas;
- rivalry with Islam;
- increased familiarity with the world's religions and the concomitant undermining of Christianity's conventional claims to unrivalled superiority;
- the modern or postmodern blossoming of radical intellectual scepticism;

- the twentieth-century revolution in attitudes towards sexuality;
- the contemporary sullying of the world's ecosphere; and
- a long-standing inability of modern and contemporary Christians to recognize that Jesus was a Jew, and that their churches are Gentile offshoots of ancient Judaism.

This book responds differently. Its working hypothesis is that theology's most intractable current problem, as it was throughout the twentieth century, is suffering – the misery and degradation wrought by violence, warfare, greed, poverty, disease, starvation and indifference. This may sound overly gloomy, but unless theologians address this many-sided problem, they will never convince their addressees that the God of whom they speak as benevolent, liberating or redemptive is worthy of anyone's belief and devotion.

Of the 22 known human species, *homo sapiens* is the only one to have survived into the twenty-first century.[5] How could theologians possibly know whether it will continue into a blissful, divinely designed future? Over 99 per cent of all animal species that have ever lived have become extinct.[6] That *homo sapiens* will outlive the suffering currently cultivated through bombs and ecological destruction cannot be taken for granted.

To speak of suffering as theology's severest conundrum is not to forget other impasses faced by the discipline. Each of the dilemmas listed above merits sustained and sober reflection.

Subsequent chapters scrutinize theologians and the fashions in which they grappled with the hitherto unseen human, intellectual and religious bafflements that the twentieth century hurled at them. The chapters are selective in the people they discuss, and cannot pretend to be comprehensive. No Eastern Orthodox theologians, for instance, have been discussed, but that does not imply that such theologians are not worthy of attention. Because the book is selective, it has many lamentable omissions. The danger in chatting about theologians is to mention this or that book written by them. I have tried in these pages to mix a cursory sampling of publications by theologians, with the much more revealing exercise of trying to convey the type of person who wrote in such a way, and for what reasons.

Now for a word on practicalities. The quotations from the Bible in this book all follow the translation of the New Revised Standard Version.[7] The endnotes can safely be ignored. Many of them refer to books in French, German, Dutch or Spanish. They are only included for readers who might wish to scrutinize a few of the bases for observations I make, or sources of quotations. A Glossary at the end of the book explains my understanding of the major ecclesiastical and theological terms I use.

I arrived to live in Oxford during December 1994. The following year I began lecturing on 'Twentieth-Century Protestant Theologians'. In 1996 I found myself teaching in the Chandler School of Theology in Emory University of Atlanta, Georgia. The university was Methodist in its original foundation, but no one there seemed to want me to talk about Protestants. My brief was to lecture on 'Twentieth-Century Catholic Theologians'. And so I did.

While living and teaching in Oxford, I have often had occasion to experiment with students during lectures ideas vaunted in this book. I ought also to acknowledge at this stage that frequently, but I hope unwittingly, I steal ideas from friends and colleagues far more insightful than I. All of which is to say that in penning these pages, I have benefited beyond calculation from conversations with, and the unfailing kindness of, Diarmaid MacCulloch, Yvan Mudry, Jennifer Cooper, Bernard Green, Peter Groves, Didier Croonenberghs, Beatrice Groves, Judith Maltby, Craig Leaper, Lucy Clark, Guy Tourlamain, Howard Clark, Richard Saynor, Barnaby Tolhurst, Samuel Hodder, Ben and Whitney Stone, Fiona Nickalls, Robert Wilson, Oliver Nickalls, Lynn Partridge, Prince Saprai, Tom Nickalls, David Earl, John Muddiman, Margaret Kennedy King, Tony Lemon, and Alex Wright of the Publishers I.B.Tauris. The last-mentioned is an editor and expert in theology whose patience and skills are unmatched. I am unable to thank him enough for his forbearance. My family, as ever, has been unfailingly supportive.

I dedicate this book to Stephen, my father.

Philip Kennedy
Oxford

list of abbreviations

AIDS	The Acquired Immune Deficiency Syndrome
b.	born
BBC	British Broadcasting Corporation
BCE	Before the Common Era (an alternative to BC, 'Before Christ')
BECs	Basic Ecclesial Communities
c.	around (*circa*)
CDF	Congregation for the Doctrine of the Faith
CE	The Common Era (an alternative to AD, 'In the year of the Lord')
2 Cor	2 Corinthians (The Second Letter of Paul to the Corinthians)
d.	died
Deut	Deuteronomy
DNA	deoxyribonucleic acid
ed.	editor/edited by
edn	edition
eds	editors
esp.	especially
Ex	Exodus
Gal	Galatians
Gen	Genesis
HIV	The Human Immunodeficiency Virus
HMS	His or Her Majesty's Ship
Hos	Hosea

Isa	Isaiah
Jer	Jeremiah
Jn	John (The Gospel According to John)
1 Jn	1 John (The First Letter of John)
Lk	Luke (The Gospel According to Luke)
Mk	Mark (The Gospel According to Mark)
Mt	Matthew (The Gospel According to Matthew)
Phil	Philippians (The Letter of Paul to the Philippians)
Ps	Psalms
RAF	Royal Air Force
Rev	Revelation
Rom	Romans (The Letter of Paul to the Romans)
1 Sam	1 Samuel
SCM	Student Christian Movement
Sir	Sirach (Ecclesiasticus, or the Wisdom of Jesus, Son of Sirach)
ST	Systematic Theology
1 Tim	1 Timothy (The First Letter of Paul to Timothy)
trans.	translated by
US/USA	United States/United Sates of America
USS	United States Ship
USSR	Union of Soviet Socialist Republics
vol.	volume
Zeph	Zephaniah

list of boxed information

The following topics are explained in this book in texts printed with a border around them – hence 'boxed information' – and interspersed throughout the general narrative of the book.

I

the twentieth century

The poor are disliked even by their neighbours,
but the rich have many friends.

Proverbs 14: 20

This book probes a panoply of twentieth-century theologians. It introduces their lives and work in the historical circumstances that generated them. What theologians say is always tinctured by their personal histories. The more that is known about their lives and dilemmas, the more light is shed on why they speak in the modes they do.

Some of the theologians are still productive. All of them drew attention to their ideas during the last century. Several achieved international recognition in universities or churches. Most were entirely unknown and unread by the majority of their contemporaries.

They were also exceptionally diverse. No two were neatly alike in terms of theological style and preoccupation. They never entirely agreed with each other about how best to talk about God. One of the more prominent features of theology over the past ten decades has been the steady evolution of an almost limitless variety of theological motifs and methods. These cannot simply and dualistically be classified in pairs of polar antitheses, such as liberal versus conservative, traditional against avant-garde, fundamentalist over enlightened, feminist fighting sexist, modern before postmodern, and conventional opposed to creative.

What all the multifarious types of twentieth-century theologies share is that the theologians who voiced them jointly and often feebly faced historical, cultural, social, intellectual and religious challenges of which earlier theologians were blithely unaware. No theologian writing before 1900 knew certainly that the universe is both expanding and much more than 10 billion years old.

Another salient feature of twentieth-century theology was its gradual social eclipse. It diminished steadily as a popular pastime and professional pursuit while the 1900s unfolded, year by startling year. Its decline in popularity and viability is linked to a far-reaching reconfiguring of modern and contemporary mentalities. These mutated under multiple stimuli as the twentieth century transpired. The reconfiguration of human experiences and understanding during the last century spawned a pervasive incredulity among many people towards Christian teachings.[1]

Theology's relatively recent enfeeblement has been particularly noteworthy in the West. Other regions have not escaped the influence of the West's by-and-large increasingly theologically indifferent world-view. Apart from social indifference, theology and belief in God today are often articulately and energetically renounced. Religious beliefs have latterly been said to share 'the same intellectual respectability, evidential base, and rationality as belief in the existence of fairies',[2] while belief in God has been dismissed as delusional.[3]

Away from the West, present-day nomadic tribes of hunter-gatherers, for all their wandering and reliance on centuries of agricultural tradition and religious customs, are often not entirely deprived of access to the gadgets, baubles and fashion accessories of occidental leisure-seekers, coupled with the latter's manifest insouciance towards theology.

What follows in this chapter is a brief consideration of the distinctiveness of the historical circumstances in which twentieth-century theologians worked. The chapter ends by proposing a thesis that is the leitmotif of the book. The thesis concerns poverty, the wretched hardship it causes, the warfare that aggravates it, and the way theologians addressed or ignored poverty during the twentieth century.

the chronological parameters: what counts as the twentieth century?

The distinct phases and historical convulsions of the twentieth century can be delineated in various ways. If one considers political changes to be all-deciding, it could be argued that the novel era of the twentieth century effectively began with the outbreak of the First World War, and ended with the destruction of the

Berlin Wall. In this schema, the twentieth century elapsed between 1914 and 1989. If engineering is regarded as the deciding factor for marking periods, the twentieth century could be dated from the completion of the Trans-Siberian railway in 1903 to the opening of the Channel Tunnel between England and France in 1994. Should sport become the measure of all things, the century might be understood to encompass the years between the first modern Olympiad, held in Athens during 1886, and the Olympic Games staged in Atlanta, USA, in 1996. Were the history of musical composition to become a decisive chronological yardstick, the last century could begin with Edward Elgar's Enigma Variations of 1899, and end with György Ligeti's Concerto for Violin and Orchestra, written in 1990.

Authors commenting on the twentieth century frequently tie its beginning to the eruption of the First World War. The following is an instance of such a practice: 'By the end of the twentieth century, people in Western Europe thought of their age as born in catastrophe, when the most powerful nations of Europe stumbled unthinkingly into war in August in 1914. It is hard to conceive of any other coherent starting point for a history of the worldwide Church in the twentieth century.'[4] A view akin to this regards the war as the collapse of the nineteenth-century reign of nationalistic empires. There are those who assert that 'The era that saw much of the world dominated by the great powers of Europe, many of them still ruled by an *ancien régime* of land-owning aristocracy, did effectively come to an end with the First World War.'[5]

Regrettably, that perceived end was not an end at all! Nineteenth-century empires were often able to continue their aggressive, colonial and expansionist ways until the Second World War and beyond. While an era of European aristocratic imperialism may have petered out early in the twentieth century, empires have not. If an empire is a sphere or domain governed by a peerless and unrivalled authority, former military and colonial empires were transformed during the twentieth century into neo-colonial, neo-liberal capitalist dominions.[6] The USA has been described, by an American, as 'a great imperium with the outlook of a great emporium', a Market Empire, and 'the world's first regime of mass consumption'.[7]

The USA is currently the most militarily powerful nation in the world.[8] The size of its massive arsenal can be glimpsed simply by looking at its navy, which includes the gigantic aircraft carrier, the USS *Kitty Hawk*. This nuclear-powered and nuclear-armed ship is as tall as a 20-storey building, and about the length of three gridiron football fields. It is home to 6,000 sailors and officers, as well as 70 lethal aircraft. To protect it and enhance its destructive powers, it is accompanied by a large battlegroup of other ships – an Aegis cruiser, frigates and destroyers – submarines and supply vessels.[9] 'The United States has thirteen of these carrier battle groups. No other country has even one.'[10] The same country now uses space-based weapons systems. Its global positioning systems satellites can guide precision bombs to their targets.[11]

The European empires of the past five centuries or so, such as those of Spain, Portugal, the Netherlands, Belgium, Great Britain and Germany, have been supplanted by imperial transnational business corporations, which 'often amass greater wealth than entire nations and enjoy a great deal of freedom from the control of even the most powerful national governments. On these grounds it could be argued that empire is primarily an economic reality, tied to the growth of global capitalism.'[12] The end of the First World War was not unambiguously the finish of the era of empires.[13]

For the purposes of this book, a simple chronological periodization will suffice: the twentieth century was constituted most obviously and basically by the 1900s.

the 1900s

The twentieth century is aptly described superlatively. It was the most populous, urbanized, scientifically informed and technologically skilled epoch of human history. It was also the most homicidal and bellicose time of any human age. It was the only period known to humanity that witnessed two genocidal global wars, and the transnational deployment of nuclear, biological and chemical weapons. The destructive power of such armaments was gruesome and ghastly, and still menaces the twenty-first century. Since the end of the Second World War, there have been at least 135 other wars on smaller scales, 'most of them in the poor world (often misnamed "developing"), and these have killed more than twenty-two million people … .'[14]

The largest cities ever constructed emerged during the past hundred years. They were populated by many millions of mobile citizens, some living in plush solar-powered penthouses; others in putrid rat-infested slums.

The growth of the human population during the twentieth century was rapid and unrelenting. The population increased from 1.6 billion in 1900 to 6 billion in 1999.[15] The enlarged population spawned a host of debilitating conditions for the world's poorest inhabitants, including scarcity of food and water, with concomitant diseases, competition for diminishing arable land, and the unavailability of housing, clothing, medicinal drugs, information and education.

The human condition changed more extensively and rapidly during the twentieth century than in any other human period. The range and pace of change separates human inhabitants of the twentieth century from all previous humans to an immense degree. During the 1900s, human beings split atoms, cloned sheep, probed space, skipped on the moon, built robots, launched satellites, flew in jets and rockets, mapped the human genome, and devised computers. The ongoing industrialization, electrification and computerization of human societies during the last century spawned globalization, that is, the technologically engineered interconnection around the globe of previously disconnected people and places.[16]

The more the current and recent human conditions differ from the historical circumstances in which ancient religions were born, the more vexing it can become for latter-day theologians of those religions to reconcile contemporary humans with the religious beliefs, discourses and practices of their forerunners living thousands of years earlier. The era when theologians spoke in Hebrew, Greek or Latin to students training to be priests, rabbis and monks in synagogues and monasteries has ceded ground to a time when theologians on holiday visiting the Great Sandy Desert of Northern Australia can use a palm-sized, wireless computer to instruct their students in Botswana.

Human beings in 1900 were entirely ignorant and innocent of the events into which they were about to be flung during the ensuing 100 years. By the end of the twentieth century it had become clear that within the span of ten decades, a world that was monarchically governed, largely agrarian, locally based and religiously traditional had been transformed into a more democratically guided, urban-based, highly mobile, and far more secularized planet. By the end of the 1900s it was evident that the culture of Christendom in Europe, which had buttressed social and political institutions for over 1,000 years, had very largely dissipated.

The near collapse of Christendom has been starkly evident in Great Britain. At the beginning of the twentieth century Britain was a markedly religious society. If was far less so by the century's end: 'In between, the strength, significance and character of British religion changed more profoundly than in any other period of

christendom   Christendom is related to, though distinguishable from, Christianity. The former is a civic and cultural expression of the latter. Christianity is a religion born of Semitic parentage in the Roman imperial province of first-century Palestine. Christendom evolved once Christianity was adopted as the religion of the Roman Empire. Its remnants remain today, but it has steadily weakened since the French Revolution and Enlightenment of the eighteenth century. Christendom is characterized by doctrinal uniformity and political power. That is, it has two principal features. First, it is a society wherein Christian doctrines are professed to be true by almost all members of the population. And second, it enjoys the support and protection of political might. The Crusades, the Inquisition and pogroms were the children of Christendom.

recorded history. The twentieth century was the first century in which weekly churchgoers fell below 10 per cent of the British population.'[17] Other parts of the world, like rural India and the Philippines, contain large populations of tradition-ally religious citizens. In Europe the situation is now very different from the time of the Reformation, and the efforts of theologians there during the twentieth century to draw people's attention to God have met with limited success.

The twentieth century was undoubtedly a time of astoundingly sophisticated intellectual accomplishments, medical discoveries, technological inventions and scientific understanding of the cosmos and its inhabitants. To illustrate with reference to a single decade: Max Planck began to formulate quantum theory in 1900, while Sigmund Freud published *The Interpretation of Dreams*. The following year, the first petrol-engined motor-bicycle was invented, as was instant coffee. Joseph Thomson had isolated the electron by 1899. Hormones were discovered in 1902. Orville and Wilbur Wright flew the first petrol-engined aeroplane in North Carolina on 17 December 1903. The ultraviolet lamp was invented in 1904; cellophane in 1905; the jukebox in 1906; the electric washing machine in 1907; the Geiger counter in 1908; a cure for syphilis in 1909; and the spectrohelograph in 1910. Discoveries and inventions continued unabated in mid-century. The first supersonic flights occurred in 1947. The commercial production of transis-tors began in 1951. With far-reaching consequences for sexual mores, a contra-ceptive tablet – the Pill – made of phosphorated hesperidin, was devised in 1952.[18]

the 1960s

Ground-breaking human ingenuity during the twentieth century, coupled with chillingly lethal military inventions and tumultuous political events, appeared to gather pace during the 1960s. Consider the following years and events:

1960:   France exploded an atomic bomb; a heart pacemaker was first devised; Theodore Maiman invented the laser; and Robert Woodward synthesized chlorophyll.

1961:   The USSR detonated a hydrogen bomb; Yuri Gagarin (of the USSR) became the first person to travel in space; the Berlin Wall was built; the Bay of Pigs invasion was launched; and Adolf Eichmann was tried in Jerusalem.

1962:   The Second Vatican Council began its deliberations; China attacked India; the Cuban Missile Crisis began; and Israel executed Eichmann.

1963:   John F. Kennedy was assassinated; Maarten Schmidt discovered quasars; and the audio cassette tape was mass produced.

1964:   China detonated an atomic bomb; the Palestine Liberation Organization was inaugurated; Nelson Mandela was sentenced to life imprisonment in South Africa; civil war erupted in Laos; and the Aswan Dam was opened in Egypt.

1965:   War began between India and Pakistan; North American soldiers arrived in Vietnam; and Robert Wilson detected microwave cosmic background radiation.

1966:   The Cultural Revolution began in China; and Raden Suharto assumed power in Indonesia.

1967:   Christian Barnard performed the first heart transplant; Jocelyn Bell Burnell discovered pulsars; Che Guevara was killed; Israel engaged in the Six Day War; and civil war began in Nigeria.

1968:   Students and labourers rioted in Paris; Martin Luther King Jr was assassinated; North Vietnam began the Tet Offensive; and Biafra was blighted by famine.

1969:   The Woodstock Folk Festival was staged; Neil Armstrong and Buzz Aldrin walked on the moon; and the supersonic Concorde jet flew for the first time.[19]

1968

Of all the years during the tumultuous 1960s, 1968 stands out as a period of dizzyingly rapid cultural change. To this day it is remembered as an emblematic signpost for social and political upheaval. It has even been observed that:

> There has never been a year like 1968, and it is unlikely that there will ever be one again. At a time when nations and cultures were still separate and very different – and in 1968 Poland, France, the United States, and Mexico were far more different from one another than they are today – there occurred a spontaneous combustion of rebellious spirits around the world.[20]

In January of that year, Israeli soldiers fought their Jordanian counterparts, and North Korean agents tried to assassinate the President of South Korea. During the following month in the Kingdom of Belgium, the government collapsed after violent clashes between Flemish- and French-speaking groups in the country; and a bomb exploded in the Soviet Embassy in Washington. During March, US soldiers massacred civilians in the Vietnamese village of My Lai, and the Czech President (Novotny) resigned. In April, abortion was legalized in Britain, and students fought police at Columbia University in New York. Paris was disrupted by major social unrest in May, while the Rector of the city's Sorbonne University asked police to end student demonstrations in the university. Social and political turmoil continued unabated around the world for the remainder of the decade.

1968 was also the year in which Pope Paul VI caused uproar internationally by publishing a letter called *Humanae Vitae* (*On Human Life*). It prohibited the use of contraception, and thereby triggered a major world-wide dismissal of papal authority.[21]

popular culture and sport

Quite apart from scientific progressions and political upheavals, the twentieth century was also a time of fertile cultural and artistic creativity. Gustav Mahler performed his Fourth Symphony in 1900. At the same time, Giacomo Puccini composed his opera, *Tosca*, and Joseph Conrad published his novel, *Lord Jim*. Human creativity was expressed in vividly alternative ways by 2000, the year in which J.K. Rowling published *Harry Potter and the Goblet of Fire*, and Ridely Scott directed the film, *Gladiator*.

Musicianship was transformed on a major scale throughout the twentieth century. By the end of the 1990s, relaxation in the concert or opera hall had become a pastime for the minority of the population in the West, while forms of music such as pop, ska, rock and roll, rocksteady, hip-hop, rock, punk, heavy metal, jazz, rap and reggae entranced major sections of societies all around the world. Discos, strobe and laser lighting, woofer basses and night clubs had become prominent aspects of metropolitan life internationally. What does the theologian have to say to such an audience and setting?

Sport also enthralled twentieth-century societies in a way and on a scale not previously witnessed. At the end of the twentieth century in Great Britain, a person could be created a Dame of the British Empire or a Knight of the Realm for winning a foot race, sailing a boat over long distances, or managing a football club. Esteemed footballers were paid tens of thousands of pounds, dollars, pesos or euros per week. They were also occasionally adulated as secular saints and sexual magnets; idealized as such in glossy magazines sold in supermarkets and on street corners throughout the world. The televising of their on-field triumphs has been one of the more lucrative of all international financial enterprises.

the end of the century and into the next

The final decade of the twentieth century witnessed an uninterrupted progression of scientific breakthroughs that characterized the century's preceding decades. The Hubble Space Telescope was launched into permanent orbit in 1990. The following year the Worldwide Web was initiated. In 1995, a brown dwarf was discovered in the constellation Lepus. Two rhesus monkeys were cloned from embryo cells in 1996. The following year the cloned lamb Dolly was born. The 38th Mersenne prime was discovered in 1999. During 2000, the first draft of the complete structure of DNA was completed.

The year after, two airliners were deliberately crashed into the World Trade Centre in New York and the Pentagon in Washington, USA, while elsewhere Macedonians fought ethnic Albanians. The world was thereby reminded that all the twentieth-century accomplishments of human beings had not taught them to renounce violence. Despite the instructive breakthroughs of the past century, the age was also clearly a period of barbarism. Last century, humans not only devised theories of relativity and quantum mechanics. They also bombed Arabs, gassed Jews, hacked Tutsis, destroyed animal species, and ravaged their ecological habitats.

The events of the twentieth century can be doubly measured by intellectual advancements and human depravity. Change and decay, progress and persecutions, insight and horror – these are the constantly twinned companions that so perplexingly and chillingly mark the history of the twentieth century. Why, when humans have been at their most knowledgeable, have they behaved so destructively? The tragedy of the twentieth century was that 'it began with the promise of bringing an end to war as an instrument of state diplomacy', but ended 'as the world's bloodiest century, with 108 million war dead'.[22] The tragedy of the twenty-first century 'may be our failure to learn anything from the previous one'.[23]

the second world war

The terrifying pivot of the twentieth century was the Second World War. The most horrific moment of the century occurred in 1945, with the dropping of an atomic bomb on Hiroshima. With that event, human beings realized the deadliest capacities of their species in a history spanning at least 100,000 years: 'The atomic bombs of 1945 were properly seen as cutting history in two: *the prior time*, when nature could recover from the greatest wounds we inflicted, and *now*, when we can inflict wounds that nature cannot heal.'[24]

In Paris' largest military museum and hospital, Les Invalides, the technology of human weaponry is illustrated as growing markedly more lethal once gun powder was invented. None of the weapons displayed in the museum remotely matches the Hiroshima atomic bomb in terms of potential for homicidal destructiveness. Before August 1945, the means for human beings to obliterate themselves and their planet eluded them. Now, only diplomacy and politics prevents the cataclysmic detonation of such armaments:

> The dropping of the atomic bomb on Hiroshima on 6 August 1945 brought humanity into a radically new historical situation. Technological advances had now placed into human hands new powers of destruction so massive that the accepted conventions of warfare as an instrument of national political policy were rendered obsolete for the great powers; and humankind entered a period of cautiously feeling its ways in international relations.[25]

1945 was not without signs of improvement for the human condition. The Second World War was brought to an end. So too was the Nazi-engineered slaughter of European Jewry.[26]

How does anyone dare to talk about God in response to genocide and obliteration bombing? Did theologians of the past century concentrate sufficiently on the dreadful extent of human suffering and misery that continues to bedevil the human race and other species? Is it possible to continue to speak about God in the conceptual categories inherited from ancient, religiously traditional societies? Ought theologians in the last century to have persisted in describing human destiny in terms of angels, devils, sin and a future heaven or hell, when their addressees were languishing or perishing because of human-generated suffering? These questions received ill-matched answers from the theologians to be surveyed in this book. For some, rescuing humans from perdition is a matter of the personal renunciation of sin, and has nothing to do with whining about economic poverty and military pugnacity. Theology in another key insists that it is not possible to speak about God in total abstraction from the hapless human world that God is professed to have created and maintained.

The twentieth century represents the sixth significant age of Christian theology.[27]

---

six ages of theology

1. The Biblical Era, in which texts of the Bible were composed and redacted.
2. The Patristic Period.
3. The Dark and Middle Ages.
4. The Reformation and Counter-Reformation.
5. The Age of Enlightenment and Revolutions.
6. The Twentieth Century and Beyond.

Enrique Dussel summarizes much of the theologies represented by these periods in the following way:

> The expansion of Latin-German Christianity gave rise to its own theology of conquest. Semitic and Christian thought of the Old and New Testaments was reduced to a process of Indo-European Hellenization from the second century onwards. Medieval European theology was able to justify the feudal world and the *ius dominativum* of the lord over the serf. Tridentine and Protestant theology had nothing to say about the Indian, the African, or the Asian ... .[28]

All of which leads to the preoccupation and thesis of this book. Theology's sixth major epoch was a partial return to the first, and is represented by the twentieth century. It is significant in the history of theology because it championed the cause of the poor in ways and on a scale unseen before, fretted about their suffering, and was increasingly intolerant of warfare. The third, fourth and fifth theological epochs, for all their accomplishments, were also noteworthy for ignominious factors: they were often massively forgetful of the poor and patient with imperial aristocratic bellicosity.

the thesis

Apart from introducing the ways twentieth-century theologians strove to discuss God, this book also advances and develops a thesis through successive chapters. The thesis is this: the greatest theologians of the twentieth century were the most negative. They were negative, or are negative in the case of those still living, in a twofold sense. First, they were vividly aware that God is best discussed in terms of what God is clearly not. For example, God is neither a man nor a Supreme Court judge. Many of the most accomplished theologians and philosophers over the past 4,000 years have been negative or apophatic thinkers. Dionysius the Pseudo-Aereopogite (c. 500 CE), Thomas Aquinas and Maimonides (Moses ben Maimon, known as Ramban [1135–1204]), fall into this category.

In the second instance, the most insightful of twentieth-century theologians were acutely aware of the bleak and harrowing negativity of human (and animal) suffering. Human beings throughout the twentieth century suffered appallingly because of poverty, malnutrition, deprivation of water, disease, banditry, warfare, fascism, distorted Marxisms, capitalism, nationalism, terrorism, racism, sexism, misogyny, homophobia, homohatred and ageism. Debilitating and death-dealing

apophasis   The adjective **apophatic** is of Greek origin and means 'negative'. It characterizes a style of speaking about God called **apophasis**. The style insists that any positive affirmation about God, such as that God is a loving parent, must be accompanied by a prohibitive or negative assertion that no human conceptual term could ever accurately designate God. Positive statements about God are called **cataphasis** (occasionally spelt as 'kataphasis'). Hence the adjective, **cataphatic**, used to label affirmative theological declarations, such as 'God is good'.

poverty was the scourge of too many human beings throughout the twentieth century. Coupled with militarily engineered slaughter, poverty rendered their lives a grisly saga of misery.

The greater theologians of the twentieth century were attentive to the problem suffering causes for fatuous discourses that God is good and cares for people. It is breathtakingly unsettling to discover how many theologians in the last century paid virtually no attention to poverty and human torment. In this, they bear no resemblance at all to the biblical prophets. Neither do they resonate with the record of Jesus' priorities. The latter, as he is remembered by Matthew's Gospel, could not have been clearer:

> You that are accursed, depart from me into the eternal fire prepared for the devil and his angels; for I was hungry and you gave me no food, I was thirsty and you gave me nothing to drink, I was a stranger and you did not welcome me, naked and you did not give me clothing, sick and in prison and you did not visit me (Mt 25: 41b–43).[29]

The judgement attributed to Jesus above mentions human hunger, thirst, alienation, lack of clothing, sickness and imprisonment. These debilitating states appear to have dogged the human race without relief from the time of Jesus until now. The growth of the human population during the twentieth century caused additional misery for the world's inhabitants. There is now not even enough water for the human population to drink.[30] Deprivation of water and dirty water currently breed disease and death inestimably.

The more vapid and unconvincing theological thinkers of the twentieth century tended to be positive, again in a twofold way. First, in that they spoke with an unfettered confidence about what God is like, what God wills, what God forbids, what God has done, what God will do, whom God hates, whom God condemns and whom God loves. They spoke with a self-assurance and apparent authority as if they had dined and danced with God every evening. What is worse, they sometimes styled themselves as God's most favoured mouthpieces.

The less insightful twentieth-century theologians were positive in a second sense, in that they reassured their audiences that all is well, or will be well, with the world.

These theologians were to a large extent unable to see that the world during the twentieth century was a dreadful dystopia.

In view of pervasive human affliction throughout the twentieth century, it is striking that theologians in the first half of the century often ignored it and spoke instead of supernatural, sacramental or ecclesiastical matters as if suffering were not germane to theology's operation. A vivid example of this oversight is contained in the *Dictionnaire de Théologie Catholique* (*Dictionary of Catholic Theology*) that was published in Paris from 1903 to 1950. The comment on the dictionary cited below illustrates clearly an absence from the dictionary of topics that began to preoccupy many theologians in the second half of the twentieth century. The dictionary lacks articles on, or contains scant treatments of, the following themes, except the last mentioned: '*Work*: nothing; *Family*: nothing; *Woman*: nothing; *Economy*: nothing: *Politics*: nothing; *World*: nothing: *Life*: an article on eternal life; *Laity*: nothing apart from an article on laicism (a heresy); *Technology*: nothing; *Sex*: nothing; *Power*: 103 columns on "the power of the pope in the temporal order".'[31]

an embarrassment of riches

Why study twentieth-century theologians with an eye to poverty and warfare rather than doctrine and orthodoxy? The answer is painfully plain. Poverty is the most lethal danger faced by human beings today:

> The 1995 World Health Report (WHO 1995) states that the world's most ruthless killer and the greatest cause of suffering on earth is listed in the latest edition of WHO's *International Classification of Diseases*, an A-to-Z of all ailments known to medical science, under the code Z59.5. It stands for extreme poverty. Poverty is the main reason why babies are not vaccinated, clean water and sanitation are not provided, curative drugs and other treatments are unavailable, and why mothers die in childbirth. Poverty is the main cause of reduced life expectancy, of handicap and disability, and of starvation. Poverty is a major contributor to mental illness, stress, suicide, family disintegration and substance abuse.[32]

If poverty is the world's most ruthless killer, and if theologians want to talk about God saving humanity, they need to be able cogently to explain how God might rescue people from the ravages of the most menacing threat to their happiness and survival. The story of twentieth-century theology is at least a tale of a gradual awakening from a cosy Christian indifference to poverty.

A study of the past, even the recent past, fuels a better understanding of the present. Without a memory of the past and its thought, current personal identity and self-understanding are impossible. Any investigation of former times and its thinkers is an antidote to collective cultural amnesia today. A consideration of twentieth-century theologians aids a comprehension of, and propels a challenge to, current theological oversights and engrossments.

As Christianity grew older over the centuries, its early traditions of antipathy to war and fretfulness about poor people were occluded as Churches gained aristocratic privileges and imperial support. While empires altered in form throughout the twentieth century, the alliance between many Christians and wealth remained strong.

The wealthiest nations of the world today and for most of the twentieth century are countries wherein the majority of their populations were or are Christian. Imagine the human population of the world in the late twentieth century clustered in a single city of gigantic proportions.

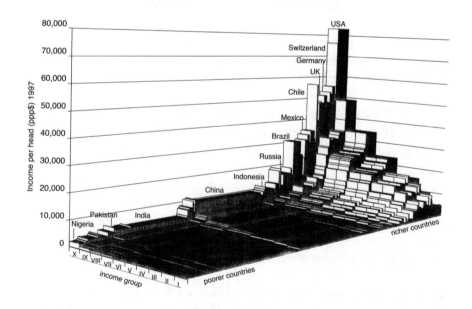

The numerals on the left-hand side of the image represent a purchasing power parity (PPP) calculated in US dollars per head of a given population. The parity compares and contrasts what a dollar will buy in far-flung locations. A dollar in Morocco buys much more than it does in Sweden.

The arresting image above illustrates the actual distribution of wealth on earth in 1997.[33] Marrying the imagined city with actual wealth, the picture shows how fortune was located in Western, North Atlantic countries in the late twentieth century. The inhabitants of the tallest skyscrapers to the right of the picture are the richest in the world. They live in countries that were and are conventionally Christian. Their opulence ought to be for them an excruciating embarrassment. They align themselves verbally with the poor and crucified Jesus Christ, while simultaneously enjoying lifestyles than can only be sustained by the subjugation of fearfully impoverished peoples in other parts of the world. Many of their clothes are made in Asian sweat shops, where most of their TVs are assembled: '80 per cent of all electronics are made in poor countries' and '100 per cent of all televisions sold in the United States are produced in poor countries'.[34] Asia also represents, and is exploited by, well-off Western regions as a plentiful source of faceless, poorly paid factory slaves: 'Wages are so low in China that even if they grew 6% per year faster than the USA in dollar terms over the next two decades, they would still only be *one tenth* of the US level.'[35]

The international economic circumstances addressed above gestated throughout the twentieth century. Despite its wonders and accomplishments, the century was a wilderness overly bereft of peace, human compassion, justice and love. The entire century can be divided into two halves, each of which faced different types of trauma. The first half, ending around 1945, was a period of international mayhem, including two World Wars. The second 'was a period of comparative calm, in which the mayhem was stilled – at least at a global level – but was overhung by nuclear terror'.[36] By the end of the century there were 32,000 nuclear weapons available for use in the world.[37] They continue to constitute a nightmarish menace for the future.

What is particularly shocking about the twentieth century is that it produced a history of suffering, degradation and poverty in an age of unbridled affluence and colossal wealth. The indifference of the affluent to the nightmares of the destitute in the last century did not produce an admirable portrait of human beings.

The theologians of the twentieth century were voices crying in a wilderness in one or both of two basic ways. Either they raised their theological utterances to attract the attention of their contemporaries in a wasteland of religious indifference, or they cried out in opposition to war, economic exploitation, the social subjugation of women, cruelty to children and other animals, and the destruction of the eco-biosphere. Some theologians defended imperial might. Others were assassinated by it.

To the theological voices raised in the desert that was the twentieth century, it is now opportune to turn.

2

Adolf von Harnack: 1851–1930

Freedom is the freedom to say that two plus two make four.
If that is granted, all else follows.

George Orwell

What is Christianity's kernel? Is it a doctrine, an ethical system, a utopian vision, God, the Church, a myth, or a terrestrial quest for an otherworldly paradise? Does the Jewish man Jesus, or a later belief about him, serve as the hub of Christianity? At the beginning of the twentieth century, the answer to these questions was not obvious, as the Christian Church continued to split into thousands of rival and frequently bitterly opposed groups. By the year 2000 CE, global Christianity included 33,820 distinct denominations and paradenominations.[1] Is it even possible to speak of Christianity's essence, in view of its unabated fissiporousness? Throughout the nineteenth and twentieth centuries theologians strove to pinpoint a core of the Christian religion that was worthy of their contemporaries' belief. Adolf von Harnack was among them, and he forms the focus of this chapter. His most widely read popular work, *The Essence of Christianity*, contributed to a prevalence of modern books devoted to specifying the pith of Christianity.[2] Their authors attempted to convince increasingly sceptical audiences that Christianity has at its centre a power to liberate anyone from aimlessness and unhappiness, as well as to inspire people with hope for a blissful future.

Harnack has been lauded, together with Origen (c. 185–254), as 'perhaps one of the two most learned theologians who ever lived'.[3] His full name was Carl Gustav Adolf von Harnack. He was at the height of his intellectual powers as the twentieth century began. Born in 1851, he spent his entire life in Germany before he died in 1930. He was appointed as the Professor of Ecclesiastical History for the University of Berlin in 1888, and remained in that post until he retired in 1921. While his learning was primarily in the field of Church history, he deployed his detailed knowledge of historical events and transformations to forge an avowedly liberal theology, that is, a discourse about God that freely modified or departed from the concepts and terminology of traditional Christian dogmatic theology.

Harnack was a Lutheran. Because of his espousal of liberal theology he incurred the suspicion of the Lutheran Church in Germany. Much of the history of twentieth-century theology has been the story of a struggle for ascendancy in Western societies between liberal, traditional, pseudo-traditional or anti-modern theologies. Scanning the history of twentieth-century theologians is like watching a prolonged tennis match. Just as two tennis players vie for ascendancy until one can claim victory in game, set and match, theologians throughout the twentieth century struggled to convince each other and far wider audiences that their interpretations of Christianity and God were more viable than others.

With regard to a principal leitmotif of this book, namely, that accomplished theologians are acutely aware of the bleakness and suffering that blight poor people's lives, Harnack never allowed his professorial career to render him indifferent to poverty. In 1903, he became the President of the Evangelical-Social Congress, an organization that included in its remit a sustained effort to establish social justice in Germany. To appreciate the significance of Harnack's life and work in more detail, it helps to consider the broader historical circumstances to which he responded.

---

lutheranism and calvinism

Lutheranism is a system of Christian life and belief stemming from Martin Luther
(1483–1546), who launched the German Protestant Reformation in protest
('Protestant' from the Latin, *protestans*, meaning 'protesting') against what were
perceived as corruptions within the Catholic Church. 'Lutheranism' was not an
appealing term to Luther himself. He was excommunicated from the Catholic Church
in 1520. By 1600, Lutheranism was established by states in Germany, Denmark,
Sweden, Finland, Iceland, Norway, Estonia, Latvia, regions of Bohemia, and Hungary.
The theological pivot of Lutheranism is a belief about the way human beings are
saved from perdition, or justified (set in a right relationship with God). For
Lutherans, people are reconciled with God through their faith, and not solely by any
observance of law or custom: 'The Lutheran proposal of dogma has one great theme:
justification by faith alone, apart from works of law. This is the heart of the matter
…'.[4] **Calvinism** is an expression of Protestant Christian faith that stems from the
writings of John Calvin (1509–64), especially his *Institutes of the Christian Religion*. It
shares with Lutheranism a belief in justification by faith alone. It affirms the
sovereignty of God and teaches that not everyone can be saved, because not everyone
is elected and predestined by God to be saved: reprobates will be consigned by God to
hell, and those whom God favours, or elects, will enter heaven.

---

modernity

Adolf von Harnack and all the other theologians discussed in this book worked in
the context of modernity and reactions to it. 'Modernity' and 'the Modern Age'
are terms that designate a chain of changes that began in northern Europe around
400 years ago. The process and era of modernity transformed territories in
Europe from insignificant cultures – when compared to the ancient civilizations
of Greece and Egypt – to the most technologically and militaristically sophisticated nation states ever known to human beings.

The chain of changes in the process called modernity had several links, includ-
ing: the European exploration and seizure of territories in the Americas; the
Protestant Reformation; the astronomy of Nicolas Copernicus (1473–1543) and
Galileo Galilei (1564–1642); the physics formulated by Isaac Newton (1642–1727);
the Enlightenment; the emergence of political democracy with the American and
French Revolutions; the philosophies of René Descartes (1596–1650), Immanuel
Kant (1724–1804) and Georg Hegel (1770–1831); the proliferation of capitalist
forms of monetary exchange; and the evolutionary vision of Charles Darwin
(1809–82). Cumulatively, these developments acted as a stimulus in northern
Europe for nations to reorganize themselves so that religion was placed at the

periphery of society, and religious beliefs were regarded as matters of private, individual opinion. Especially after the eighteenth century, these societies reconfigured themselves so that public and political life were regulated according to principles of individual freedoms and human rights.[5]

Theologians working at the beginning of the twentieth century were heirs to at least 300 years of political upheaval, intellectual ferment and far-reaching social change. Throughout the nineteenth century, human beings militated around the world, and especially in Europe, to end imperial, aristocratic rule in favour of democratic government. They laboured for improved material living conditions, strove for the eradication of illiteracy, fought for state-protected freedoms of speech and religion, struggled to abolish slavery, and sought the control of disease through medical science.

By 1900, theologians were well aware that their times and cultures differed starkly from those in which their authoritative religious traditions were born thousands of years earlier. The overall novelty and distinctiveness of thought during the last century was captured by the North American theologian, Helmut Richard Niebuhr (1894–1962), writing in 1941:

> No other influence has affected twentieth century thought more deeply than the discovery of spatial and temporal relativity. The understanding that the spatial-temporal point of view of an observer enters into his knowledge of reality, so that no universal knowledge of things as they are in themselves is possible, so that all knowledge is conditioned by the standpoint of the knower, plays the same role in our thinking that the idealistic discoveries of the seventeenth and eighteenth centuries and the evolutionary discovery of the nineteenth played in the thought of earlier generations.[6]

The vivid differences between the knowledge and experiences of people living in Paris or London at the dawn of the twentieth century, and of those eking out a living in the agrarian Roman imperial province of Palestine in the first century, spawned an unnerving chain of questions for theologians of the early 1900s: should theology be practised as it has been in the past? Or ought it be attempted with entirely new methods? Are biblical texts written in Hebrew, Greek or Aramaic too conceptually and experientially alien to be translated intelligibly for modern urbanites acquainted with the works of Copernicus, Galileo, Newton and Darwin? Is the Christian doctrinal tradition that was articulated in Greek and Latin, and forged in the Roman and Byzantine empires, intellectually defanged? Has the historical figure of Jesus been lost, or abandoned, in the modern, bourgeois burgeoning of thousands of competing Christian churches and denominations?

religious violence

Another reason why theologians during the past two centuries struggled to delineate Christianity's identity stems from a long history of religiously motivated violence, exemplified shockingly in the Thirty Years War (1618–48). If Christianity is a religion of life, love, justice, mercy and peace, why do its devotees so often kill each other and persecute others? During the Thirty Years War, Catholics and Protestants fought each other savagely in Europe, with each group hoping to vanquish the other. When the conflict ended with the Peace of Westphalia, signed in 1648, neither side had triumphed unilaterally.[7] This conflict bred not only anxiety and uncertainty among Christians, with a now clearly divided Church in the heartlands of Europe. It also spawned a revulsion against Christianity among people there who were unable to reconcile putative belief in a loving God with violent bloodletting by and among those Christians professing belief in such a God. To this day, violent religious people render it far more difficult if not impossible for the religiously indifferent or uncommitted to be convinced that religion is worthwhile. Their homicidal actions directly nullify their attestations of belief in a God of Life and Love. An unforeseen consequence of the Thirty Years War was that it became one of the catalysts that caused several European nations in the nineteenth and twentieth centuries to reorganize their cultures so that Christianity was pushed to the margins of society and religious beliefs were purged from the daily working of politics and government. This purgation started in earnest with the French Revolution (1789–1815). The Catholic Church has never regained the social prominence it enjoyed in France before 1789. By the twentieth century, theologians were hamstrung by a long history of religiously generated violence. In Europe they worked in cultures wherein Christianity no longer dominated the lives of every citizen. Texts charting the historical process by which Europe became, governmentally speaking, more secular, often designate the rise of modern science and technology as the motor force causing Europe's inhabitants to doubt the viability and truthfulness of Christianity. The contribution of religious violence to this secularizing process is often not as fully acknowledged as it might be.

the essence of christianity

The modern proliferation of works focused on finding Christianity's core illustrates both the unrelenting and unsettling extent of social change during the period, and the concomitant uncertainty or difficulty theologians met in attempting to answer the interrogative, What is Christianity? Ludwig Feuerbach

(1804–72) answered that question in 1841 with his monograph, *The Essence of Christianity*.[8] He judged that Christianity's fundament is anthropology. In his terms, when theologians speak about God, they are really talking about themselves. By a process of intellectual projection, they unconsciously apply concepts that properly depict people to an objectified, though ultimately illusory, reality they call God.

Feuerbach's thought on Christianity's nature is summed up in his Latin maxim, *Homo homini Deus est* – 'man is the God of man',[9] or 'the human being is God to human beings'. Feuerbach also refers to 'God as the mirror of man'.[10] In so doing, he turns on its head the biblical teaching that humans are made in God's image (Gen 1: 26–7). He teases out what he means by *Homo homini Deus est* at different stages of the book: 'The divine being is nothing else than the human being, or rather the human nature purified, freed from the limits of the individual man, made objective – *i.e.*, contemplated and revered as another, a distinct being. All the attributes of the divine nature are, therefore, attributes of the human nature.'[11]

Bitingly, Feuerbach observes that 'Prayer is the self-division of man into two beings, – a dialogue of man with himself, with his heart.'[12] In his terms, the substance of Christianity is entirely human: 'The fundamental dogmas of Christianity are realised wishes of the heart; the essence of Christianity is the essence of human feeling.'[13]

harnack's life and thought

Feuerbach is a rare example of an atheist (a label he rejected) in the nineteenth century who was educated in both theology and philosophy at universities. Thus equipped, he was a particularly intimidating foe for defenders of traditional Christian doctrines. The publication of his interpretation of Christianity's nature generated an intellectual maelstrom in Europe. What he lacked was the scope of Harnack's vast knowledge of past history.

Harnack was an extraordinarily energetic and productive man. A bibliography of his writings lists 1,611 items.[14] Apart from his professorial duties in Berlin, he served as the director of the Prussian State Library (*Staatsbibliothek*) between 1905 and 1921. In 1890 he was admitted to the Prussian Academy of Sciences. He was ennobled by Kaiser Wilhelm II in 1914, and thereafter bore the name Adolf von Harnack, rather than Adolf Harnack. As an historian and biblical critic, Harnack articulated both a discourse about God and an interpretation of Christianity at the end of the nineteenth and the beginning of the twentieth century that launched him as one of the latter century's most erudite and intellectually perceptive theologians. His academic nemesis, the Swiss Reformed theologian, Karl Barth, was still able to concede that Harnack was '*the* theologian of the day'.[15]

Adolf von Harnack was born in Dorpat on 7 May 1851, the year in which Verdi composed his opera, *Rigoletto*, Herman Melville wrote *Moby-Dick*, and Isaac Singer built the first modern sewing machine.[16] Dorpat was a Baltic German town that is now in Estonia and called Tartu. He was one of four children, with a twin named Axel. His mother died when he was seven. His father, Theodosius Harnack, was the Professor of Homiletics and Historical Theology in Dorpat's university.[17]

While a very young man, Adolf Harnack decided to become a theologian. To achieve his goal he enrolled in Dorpat University during 1869. He succeeded in becoming a theologian: 'But a theologian with a difference, for Harnack was to be first and foremost an historian trained in the discipline of classical philology.'[18]

Harnack moved to the Lutheran University of Leipzig in 1872 and remained there for seven years. While doing so he studied Greek and Latin Fathers assiduously. He successfully completed a doctoral dissertation and *Habilitationsschrift* ('Habilitation text', a thesis qualifying him to work as a university lecturer). He began his career as a university teacher in 1875. He worked first as an unsalaried lecturer (*Privatdocent*), before becoming a probationary, or Extraordinary Professor of Ecclesiastical History in 1876. He worked as a full professor from 1879 in Giessen (or Gießen), and from 1886 in Marburg. He taught as a professor in Berlin between 1888 and 1921, the year of his retirement. He married Amalie Thiersch, a Catholic, in 1879.

While in Giessen, Harnack began to become estranged from his father for doubting whether Jesus Christ was pre-existent and asking whether Christians need to believe in the Logos and the Trinity.[19]

Harnack was above all a specialist in patristics. His command of ancient languages enabled him to study the Bible critically as well. His primary innovation in the history of modern theology was his argument that orthodox Christianity is an historical offspring and continuation of ancient Hellenistic culture. Such an argument may serve to fan the suspicion that Christendom is alien to the life and work of Jesus Christ.

harnack's essence of christianity

Sixty years after Feuerbach's publication of *The Essence of Christianity*, Harnack followed him in the age-old quest for the *essentia religionis christianae* ('the essence of the Christian religion'). During the winter of 1899–1900, Harnack delivered a series of 16 lectures at the University of Berlin (Humboldt-Universität), which was founded in 1810. They explored what Harnack termed the nature, character or essence (*Das Wesen*) of Christianity. He presented them to about 600 students from all the faculties of the university. Remarkably, they were delivered extempore. Harnack's mind worked like a camera. His memory was so reliable and precise that he could recall and repeat a full page of Greek text after having seen it only once.[20] While he was lecturing, one enterprising student recorded his words in shorthand. Shortly after the course of lectures had ended, the student amazed his professor by presenting him with a complete transcript of the oral delivery.

Harnack corrected the text slightly and published it in German in 1900 as *Das Wesen des Christentums* ('The Essence of Christianity'). It appeared in English translation the following year as *What Is Christianity?*[21] Subsequent page references to it will be included between parentheses in the body of the text which follows. In the opening pages of the book Harnack announces that 'the Christian religion is something simple and sublime; it means one thing and one thing only: Eternal life in the midst of time, by the strength and under the eyes of God' (8).

Harnack explains in the first of his lectures that he wishes to consider Christianity's essence as a purely historical theme (9). His initial lectures explore Jesus' historical identity and teachings. They take as their primary sources Jesus himself and the gospels of Matthew, Mark and Luke. John's Gospel is discounted as a reliable historical witness (10 and 19). Later lectures explore the gospels in relation to issues such as poor people, law, work and doctrine. They also consider the way Jesus' gospel has been construed in subsequent stages of history, beginning with the earliest Christian age and ending with Protestantism.

That Harnack is not attempting a dogmatic account of Jesus in his lectures becomes arrestingly evident in Lecture I. There he acknowledges in his own terms what Helmut Richard Niebuhr observed four decades later as the most significant influence in all twentieth-century thought: the recognition that 'all knowledge is conditioned by the standpoint of the knower' (cited above). Harnack's words struck a new chord for an audience fed on a diet of dogmatic Christology, according to which Jesus was and is the pre-existent Logos – Word, or Son of God – and hence omniscient:

> Jesus Christ and his disciples were situated in their day as we are situated in ours; that is to say, their feelings, their thoughts, their judgements and their efforts were bounded by the horizon and the framework in which their own nation was set and by its condition at the time. Had it been otherwise, they would not have been men of flesh and blood, but spectral beings (12).

For Christian dogmatic theologies of Eastern, Western, Catholic, Protestant and Anglican traditions, Jesus Christ is the divine and human Pre-Existent Logos of God. As such, his knowledge is unconstrained in any way.

In Harnack's 11th lecture he takes issue with the early Christian identification of Jesus with the Logos, but before he does he sketches for his readers an historical portrait of Jesus and his proclamation. These he will identify as the essence of Christianity.

Harnack informs his listeners about

> **logos** The Greek term λογός ('logos') means 'word', 'message', 'reason' or 'discourse'. It is a prevalent concept in ancient Greek philosophy, especially Stoicism. In Hellenistic philosophy the logos is understood as a rational power suffusing or permeating the universe. Early Christian thinkers, such as the author(s) of John's Gospel, identified Jesus as the Logos. After the Council of Nicaea in 325 CE, Christian theologians used the terms 'Logos' and 'Son of God' alternatively to designate the second person of the Trinity.

Jesus' historical identity in his second lecture, which he begins by debunking the possibility of miracles: 'we are firmly convinced', he says, 'that what happens in space and time is subject to the general laws of motion, and that in this sense, as an interruption of the order of Nature, there can be no such things as miracles' (26). Speaking thus, Harnack revealed himself as an exponent of liberal theology, which evolved throughout the nineteenth and twentieth centuries. The principal features of modern liberal theology will be considered in the final phases of this chapter.

who was jesus?

Harnack begins his historical portrayal of Jesus with a stark admission that 'We know nothing of Jesus' history for the first thirty years of his life' (30). On that basis he remains convinced that available historical sources provide a clear picture of Jesus' teaching, the way his life unfolded, and the impression he made on his disciples. He concludes that statements can be made about Jesus negatively. He presents his audience with four negative and two positive propositions (negative or positive in the sense of denying or affirming who Jesus was or what he did):

- it is very unlikely that Jesus was instructed in a rabbinical school;
- Jesus would have no relations with Essenes;
- he never experienced a crisis through which to break with his past;
- Jesus' life and discourses do not stand in any relation to a Greek spirit;
- he was absorbed by religion. All of his feelings and thoughts were absorbed in a relation to God; and

- he regarded the world and spoke his message 'with a clear view for the life, great and small, that surrounded him' (35; 31–7 for all points listed).

In his third lecture Harnack turns his hand to describing Jesus' teaching and concludes that 'the essence of Christianity is Jesus' own message ...'.[22] He summarizes it with reference to three of its cardinal themes: the kingdom of God and its arrival; God the Father and the human soul's infinite value; and what he calls 'the higher righteousness and the commandment of love'.[23] The higher righteousness referred to is essentially the relation between God and the individual that is expressed through love of others. The kingdom of God which Jesus preached is defined by Harnack as 'the rule of the holy God in the hearts of individuals; *it is God himself in his power*'.[24] Both the essence of Jesus' Gospel and of Christianity are for Harnack condensed in a small cluster of ideas: 'In the combination of these ideas – God the Father, Providence, the position of men as God's children, the infinite value of the human soul – the whole Gospel is expressed.'[25]

Harnack represents the Gospel of Jesus as an ethical phenomenon. In his sixth lecture he broaches the topic of Jesus and poverty: 'The Gospel is a social message', he declares, 'solemn and overpowering in its force; it is the proclamation of solidarity and brotherliness, in favour of the poor' (101). For all Harnack's talk of the value of the human soul (63), he does not allow Christians to regard their religion as a purely individualistic way of living:

> People ought not to speak of loving their neighbours if they can allow men beside them to starve and die in misery. It is not only that the Gospel preaches solidarity and the helping of others; it is in this message that its real import exists. In this sense it is profoundly socialistic, just as it is also profoundly individualistic, because it establishes the infinite and independent value of every human soul (99–100).

While Harnack does not portray Jesus as a social reformer (97–98), he speaks very strongly about how Jesus would relate to poor people in the twentieth century:

> There can be no doubt, therefore, that if Jesus were with us to-day he would side with those who are making great efforts to relieve the hard lot of the poor and procure them better conditions of life. The fallacious principle of the free play of forces, of the 'live and let live' principle – a better name for it would be 'live and let die' – is entirely opposed to the Gospel (100).

The seventh of Harnack's lectures is the pivot of the book. It raises what Harnack calls 'the Christological question'. He means by that the issue of how

Jesus regarded himself and wished to be accepted by others (124). Christology is the theological discipline that attempts discursively to clarify the identity and significance of Jesus. The most significant of all Christological doctrines was formulated by the Council of Chalcedon in 451 CE. According to this Greek-speaking assembly of bishops, Jesus is truly God and truly a human being in the same person of the Logos of God. Harnack is highly critical of Christological dogma, like that of Chalcedon. He even describes the history of Christology as 'a gruesome story': 'On the question of "Christology" men beat their religious doctrines into terrible weapons, and spread fear and intimidation everywhere' (125).

Rather than interpreting Jesus as a human and divine person, Harnack portrays him as utterly focused on a father God. He acknowledges that Jesus was uniquely aware of being God's Son, but this awareness is simply a heightened conviction on Jesus' part that 'he knows God in a way in which no one ever knew him before ...' (128).

In Harnack's 11th lecture he takes direct aim at dogmatic Christology by focusing on the way Christology identified Jesus Christ with the Logos. For Harnack, this linkage is illegitimate. He concludes that the identification of Jesus Christ with the Logos was a fusion of Greek philosophy with original Christian testimonies, and is confident in stating that 'Most of us regard this identification as inadmissible, because the way in which we conceive the world and ethics does not point to the existence of any logos at all' (204–5).

The published version of Harnack's lectures of 1899–1900 has been described as 'one of the most popular theological works ever written'.[26] It was so popular in its day that it coursed through 15 successive editions. In the history of twentieth-century theology it is significant for the way in which it sought to wean modern interpretations of Jesus' identity and worth from Hellenistic philosophies of the Logos. In this, it typified the liberal theology that emerged and developed in the nineteenth century and afterwards.

Das Wesen des Christentums is Harnack's best known and theologically most accessible book. His other significant writings include a long survey of the history of Christian doctrine up until the Reformation. It was published between 1886 and 1890 as a *Lehrbuch der Dogmengeschichte*, literally translated as 'Textbook of the History of Dogma'. An English translation, *History of Dogma*, was produced in 1899. A dominant aim of this work is to draw attention to the gradual Hellenization of Christian teachings: 'If dogma is originally the formulation of Christian faith as Greek culture understood it and justified it to itself, then dogma has never indeed lost this character, though it has been radically modified in later times.'[27] Harnack was keen to relegate dogmatic theology to a secondary position in relation to his reconstruction of Jesus' original teachings:

The Gospel entered into the world, not as a doctrine, but as a joyful message and as a power of the Spirit of God, originally in the forms of Judaism. It stripped off these forms with amazing rapidity, and united and amalgamated itself with Greek science, the Roman Empire and ancient culture, developing, as a counterpoise to this, renunciation of the world and the striving after supernatural life, after deification. All this was summed up in the old dogma and in dogmatic Christianity.[28]

Most of Harnack's other significant books explored either biblical texts or the history of ancient Christianity. They include *The Mission and Expansion of Christianity during the First Christian Centuries* (2 vols, 1902); the tripartite study, *The History of Ancient Christian Literature* (produced between 1893 and 1904); *The Sayings of Jesus* (1907); *Luke the Physician* (1907); and *The Acts of the Apostles* (1908).

liberal theology

Adolf von Harnack laboured as a university teacher for 46 years. During all that time he was not an academic soloist. Intellectually, he worked in concert with a coterie of German professors, who have come to be known as liberal or Ritschlian theologians – the latter term stemming from the name, Albrecht Ritschl (1822–89).

Modern liberal theology is not a homogeneous school of thought. Its practitioners differed and quarrelled among themselves, but exhibit enough commonalities in their diverse publications to allow a general characterization of the type of theology they tended to exemplify.

Liberal theology is in some measure synonymous with modern theology in counterpoint to traditional dogmatic theologies shared by Catholic, Protestant and Eastern Orthodox thinkers. It is common for Friedrich Schleiermacher (1768–1834) to be crowned as the 'Father of Modern Theology', and hence a liberal. Yet Schleiermacher's work was a response to the oeuvre of the Prussian philosopher Immanuel Kant. With Kant's *Religion within the Limits of Mere Reason* (1893), he presented his readership with a reading of religion, Christianity, Jesus and theology shorn of dogmatic theological traditions. If Jesus need not be interpreted in the conceptual categories of Chalcedon and the Logos, theologians following Kant were often motivated by him to illustrate Jesus' identity in novel ways. Schleiermacher was one of the first major theologians to do so. He nominated the distinctiveness of Jesus as the latter's heightened consciousness of God: 'to ascribe to Christ an absolutely powerful God-consciousness, and to attribute to Him an existence of God in Him, are exactly the same thing.'[29] Such is Schleiermacher's mode of interpreting the age-old teaching of Jesus Christ's divinity in non-dogmatic categories.

The central concept of all liberal theology is freedom. The word 'liberal' comes from the Latin noun *libertas* (freedom), the adjective *liberalis* (free), and anyone who is *liber* (free). Interestingly, the Latin word for children – *liberi* – also has the meaning of freedom at its core. A child is someone who lives in an unencumbered way in a patiently tolerant community or family.[30]

The freedom of which liberal theology speaks is twofold. It refers to the freedom of God and the freedom of human beings. In this scheme, God is envisaged as an absolute (or unlimited) freedom, who creates people as situated, limited and localized freedoms.

Freedom was one of the overarching ideals of the French Revolution. '*Liberté, Egalité, Fraternité*' ('Freedom, Equality, Fraternity') was the most famous of the revolutionaries' battle cries, as they tore down the trammels of the French monarchy and reduced the Church in France to its weakest institutional state in more than 1,000 years.

The freedom sought and esteemed by nineteenth- and twentieth-century liberal theologians was not the liberty to butcher nobles and priests, but to discourse about God, Jesus, Christ, and the drama of human destiny without the control, punitive reaction or censorship of the Church and its dogmatic traditions.

If enthusiasm for intellectual and political freedom, a freedom lionized by the American and French Revolutions, is one facet of liberal theology, a second is a broad consensus among its practitioners that the Enlightenment was a much-to-be-welcomed improvement of the human condition. The Enlightenment began in Europe during the middle of the seventeenth century and reached the zenith of its historical influence around the end of the eighteenth century. It was a general period of intellectual and cultural history with many, although by no means all, of its devotees resolutely anti-religious and anti-Christian.

As the very word suggests, the Enlightenment was an era convinced that the lives of human beings could be illuminated so as to free themselves from the shackles of ignorance, superstition, bigotry, religious infantilism and fear, redolent, it was thought, of previous centuries. The faculty of illumination prized by enthusiasts of the Enlightenment was human reason, rather than divine revelation. The Enlightenment was the first significant social and intellectual movement to evolve independently of the political control of the Church in Europe for over 13 centuries.[31] Before the genesis of the Enlightenment, Christendom was normally able to use its political arm to strike down deviants from ecclesiastical doctrine.

Other general features of modern liberal theology are an acceptance of Kant's theory of knowledge, according to which God is beyond the ken of human rational knowledge; a keenness to use the insights of modern biblical research in theology and to regard the Bible as a product of human derivation; and a fervour for hermeneutics, the methodical investigation of the most appropriate way to discern the meaning of language. Dogmatic thinkers occasionally tend to assume that the meaning of a teaching is unambiguous, while hermeneutically-minded liberals, in response to questions such as 'Do you believe in God?', may be inclined to respond by stating: 'It depends what you *mean* by "believe" and "God".'

harnack and the first world war

Adolf von Harnack typified in his own way the facets of liberal theology outlined above. The strength of his work, as a Christian theologian, was his focus on Jesus' own proclamation, and its concomitant invitation for love to be shown in actions. As he said in his conclusion to his lectures of 1800, 'the goal of all Christian work, even of all theological work, can only be this – to discern ever more distinctly the simplicity and seriousness of the gospel, in order to become ever purer and stronger in *spirit*, and ever more loving and brotherly in *action*.'[32]

Liberal theologians are often accused of betraying Christian tradition by uncritically imbibing the zeitgeist of their times. Harnack stupefied many of his students and former students in 1914 when he publicly supported the declaration of his Emperor to wage war, on the eve of what became the First World War. If nothing of the above has led to the conclusion that Harnack was a great twentieth-century theologian, then the following observation might. Harnack taught two of the theological lodestars of the twentieth century – Karl Barth and Dietrich Bonhoeffer. Unlike their teacher, both opposed regimes of war, and Bonhoeffer was put to death for his troubles.

3

Alfred Firmin Loisy: 1857–1940

The truth is rarely pure, and never simple.
Oscar Wilde

Imagine the prospect of being buried largely unloved and unmourned in a grave already occupied by a rotting corpse. Envisage what it would be like to end your life publicly shunned and vilified. Conceive of being spat upon while walking down the street. Contemplate the suffering involved in being rejected by an institution to which you had devoted your life and allegiance. Such was the fate of the subject of this chapter, Alfred Loisy. The story of his life and learning is heartrending. He left a detailed account of it. Between 1930 and 1931 he published a lengthy autobiography in three volumes that recounts his interpretation of events and characters in his life. He called it *Mémoires pour servir à l'histoire religieuse de nôtre temps* ('Memoirs in the service of a religious history of our time').[1]

Loisy dedicated his entire life to the Catholic Church, only to be excoriated by its Roman leadership. In the first decade of the twentieth century he was excommunicated by order of Pope Pius X as a *vitandibus* – a psychologically brutal Latin term meaning 'someone who ought to be avoided'. Loisy incurred the penalty of major, as opposed to general, excommunication. The former requires Catholics publicly to shun the excommunicant, while the latter is a published denunciation.[2] His crime? To be a liberal thinker, labelled in Catholic circles as a Modernist, that is, as someone who attempted to reconcile Catholic doctrines and life with modern sciences, biblical studies and philosophies, the Enlightenment, and democracy. His judges in Rome accused him of distorting Christian faith by teaching falsehoods. The idea that a pope ought to align himself with modernity was clearly condemned in 1864 by Pope Pius IX in his *Syllabus Errorum* ('Syllabus of Errors'). This text was a denunciation of nineteenth-century theologies, philosophies and democratic government. It takes the form of 80 propositions, the last of which assails the assertion that 'the Roman pontiff can and ought to reconcile himself with progress, with liberalism, and with modern civilization'.[3]

Loisy was a Catholic priest who enjoyed a distinguished career in Paris as a professor of biblical studies and of the history of religions. Over time, the Christian faith of his youth became sorely tested by the results of his biblical research and its implications for dogmatic theology. Despite his excommunication and estrangement from the Church into which he had been initiated as a baby, he has a great deal to teach anyone interested in Christian theology. He did not abandon Christian faith, but a particular expression of it. As an adult he rejected late nineteenth-century formulations of medieval theology, called medievalism or neo-scholasticism. He was not disenthralled with medieval thought, but with reinterpretations of it in his own time that strove to ignore modern forms of knowledge. Loisy's great strength was his erudition. He knew far more about the history of the Church, the Bible and religions of the world than the French and Roman hierarchs who denounced him.

the life and times of alfred loisy

Loisy was born on 28 February 1857, and baptized the following day with the names Alfred Firmin. He entered the world as a neonate near the village of

Ambrières in the province of Champagne, in the French department of the Haute-Marne. The village had no more that 250 inhabitants. His father was Charles-Sebastian Loisy, a farmer, and his mother, Justine Desnalis, was a distant cousin of her husband, sharing a great-great-grandfather with him. Loisys had lived in the valley of the Marne for centuries.[4]

Albert was the second of three children to be born. He had an older brother and a younger sister. He grew up on the family farm on the outskirts of Ambrières. His childhood was not idyllic. Unlike his older brother, he was a weakling who was frequently humiliated by the sight of the more robust musculature of local farming boys. Throughout his childhood he suffered from chronic enteritis and was too frail to work planting or harvesting crops in the farm's fields. Consigned to home, he relaxed frequently with his sister and her friends and became adept at sowing dolls' clothes.

As a boy, Alfred enjoyed a religious disposition, even though his father was a sceptic in matters of religion, and his grandfathers and great-grandfathers, while attending liturgies from time to time, were not church-attending Catholics.

In 1869, a year before France declared war on Prussia, Alfred enrolled at a school in Vitry-le-François, which was close to his local village of Ambrières. Although the more brawny boys of his school taunted him with the name, 'le petit Loisy' ('the little Loisy'),[5] it was clear to his teachers that he was abnormally intelligent. After the Franco-Prussian war broke out in July 1870, Loisy once saw the Emperor Napoleon passing through Vitry on the way to the main theatre of war. The following August, enemy infantry occupied Ambrières and remained there until 1871. Albert's institutional education was thereby interrupted for two years. He was compelled to study at home with the help of his parish priest.

In October of 1872, he enrolled in an ecclesiastical college in Saint-Dizier. He formed a close friendship with a student called Alexandre Pitoye, whom Loisy later remembered as 'un brave garçon' ('a nice boy'). Loisy insisted that their friendship was above reproach, but it caused a scandal in the college that was irksome for them both.[6]

During October 1873, Loisy decided to become a priest. To that end, he left school the following year without the standard qualification of the baccalaureate, and entered the Grand Séminaire ('major seminary') of the diocese of Châlons-sur-Marne. He was not exceptional in this because the French Catholic Church of the day was experiencing a major rejuvenescence after its traumas in the wake of the French Revolution. It experienced few difficulties attracting teenagers to its seminaries. Between 1830 and 1870 the number of diocesan priests (as distinct from priests in religious institutes, such as the Benedictines) 'swelled to nearly 56,000, an increase of 39 per cent during a period when the overall population grew by only 17 per cent. ... In 1851 there were 34,000 nuns in France; twenty-five years later there were almost 128,000 ... .'[7]

When Loisy began his studies at Châlons he donned a soutane (a black cassock), which he was obliged to wear for the next 34 years of his life.[8] The education offered in the seminary was appallingly blinkered and reactionary. Loisy's teachers ignored mathematical and physical sciences and showed no interest even in ecclesiastical art. They disregarded the work of philosophers like Immanuel Kant (1724–1804) and Auguste Comte (1798–1857), and were fond of decrying Voltaire (1694–1778) as well as the French Revolution.[9] In the last quarter of the nineteenth century when Loisy undertook his ecclesiastical training, his seminary instructors favoured a neo-scholastic pedagogy.

Loisy stayed at Châlons for five years. He applied himself to study the Bible's Book of Genesis in Hebrew, as well as in Greek and Latin translations. He began a formal study of theology in 1875. He regarded his theological studies as tedious and he became distressed by religious doubts. He later described the period of 1875–9 as one of perpetual anxiety on his part.[10] He fretted about whether Christian doctrines concerning a Triune God and Jesus Christ were mere theories that do not refer to realities.[11]

Despite inner turmoil, in June of 1878 he was ordained a subdeacon (a clerical order abolished by the Second Vatican Council). He was 21 at the time. His ordination required him to remain celibate and daily to recite a breviary. He subsequently came to regard submitting to ordination as the worst mistake of his life.[12]

When his seminary days finished he moved to Paris in 1878, the year in which bishops established a Catholic university there. Loisy was enrolled in the first class of its faculty of theology. In 1880, the French government denied the institution the privilege of calling itself a university. Thereafter it was known as the Institut Catholique de Paris ('Catholic Institute of Paris').

neo-scholasticism   Scholasticism was a medieval form of learning that flourished in Europe between the eleventh and thirteenth centuries. It applied principles of logic to the interpretation of the Bible and patristic writings in order to elucidate or resolve contradictions in the texts. Neo-scholasticism was a repristination of scholasticism that gained ascendancy in Catholic seminaries during the late nineteenth and early twentieth centuries. It was a theological movement that largely ignored modern biblical research and post-Enlightenment philosophies. In 1879 it was sanctioned by Pope Leo XIII in his encyclical, *Aeterni Patris* ('[Of the] Eternal Father'). The net effect of this missive was that scholastic theology and philosophy (in a neo-scholastic guise) became a compulsory approach to study in seminaries up to the Second Vatican Council (1962–5). Thomas Aquinas' thought dominated neo-scholasticism.

Loisy soon met Louis Duchesne, the Institute's Professor of Ecclesiastical History. Duchesne was an advocate of applying an historical-critical method to the interpretation of texts.

---

historical-critical method   This method is a procedure for interpreting the Bible (and dogmas) that has ancient origins, but was developed in a modern form especially in the nineteenth century. Its historical roots can be traced to Scholiasts (scholars who annotated time-worn literary texts) in the ancient library of Alexandria. There they commented on Greek epics and poets. In its modern guise, it is an *historical* method of interpretation in that it regards all texts, including biblical and dogmatic ones, as human products of particular times, locations, cultures and personalities. It is *critical* in that it is a task of analysis rather than reverential citation or exposition. The historical-critical method does not take as its starting point the assumption that the Bible is a compendium of divine dicta which are comprehensible without attention to the historical provenance of particular texts. The method begins with introductory questions applied to a text: Is it authentic? Has it been edited? Where and when was it composed? What is the literary style of the text? Why was it written? What is its historical background? With prefatory questions considered, the method then proceeds to consider such matters as deciphering the original language of a text, the sources it has relied upon, concepts that are prominent, and, if applicable, the way writers subsequent to a text's original author have modified it.[13]

Loisy became nervy and homesick in Paris. He returned to Ambrières in January of 1879. His bishop was displeased with him. As soon as Loisy was ordained a priest in June of that year, the bishop punished him by assigning him to a remote and run-down parish with virtually no worshippers. After six months he was assigned closer to home.

Loisy's health improved while he worked as a rural curé. So much so that, with his bishop's approval, he took up residence again at the Institut Catholique on 12 May 1881, after an absence of 30 months.

The bright star in his life in Paris was Duchesne, the most competent and inspiring of his professors. Duchesne's specialized field of research work was the history of the early Church. He was a rarity in Catholic academic circles of the time because he was also adept at higher biblical criticism, which sought to decipher the original authorship and provenance of biblical texts. It is distinguishable from lower biblical criticism, which analyses topics in texts. Higher biblical criticism as it was practised in the nineteenth century by Duchesne, Loisy and Liberal Protestants involved three principal methods of investigation – source criticism, form criticism and redaction criticism. The first strives to uncover the historical identity of the authors of biblical texts. It also hopes to understand the original intentions that motivated authors to write in the ways they did. Source criticism aims to delineate the original localities and circumstances in which texts were produced.[14]

Inspired by Duchesne, Loisy began to study the Bible critically. His boyish enthusiasm for traditional Christian doctrines was about to become unhinged. His studies convinced him that conventional ecclesiastical doctrines were in need of radical reform. He continued to be afflicted by a chronic disquietude over his faith. By 1886, his ties to traditional Catholicism had become severely tested, but he maintained links with the Catholic Church in the hope that it could be infused with modern patterns of thought. Apart from his uncertain religious faith, his physical health began to fail him again. In 1886 he was diagnosed to be in the early phases of pulmonary tuberculosis. He recovered sufficiently to return to Paris after a period of four months' rest at Cannes.

Loisy's work in Paris laid the foundation for a long and distinguished academic career. He formally and successfully defended a thesis in Paris on 7 March 1890, and was awarded the degree of Doctor of Theology. His dissertation commented on the Hebrew Bible and became his first book. For the rest of his life he studied and published tirelessly, producing 60 books and about 300 articles in journals.[15]

As soon as Loisy became a Doctor of Theology he was appointed as the Professor of Sacred Scripture at the Institut Catholique.[16] Trouble with ecclesiastical authority was looming. His lectures and their critical approach to biblical studies incurred the displeasure of Henri Icard, a priest in charge of seminarians in Paris who belonged to the Society of Saint Sulpice (a religious institute established in Paris in 1642 to educate priests). Icard forbade his seminarians from attending Loisy's lectures. The Archbishop of Paris, Cardinal François Richard de la Verge, became an even more powerful opponent of Loisy's ideas than Icard.

The upshot of the combined opposition of Icard and Richard de la Verge was that Loisy was forced to resign from teaching. The published results of his critical examination of the Bible irritated the cardinal.

The day of his resignation illustrates well why he found himself at odds with the highest of his ecclesiastical authorities. He resigned on 18 November 1893. On the same day, Pope Leo XIII promulgated an encyclical (circular letter) devoted to the study of sacred scripture. It bore the title *Providentissimus Deus* ('Most Provident God'). Leo proffered the view in this text that God was the author of the books of the Bible. Commenting on this view, Loisy could hardly have been more scathing: 'The idea of God as author of a book is more contradictory, more absurd in itself, than the idea of a toad-man or a snake-woman. It is an infantile myth.'[17]

Calling a papal teaching an infantile myth was and is a certain recipe for trouble. Unable to teach seminarians, Loisy began work in 1894 as a chaplain to a convent of Dominican nuns in Neuilly-sur-Seine, a suburb on the northern borders of Paris close to the beguilingly beautiful park, the Bois de Boulogne.

loisy's rejoinder to harnack

Loisy began lecturing in Paris once more in 1900 with an appointment to the École Practique des Hautes Études ('Practical School of Higher Studies'). This was the same year in which Adolf von Harnack was lecturing in Berlin on Christianity's essence. Loisy was well aware of Harnack's work, so much so that he published a response to Harnack's *Das Wesen des Christentums*. Loisy's reply was issued as a book in 1902, with the title *L'Évangile et l'Église* ('The Gospel and the Church').

Harnack's book grabbed public attention in Europe. It was reprinted 70 times and translated into 15 languages. It was a particularly discomforting treatise for the Catholic Church. The Catholic hierarchy of the day insisted that the structure and rituals of the Church are not derived from Greek culture, but stem directly from Jesus' intention to establish a Church.[18]

Loisy decided to counter Harnack with a different historical account of the Church's origins. In *L'Évangile et l'Église* he argued that Harnack was mistaken to discount so drastically doctrinal developments after Jesus' death. He observed that the substance of Christianity resides in the Church's faith that develops over centuries under the impulse and guidance of God's Holy Spirit.

Harnack based the central argument *Das Wesen des Christentums* on a text from Matthew's Gospel that recounts Jesus speaking of himself in relation to God designated as Father: 'All things have been handed over to me by my Father; and no one knows the Son except the Father, and no one knows the Father except the Son and anyone to whom the Son chooses to reveal him' (Mt 11: 27). On this verse Harnack based his entire book and its central thesis that Jesus' consciousness of divine paternity is the substance of Christianity.

Harnack spoke as an historian, and it is for this reason that Loisy intended his rejoinder as an historical inquiry. To devastating effect, he used historical criticism to show that the text of Mt 11: 27 was a late interpolation into the gospel after it had been originally composed. On historical grounds, the text could not be used as evidence of Jesus' awareness of God as Father. Loisy recoiled at the idea of reducing the history and essence of Christianity to a single verse.

Loisy also accused Harnack of extruding Jesus from his historical context by ignoring the eschatological tenor of Jesus' teaching. He insisted that Jesus pined for the coming of God's kingdom and in so doing belonged firmly to a Jewish tradition.[19]

Speaking historically, Loisy was clear that Jesus did not establish the Church, establish a hierarchy, devise sacraments, or bequeath dogmas to later generations. He concluded instead that it was only natural that the structures and teachings of the Church would evolve from the gospel of Jesus. The principal thesis of his book was that the Church would inevitably grow from the gospel. To the question of why a hierarchy emerged, Loisy responded that all societies, including Christian communities, need authority and authoritative structures.

---

eschatology   Eschatology is one of the most difficult fields of theological discussion. It is taxing because it strives to speak of matters of which living human beings have no experience – what happens after death and the end of human history. The word 'eschatology' comes from two Greek terms: *eschata* ('the last things') and *logos* ('word'). Eschatology is a human discourse about the ultimate destiny of the world and its inhabitants.

One of the most frequently quoted and usually misunderstood aphorisms of his book is the phrase, 'Jesus announced the kingdom, and it was the Church which came' ('Jésus annonçait le royaume, et c'est l'Église qui est venue').[20] Loisy did not intend this comment to be a rebarbative slighting of the Church, as is often thought.[21] The phrase was part of a wider strategy to argue that the evolution of the Church was inevitable.

Fatefully for Loisy, he argued in this book that Jesus did not institute any sacraments. The text was condemned by the Archbishop of Paris. Loisy continued to publish his ideas. In 1903 he produced two books – *Autour d'un petit livre* ('On a Little Book') and *Le Quatrième Évangile* ('The Fourth Gospel'). Both texts were placed on the Index of Forbidden Books by Pope Pius. This meant that no Catholic student of theology was permitted to consult them.

Autour d'un petit livre refers in its title to *L'Évangile et l'Église* ('un petit livre') and is a lively defence of the earlier book. Like 'the little book' to which it refers, *Autour d'un petit livre* concludes that the idea that Jesus instituted seven sacraments does not stand up to critical historical investigation.[22] It was therefore condemned. On 18 December 1903, the Vatican's Holy Office ordered that five of Loisy's books be placed on the Index.[23]

In 1904, Loisy diplomatically and regretfully resigned from his lectureship and went to live in the country. He abandoned all priestly duties and activities in 1906, but continued to study and write. During 1907 and 1908 he published a large two-volume study of Christian scriptures called *Les Évangiles synoptiques* ('The Synoptic Gospels', that is, the Gospels According to Mark, Matthew and Luke).

On 1 November 1906, Loisy celebrated Mass, as all priests of the time were required to do on a daily basis. He never celebrated Mass again.[24] He invested his energies in research and lecturing. By the time he died, he had spent six decades studying the Bible and its implications for theology and Christianity.

the modernist crisis

The critical investigation of the Bible flourished in German, mostly Protestant, universities throughout the nineteenth century. Those Catholic scholars who tried to learn from it and develop it have come to be remembered as Modernists.

---

modernism   Modernism is a Catholic cousin of Protestant theological Liberalism. Modernists and liberals at the beginning of the twentieth century shared the conviction that traditional Christian theology needed to be reinvigorated and reinterpreted by accommodating the findings of modern biblical criticism, archaeology and science. Modernism was an amorphous phenomenon without a clearly defined set of doctrines. It was more an intellectual temperament or tendency than a school of thought. It involved an enthusiasm for the philosophy of Kant, democracy, the historical-critical examination of the Bible, empirical sciences and freedom of academic investigation. As its very name connotes, Catholic Modernism was an attempt by a handful of intellectuals to marry Catholic life and thought with modern cultures and forms of knowledge. They were also keen to see medieval forms of governance in the Church reconstituted along more democratic and less autocratic or plutocratic principles. Modernists and liberals were emboldened to reconcile Christianity with the knowledge and experiences peculiar to their time.

Loisy was the most prominent Modernist thinker, but no two Modernists shared exactly the same ideas. Others linked to Loisy as Modernists include the Irish Jesuit, George Tyrrell, and Edouard Le Roy. Baron Friedrich von Hügel was a friend to and sympathizer with Modernists, but escaped censure himself.

To speak of a Modernist Crisis is to refer to the way the hierarchy of the Catholic Church responded to thinkers like Loisy and Tyrrell and to the reactions of the latter. The Papacy of 1907 saw Modernism as corrosive of its authority, and sought to suppress it. Modernists and liberals were perceived by Pius X and many others as a threat to the religious and social stability of Europe. For over 1,000 years, church and civil authorities there had invoked divine legitimization for their hierarchical and aristocratic domination of peoples, a legitimization of which Modernism was mistrustful.

The response of the hierarchy to Modernists was not dialogue or acceptance of new thoughts, but relentless denunciation, hounding, policing and spying. Late in the twentieth century, Rosemary Haughton described the Modernist controversy and the fashion in which Modernists were treated in these terms: 'This episode of Catholic history does not have the horror of the Spanish inquisition or the medieval persecution of the Jews, but for ruthlessness and psychological brutality, for sheer inhumanity and lack of basic decency, it is hard to forgive.'[25]

On 3 July 1907, the Vatican condemned Modernists in general and Loisy's ideas in particular, although it did not mention him by name. On this day, the Vatican's Holy Office, now called the Congregation for the Doctrine of the Faith, published a text of 65 propositions condemning Modernism. It was called *Lamentabili Sane Exitu* ('With truly lamentable results'). Three years earlier, Cardinal Richard of Paris had enlisted a group of Parisian theologians to assess two of Loisy's works – *L'Évangile et l'Église* and *Autour d'un petit livre*. The conclusions of the group were used to compose *Lamentabili*.[26] Of its propositions, 24 focused on biblical matters; two dealt with the nature of faith; 11 concentrated on the identity of Jesus Christ; 13 discussed sacraments; and the others focused on the Church. It opposed the notions that the Bible can be interpreted independently from ecclesiastical authorities and it insisted that Christian truth is immutable.

Two months after the promulgation of *Lamentabili*, on 8 September 1907, Pius X joined in with his own denunciation. It was contained in his encyclical published on that day, *Pascendi Dominici Gregis* ('Pasturing or looking after the Lord's flock').

Pascendi offers a summary of what it takes to be central Modernist ideas, without naming individual Modernists, and clearly signals to the Catholic bishops of the world that they are to ferret out and silence Modernists in their dioceses. This papally inspired purge of Modernists was to afflict Catholic theologians until 1967. After the publication of *Pascendi*, between 1910 and 1967 all bishops, teachers in seminaries and theologians in Catholic institutes of higher learning were compelled to take an anti-Modernist oath.[27] The Second Vatican Council ended the purge, and once more Catholic instructors and theologians could work without fear of being denounced and spied upon (for a while at least).

Pius X coined the term 'Modernism' to designate the pattern of thinking denounced in *Pascendi*: 'Can anybody who takes a survey of the whole system be surprised that We should define Modernism as the synthesis of all heresies?'[28] He described and execrated what he regarded as the four objectionable pillars of Modernist thought – agnosticism, immanentism (the view that familiarity with God derives from personal experience rather than revelation), evolutionism (the belief that doctrines as human products change over time) and democratism (the denial that Jesus was the founder of the Church).[29]

Pius X's *Pascendi* inaugurated an inglorious phase in the history of the Catholic Church:

> The encyclical caused an immediate crisis throughout the Catholic Church. It inaugurated a period of ecclesiastical McCarthyism when 'modernists' were hunted down with a zeal that was as pathological as the paranoia that fed it. ... Career-orientated priests denounced their colleagues. A climate of fear prevailed throughout the Church.[30]

Loisy and Tyrrell, the principal thinkers targeted as Modernists, riposted by declaring that they did not recognize their thought in the characterizations of *Pascendi*. Both sought to explain their ideas in published rejoinders. Tyrrell was publicly denounced as a Modernist by the Primate of Belgium, Cardinal Mercier. He responded with his book, *Medievalism: A Reply to Cardinal Mercier*, written in refined English prose deploying devastating wit and rhetorical power.[31] Loisy sought to justify his ideas and method of research by publishing *Simple Réflexions sur le décret du Saint-Office 'Lamentabile sane Exitu' et sur l'encyclique Pascendi Dominici gregis'* ('Simple reflections on the Holy Office's decree and on the encyclical').[32]

To make sure Loisy was finally and properly muzzled, on 7 March 1908, Pius X excommunicated him. The penalty of major excommunication meant that Loisy's Catholic housekeeper had to leave the home and avoid all contact with him. She had been persuaded by her local curé that, were she to become gravely ill in Loisy's house, she could not receive sacraments and her soul would be in danger of perdition. After six weeks away she ignored the decree of excommunication and returned to cook and care for Loisy. She no longer worried about her salvation and set to work altering his soutanes and changing them into frock coats.[33]

Papal muzzling did not work. Loisy deftly transformed adversity into opportunity. In 1909 he accepted an appointment as the Professor of the History of Religions in the state-run Collège de France.[34] He remained in that post until 1932 and published a string of books devoted to the historical origins of Christianity and the comparative history of religions. These works included *La Religion* ('Religion', 1917); *Les Acts des Apôtres* ('The Acts of the Apostles', 1920); and *Essai historique sur le sacrifice* ('Historical Essay on Sacrifice', 1920). He also produced two autobiographical studies: *Choses passées* ('Past or dated things', 1913); and the previously cited *Mémoires pour servir à l'histoire religieuse do nôtre temps*. The last text mentioned contains Loisy's interpretation of Modernism.

He delivered his final lecture at the Collège de France on 16 April 1932, and retired to live in Ceffond, close to the place of his birth. In retirement he imposed on himself a rigorous programme of research. He published eight books in the initial seven years of his retirement. He penned his final interpretation of the Gospels and early Christian literature in *La naissance du chistianisme* ('The Birth of Christianity', 1933).

The final decade of Loisy's life was blighted by excruciating loneliness. He died of uraemia on 1 June 1940. When he was buried there were only three mourners at his funeral: his niece and two young working-class people. His burial was devoid of religious ritual. His coffin was lowered into the grave of Maria Maulandre, who had been buried there 70 years previously. Underneath her name on the stone marking her grave were chiselled the words: 'Alfred Loisy/Prêtre/Retiré du Ministère/et de l'Enseignment/Professeur au Collège de France/1857–1940/ Tuam in Votis/tenuit Voluntatem': 'Alfred Loisy/Priest/Retired from Ministry/ and from Teaching/Professor of the College of France/1857–1940/He who observed your will by keeping his vows.'

This inscription is remarkable. It was composed by Loisy himself. Even though he had resigned from all sacramental responsibilities, at the point of death he still regarded himself as a priest. He no longer performed ecclesiastical rituals, but all his adult life he was convinced that he exercised a priestly ministry by serving and instructing students, as well as illuminating colleagues. The final Latin phrase of his inscription comes from a prayer in the then current Catholic rite of burial that was denied to him.

Loisy was a pioneer in Catholic thought. His views that God did not write the Bible, that apostles of Jesus did not write the Gospels, that there is a difference between the teachings of Jesus and many teachings of the Church, are now commonly accepted by theologians and biblical scholars. The historical-critical method of studying the Bible and investigating the history of the Church has uncovered too much information to be dismissed. It is not the only way of interpreting the Bible, yet it finally received papal approbation by Pope Pius XII in 1943.

After Loisy was excommunicated and socially shunned by other Catholics, he received a letter from a kindly disposed and youthful Protestant pastor. Loisy ends the second volume of his memoirs by quoting him, but he does not record the pastor's name. The letter was written in French on 5 June 1908. It contained the following observation: 'I do not know if I understand the signs of the times, but I believe that, for Protestantism as for Catholicism, the ideal, is to disappear and to give way to something which will be worth more than Catholicism and Protestantism.'[35] This young man's rueful observation and consoling words to Alfred Firmin Loisy, written over 100 years ago, have lost none of their aptness and prophetic perspicacity.

4

Evelyn Underhill: 1875–1941

We had the experience but missed the meaning.
T.S. Eliot

'I believe in God and think it is better to love and help poor people around me than go on saying that I love an abstract spirit whom I have never seen.'[1] The author of these arresting words was a 17-year-old student writing in London during the final decade of the nineteenth century. She lived long enough to witness the First World War and the outbreak of the Second. Her name was Evelyn Underhill. She is rarely discussed in books devoted to theology, and is occasionally categorized as not being a theologian at all.[2] She may well have been inclined to think the same, yet John Macquarrie's survey of twentieth-century religious thought counts her among the three most significant female religious thinkers of the century.[3] She was in any case a prolific author of books and articles. The bibliography of her published works contains around 390 items, including 40 books, devoted to Christian, theological and generally religious themes.[4] It also lists a series of novels. She displayed an aptitude for creative writing even as a teenager.[5]

The intellectual task for which she is most noted is the investigation of the particular form of religious experience known as mysticism. Underhill intuited at the age of 17 that mysticism is not a magical or occult phenomenon, but is inseparable from practical engagement to improve the lives of other people.

---

mysticism   The word 'mysticism' comes from the Greek term for 'mystery' (μυστήριον/'mysterion').[6] The Greek word is rooted in the verb 'to close', as in closing access, or refusing admission. A mysterious community is one that is secret, closed off or inaccessible to outsiders. Religious cults often have secret rites that are only available to people who have been initiated into the groups. For early Christians, a mystery was not so much an intellectual conundrum, but a truth that was inaccessible to human beings unless it had been revealed to them from God in the figure of Jesus Christ. A mystic is someone who seeks such truth. The scrutiny of mysticism is typically known as mystical theology. Its main task is to explore mystical experiences that individuals report. Simply stated, a mystical experience is a form of human perception that the experiencing individual interprets as an encounter with either the reality of God or, more amorphously expressed, Ultimate Reality. Mystical theology is an investigation of a human experience which is interpreted by the experiencing individual as a divine-human encounter, or a human perception of that which is ultimately or fundamentally real. A mystical experience, by definition, is intensely individualistic in the sense that no one can share, prove or discount what another person believes he or she is perceiving. In these terms, each and every type of human experience has the potential to be regarded by its experiencer as mystical, whether it be listening to Beethoven's last piano sonatas, nursing a child, smelling a rose, marching along streets protesting against nuclear weapons, or fretfully languishing in a prison cell.

Evelyn Underhill was not a celibate priestly theologian. Nor was she a university professor. She was a married woman who studied and worked at home in London. For much of her adult life she did not worship in a church community. During the final stages of her life she became a pacifist, at a time when the churches she knew were broadly supportive of military endeavours in the period leading to the Second World War. During her adult life she took particular care to spend extended periods each week visiting and helping poor families in the slums of London's North Kensington.

Why is such a woman considered in this book in the company of the great and famous historian and theologian, Adolf von Harnack? Because too often definitions of who a theologian is, and what theologians do, are overly narrow and restrictive. A standard profile of a theologian is that of a highly erudite male priest or pastor who has been extensively educated in a seminary, monastery or university. For most of Christian history, theologians hailed as Doctors of the Church in the Church of the Roman Rite have been priests, bishops, and monks. A book published late in the twentieth century discusses what its author regards as the seven greatest theologians in the history of Christianity. They are all men: Paul (d. c. 62–5 CE), Origen (c. 185–c. 254), Augustine of Hippo (354–430), Thomas Aquinas (c. 1225–74), Martin Luther (1483–1546), Friedrich Schleiermacher (1768–1834) and Karl Barth (1886–1968).[7] Another text, published in 2004, discusses what its authors esteem as 50 key Christian thinkers over the past two millennia. Of the 50 thinkers discussed, only two women are mentioned, and both were born in the 1930s. No woman before the twentieth century is treated as a key Christian thinker.[8] Both books illustrate how the long-standing preponderance of male voices in the history of theology has been regulative.

In the twentieth century, women in the West were more readily able to vote, to work for salaries, to be governmental ministers, prime ministers and presidents, and to pursue professional careers independently of the context of marriage. They also gained far better access to higher education, especially in the latter half of the century. By the century's end, a large and internationally dispersed body of female theological professors had gained widespread public attention with their interpretations of Christianity. The task of a theologian is no longer so tightly the preserve of clerical men as it was in the past.

Evelyn Underhill never received a formal seminary training in theology. A university degree in theology was never conferred on her for having undertaken a prescribed course of studies. Women in England at the beginning of the twentieth century were not eligible for degrees. In the USA right up until the 1960s, women could not study for degrees in Catholic theological faculties.

early years

Evelyn Underhill was born on 6 December 1875, the same year as Albert Schweitzer (1875–1965) and Carl Gustav Jung (1875–1961). She was born in Wolverhampton. She was the only child of Alice Lucy Ironmonger and Arthur

---

women and doctors of the church   The extent to which women have been considered ineligible to teach theology or doctrine to anyone is exposed by the ecclesiastical tradition of honouring learned and pious Christians with the title of 'Doctor of the Church'. The Catholic, Anglican and some Orthodox Churches recognize the title. In academic and ecclesiastical settings, a doctor is one who teaches (from the Latin, *doctor* ['teacher', 'instructor']). A lecturer is a person who reads prepared notes so as to educate students (from *lector* ['reader']). The word 'doctor' is linked etymologically to the term 'doctrine', which simply means 'a teaching' (Latin: *doctrina*). The Doctors of the Church are canonized saints – baptized Christians declared to be holy (or devoted to God) by a pope or ecumenical (universally representative) council of bishops. They include Ephraem of Edessa (306–73), Gregory Nazianzus (330–90), Augustine of Hippo (354–430), Bernard of Clairvaux (1090–1153), Thomas Aquinas (c. 1225–74), John of the Cross (1542–91) and Robert Bellarmine (1542–1621). *The New Catholic Encyclopedia*, published in 1967, observed correctly at the time that no woman had ever been proclaimed a Doctor of the Church. It also opined 'it would seem that no woman is likely to be named because of the link between this title and the teaching office, which is limited to males'.[9] Three years later, in 1970, Pope Paul VI named Catherine of Siena (1347–80) and Teresa of Avila (1515–82) as Doctors of the Church. Thérèse of Lisieux (1873–97) was similarly honoured in 1997 by Pope John Paul II, although she is not known for her erudition in the same way as other Doctors, such as Albert the Great (1220–80) and Bonaventure (1217–74). There are currently 33 Doctors of the Church, only three of whom are women, and all three were thus nominated in the second half of the twentieth century.

Underhill. Her father was an accomplished barrister whose career was based in London. As a child she was baptized and confirmed in the Church of England. Her parents showed no interest in attending church regularly, and before the 1920s, Evelyn was reluctant to align herself publicly with the Church of England. By 1921, however, she had reached the stage of being able to regard the Anglican Church as her primary religious community.[10] She once decided to become a Catholic, but changed her mind after the publication of a papal condemnation of modern ideas – of which, more in a moment.

Her childhood was lonely, partly because she was initially schooled privately without much contact with other children. After her private education she was sent to study at Sandgate House, near Folkstone. While growing up in London and leading a solitary life, she did manage to make friends. Her closest ones as a child were two boys, who were brothers – Jeff and Hubert Stuart Moore. The latter became her husband. She married Hubert, a barrister, in 1907 when she was 31.

After leaving school she enrolled in the Ladies' Department of King's College, London. At the time, the College was not empowered to confer degrees in its own right. There she studied languages, history, art and botany.[11] Her interest in languages had been stimulated by her frequent holidays with her mother. The two would often visit France and Italy. These travels also fired her fascination with the religious experiences of different cultures.

During the four decades of the twentieth century in which she was alive, she engaged in three primary interrelated religious activities: (1) writing and publishing; (2) leading retreats, that is, instructing groups of people who gathered together away from their habitual settings for extended periods of prayer and reflection; and (3) what she called spiritual direction – giving advice on religious matters to people who sought it. She died in London in 1941 as the Second World War raged.

an age of suspicion

The historical context of Evelyn Underhill's life was one of constant social change and intellectual ferment. She was born 16 years after Charles Darwin published *On the Origin of Species* (1859), and grew up in London amid fervid intellectual debates over biblical accounts of creation considered in relation to Darwin's theory of evolution by natural selection. She was alive while Friedrich Nietzsche charged Christianity with moral turpitude, and Sigmund Freud insisted that religious allegiance leads to mental illness. When she was a young woman, London was the largest city in the world, its population having reached 4.5 million by 1901.[12] She saw at first hand the transformation in urban daily life wrought by urbanization, secularization and the electrification of streets and households.

Above all, she existed in a time and place wherein religious and governmental authorities were challenged and

suspicion   The English word 'suspicion' comes from the Latin verb *suspicere*, which means 'to look up at'. It suggests a spatial metaphor of a person looking up from beneath something to see what underlies it. Peering upwards from beneath floorboards might reveal that they are rotting with worms. They may appear solid and strong, but in reality are about to collapse. Applied to religion, closely scrutinizing ancient doctrines may well show that they are based on falsehoods and misunderstandings, and thereby prone to implosion. The nineteenth century produced a **hermeneutics of suspicion** with regard to Christian doctrines. Feuerbach's *The Essence of Christianity* (1841) is the archetypal textbook of a hermeneutics of suspicion.

called into question at their respective cores. She lived through an age of suspicion towards ecclesiastical authorities and the doctrines they sought to convince their audiences were true.

Modern biblical studies in particular fuelled the mistrust that the biblical bases for many Christian doctrines were unstable. In the nineteenth century it was widely believed that the Bible was the oldest known collection of writing, inspired by God, and hence unlike any other text. Such a view was torpedoed in the latter half of the nineteenth century by Assyriologists who had learned to decipher cuneiform script found in Mesopotamia. They discovered a narrative that contains many of the details found in the biblical story of the flood, and yet predates the Bible. The Bible's story had obviously been inspired by two Mesopotamian texts – the Epic of Gilgamesh (late second century BCE) and the Poem of the Supersage (*Atrahasis*, seventeenth century BCE).[13] Biblical scholars in the nineteenth century also exposed a multitude of factual errors and textual contradictions in the Bible. The intellectual and religious ferment of Underhill's time eventually dragged her into a profound personal turmoil.

life and works

Underhill began to publish before she married. Her first book, *A Bar Lamb's Ballad Book*, was issued in 1902. It is a witty commentary on convoluted English legal customs, which is not altogether surprising in view of the profession of both her father and husband.[14]

Her sense of isolation as a child continued throughout her adult life because neither her parents, nor her husband, were interested in her religious investigations and publications. She had to undertake her work at home without the accoutrement of an academic's office.

In February of 1907, Evelyn stayed in the Franciscan convent of St Mary of the Angels, located in Southampton. There she contemplated the future direction of her life, and experienced a strong desire to be initiated into the Catholic Church.[15]

Thus began the first major emotional turmoil of her life. 1907 was a time of crisis for her. Her husband was resolutely opposed to her desire to convert to Catholicism. She married him in July of 1907. On 8 September of the same year, Pope Pius X condemned Modernism (discussed in the previous chapter). His denunciation helped Evelyn Underhill map her future and lead her out of an emotional impasse. His actions inadvertently convinced her that she could not betray her interest in modern life and thought. She decided not to become a Catholic.

mysticism examined

The crisis she underwent in 1907 fired her interest in mysticism. So too did a cluster of texts published early in her career. These included William Inge's *Christian Mysticism* (1899), William James' *Varieties of Religious Experience* (1902), Baron Friedrich von Hügel's *The Mystical Element in Religion* (1908), and Henri Delacroix's *Études d'Histoire et de Psychologie du Mysticisme: Les Grands Mystics Chrétiens* ('Studies of the History and Psychology of Mysticism: The Great Christian Mystics', 1908). She set about gathering and studying these and a host of other texts by mystical writers. The fruit of her labours is her most significant book. It was published in 1911 as *Mysticism: A Study in the Nature and Development of Man's Religious Consciousness*. In this and two other early works, *The Mystic Way* (1913) and *Practical Mysticism* (1914), she undertook a theological and psychological analysis of reports of mystical experience.

It is important to note that her response to the religious and intellectual turmoil of her day, sparked by constant social change, new science and the philosophical debates stemming from the Enlightenment, led her to present the essence of Christian life to her readers as an *experiential* rather than *purely rational* endeavour. After Immanuel Kant debarred the idea that theoretical reason furnishes knowledge of God, Friedrich Schleiermacher responded by asserting that the pith of religion is not rational knowledge, but the experience or feeling of absolute dependence on God. As he says: 'The common element in all howsoever diverse expressions of piety, by which these are conjointly distinguished from all other feelings, or, in other words, the self-identical essence of piety is this: the consciousness of being absolutely dependent, or, which is the same thing, of being in relation with God.'[16]

Evelyn Underhill stands in the shadow of Schleiermacher. In the preface to the first edition of her book, *Mysticism*, she indicates clearly that in her terms, mysticism is the highest form of human consciousness. This explains why she devotes a good deal of attention in the book to a psychological probing of mystical experiences. She understands the subject of mysticism as a life process rather than an intellectual speculation. She defines mysticism broadly as 'the expression of the innate tendency of the human spirit towards complete harmony with the transcendent order'.[17] As such, it is a human movement towards, and desire for, an end which may variously be called the God of Christianity, the World-soul of Pantheism (the belief that God is in all things), or the Absolute of Philosophy.[18]

Mysticism is an erudite book. It has an Appendix charting the entire history of Western mysticism and an extensive bibliography listing multiple writings by mystics, general studies of mysticism, and treatises on theology, psychology and philosophy. It also contains works devoted to magic. It is not a dispassionate study of mysticism, but a deeply felt pleading on behalf of its author to encourage her readers to accept that mysticism, as an intense form of religious experience, is the highest achievement that human beings can realize in their lives. It is not the privilege of an elect few, but is potentially attainable by anyone. She confirms this view in *Practical Mysticism*: 'the contemplative consciousness is a faculty proper to all men, though few take the trouble to develop it.'[19]

Mysticism is divided into two parts, called respectively, 'The Mystic Fact' and 'The Mystic Way'. The first part provides a general introduction to the topic of mysticism, while the second is decidedly psychological in the sense that it attempts to elaborate a theory of the nature of human beings' mystical consciousness. It attends to the different experiential stages a mystic might traverse before reaching his or her goal of conscious union with God or Ultimate Reality. Part one considers mysticism in relation to vitalism (the belief that life does not emerge from purely physical processes), psychology, theology, symbolism and magic. Its fourth chapter is crucial because it outlines Underhill's understanding of mysticism's main features. Here, she restates a position made earlier in the book that 'Mysticism, in its pure form, is the science of ultimates, the science of union with the Absolute, and nothing else, and that the mystic is the person who attains to this union, not the person who talks about it. Not to *know about*, but to *Be*, is the mark of the real initiate.'[20]

Later in this pivotal chapter she designates four cardinal characteristics of mysticism, deliberately distancing herself from William James. He had delineated four marks of mystical experience: ineffability, noetic (relating to knowledge) quality, transciency and passivity. In counterpoint to these, Underhill teaches that authentic mysticism is in the first place 'active and practical, not passive and theoretical'.[21] Expressed differently, mysticism for her is not fidelity to an intellectual opinion, but a way of living. Secondly, mysticism is entirely spiritual and transcendental. It is not concerned with exploring anything in the visible world. Third, the object of mystical experience is both 'the Reality of all there is' and 'a living and personal Object of Love'. Finally, a person's experience of living in union with the One (God/Ultimate Reality) is a form of enhanced life which is achieved through an arduous psychological process that may lead to ecstasy, which Underhill terms 'the Unitive State'.

All this may appear an occult mush of meaningless to a dispassionate inquirer into mysticism. All that really needs to be said to diffuse such an impression is that Underhill's understanding of mysticism is as an intense experience of human love, which the experiencer interprets religiously as an encounter with God, understood as Love:

Mysticism, then, is not an opinion: it is not a philosophy. It has nothing in common with the pursuit of occult knowledge. … it is not to be identified with any kind of religious queerness. It is the name of that organic process which involves the perfect consummation of the Love of God: the achievement here and now of the immortal heritage of man. Or, if you like it better – for this means exactly the same thing – it is the art of establishing his conscious relation with the Absolute.[22]

Three words summarize Underhill's understanding of mysticism: reality, life and love. In her terms, mysticism is an intense experience of reality as love which results in an augmented quality of life and ultimately in union with the life of God. The aim of developing a mystical consciousness is always union with God. Underhill outlines five psychologically distinct steps which an individual needs to traverse in order to attain a consciousness of being united with God. These steps are explained in the second part of *Mysticism*, as well as in the books *The Mystic Way* and *Practical Mysticism*.

The five steps are conversion, purification, illumination, darkness and union. The first involves a psychological experience of conversion from being unaware of Ultimate Reality to being awakened so as to be conscious of the divine. The second involves a vivid awareness of contrast a person experiences between God and

---

religious experience   Theologians often regard religious experience as a resource for talking about God, while philosophers occasionally ask whether religious experiences provide an evidential basis for belief in God. Expressed simply, a religious experience is a form of perception interpreted by an individual as an encounter with divine reality. Any human experience has the potential to be religious. The English word 'experience' is related to the Latin term, *experientia* ('experiment, trial or proof'; the prefix 'ex' means 'out of'). Inherent in the notion of experience is the suggestion of a person undergoing a trial, test or journey, and emerging therefrom with perception or knowledge gained by way of the test. An experience is a perception generating knowledge that a person attains through and after direct encounter with things in the world. An experience always involves a process of interpretation in which an individual decides precisely what is encountered. What renders an experience *religious* is *negativity*. Experience of mortality, suffering, despair and loneliness are all negative in the sense that they involve the absence of something or someone life-enhancing. The very negativity of such experiences is simultaneously suggestive of its opposite – life, love, health, compassion and friendship. To be religious is to be bound to another (from the Latin *religare*, 'to tie together'). Any experience which evokes what is absent simultaneously pines for a presence. In the case of theology and mysticism, the presence hoped for is God's.

himself or herself. The sense of disparity invites penance and mortification to detach a person from all that is other than God. The third step is captured in the image of betrothal: after a long, possibly lifelong process of purification, an individual can develop a sense of being in God's presence, but not yet united with God. The fourth step, darkness, is crucial to an understanding of mysticism as a form of religious experience. It is evoked by the phrase, 'the dark night of the soul'. It is a prelude to experiencing union with God and involves a person feeling weighed down by sentiments of solitude, emptiness, uselessness and stasis. From this stage the mystic progresses to a final stage of union with the love of God, symbolized by marriage.

The entire five-stage progress of developing mystical consciousness can be explained simply as a development of a person's capacity to love. This explains why Underhill was adamant that the experience of mystical union is not attained in sequestered isolation, but among human beings in their messy worlds. She was encouraged to think this way after she sought the spiritual advice of Baron Friedrich von Hügel. They became friends after he showed an interest in her work. She sought spiritual direction from him from 1921 until his death in 1925.

Von Hügel had written extensively on mysticism himself. He encouraged her to seek mystical awarenees by undertaking three major daily activities: praying regularly; visiting the poor; and purposefully developing mundane yet enjoyable activities like cooking and gardening.[23]

god as absolute spirit

In the latter half of Underhill's life she began to write more on prayer and spirituality. If God is imagined as a spirit, indeed as the Absolute Spirit, spirituality is the human activity of seeking to discern God in the world. Prayer, contemplation and worship are all forms of spirituality.

It is very noticeable that Underhill often avoids using the word 'God', speaking instead of Ultimate Reality or Absolute Spirit. Her way of discussing God belies the influence of one of the greatest of all Western philosophers – Georg Wilhelm Friedrich Hegel (1770–1831). Kant was a metaphysical dualist. He conceived of reality as made up of two realms: a perceptible, visible world of phenomena as they appear in human experience and an unknowable, supernatural world. In counterpoise, Hegel was a metaphysical monist: he envisaged all reality as an interconnected whole or oneness. Whereas for Kant, God is transcendent (lies beyond) the world, according to Hegel, God is a Spirit with a history in the world. Underhill resonates with Hegel in conceiving of God as the Reality in and behind all things. In her own words:

> Normal consciousness sorts out some elements from the mass of experiences beating
> at our doors and constructs from them a certain order; but this order lacks any deep
> meaning or true cohesion, because normal consciousness is incapable of
> apprehending the underlying reality from which these scattered experiences
> proceed. The claim of the mystical consciousness is to a closer reading of truth; to
> an apprehension of the divine unifying principle behind appearance. ... To know
> this at first-hand – not to guess, believe or accept, but to be certain – is the highest
> achievement of human consciousness and the ultimate object of mysticism.[24]

Thus construed, mysticism is 'an experience of the interconnectedness and rela-
tionality of all reality'.[25] A contemporary nuclear physicist or astronomer may
well be included to depict reality similarly in the light of quantum mechanics. In
Underhill's terms, the whole point of religion and mysticism is not to produce
doctrines, establish institutions or teach ethics, but to engage with reality and
ultimately Absolute Reality. Her preferred way of explaining this engagement
was by way of an analogy of love: in love, humans undergo a changed consciousness and way of life.

Late in her life, Evelyn Underhill was widely regarded as the foremost authority on mysticism in Great Britain. *Mysticism* passed through several editions and
is still in print. The last years of her life were traumatized by the Second World
War. It afflicted her with considerable emotional and spiritual distress, and caused
fraught relations between her and Christian Churches. She was appalled by the
readiness of so many of her Christian contemporaries to support warfare. In one
of the last published works she penned, she observed: 'We are forced to the bitter
conclusion that the members of the Visible Church as a body are not good
enough, not brave enough to risk everything for that which they know to be the
Will of God and the teaching of Christ.'[26] In the same text she explains why pacifism is incumbent on Christians:

> We are moving – perhaps more rapidly than we realize – towards a moment in which
> the Church, if she is to preserve her integrity and spiritual influence, will be
> compelled to define her attitude towards war; to clear her own mind as to the true
> reason why her members, by the mere fact of their membership, are bound to
> repudiate war, not only in principle but also in fact. The reason, for there is only
> one, is simple and conclusive. The Christian Church is the Body of Christ. Her
> mission on earth is to spread the Spirit of Christ, which is the creative spirit of
> wisdom and love; and in so doing, bring in the Kingdom of God. Therefore she can

never support or approve any human action, individual or collective, which is hostile to wisdom and love.[27]

On this matter, her voice was widely ignored by her co-religionists. The recognition she earned came more from her publications on mysticism and spirituality coupled with her labours as a retreat director and spiritual advisor.

Evelyn Underhill achieved a great deal in her life. In 1921 she delivered the Upton lectures at Oxford University's Manchester College, and thereby became the first woman lecturing on religion to appear in the published list of lectures of the University of Oxford. She also became a Fellow of King's College in London, and was acclaimed as an honorary Doctor of Divinity in the University of Aberdeen.

Why would anyone living in the twenty-first century benefit from engaging her theological thought? For a cluster of reasons. First, she did not presume to explain who or what God might be in precise detail. Second, she bothered to mine the wisdoms of previous generations, most notably of medieval mystics. Her favourite mystic was Ruusbroec. Third, she saw the absurdity of Churches supporting programmes of war. Fourth, she realized that it is not possible to speak of loving God without first loving particular people, especially people suffering in poverty. Finally, she did not dichotomize life into religious and non-religious zones.

The twentieth century might have elapsed differently and far more happily had voices like Evelyn Underhill's been savoured. Instead, wars and armed skirmishes prematurely ended the lives of millions of people throughout the twentieth century.[28] Evelyn Underhill's opposition to war has become more, not less, incumbent on human beings today.

5

Albert Schweitzer: 1875–1965

Schweitzer in Africa, 1965 – the last year of his life

Truly I tell you, there are some standing here who will not taste death
until they see that the kingdom of God has come with power.

Mark 9: 1

It is difficult to imagine a more polymathic person than Albert Schweitzer. As
a young man he decided to use his prodigious knowledge and bountiful skills
practically to help people festering with sickness and penury. His decision became
clear to others when he reached the age of 30. On 13 October 1905, he dropped
a bundle of letters into a letter box on Paris' Avenue de la Grande Armée. The

correspondence informed his parents and some of his close friends that he had decided to train as a medical doctor to work in a French colony in equatorial Africa.[1] He had not consulted them before announcing his plan. At the time, he was a lecturer in theology at the University of Strasbourg, a Doctor of Philosophy, an ordained Lutheran minister, the rector of a seminary (the Collegium Wilhelmitanum) in Alsace, a recital organist, and a student of the pipe organ under the French composer, Charles-Marie Widor (1844–1937). His primary contribution to theology lay in the critical study of the Bible, the historical investigation of the life of Jesus, and the implications that life poses for those who aspire to be Christians today.

Schweitzer lived a long and eventful life, from 1875 to 1965. Of the several books he published, he regarded his autobiography as the most important. It was released in German as *Aus meinem Leben und Denken* (1931) and translated into English with the title *Out of My Life and Thought: An Autobiography*.[2] Further references to page numbers of this book will appear in the body of the text between parentheses. Schweitzer is often described as a missionary. He did indeed work for a mission station in Africa, but his autobiography explains that his primary reason for leaving Europe was to work as a physician, not as an evangelizing missionary. His motive for training to be a medical doctor, in the midst of a promising career as a lecturer and musician, was to press himself into the practical service of poor and enfeebled human beings. 'I wanted to be a doctor', he says, 'so that I might be able to work without having to talk'. With great joy he had been active as a preacher and theological teacher, but he hoped that medical work 'would consist not in preaching the religion of love, but in practicing it' (92).

Schweitzer first travelled to Africa in 1913. This was the beginning of 14 sojourns there, which were interrupted by trips back to Europe. The first interruption occurred in 1917 when he returned to Europe with his wife, as a prisoner of war. By the time of his death his bountiful giftedness as a musician, theologian, physician and philosopher had been amply recognized internationally. In October 1953, he was awarded the Nobel Prize for Peace for the year 1952. Apart from receiving doctorates in philosophy and medicine in Strasbourg, during the course of his adult life he had at least 12 honorary doctorates conferred on him in the fields of music, medicine, theology, law and philosophy.[3]

early years and education

Albert Schweitzer was born at Kaysersberg in Upper Alsace on 14 January 1875. Since the end of the First World War, Alsace has been part of France. When

Albert was born, it was part of the German Empire, as it had been since 1871, in the aftermath of the Franco-Prussian War. Schweitzer was thereby a German, even though he was able to speak French since his early childhood. When he later corresponded from afar with his parents he always wrote in French. His father, Louis Schweitzer, was a Protestant pastor who died an elderly man in 1925. His mother was Adele Schillenger. Her father was also a Protestant pastor in the Münster Valley of Upper Alsace. She suffered a violent death in 1916 when cavalry horses ran over and killed her on a road (1–2). The First World War was by then well under way. Both sides of Albert's family were Lutherans living in a predominantly Catholic Alsace. Albert was the second of five children to be born. He had three sisters, Louise, Margrit and Adele, as well as a younger brother named Paul.

Within weeks of Albert's birth his family moved to Günsbach in the Münster Valley so that his father could work there as a local church minister. When Albert was five, his father began to teach him music on the piano. By the age of nine he was able to play the organ during a church service in Günsbach. He practised, played and performed as a musician for the rest of his life.

In 1885, he enrolled at the local Gymnasium at Mülhausen (Alsace). Such a school was required to teach Greek and Latin in addition to other subjects. Once ensconced at the school, Albert began to study music, Hebrew, Greek, Latin, history, mathematics and natural science. His studies continued there for eight years. In June of 1893 he passed his final examinations (2–4).

1893 was an eventful year in his life. During October he went to stay in Paris so that he could meet Charles-Marie Widor. Albert had been taught to play the pipe organ by Eugène Münch while he was a schoolboy in Mülhausen. He began his studies of the organ in earnest when he was 15. He played for Widor when they first met. He was 18 at the time.[4] Widor was a professor at the Conservatorium of Music in Paris, and for 64 years the principal organist at the Church of St Sulpice in Paris. St Sulpice has a strong case for being awarded the accolade of housing one of the finest pipe organs in the world. Schweitzer certainly thought as much (74). Its organ was built by Aristide Cavaillé-Col, who completed the task in 1862. He also constructed the organ for the more internationally famous site in Paris of the Basilica of Notre Dame. Widor normally only taught the organ to classes of students at the Conservatorium. He was so impressed by how well Albert played, and had been taught, that he agreed to take him on as a private pupil. Young Albert had his first lesson with Widor in the same month they met.

Widor remained a friend of Schweitzer until he died in 1937. When the young Schweitzer told him by letter that he was going to live and work in equatorial Africa, Widor accused him of behaving like a general who, instead of commanding

Schweitzer as a university student

a battle, took up a position with a rifle on the front line of battle with infantry (86). Schweitzer was undeterred.

Late in October of 1893, Albert started studying theology and philosophy at the University of Strasbourg. He lived in Strasbourg's St Thomas Theological Seminary (the Collegium Wilhelmitanum). From there he could easily find his lectures in the university. He began to attend the lectures of Heinrich Julius Holtzmann on the Synoptics, that is, the Gospels according to Matthew, Mark and Luke. They are called 'synoptic' ('with one eye') because if their texts are aligned next to each other in columns it is possible to study them together in a single glance. With such a method of scrutinizing passages arranged in parallel columns their commonalities and disparities become clearly detectable.

In the Bible, the four Gospels ('texts announcing good news') are arranged in sequence beginning with Matthew, which is followed by Mark, Luke and John. Before Holtzmann's work, Matthew was thought to be the first gospel to be written. Holtzmann pioneered the thesis, now widely accepted, that Mark was the first gospel and served as the basis for the authors of Matthew and Luke (7).[5]

the problem of matthew

While attending Holtzmann's lectures, Schweitzer became troubled by intellectual problems generated in Matthew's Gospel. He was particularly vexed by the tenth and 11th chapters of Matthew, which are not found in the other Synoptics. Chapter 10 recounts Jesus sending out 12 apostles on a mission to Israel with the command to proclaim 'the good news, "The kingdom of heaven has come near"' (Mt 10: 7). Jesus warns his apostles that they can expect to be persecuted for being his disciples (Mt 10: 16–22). He then states: 'When they persecute you in one town, flee to the next; for truly I tell you, you will not have gone through all the towns of Israel before the Son of Man comes.'

the difficulty of studying jesus   Twenty centuries after Jesus lived, it is exceptionally difficult for anyone now (as it was for Schweitzer) to apply historical methods to investigate his life, words and activities. This is so because historical sources are extremely scant. Nothing written by Jesus has survived to this day. His immediate circle of followers were not scribes, and left nothing written about him. Christianity did not begin as a bookish religion. After Jesus' death, stories about him were circulated in Palestine and beyond in oral form. The earliest written text about him is Paul's First Letter to the Thessalonians. There is no evidence that Paul ever met Jesus. Written historical sources are meagre. The most significant ones are the Gospels contained in the Bible and the letters of Paul. Gospels excluded from the Bible may or may not shed some reliable information. There are no extant copies of the most important literary sources about Jesus. All that remains of these sources are copies, the oldest of which date from around 200–10 CE. This means that there is a gap of at least 170 years between the death of Jesus (around the beginning of the fourth decade CE) and the first available textual discussion of him. The copies diverge in detail, and were written in Greek, which may not have been the language in which the originals were produced. Aramaic, rather than Greek, was most likely the language of Jesus and his Galilean followers. A small surviving fragment (Papyrus 52) of the 18th chapter of John's Gospel dates from around 125 CE. Nothing written has survived that stems from an eye witness to Jesus' life. The earliest Gospel, Mark, may have been written as late as the fourth decade after Jesus' death (around 70 CE). The identities of the authors of the Gospels are unknown. The titles 'Matthew', 'Mark', 'Luke' and 'John' were added to manuscripts in the second half of the second century, thereby creating the impression that they were especially authoritative because they were written by four apostles who knew Jesus. Of the four Gospels included in the Bible, no two record the same details of Jesus' life. In places they contradict each other.[6]

'The Son of Man' (or 'the Son of the Man') is the title Jesus is depicted in the Bible as using most frequently to refer to himself. It appears 72 times in the Synoptics, and 13 in John's Gospel. Its meaning is unclear. Schweitzer interprets it as a messianic title. Historically he concludes that Jesus, in common with other Jews of his time, lived with a heightened expectation that a messiah would inaugurate God's kingdom at the end of the world: 'Like His contemporaries, Jesus identifies the Messiah with the "Son of Man", who is mentioned in the Book of Daniel, and who speaks of His coming on the clouds of heaven. The Kingdom of God he preaches is the heavenly Messianic Kingdom, which will be established on earth when the Son of Man comes at the end of the natural world' (37). For Schweitzer, Jesus does not yet think that he is the messianic Son of Man: 'He is convinced that only at the appearance of the Messianic Kingdom, when those predestined enter the supernatural existence intended for them, will He be manifested as the Messiah' (39).

The dilemma that the tenth chapter of Matthew poses for Schweitzer is this: Jesus told his disciples to expect the imminent arrival of the Son of Man, and hence the end of the natural world, and no such arrival or end transpired. Nor were the disciples persecuted. They returned from their mission quite safely. How could Jesus tell his apostles of events that did not eventuate? Holtzmann attempted to relieve the discomfort such a question poses for traditionally minded Christians by concluding that Matthew's story of the apostles' mission was not an historical narrative, but was made up at a later stage (7). Schweitzer concluded that the text was historically accurate and that Jesus was mistaken in his prediction (59).

On 1 April 1894, Schweitzer began a compulsory year of military service, but his military regime was so benign that he was permitted to continue attending lectures. While on manoeuvres he found time to read sections of the Bible written in Greek. By the end of his service he had become certain that, historically speaking, Jesus announced a divinely dominated kingdom that would be established in history, not by himself or his followers. It was to be a kingdom 'that was to be expected as coming with the approaching dawn of a supernatural age' (10).

the problem of the last supper

Schweitzer pushed on with his studies of the Gospels and the life of Jesus. He focused on the texts in the Bible that tell of Jesus enjoying a final meal with his apostles before he was executed. All of the Gospels narrate the story of this Last Supper. Schweitzer's investigations presented him with yet another dilemma. He read Friedrich Schleiermacher's earlier interpretation of the Last Supper. Schleiermacher pointed out that the two earliest Gospels, Mark and Matthew, do not record Jesus telling his followers to repeat what transpired at the Last Supper.[7] Schweitzer inferred that the final meal Jesus shared was not the inauguration of Catholic Masses or Protestant celebrations of the Last Supper that continue to be conducted today. Correctly understood, it was an anticipation of 'the Messianic feast to be celebrated in the Kingdom of God, which was soon to appear' (14).

Schweitzer passed the first of two state examinations in theology on 6 May 1898. He then set his mind to preparing a dissertation for a doctorate in philosophy. The subject he chose for his doctorate was the religious philosophy of Immanuel Kant.

In October of 1898, he travelled to Paris once again to study philosophy at the Sorbonne University and to continue his organ lessons with Widor. Boundless in energy, he also began a sustained study of the piano with two teachers – Isidor Philipp and Marie Jaël-Trautmann, who had been a pupil of Franz Liszt. In the summer of the following year, Schweitzer took himself off to Berlin where he attended the lectures of Adolf von Harnack. He kept in contact with Harnack until the latter's death.

In July of 1899, Schweitzer received his doctorate in philosophy. During the following December he was appointed as an assistant vicar to the Church of St Nicholai in Strasbourg (25). In July of 1900, he passed his second state exam in theology and received a licentiate degree in theology with a thesis devoted to the problem of the Last Supper (33). He was ordained a regular curate on 23 September 1900.

the history of the study of the jesus of history

Schweitzer began his career as a university lecturer in theology at Strasbourg on 1 March 1902. His engrossing intellectual passion at this stage of his life was the history of research into the life of Jesus. His methodological approach to this work was directly influenced by Aristotle. In Aristotle's treatise, *Metaphysics*, he explores philosophy by discussing and criticizing earlier philosophizing (118). In a similar vein, Schweitzer decided that he needed to examine the history of previous research on Jesus before he could decide for himself who Jesus was as a figure in history. His own research formed the basis for his best known book, *The Quest of the Historical Jesus* (1906).

Studying Jesus as an historical figure is a modern enterprise. Before the eighteenth century, Christians generally accepted as unproblematic the doctrine that Jesus was the Second Person of a divine Trinity incarnate in history, and that everything the Bible says about him and attributes to him is infallibly accurate. From the fifth to the eighteenth centuries, by far the majority of Catholics, and after the sixteenth century most Protestants, accepted the teaching of Chalcedon that Jesus is truly God and truly a human being.

The pervasive acceptance of Chalcedon in the Church was unsettled in 1878 with the posthumous publication of a text by Hermann Samuel Reimarus (1694–1768), a professor of Oriental languages in Hamburg. His text, 'The Intentions of Jesus and His Disciples', unleashed a flood of publications devoted to the historical investigation of the life of Jesus that has not subsided today. Reimarus stands as an instigator of a modern history of the study of the Jesus that has continued for over two centuries. He was unconvinced by conventional Christian teaching that Jesus is the founder of Christianity, and was moved to discern the identity of the historical Jesus as distinct from any dogmatic portrait of Jesus. To speak of 'an historical Jesus' is merely to differentiate between a sketch of Jesus as he lived in human history drawn from available historical sources, and depictions of him that are legendary, mythical, fabulous or fictitious.

Reimarus' fragments launched the modern attempt to compose an accurate historical portrait of Jesus with two primary observations. First, he concluded that there is a disparity between what the Bible says about Jesus and who Jesus actually was. It follows from this that the challenge for an historian is to devise methods for investigating who Jesus was in contrast to whom the Bible states he was. Second, Reimarus' text is the first extant document to argue that Jesus shared an eschatological Messianic expectation with his contemporaries.

Reimarus depicted Jesus as a Messianic pretender who stove practically to undermine Roman rule in Palestine and to restore the sovereignty and unity of Israel. He further observed that Jesus was a failure. His life and mission came to an end when he was captured and executed by order of Pontius Pilate. Shamed and humiliated, so Reimarus hypothesized, his disciples stole his dead body from its tomb and fabricated the story that Jesus had been raised from death by God into a divine dimension of existence. If that was so, then Christianity was not established by Jesus Christ. It was the fraudulent concoction of his disciples.[8]

Spurred on by the example of Reimarus, William Wrede (1859–1907), a professor of theology in Breslau, set about writing his own account of the historical Jesus. The fruit of his labours appeared in 1901 with the publication of his treatise, *The Messianic Secret of the Gospels*. Therein he argued in counterpoint to Reimarus that Jesus did not entertain any eschatological or Messianic ideas about himself. Instead, his disciples proclaimed him to be the Messiah after his death. The notion that Jesus regarded himself as the Messiah but kept his self-awareness a secret was, in Wrede's terms, an invention of primitive Christianity after Jesus' death. Wrede was insistent that Jesus regarded himself as the master of the disciples but not as the Messiah. He only became the Messiah in the disciples' imagination after he was killed (45 and 49).[9]

Reimarus and Wrede stand as polar opposites on the question of Jesus' historical identity. For the former, Jesus saw himself as a politically motivated Messiah. According to the latter he was not. For this reason Schweitzer included the names of both scholars in the title of his investigation into the history of modern research into the life of Jesus, which was published in 1906 as *Von Reimarus zu Wrede: Eine Geschichte der Leben-Jesu-Forschung* ('From Reimarus to Wrede: A

History of Life of Jesus Research').[10] This book became in English *The Quest of the Historical Jesus*, the first edition of which was published in 1913. Schweitzer published a second German edition in 1913 with substantial additions.[11]

the quest of the historical jesus

The University of Strasbourg was an ideal place for Schweitzer to investigate modern historical studies of Jesus. Its library contained 'a virtually complete collection of literature on the life of Jesus' (44).

When Schweitzer was undertaking his research he was the director of the Seminary of St Thomas. He could take books there from the library and methodically make his way though the numerous volumes devoted to Jesus' life – which he called Lives of Jesus. Having read a great deal, he was stymied by difficulties encountered while trying to organize his book into chapters that incorporated comments he wished to make on each of the authors he had studied.

To overcome this hurdle he simply designated separate places on his seminary study's floor and grouped all the library books into piles, with each pile representing a successive chapter in the text he was preparing to write. He kept his study in such a state for many months (46).

The first sections of *The Quest of the Historical Jesus* discuss the first practitioners of an historical-critical method and their attempts to explore the existence of Jesus. The method took the Gospels as its primary source material. Schweitzer describes the initial results of historical-critical analyses of the Gospels in his autobiography:

> Genuine historical research begins with critical analysis of the Gospels to determine
> the historical value of their accounts. This effort, which began in the nineteenth
> century and continued for several decades, had the following results: The picture
> given by the Gospel of John is irreconcilable with that of the other three; the other
> three are the older and therefore the more credible sources; the material they have
> in common with one another is found in its earliest form in the Gospel of Mark; and,
> finally, Luke's Gospel is considerably later than those of Mark and Matthew (47).

In surveying the lives of Jesus penned during the eighteenth centuries, Schweitzer noticed that they ignored Reimarus' endeavour to interpret the sayings of Jesus in the context of late Judaism and its anticipation of an eschatological Messiah. Instead, these lives spoke of the kingdom of God which Jesus preached as a spiritual reality, that is, a phenomenon in individuals' lives and not a practical termination of human history. These studies of Jesus also dismissed the miracle stories of the gospels as purely natural events that could be explained rationally (47).

Schweitzer then turns his attention to the work of David Friedrich Strauss, who published a large examination of the Gospels in 1835. It was called *The Life of Jesus Critically Examined*. Despite its title, it is not a biography of Jesus. It is clearly not a dogmatic Christology. It is a detailed examination of successive passages of the Gospels.[12] Its main conclusion is that much of the material in the Gospels is mythical by nature and that stories of miracles are best interpreted as myths. He only accepted portions of Mark and Matthew as trustworthy sources of historical information about Jesus. The rest he designated as mainly mythical.

christology   Attempts to interpret the identity and significance of Jesus have traditionally been designated as Christologies. Strauss was dismissive of them. The word 'Christology' derives from two Greek terms, *Christos*, meaning 'one who is anointed', and *logos*, connoting 'word'. A Christology is a discourse about 'Christ', one of the many honorific titles predicated of Jesus in the Bible. The titles given to Jesus in the Christian Scriptures, normally designated as the New Testament by Christians, include 'Son of Man', 'Son of God', 'Lord', 'Master' or 'Rabbi', and 'Messiah'. The English word, 'Messiah', translates the Hebrew term, *Massiah*, which has the same meaning as *Christos*. A Messiah or a Christ is a person chosen and favoured (anointed) by God. The word 'Christ' is not a surname for Jesus. It is a title of esteem and veneration. The authors of the Christian Scriptures borrowed titles of distinction from their surrounding Greek, Hebrew and Roman cultures in order to specify what they regarded as unique and superlative about Jesus.

As Schweitzer continued to make his way through the piles of books devoted to Jesus' life that he had stacked on his study floor, he noticed that from the middle of the nineteenth century onward scholars tended to spiritualize Jesus' preaching about the Kingdom of God. To spiritualize it is to turn it into an individualistic and interior matter: the life and love of God's kingdom becomes present within particular human beings. Schweitzer decided that such a view is untenable. He insisted that Jesus in the Gospels 'speaks in a quite realistic way of the coming of the Son of Man and the Messianic Kingdom when this world comes to an end' (48), and that 'the preaching of Jesus had been entirely determined by the imminent end of the world and the advent of the supernatural Kingdom of God' (118).

Such a conclusion was something of a shock for liberal Protestantism of his day: 'Throughout the nineteenth century it had been widely thought that

Jesus had founded the Kingdom of God as an inward spiritual reality, a seed growing secretly in the heart of believers.'[13]

By the end of the nineteenth century, Schweitzer observed, the view that Jesus' preaching was determined by an eschatological expectation had become increasingly perceived among scholars writing Lives of Jesus. Johannes Weiss, for instance, underscored the eschatological nature of Jesus' words in his book of 1892, *Jesus' Proclamation of the Kingdom of God*.[14]

The Quest for the Historical Jesus is not an elaborate presentation of Schweitzer's own thoughts on who Jesus was and what he did. Most of the book surveys and assesses the opinions of others. Only in the concluding chapter of the treatise does Schweitzer deploy his own account of the Jesus of history. He concludes that Jesus, in his words and actions, was driven by an ardent hope that the Son of Man as a long anticipated Messiah would end human history and thereby inaugurate God's supernatural kingdom as an eschatological reality.

The lynchpin in Schweitzer's interpretation of Jesus is eschatology. He charged that late eighteenth- and nineteenth-century Lives of Jesus were blind to the eschatological expectation suffusing Jesus' life and thought. Schweitzer's most elaborate study of Jesus and eschatology is deployed in his first significant publication on the historical Jesus which dates from 1901 and in English is called *The Last Supper in Connection with the Life of Jesus and the History of Early Christianity*. This study was published in two parts, the second of which was called *The Secret of the Messiahship and Passion – A Sketch of the Life of Jesus*. The second part was published in English in 1913 with the title, *The Mystery of the Kingdom of God*.[15] It clearly elaborates Schweitzer's conviction that Jesus' life was driven by an eschatological expectation that God's kingdom would arrive immanently and constitute a supernaturally wrought caesura with the past.[16] Schweitzer concluded that modern Lives of Jesus were unable to recognize the historical Jesus because late Jewish eschatology was alien to their thought.[17]

Schweitzer uses his conclusion to defend the accounts of Mark and Matthew. Both Gospels, he holds, present Jesus in a thoroughgoing eschatological way. They may therefore be regarded as historically reliable. Concluding thus creates an acute difficulty for many modern and contemporary Christians. If Jesus pined for an eschatological Messiah to end the history of the world, and if he expected that end to eventuate while his disciples were still alive, he was clearly mistaken. Schweitzer asserted that the Christianity of his day found itself in a difficult situation because it had neglected to pursue historical truth 'again and again in the past' (54). He tries to convince his readers that they have nothing to fear from historical truth because it is a gain for spiritual truth (54).

human suffering

Schweitzer was 31 when *The Quest of the Historical Jesus* was published. Ten years earlier, he was still a schoolboy. In 1896 he decided that he would devote his life to scholarship and the arts, and thereafter to what he called 'direct human service'. He recalled his happy life as a boy and ruminated: 'It struck me as inconceivable that I should be allowed to lead such a happy life while I saw many people around me struggling with sorrow and suffering' (82).

Schweitzer kept to his decision. He never abandoned his intellectual and musical pursuits, but once he reached the age of 30 they were subservient to his desire to help suffering human beings practically on a daily basis. To that end, in 1905 he commenced studies in medicine in the University of Strasbourg. These continued until 1912, the year he married Helene Bresslau. He received the degree of Doctor of Medicine in 1913 with a dissertation exploring the question of whether Jesus was mentally ill.[18] Schweitzer used his historical research into the life of Jesus to argue that Jesus was not psychiatrically unwell, but whose thought was driven by eschatological hope. Schweitzer felt partly responsible for generating a body of literature devoted to the question of Jesus' mental health, because he had underscored so well Jesus' apocalyptic and eschatological disposition.[19]

life as a jungle doctor at lambaréné

Well before Schweitzer qualified as a physician he prepared himself for the direct service of suffering people. In 1904 he read an article in a magazine published by the Paris Missionary Society (*La Société Evangélique des Missions à Paris*). The article complained that there were not enough people to support a missionary endeavour in Goboon, which was a part of what was known then as the French colony of the Congo. A few months after Schweitzer's 30th birthday he resolved to work in equatorial Africa and offered his services to the Paris Mission Society. The eventual location of his work was a mission station called Lambaréné. It was set by the river Ogowé in the northern regions of the Congo. It had been established by North American Missionaries in 1876. When the area became a French territory, the Americans had to leave because they could not obey a government order that all schooling was to be conducted in French.

Schweitzer and his wife left Europe from the port of Bordeaux on 26 March 1913. They travelled with 70 packing cases full of medical equipment, surgical instruments, and enough medicines and drugs to support a field hospital for a year. They arrived at Lambaréné on 16 April.

Life for many of the local people of Lambaréné was an ordeal. They were impoverished and blighted by diseases. Schweitzer set up his first medical consulting room in a disused chicken coop. He later moved it to a corrugated iron building. From the time of his arrival he had to cope with diseases such as leprosy, malaria, dysentery, frambesia, sleeping sickness, as well as phagedenic ulcers, pneumonia, and diseases of the heart and urinary tract. He had to employ by his own account modest surgical skills to treat cases of hernia and elephantiasis tumours (137).

For the rest of his life he divided his time and energies between the people he encountered in equatorial Africa and visits to Europe. While in Europe he continued to work with Widor on a critical edition of Bach's organ compositions, and to arrange for the publication of books he had been preparing. The sixth and final volume of Bach's Complete Organ Works was published in 1954. Schweitzer's study of the thought of Paul of Tarsis was published in 1930 as *The Mysticism of Paul the Apostle*. His autobiography is the only book he wrote in Africa.

schweitzer's bleak view of humanity

It is surprising to some to discover that despite Schweitzer's commitment to help others, he entertained a disapproving assessment of his contemporaries. In the early stages of his life in Africa he became troubled by what he termed the problem of civilization. He concluded that his contemporaries had regressed in their behaviour, compared with more civilized peoples of the past. This led him to explore the nature of civilization. Unlike many other liberal theologians, Schweitzer did not think that humanity in his day was steadily improving its condition. His suspicion was quite the reverse. He observed that intellectually and spiritually his generation had 'sunk below' the level of past peoples (146). He complained that he had seen on a number of occasions 'public opinion failing to reject officially proclaimed theses that were barbaric; on the contrary, it approved inhumane conduct whether by governments or individuals' (145).[20]

reverence for life

Schweitzer's proposed solution to the problem of declining civilization came to him during December of 1915, while he was travelling along the Ogowé river to treat the ailing wife of a missionary. On the third day of his journey the phrase 'reverence for life' presented itself to him as a fundamental principle of ethics that could promote human civilization. He became convinced that an estimation of life and ethics intertwine indissolubly and thus form the basis of civilization. This meant for him that civilization was not founded on the accretion of techno-logical power and science. More fundamentally, it flowed from an individual's reverence for life, developing, promoting and preserving life in all its forms – plant, animal and human (see 157–159). Schweitzer mulled over his ideas con-cerning civilization for several years. He shared his thoughts in 1923 with the publication of *The Philosophy of Civilization*.[21] His book, *Reverence for Life* ('Strassburger Predigten') was published posthumously.[22]

Schweitzer lived through two world wars and the development of the H-Bomb, an invention that appalled him as an offence to reverence for life. In Oslo on 4 November 1954, Schweitzer accepted the Nobel Peace Prize for the year 1952 with the speech, 'The Problem of Peace in the World Today'.

Schweitzer died at Lamberéné on 4 September 1965, in his 90th year. Despite his gifts and achievements he was neither faultless nor infallible. He was keen to help Africa, but did not show many signs of learning from African cultures. Hence the charge that he was paternalistic. His studies of the Synoptics may have overestimated the problems constituted by the tenth chapter of Matthew.[23] His focus on Mark and Matthew as the most reliable sources for historical knowl-edge about the life of Jesus may have blinded him to the fact that all four Gospels are theological proclamations based on oral traditions that passed on historical reminiscences of people who knew Jesus. John's Gospel is certainly a theological proclamation from beginning to end. So too are the other three. It also contains reliable historical data not found in the Synoptics, such as its mention of the pool of Siloam in Jerusalem (Jn 9: 7), which has been unearthed by archaeologists.[24]

The driving force of Schweitzer's life was a passion he inherited from Lutheranism. It was an intense and abiding loyalty to the way Jesus lived and what he taught. That explains why Schweitzer devoted so much of his university career to unearthing historical information about Jesus. His conclusion that Jesus fervidly expected the immanent world-transforming arrival of the kingdom of God appears accurate. Because Jesus was an eschatologically impassioned fire-brand – why else was he brutally crucified? – he remains somewhat awkwardly unfamiliar to the inhabitants of the twentieth and twenty-first centuries. By and large, these inhabitants have not yet expected God immanently to end human his-tory and to overturn current economic pecking orders. Those who do are more likely than not to be dismissed as sectarian religious lunatics.

6

Karl Barth: 1886–1968

If gods did care, the good would prosper, and the bad
Would suffer; that's not the way of things.

Telamon

If God is the compassionate Creator of the universe and its inhabitants, why has
the Earth been for so long a grotesque theatre of war, disease, animal predation,
torture and genocide? Could such a God have created a world devoid of the starvation and misery that render the lives of vast swathes of its human population a
kaleidoscope of horrors, and a terrifying, sorrow-wracked drudgery? Theologians
working in the first half of the twentieth century met the full force of these

questions as they attempted to speak about a God they regarded as paternal during and after two chillingly cataclysmic world wars. These global conflagrations involved human beings systematically gassing, bayoneting, bombing, maiming, and annihilating each other in their millions. The Swiss Protestant theologian, Karl Barth, lived in central Europe throughout the wars. His reflections during the inter-bellum on human behaviour led him to turn his back on liberal theology.

After the outbreak of the Great War in 1914, Barth decided that liberal theology was bankrupt. He effectively charged that its practitioners in the nineteenth century had been overly enthused by the Enlightenment. Their enthralment with human reason, freedom and ingenuity blinkered them to the tyrannies that unbridled human arrogance, greed and power can produce. With the Great War, reason led to ruin. Science devised mustard gas. Technologies produced bombs. Freedom became a free-for-all to slaughter enemies and innocents. Could it be that such behaviour is an affront to, not licensed by, a benign Creator?

The European (and North American) Enlightenment was an ambiguous phenomenon. Its shibboleth was progress. Its devotees hoped that technologies could build machines to explore, subdue and carefully control the natural world, providing wealth and material resources to improve and perfect the human condition. With the Great War of 1914–18, the Machine of Progress became the Machine Gun of trench warfare. The idea that human ingenuity inexorably leads to progress was blown to oblivion.

Karl Barth rocketed forth an alternative style of theology to Protestant liberalism from the barbaric chaos of the First World War. The method he came to decide was ideal for talking about God was based four-squarely on the Bible, not on philosophy, speculation or the vaunted notion that human intelligence can decipher all there is to be known about God. How he did so is best grasped by attending to the way his life unfolded.

the life and tribulations of karl barth

Barth's childhood was peaceful. He was born on 10 May 1886, in the beautiful city of Basel, which lies in the upper northwest corner of Switzerland. So situated, Basel is a conduit to the Swiss for French, German, Belgian and Dutch cultural influences. It was the home of Nietzsche (until 1900), and has been a member of the Swiss Federation since 1501. Barth spent most of his life in Basel, and died there in 1968.

He was born into an observant Christian family. His mother was Anna Katharina Sartoris. Her father was a pastor in the Reformed Church – a

Protestant denomination enthused by the theology of John Calvin. Karl's father was Johann Friedrich Barth, commonly called Fritz by those who knew him. He taught in Basel's College of Preachers. Both Karl's maternal and paternal grandfathers were Protestant pastors in Basel. In 1888, Fritz Barth moved with his family to the Swiss city of Bern where he began to teach in the city's university. There he lectured on the Christian Scriptures (the 'New Testament') and the history of the Church.

Karl spent most of his youth in Bern. In 1904, when he was 18, he enrolled in the theological faculty of the university. His ambition was to prepare for ordained ministry in the Reformed Church. During the initial stage of his studies he read avidly the works of Immanuel Kant and Friedrich Schleiermacher – two lodestars for liberal theologians of the time. Karl also became familiar with the historical-critical method of interpreting biblical texts. As a consequence of the first stage of his university studies he began to dissociate himself from his father's style of orthodox Protestant theology and biblical exegesis.

While still enrolled in Bern, Karl informed his father that he would like to spend time studying in the German university of Marburg. His father refused to grant permission, so Karl visited Berlin instead, where he was taught by Adolf von Harnack. After attending Harnack's lectures, Karl returned to Bern for another semester of work and to serve as an intern in a parish. Then he went back to Germany to study in Tübingen. Finally, he realized his hope of studying in Marburg in 1908. While there, he was strongly influenced by the liberal theologian Wilhelm Herrmann (1846–1922). Herrmann was the Professor of Systematic Theology in Marburg, and was closely aligned with the work of Albrecht Ritschl. He argued that people become aware of God because of divine revelation, yet he insisted that God's manifestation to people is not presented in the form of propositional information about God. Revelation for Herrmann was a non-conceptual divine revelation of Godself to human beings. This understanding of revelation lay seeds for the evolution of Barth's later decision to distance himself from theological liberalism.[1]

As in the case of Barth, it is still common for Swiss students of theology to prepare for their first degree in theology in a variety of universities. After learning from Herrmann (and others) in Marburg, Barth returned to Bern, the primary base of his education. He passed his final university examinations in 1908. In that year his father ordained him to the pastorate in Bern's principal church.

Here is how Barth described his theological education at this stage of his life:

> I had made myself a committed disciple of the 'modern' school, which was still dominant up to the time of the First World War, and was regarded as the only

revelation   Appeal to a divine revelation has been by far the predominant method for Christian theologians in the past to talk about God. To the question, 'How do human beings know God?', a standard orthodox response for Christians for most of their history has been: 'Because God has been and is revealed to human beings.' The word revelation is linked to the Latin noun, *velum* – 'a veil' – and to the verb, *revelare* – 'to remove the veil'. The Greek word for revelation is *apocalypsis*. Apocalyptically minded people live in expectation that God is soon to be revealed to them. **Apocalyptic eschatology** is a discourse about how God will be revealed at the end of the world. The root meaning of revelation is the idea of an obscured face that is made manifest by the removal of a veil covering it. In Christian theology of the past, this process of the unveiling of God is understood as an initiative of God, not humans. God's unveiling is a self-disclosure. It is also construed as only a partial uncovering: God is neither fully known nor directly encountered in human history. Over past centuries, Christians have understood divine revelation in a variety of ways. For some, the People of Israel stand as a revelation of what God is like in human history. For others, the Bible is a form of revelation. Jesus Christ, too, is worshipped by Christians as the unveiler of God. Since the Middle Ages, it has been customary for theologians to distinguish between **natural and revealed theologies.** The former understands theology as the process by which human reason or human nature attains knowledge of God. The latter associates revelation with the Bible and Christian tradition. The notion of divine revelation was taken for granted for most of Christian history. It was severely called into question during and after the Enlightenment, and following the development of modern biblical criticism which raised questions about whether the Bible is a reliable source of information. If it contains historical errors and textual contradictions, how could it be a divine revelation?

school worth belonging to. In it, according to the teaching of Schleiermacher and Ritschl, Christianity was interpreted on the one hand as an historical phenomenon to be subjected to critical examination, and on the other hand as a matter of inner experience, of a predominantly moral nature.[2]

It was predominantly from Friedrich Schleiermacher that Barth had ingested the notion that the essence of religion resides in an individual's feeling of being dependent on God.

After finishing his studies in Bern, Barth spent a year back in Marburg working as an assistant editor to Martin Rade (1857–1940) on the journal, *Christliche Welt* ('The Christian World').[3] Rade was a liberal religious thinker and the journal was concerned with the political and social implications of Christian faith.

Barth as a student in Marburg – 1909

Barth returned to Switzerland in 1909 and began to work in Geneva. In the same year, Austria annexed Bosnia. Tensions leading to the Great War were already percolating. The German Chancellor, Otto von Bismarck, had previously advocated in 1887 that the German army needed to be enlarged. Barth worked as an assistant pastor in Geneva's German Reformed church. In Geneva he encountered the daily duress of hard-pressed workers who struggled to eke out a living on very low pay.

He was not overly excited by his daily round of duties in Geneva. In 1911, the year in which Barth became engaged to Nelly Hoffmann, and Italy declared war on Turkey, he moved to the Swiss village of Safenwil in the north-central canton of the Argau. When Barth arrived in Safenwil to serve as the pastor for the local Reformed church, the town boasted a population of about 2,000 inhabitants, most of whom were factory workers. Barth spent the next decade of his life in Safenwil. The village had formerly been under the control of the Lords of Berne, who exploited the villagers financially by requiring them to pay tribute. The village's pastors were expected to collect the tribute for the Lords. This system had been abolished by the time Barth arrived in Safenwil, but the village did not enjoy a tradition in which its pastors defended the rights of factory workers.

During Barth's tenure at Safenwil, the town was effectively ruled by two factory owners. Once boys and girls of the village reached the age of 14–16 it was customary for them to begin work in the factories. There they were required to labour for more than 12 hours a day. They were paid a paltry sum for their labours, which forced them to scrimmage for a frugal living. Barth broke with the tradition established by the pastors who preceded him, and aligned himself with the poor and oppressed inhabitants of Safenwil.[4] He enrolled as a member of the Social Democratic Party and established contact with a group of Swiss Christians who were members of a socialist political party. Leonhard Rogaz (1868–1945) was among them.

Religiously and intellectually, the decade proved to be a time of turmoil and far-reaching change in Barth's life. Living among labourers, and engaging with Christian social thinkers, he came to question the appropriateness of the bourgeois lifestyles of his theological masters in Germany. When he arrived in Safenwil, he had hoped that his pastoral experience would help to prepare him well for professional theological reflection in an academy. Instead he was catapulted by his surrounding circumstances in Europe into a convulsive personal and theological crisis. It was in Safenfil that Barth unexpectedly charted a new trajectory for twentieth-century theology.

Barth spent the course of the Great War in Safenwil. The task of having to preach every Sunday to factory workers burdened by poverty and overshadowed by warfare focused him intently on the Bible. While preparing to preach, he discovered that his liberal theology professors in Germany had not furnished him with a language to talk about Christianity in a way that would enlighten his parishioners in a time of war. Switzerland remained neutral during the War, but this did not prevent its inhabitants from fretting about the War's dreadful consequences.

1914

The bedlam of the Great War broke out in a single month. On 1 August 1914, the German Emperor, Wilhelm II, acting on Germany's behalf, declared war on Russia. His declaration triggered a chain of similar proclamations on successive days in August. On 4 August, Germany declared war on France and proceeded to invade Belgium and France. On the same day Britain declared war on Germany. The Austro-Hungarian Empire joined the fray on 6 August by declaring war on Russia. In the course of the same day Serbia and Montenegro proclaimed war on Germany. France then declared war on Austria (10 August), while Britain declared war on the Austro-Hungarian Empire. On 28 August, the Austro-Hungarian Empire announced war against Belgium. Barth was jolted to discover that on the day Kaiser Wilhelm II first declared war, 93 German intellectuals published a manifesto supporting the Kaiser's aggressive policy. Among the signatories to the manifesto were Barth's former liberal teachers, Adolf von Harnack and Wilhelm Herrmann. Harnack went so far as to help the Kaiser in drafting the formal declaration of war.

Desire for war among German generals was fanned by Friedrich von Bernhardi who, since 1907, had commanded the Seventh Corps of the German Army. He was also a military historian. Two of his best-known books were published in 1912: *On War Today*, and *Germany and the Next War*.[5] In the second book, General von Bernhardi informed his readers that Germany was obliged to go to war, lest it decline as a nation. He argued that it was a biological necessity and historic duty for Germany to wage war because its peerless culture, so he surmised, could and should be established elsewhere.[6]

---

great war   A cluster of historical catalysts led to the Great War, which later came to be called the First World War, to distinguish it from the Second World War. Before the Great War, its eventual prominent combatants, as colonial powers, frequently argued over their colonies. In the pre-war period, Austria-Hungary and Russia each showed interest in taking over Balkan lands as the Ottoman Empire receded there. Germany began to build a much lager navy to challenge Britain's naval superiority. Britain had become a very powerful industrialized nation throughout the nineteenth century, but by the end of the century Germany had succeeded in surpassing Britain's industrial output. Rivalries between such competitive nations spawned military and diplomatic alliances. Germany and Austria-Hungary formed the Central Powers, while Britain aligned itself with France and Russia to create the Triple Entente. This group was later joined by Italy in 1915. Intense preparations for war by both affiliations were set in train by a political assassination. On 28 June 1914, the Archduke Franz Ferdinand, heir to the crown of Austria-Hungary, and his wife were assassinated by a Bosnian Serb student, Gavrilo Princip, in Sarajevo, Bosnia. The ensuing four-year war lasted until an armistice between the Allies and Germany came into force on 11 November 1918. More than 8 million soldiers were killed during the war. Another 20 million were wounded.[7] The Great War led to the collapse of four empires – the German, Russian, Austro-Hungarian and Ottoman.

Later in Barth's life he noted the consequence for him of his teacher's support for the Kaiser: 'An entire world of theological exegesis, ethics, dogmatics, and preaching, which up to that point I had accepted as basically credible, was thereby shaken to the foundations, and with it everything which flowed at that time from the pens of the German theologians.'[8] The North American theologian, Helmut Richard Niebuhr (1894–1962), chimes with Barth in voicing misgivings about liberal theology. He accused it of proposing that 'A God without wrath brought men without sin into a kingdom without judgement through the ministrations of a Christ without a cross.'[9]

barth's retort – the letter to the romans

Once Barth became disillusioned by the style of theology in which he had been instructed, he entered a phase of intense rumination. This involved a sustained meditation on the Bible, and more particularly on Paul's *Letter to the Romans*, which had been composed almost 19 centuries earlier. Dispirited by liberal theology, he sought an alternative way of talking about God in relation to human beings.

The first fruits of Barth's quest to formulate theology in a new key appeared in 1919 when he published the book, *The Epistle to the Romans (Der Römerbrief)*. This volume was never translated into English. Barth reworked it with extensive changes. A second edition was published in 1922 and translated into English in 1933.[10] It is not an historically-critical exegetical examination of each verse in *Romans*, but an energetically sustained elaboration of cardinal theological themes in the letter, and a verse-by-verse meditation on the text. Uppermost among these themes was the issue of how human beings imagine they encounter God in their lives.

The first chapter of the Letter of Paul to the Romans graphically records its author's keen awareness of the sinfulness of human beings who had not acknowledged God: 'They were filled with every kind of wickedness, evil, covetousness, malice. Full of envy, murder, strife, deceit, craftiness, they are gossips, slanderers, God-haters, insolent, haughty, boastful, inventors of evil, rebellious towards parents, foolish, faithless, heartless, ruthless' (Rom 1: 29–31). With sinfulness acknowledged, Paul underscores 'the righteousness of God'. The English words 'righteousness' and 'justification' both translate a Greek term, *dikaiosunē*, which in the Bible can refer to the condition of a person being right or true when tested or judged by God.

In the ninth chapter of *Romans*, Paul declares: 'Gentiles, who did not strive for righteousness, have attained it, that is, righteousness through faith; but Israel, who did strive for the righteousness that is based on the law, did not succeed in fulfilling the law. Why not? Because they did not strive for it on the basis of faith, but as if it were based on works' (Rom 9: 30b-32a). For Paul, and later for Martin Luther, a person achieves the status of being in a good or right condition before God by professing faith in Jesus Christ, rather than by a religious observance (work) such as obeying the ancient laws of Israel.

Pondering *Romans*, Barth began to surmise that in Europe of the early twentieth century God had moved away from Christians and had come close to non-Christians. Those Christians who supported Kaiser Wilhelm's war policy did not know God as they thought. Their religious practices and their theological concepts failed to espy God. Barth learned around 1914 from a Jewish friend, Franz Rosenzweig, that the distinctiveness of God in relation to people had to be asserted.[11]

Avowing God's distinctiveness became the pulse of Barth's entire theological output. His *Romans* is a manifesto calling on its readers to recognize God's sovereignty and asiety: God is not as people imagine; or where they think; God cannot be grasped by concepts; and an individual's experience is not the seedbed for acquaintance with God. Barth's *Romans* reverses the anthropological starting point of liberal theology: a person can apprehend nothing of God through his or her experiences. The only way for humans to encounter God, however partially, is as a result of God's self-revelation.

Barth's shift from an anthropological basis for theology to a forthright recognition of divine sovereignty is trumpeted with rhetorical force in his *Römerbrief* when he contemplates the 18th verse of *Romans'* opening chapter, which reads: 'For the wrath of God is revealed in heaven against the ungodliness and wickedness of those who by their wickedness suppress the truth.' This verse elicited the following comment from Barth:

> Our relation to God is *ungodly*. We suppose that we know what we are saying when we say 'God'. We assign to Him the highest place in our world: and in so doing we place Him fundamentally on one line with ourselves and with things. … We dare to deck ourselves out as His companions, patrons, advisors, and commissioners. We confound time with eternity. This is the *ungodliness* of our relation to God. Our relation to God is *unrighteous*. Secretly we are ourselves in this relationship. We are not concerned with God, but with our own requirements, to which God must adjust Himself.[12]

In *Romans*, Barth declares that God is *ganz anders*, or *Totaliter Aliter* ('Totally Other'), from anything human or finite.[13] God is completely different from all human desires, concepts and expectations. In speaking thus he is indebted to the Bible, Martin Luther and Søren Kierkegaard (1813–53). With *Romans*, Barth even abandoned attempts to explain who or what God might be. A frequent leitmotif of his book is that 'God is God' – a tautology that recoils from providing any information about God.

The historical significance of Barth's recoiling in the face of divine sovereignty is that it represents a pendulum swing away from liberal theology's focus on human religiosity and points to God's ineffable Otherness. For Barth, only when humans discover that they are guilty before God will they ever be in a position to recognize God's sovereignty and faithfulness. He was clear that liberal theologians utterly failed to prepare their students for the brutal harshness of contemporary human existence.

Barth's theology came to be called neo-orthodox and dialectical. It is dialectical or paradoxical because it highlights the contrast between God and people: God is *revealed to* human beings, but is not grasped *by them* in revelation. Nothing in them discovers God. Instead, they are confronted *by God*. Barth's thought has also been labelled as a crisis theology: it demands a decision to recognize that God is 'Wholly Other'.

In Barth's later work, *God, Grace, and Gospel*, he described the discovery he made after contemplating *Romans*. He realized that –

> the theme of the Bible – contrary to the critical and the orthodox exegesis in which
> we had been brought up – definitely could not be man's religion and religious ethics
> – could not possibly be his own secret godliness, but was the *rocher de bronze* on
> which we first struck – the Godness of God, precisely God's Godness, God's own
> peculiar nature over against not only the natural, but also the spiritual cosmos,
> God's absolutely unique existence, power and initiative, above all in his relationship
> to man.[14]

In 1921, Barth was appointed as an associate professor of Reformed theology in the University of Göttingen. Once there, he began to study Reformed theology in depth. From 1925 to 1930, he worked as a professor of dogmatics and New Testament exegesis in the University of Münster. There he made a study of Catholic theology. In 1930 he went to the University of Bonn to teach as a professor of systematic theology. In 1931 he published a book that, together with *Römerbrief*, was an unambiguous sign that he had distanced himself from liberal theology. It was a study of the theology of Anselm of Canterbury (1033–1109) called *Fides Quaerens Intellectum* ('Faith Seeking Understanding').[15] Barth described this work as a 'farewell to the last remnants of a philosophical, i.e., anthropological exposition of Christian doctrine.'[16]

the struggle with nazism

In 1933, Adolf Hitler and his National Socialists acceded to political power in Germany. For a second time in Barth's life, he was deeply unnerved by

Kulturprotestantismus ('Cultural Protestantism') – the association of Protestant Christianity with (German) society and culture. He reacted sharply against pro-Nazi Christians, concluding that they had fatally compromised the gospel by marrying faith and culture. He objected to the way the German Evangelical Church began to conform to and support the Nazi government.[17]

In the weeks before Christmas 1933, Barth preached a sermon centred on the fifteenth chapter of Romans, and pointed out that the Son of God in the form of Jesus had assumed Jewish flesh and blood – an uncomfortable reminder for Nazis. Barth sent a copy of the sermon and an accompanying letter directly to Hitler, pointedly advising Hitler to learn about the Christian Church.[18] Trouble was brewing for him.

He spoke before a meeting of 150 Protestant pastors in Berlin on 31 October 1933. He strove to elucidate that the Church could not serve two masters, God and a state power. Were the Church to align itself with a worldly master it would then ask itself: 'What took place in the concentration camps? What happened to the Jews? ... Has the Church not also become guilty in all this by keeping silent? Whoever proclaims the Word of God has to speak what the Word of God says about such actions.'[19]

Hitler became both Chancellor and President of Germany in August 1934, and required all state officials (including university teachers) to take an oath of loyalty to him. Barth objected to the wording of the oath and was dismissed from teaching in November and forbidden to speak in public. He was expelled from Germany the following year.[20] From Bonn he moved to Basel, and began teaching in its university. His birthplace served as his base for the rest of his life.

Back in Basel, Barth worked tirelessly. He laboured in peace movements and became an articulate decrier of nuclear weapons. He travelled throughout Europe, to England, and to the USA. He preached regularly in Basel's prison. He also strove to support churches and friends in Eastern Europe. He retired in March 1962 at the age of 76. He travelled to Rome in 1966 for discussions with Pope Paul VI.

human encounter with god

Before Barth was expelled from Germany he entered into a public dispute with Emil Brunner, a Swiss Reformed professor of theology in Zürich. In 1934, Brunner published a pamphlet called *Natur und Gnade: Zum Gespräch mit Karl Barth* ('Nature and Grace: Towards a discussion with Karl Barth').[21] The pamphlet broaches the contested theological question of whether and how human beings are able to encounter God in the World. The word 'nature' in the title of Brunner's text refers to humans and the world they inhabit. 'Grace' is a Christian theological term that designates God's free, benevolent disposition towards humanity. It is more of a loving disposition than a quantifiable thing.

Brunner had meditated on a text in the Book of Genesis which states: '[So] God created humankind in his image, in the image of God he created them; male and female he created them' (Gen 1: 27). The notion that human beings are set apart from other animals because they are created in the image of God (*Imago Dei*) is a major facet of Christians' understanding of the world as a divine creation. Brunner concluded that no matter how sinful, corrupt or deprived humans might be, there must be an element of their identity that refracts or mirrors the reality of God in their lives. Brunner called this element an *Anknüpfungspunkt*,[22] that is, a 'point of contact', between human nature and divine grace: there is a dimension of human nature that enables humans to encounter their Creator. This dimension forms the basis of natural theology – a way of discoursing about God by relying on a human feature such as reason which is understood as an image of divine reason.

Barth reacted angrily and argued that there is nothing in the human being that establishes a point of contact with God. He did not deny that God and humans contact one another, but they are only able to do so because of God's gracious initiative in divine revelation: God establishes the contact; not human beings. The title of Barth's rejoinder indicates his irritation: *Nein! Antwort an Emil Brunner* ('No! Answer to Emil Brunner').[23]

church dogmatics

By far the greatest preoccupation of Barth's mature work in Basel was the publication of his 13-volume work, *Church Dogmatics*. This work is one of the longest theological treatises in Christian history. It is twice as long as Thomas Aquinas' *Summa Theologiae*, and nine times the length of Calvin's *Institutes*. It contains nearly 10,000 pages bound in 13 volumes. The volumes are divided into five major parts: I, The Doctrine of the Word of God (two volumes); II, The Doctrine of God (in two volumes); III, The Doctrine of Creation (in four volumes); IV, The Doctrine of Reconciliation and V, Index and Aids to the Preacher.[24]

As long as it was, Barth never finished it. He stopped working on it in 1967. He died on 10 December 1968 in a year that nearly saw the Nato world become unhinged, and which witnessed student riots throughout Europe.

Barth's vast theological disquisition in *Church Dogmatics* centres on four cardinal and interrelated themes: theology understood as an activity of the Church for the Church; the sovereignty of God; divine revelation; and Jesus Christ. Barth was clear: 'there is no possibility of dogmatics at all outside the Church'.[25] For those daunted by the prospect of reading *Church Dogmatics*, a condensed presentation of his thought is contained in *Dogmatics in Outline*, which is based on a series of lectures he delivered in Bonn in 1946.[26]

Barth calls theology dogmatics. He understands dogmatics as that theological endeavour by which Christians test their language about God to see whether it conforms to the Bible's theological terminology: 'As a theological discipline dogmatics in the scientific self-examination of the Christian Church with respect to the content of its distinctive talk about God.'[27] Atheists, agnostics, monks, mendicants, bishops and prostitutes can all be found discussing God. Do they ever succeed in speaking about God tellingly, accurately or truthfully? Or do they really chatter about idols? Barth uses the Bible as a yardstick for determining truthful ways of talking about God. By dogmatics, Barth does not designate a type of authoritarian ecclesiastical dogma. Rather, dogmatics consists in a contiguity between what Christians now say about God and the Bible's witness to God. For Barth, theological reflection must be earthed in what the Bible says of God: '*Dogmatics is the science in which the Church, in accordance with the state of its knowledge at different times, takes account of the content of its proclamation critically, that is, by the standard of Holy Scripture and under the guidance of its Confessions.*'[28] He was adamant that theology must take its problems from Scripture and from Scripture alone.

Unlike many other theologians of his time, Barth does not begin his massive theological treatise with an attempt to explain how theology works, or to legitimate theology according to the criteria of other disciples such as philosophy or empirical sciences.[29] Instead, he begins by speaking directly of the Doctrine of the Word of God: 'The Bible is God's Word as it really bears witness to revelation, and proclamation is God's Word as it really promises revelation.'[30] He does not try to engage sceptical readers, but declares that the Bible is the Word of God.

Barth's entire theological edifice is built on the concept of revelation: 'In dogmatics the Church has to measure its talk about God by the standard of its own being, i.e., of divine revelation.'[31] Humans can only ever claim to know anything of God because God has taken an initiative partially to reveal Godself to humankind – hence the title of Part I of the Dogmatics, 'The Doctrine of the Word of God'. By locating revelation as the foundation of theology, Barth attempted to underscore God's complete priority over human reflection and experience: all knowledge of God depends on God's address to people and not their reflection about God. According to Barth, God and humans relate to each other dialectically, as thesis to antithesis. God and humans are not on the same ontological plane.

If Barth's theology is based on an understanding of the revelation of a God who is Wholly Other, what, more precisely, does he mean by revelation? To begin with, revelation is not a dossier of propositions taught by the Church. Revelation is an activity of God, not human beings. Expressed compendiously, Barth understands revelations as a tripartite form of the Word of God. In the first place, God is revealed in Jesus Christ. In the second instance, revelation is linked to the Bible, in so far as the Bible is a witness to the event of Jesus Christ. The third form of revelation understood as the Word of God is the witness of the Church to the Jesus Christ proclaimed by the Bible. Revelation, therefore, is Jesus Christ, scriptural witness to him, and the Church's witness to the Jesus of the Bible.[32]

On the basis of the previous sentence, it would be reasonable to conclude that Barth associates divine revelation exclusively with Christianity. *Church Dogmatics* is replete with surprises and one of its more striking comments on revelation is this: 'God may speak to us through Russian Communism, a flute concerto, a blossoming shrub, or a dead dog.'[33] What does Barth mean? He may be asserting that as far as Christians are aware, God is revealed to them by Jesus and the Bible, but that does not enable them to constrain God. For all they know, God may be revealed to other entities on other planets, or through a dead dog in Patagonia.

jesus christ

It is not misleading to conclude that Karl Barth's entire theological output is an elephantine commentary on a single verse from the first chapter of John's Gospel: '[And] the Word became flesh and lived among us, and we have seen his glory, the glory as of a father's only son, full of grace and truth' (Jn 1: 14). He states: 'I had come a long way (or round a detour!) before I began to see better and better that the saying in John 1: 14 is the centre and theme of all theology and indeed is really the whole of theology in a nutshell.'[34] That Jesus was a divine incarnation in human history is, for Barth, both 'the whole of theology in a nutshell' and the core of Christianity. Barth recorded the extent to which he was gripped and excited by the central idea of Jn 1: 14 while lecturing in Bonn during 1946: 'It really is a sensational story, more sensational than anything else. And that is the centre of Christianity, this infinitely surprising thing, that never existed before and cannot be repeated.'[35]

Barth's understanding of Jesus as a deity who became flesh is a resolute retelling of high Chalcedonian Christological orthodoxy: Jesus is the divine and human manifestation in history of the transcendent Creator of the universe. In Barth's terms, Jesus is primarily the Word of God who reveals to human beings the humanity of God, as well as manifesting to humans the archetype of their own humanity.

Central to Barth's understanding of the identity and significance of Jesus is a doctrine of election. According to Barth, each and every teaching of Christian theology must begin and end with what the Bible teaches about Jesus Christ and election. The fourth volume of the Church Dogmatics (II/2) is devoted to the doctrine of election. Central to the doctrine is the notion that God has selected, chosen, or elected certain people as worthy of divine compassion and revelation. It is basically a way of speaking about a covenant between God and people brought about because Jesus Christ as a God-man elected or decided to associate himself with sinful people.[36]

the trinity

The God of whom Barth's theology discourses at length is Triune as well as Wholly Other. The Christian teaching that God is Triune developed in the fourth century. It is not taught by the Bible. The doctrine's classical terminology of three divine persons in one divine substance stems from Greek meta-physics. Because it is not contained in the Bible it became vulnerable to being regarded as peripheral by liberal theologians of the nineteenth century. Barth regards it as indispensable to Christian Faith. He begins to elaborate the doctrine in the first volume of the *Church Dogmatics*, and continues in the fourth. A distinctive feature of his interpretation is that he avoids speaking of three 'persons' in God. This is so because he concludes that the word 'person' for modern ears can connote 'an individual'. This would mean that there are three individuals in God – three Gods. Barth substitutes the expression 'mode of being' (*Seinsweisen*) for person to overcome possible ambiguities and any suggestion that there are three Gods. He concludes that there is one God in three 'modes of being'. As explained by Eberhard Busch, 'The One God, as Father, Son, and Holy Spirit, has a specific function in these three distinct ways of being: the Father is God in his sovereignty, the Son is God in his humility, and the Spirit is God in the connection of Father and Son.'[37] Thus, this one God is God thrice in different senses.[38]

conclusion

Barth was a mighty theologian for decrying the destructiveness of human hubris, and for constantly drawing attention to God's Otherness and sovereignty. He was an illustrious theologian of the twentieth century because he was negative in a double sense. First, his 'No!' to Emil Brunner slighted people's attempts to grasp God from the bases of their own natures and intellectual resources. He was well aware that all doctrines, including that of the Trinity, are human estimations, not determinations of God. The doctrine of the Trinity might refer to God, but it is not God. Second, Barth used the Bible as a negative sword of judgement hanging over those who wage war and exploit the poor.

Barth was a precursor of what in the 1970s became known as theological postmodernism (addressed in Chapter 20 below) – the view that theology needs to take account that the modern project of the Enlightenment had become shipwrecked by its enthralment with human reason and ingenuity, and by its blindness to the bestial brutality at which humans are cruelly adept.

As distinguished as Barth's theological voice might have been, it was limited, as every theology is. He was fully cognizant of higher biblical criticism, but did not allow it to control his theologizing. Had he done so, he may have produced an entirely different reading of Jn 1: 14. If the first 18 verses of John's Gospel are cast in poetic form, a liberal theologian might well be justified in concluding that they are symbolically imagistic, not literally descriptive.

Barth's theology was also confined to the Church: dogmatics is a work of the Church for the Church. What if theology could be shaped by a variety of addressees, not simply the Church? In 1981, the North American theologian David Tracy advanced the view that theology has three major publics or audiences – Society, the Academy and the Church.[39]

The first two might not be persuaded by anything Barth says because he recoiled from justifying why the Bible ought to be venerated as a communication from God. He judged that it is, and expected others to accept his and the Church's authoritative adjudication. This amounts to saying, 'I am right because I know I am.' Barth's adulation of the Bible as the governing norm and fundamental fulchrum of theology was also the necrosis of his theology. The Bible prescribes too much homicide, genocide and execution to be regarded as the Word *of* God. If it is *God's* Word, God is demoted to the status of an all-too-familiar aggressor. Ironically, Barth's exaltation of the Bible as God's Word *reduced* rather than safeguarded any qualitative distinction between God and humans.

7

Dietrich Bonhoeffer: 1906–45

Whoever loves father or mother more than me is not worthy of me;
and whoever loves son or daughter more than me is not worthy of me;
and whoever does not take up the cross and follow me is not worthy of me.

Matthew 10: 37–8

People today were robbed of the potential gifts of Dietrich Bonhoeffer when he was hanged by the Gestapo on 9 April 1945, with the express consent of Adolf Hitler. He was 39 at the time. The woman he had engaged to marry heard of his execution the following June. She had no idea where he had been in the time between, as she searched for him in the western regions of Germany. His parents discovered in July that he was dead.[1]

Bonhoeffer was an academic theologian – trained in fine universities, and amply rewarded with their laurels. He was a gifted pianist and adept at athletics. He became a victim of Hitler specifically, and of the Second World War more generally, because he was convinced that anyone wishing to live as a disciple of Jesus Christ in the twentieth century could not possibly countenance the maniacal killing of Jews that was engineered by the Nazis.

Bonhoeffer was a casualty of his time, place and faith. Born in Germany, he lived through the nightmare of the First World War only to become ensnared in the maddening intrigues of the Second. Had he lived elsewhere and otherwise, he might have reached an old age and developed the many seminal theological ideas he sketched before he met his hangman. He was cruelly cut off in his prime. What he did manage to pen before his demise is still both starkly sobering and vividly stimulating for anyone interested in theology, and in how to correlate an ancient Christian tradition with a manifestly modern world.

A potent cocktail of causes generated the Second World War. Hitler's bellicosity was prominent among them. He consented to Bonhoeffer's execution on 5 April 1945, five days before it took place.[2] Why would the Chancellor of the German Third Reich, and one of the principal protagonists of the Second World War, want to kill a theologian? Because the latter militated furtively and publicly against the genocidal tyranny of the former.

bonhoeffer's early years

Dietrich Bonhoeffer was born on 4 February 1906, in the German city of Breslau (now part of Poland). He was the sixth of eight children. He had three older brothers (Karl-Friedrich, Walter and Klaus) and two older sisters (Ursula and Christel). His twin sister, Sabine, followed moments after his birth. Susanne was the youngest child in the family.

Dietrich's mother was Paula von Hase. Her grandfather, Karl August von Hase (1800–90), was a widely known Church historian of the nineteenth century. Dietrich's grandfather on his mother's side, Karl-Alfred von Hase (1842–1914), was court preacher to Kaiser Wilhelm II. His grandmother was the Countess Kalckreuth (1851–1903). She was prodigiously gifted as a pianist, so much so that she was taught to play the piano by Franz Liszt and Klara Schumann. Her virtuosic musicianship bore great fruit in Dietrich, who was able to perform Mozart piano sonatas by the age of ten. As a boy he also accompanied his mother and sister, Ursula, on the piano as they sang *Lieder* by Schubert, Schumann, Brahms and Hugo Wolf.[3] Dietrich's father, Karl Ludwig Bonhoeffer, was a distinguished physician who eventually became the Professor of Psychiatry and Nervous Diseases in the University of Berlin. Karl Ludwig was the son of Friedrich Bonhoeffer (1828–1907), the President of the High Court in Tübingen, and Julie Tafel (1842–1936), who came from Swabia. The Bonhoeffer clan originally migrated from Nijmegen in the Netherlands. They settled in Schwäbish-Hall in 1513.[4]

Dietrich's immediate family moved to Berlin in 1912, when he was a boy of six. It was not at all inevitable that he would eventually become a theologian of national notoriety and international distinction. His family did not participate in weekly worship at their local church. His father especially had become disenthralled with the Church of the Old Prussian Union (a combination of Lutheran and Reformed traditions). His parents concluded that their Church suffered from three maladies. First, it was closed to, and immured from, profound intellectual challenges of the day. Second, it was a manifestation of a self-centred bourgeois culture. And third, it was unable to redress the most severely debilitating social disorders in its surrounding culture.[5]

Despite the low esteem in which Dietrich's parents held the Church of the Old Prussian Union, a budding interest in theology gestated in him primarily because of his mother, Paula. Her father was a professor of practical theology in Breslau. She was 'consistently concerned that her children encounter stories of the Bible, learn the great hymns of the Christian tradition, offer grace before meals, participate in evening prayers, and be baptised and confirmed in the faith.'[6] By the time Dietrich was a young man, he had already acquired from his father a respect for the opinions and feelings of others. From his mother he had imbibed a love of God and a keen interest in people.[7]

In Berlin, Dietrich's family settled in a suburb populated by academics. Their neighbours included the physicist, Max Planck, and the theologian-historian, Adolf von Harnack. Thus situated, Dietrich grew up in a large family immersed in art, music, theatre, domestic religious devotion and lively intellectual discussions.

When Dietrich was 14 he announced to his family that he wanted to become a theologian and a Christian minister. At first, his brothers and sisters could not regard his decision seriously, and argued that the Church to which he proposed to devote his energies was a boring, feeble, petty bourgeois institution. To which he replied confidently, 'In that case I shall reform it!'[8]

university studies

As a boy of 14, Dietrich set himself on a path to become a theologian. When he was 17 he left home to study theology at Tübingen University, which at the time was an intellectual power-house and one of the academic glories of Germany. His father had previously been a student there, as were Hegel and David Friedrich Strauss. It is still a major centre for theological instruction and research. Dietrich remained in Tübingen between 1923 and 1924, studying Christian biblical texts with Adolf Schlatter (1852–1938), and the liberal theologies of Friedrich Schleiermacher and Albrecht Ritschl with Karl Heim (1874–1958).

Dietrich was constituted with a strong physique, which served him well, not only in his love for sports, but during long fatiguing hours of reading tomes in his study – and later in his life while he was imprisoned and interrogated by the Gestapo.

Bonhoeffer's many-sided and attractive character is well attested by his brother-in-law, Gerhard Leibholz (the husband of his twin, Sabine):

> Bonhoeffer was as open as any man could be to all the things which make life beautiful. He rejoiced in the love of his parents, his sisters and brothers, his fiancée, his many friends. ... But what marked him most was his unselfishness and preparedness to help others up to the point of self-sacrifice. Whenever others hesitated to undertake a task that required special courage, Bonhoeffer was ready to take the risk.[9]

Finishing at Tübingen, the young Bonhoeffer left Germany and travelled for three months with his brother, Klaus. Together they visited Italy and North Africa (Libya). Their visit to Rome made a lasting and deep impression on Dietrich. It was there that he acquired a perdurable sense of a universal ecclesial community, rather than a German one, even though he was repelled by what he took to be Roman dogmatism. Of his visit to Rome he noted: 'Palm Sunday ... the first day on which I understood something real about Catholicism. It has nothing to do with things like Romanticism. No, I think I am beginning to understand the concept of "church".'[10]

Later in 1924, Dietrich returned to Berlin to embark on higher studies in theology. He enrolled in the University of Berlin where he was taught by Adolf von Harnack, and the renowned interpreter of Martin Luther, Karl Holl (1866–1926). In 1927, when he was only 21, he successfully defended his doctoral dissertation which he had prepared under the direction of Reinhold Seeberg (1859–1935). It was called 'Sanctorum Communio [The Communion of Saints]: A Dogmatic Enquiry into the Sociology of the Church'. Therein he describes the church as 'Christ existing as community'. Karl Barth's influence is discernible in the dissertation, but Bonhoeffer worried that Barth's understanding of revelation diminished the significance of the Church.[11]

Sociology is now an established field of academic enquiry, but it was in its youth when Bonhoeffer was a doctoral student in Berlin. An abiding significance of Bonhoeffer's doctoral dissertation is that it represents the first major attempt by a theologian to speak of the Church by engaging insights from sociology. Three decades before the Second Vatican Council, Bonhoeffer emphasized the essential sociality of the Church, and warned that the Church cannot be equated directly with the kingdom of God. Before Vatican Two, the leadership of the Catholic Church tended to identify the Church explicitly with the kingdom of God on Earth.

Bonhoeffer in Rome, May 1924

In Berlin, Bonhoeffer encountered three major influences. From Harnack, he became intimately acquainted with theological liberalism. With Karl Holl, he probed the works of Martin Luther. And thirdly, he began an intensive study of the theological output of Karl Barth.

Dietrich intermitted his academic work to spend the year of 1928 living in Spain, where he worked as a curate for Barcelona's German-speaking Lutheran church.

His liking for the people he met in Catalonia is evident in a letter he wrote to a friend, Helmut Rössler, at the mid-point of his Spanish sojourn:

> I'm getting to know new people every day; here one meets people as they are, away
> from the masquerade of the 'Christian world', people with passions, criminal types,
> little people with little ambitions, little desires and little sins, all in all people who
> feel homeless in both senses of the word, who loosen up if one talks to them in a
> friendly way, real people.[12]

from berlin to new york

Dietrich returned to Berlin in 1929 to commence work on his *Habilitationsschrift* (a second advanced dissertation), which was later published with the title, *Act and Being*. This book, first published in German in 1931, is a treatise on philosophy, theology and ecclesiology. It is by far Bonhoeffer's most difficult work to engage.

It discusses the thought of the German philosopher, Martin Heidegger (1889–1976), and is basically addressed to philosophers.[13]

At the age of 24, Dietrich began to lecture in the University of Berlin. No sooner had he begun expostulating before students than he decided that he was not ready to teach. So he set out, in 1930, to pursue post-doctoral studies for one year as a Sloane Fellow at the Union Theological Seminary in New York City. He soon came to the conclusion that the seminary's theological ethos was shallow and tiresomely innocuous. He was disappointed that students did not appear to be taking theology seriously. He concluded that they were thereby intellectually ill-prepared for ministry. He was particularly upset by an incident during a lecture:

> A seminary in which it can come about that a large number of students laugh out loud in a public lecture at the quoting of a passage from Luther's *De Servo Arbitro* on sin and forgiveness because it seems to them to be comic has evidently completely forgotten on what Christian theology by its very nature stands.[14]

All was not lost. While in Manhattan, Bonhoeffer came under the influence of a French Lutheran, Jean Lassere, who was a strict pacifist. Lassere taught Bonhoeffer not to read the biblical text called the Sermon on the Mount (Mt 5–7) as if it were an intellectually intriguing theological treatise, but as a deeply unsettling programme for Christian discipleship and social action.

Bonhoeffer returned to Berlin in 1931 and began to lecture on the history of systematic theology in the twentieth century, the essence of the Church, creation and sin, Christian ethics, and Christology. In the same year he met Karl Barth in Bonn. In November he was ordained a Lutheran pastor in Berlin.

Ominously, the direction of Bonhoeffer's life changed decisively on 30 January 1933, when Adolf Hitler became the Chancellor of the Third Reich. Bonhoeffer not only appropriated from his family a taste for fine music. He also inherited from his parents and grandmother, Julie, an implacable opposition to Hitler and German National Socialism. Julie Bonhoeffer bravely defied German law and continued to buy commodities in Jewish shops after Hitler forbade the practice on 1 April 1933.

Julie Bonhoeffer died four years after her initial refusal to comply with a Nazi order not to shop in premises owned by Jews. Dietrich preached at her funeral and informed his congregation: 'She could not bear to see the rights of a person violated. ... Thus her last years were darkened by the grief that she bore about the fate of the Jews in our country, which she suffered with them.'[15]

second world war By the late 1930s, Hitler and Imperial Japan were expressing ambitions to expand their territories so as to compete with the colonial power of nations such as Great Britain and France.

In 1938, Hitler advanced his ambitions by annexing Austria and sections of Czechoslovakia. The Second World War began when he invaded Poland in 1939, and both Britain and France mobilized to oppose him. Germany surrendered on 7 May 1945, following the landing of Western Allied troops in Normandy on 6 June 1944, and the arrival in Berlin on 30 April 1945 of Soviet, British and American soldiers.

War continued to rage in the Pacific. By order of the American President, Harry Truman (1884–1972), a warplane dropped an atomic bomb on the Japanese city of Hiroshima. Two days later, another such bomb was unleashed on Nagasaki. The Emperor Hirohito capitulated five days afterwards, and declared Japan's surrender.

The devastation wrought by the Second World War was nightmarish. Roughly 7 million Soviet solders were killed, and 3.5 million Germans. Poland had 6 million of its people slaughtered, and Great Britain about 400,000.[16] The Nazis killed about 6 million Jews, as well as homosexuals and people with physical or mental impediments and challenges. Added to deaths, tens of millions of people were displaced and rendered homeless throughout Europe, and major cities were razed by bombs in England and Germany. 1945 was the last time an atomic bomb was used to vaporize and annihilate civilian populations. Since then, the world has lived with dread and anxiety that the practice will be repeated.

Many citizens of the Allied nations that defeated Hitler found it effortless subsequently to demonize him, in company with Mussolini and Hirohito, and expedient to excuse the practice of bombing civilians. In this context, the voice of the Second Vatican Council is sobering. Its participants declared on 7 December 1965 that 'Every act of war directed to the indiscriminate destruction of whole cities or vast areas and their inhabitants is a crime against God and humanity, which merits firm and unequivocal condemnation.'[17]

Emboldened, Bonhoeffer took to the radio on 1 February 1933 – two days after Hitler became Chancellor – and delivered a pointed address. It was called 'Changes in the Concept of "Leader" in the Younger Generation'. He warned his listeners against the perversion of an idolatrous Fürher principle. For Bonhoeffer, 'Hitler was the Antichrist, the arch-destroyer of the world and its basic values, the Antichrist which enjoys destruction, slavery, death and extension for its own sake, the Antichrist who wants to pose the negative as positive and creative.'[18] Predictably, Bonhoeffer was cut off the air before he could finish his speech.

the aryan clause

There was more, and worse, to come. The suffering of Jews in Germany governed by Hitler began in earnest in 1933. He enacted a law on 7 April, called the 'Law for the Re-establishment of the Professional Civil Service'. Article 3 of this law became known as 'the Aryan Clause'. It required the removal from Germany's civil service of anyone of 'non-Aryan descent'.[19] This clause was then used by the Nazis to dismiss Jews from other professions throughout Germany. Those who proclaimed it mistakenly thought that Jewishness is a matter of ethnicity, which is clearly wrong because anyone can, under prescribed circumstances, convert to Judaism.

The Aryan Clause raised an immediate problem for the Evangelical Church of Germany: what was to be done with those of its ministers who were baptized Jews, or Jewish Christians? Because the Evangelical Church of Germany was a state Church, its pastors could be regarded as state officials. Bonhoeffer refused to accept that pastors were state officials, and he was the first Protestant theologian clearly to oppose the legislation imposing the Aryan Clause.[20] His opposition was stymied: in September the Synod of the Old Prussian Union accepted the Aryan Clause in the Church.

Bonhoeffer left Germany in October and went to London where he began to minister among two German-speaking communities. In England he befriended Bishop George Bell of Chichester, to whom Bonhoeffer later sent a message just before he was hanged. Bell became an opponent of the practice of blanket-bombing – the indiscriminate destruction of cities and towns and their civilian populations.

finkenwalde seminary – costly discipleship

Karl Barth wrote to Bonhoeffer and encouraged him to return to Germany. Bonhoeffer did not return immediately, but stayed in London for a further 18 months.[21] By 1935, he was back in Germany, where he was appointed as director of an illegal seminary for preachers in the town of Zingst during the month of April 1935. In June of the same year the seminary was moved to the village of Finkenwalde, near Stettin. It was in the setting of Finkenwalde that Bonhoeffer wrote one of his most acclaimed works, called *Die Nachfolge Christi* ('The following, imitation, or discipleship of Christ').[22] It is discussed below. At Finkenwalde, he entreated his students to defend persecuted Jews.[23]

The seminary was shut down by the Gestapo in 1937, provoking Bonhoeffer to write a little book called *Life Together* (1938).[24] It enunciates the seminary's vision for Christian living. It envisages a way of life forcefully focused on prayer, personal and communal meditation, Bible study, solitude, companionship, singing, relaxing, ministry, worship, the Eucharist, spiritual care and confession. The Gestapo suppressed all subsequent publication of Bonhoeffer's ideas, apart from a short work on the Psalms.

On 9 November 1938, Nazi gangs in Germany destroyed more than 7,000 Jewish shops, burned synagogues, killed more than 90 Jews, and transported roughly 20,000 to concentration camps. In his Bible, Bonhoeffer underlined Psalm 74, verse 8: 'They said to themselves, "We will utterly subdue them"; they burned all the meeting places of God in the land.'[25]

Unwilling to be enlisted in the German army, Bonhoeffer returned to New York in June 1939. He was unable to settle, and returned to Germany the following month. He wrote to Reinhold Niebuhr, explaining his decision with these words: 'I have made a mistake in coming to America. I must live through this difficult period of our national history with the Christian people of Germany. I will have no right to participate in the reconstruction of Christian life in Germany after the war if I do not share the trials of this time with my people ... .'[26]

resistance

Back in Germany, Bonhoeffer became a civilian member of the Abwehr, the counterintelligence agency of the German army. That meant he was to become something of a double agent. Outwardly he worked for the army, while secretly he laboured for the German underground resistance to Hitler. Thrice he travelled to Switzerland, trying to arrange for Jews to be smuggled out of Germany. His most dangerous trip came in 1942 when he travelled to Sweden to meet Bishop Bell. He wanted Bell to inform Winston Churchill and President Roosevelt that the German resistance movement was plotting to overthrow Hitler.[27]

On 13 January 1943, Dietrich became engaged to Maria von Wedemeyer, but could never share a home with her as a result of his clandestine opposition to Hitler. He joined Hans von Dohnanyi, his brother-in-law, in secretive anti-Nazi activities. These culminated in two unsuccessful attempts to kill Hitler during the month of March.[28]

tegel prison

The Gestapo reacted swiftly. On 5 April 1943, Dietrich was arrested and locked up in Berlin's Tegel military prison. His cell measured a mere six feet by nine feet

*Looking into Bonhoeffer's cell
at Tegel prison*

(almost two metres by three). In this hell hole, some of the more innovative ideas of twentieth-century theology were penned. From his cell, he wrote several letters, theological jottings and poems, which were smuggled out and subsequently published as *Letters and Papers from Prison*. In a letter to him, his parents once asked him to describe his cell. To which he replied: 'To picture a cell does not need much imagination – the less you use, the nearer the mark you will be. ... Our day lasts fourteen hours, of which I spend about three walking up and down the cell – several kilometres a day, besides half an hour in the yard. I read, learn, and work.'[29]

On 8 October 1944, Bonhoeffer was transferred to the Gestapo prison in Prinz-Albrecht-Strasse in Berlin. In February 1945, he was transferred to Buchenwald concentration camp. A prisoner in Buchenwald, Captain Payne Best (of the British Secret Service), wrote of Bonhoeffer at the time, observing that he 'always seemed to diffuse an atmosphere of happiness, of joy in every smallest event in life, and a deep gratitude for the mere fact that he was alive. ... He was one of those very few men I have ever met to whom his God was real and ever close to him.'[30]

On 3 April 1945, Bonhoeffer was dispatched to Flossenbürg extermination camp. His prison van broke down on the way at the little Bavarian village of Schönberg. The prisoners were detained in the village schoolhouse. Since it was Sunday, the prisoners asked Dietrich to lead them in prayer. He obliged, yet, while praying, two Gestapo officers burst through a door and demanded that he follow them. This could only have meant one thing. He was about to be executed. He calmly took his time to bid farewell to each prisoner.

He drew aside his English friend, Captain Payne Best. He wanted Best to pass on his final thoughts and good wishes to Bishop Bell. Bonhoeffer declared to Best: 'This is the end – for me the beginning of life.'[31] These are Bonhoeffer's last recorded words.

Early the next morning, on 9 April 1945, he was hanged in Flossenbürg camp. The camp was liberated a week after by General Patton's army. Three weeks later, Hitler was dead. Maria still did not know what had happened to Dietrich. In his *Letters and Papers from Prison*, he noted:

Again I've had a marvellous letter from Maria. The poor girl has to keep writing without getting a direct response from me. That must be hard, but I delight in every word about her and every small detail interests me because it makes it easier to share what she is doing. I'm so grateful to her. In my bolder dreams I sometimes picture our future home.[32]

major themes in bonhoeffer's theology

Bonhoeffer never published a fully elaborated theology. He died too young to develop the seminal ideas sketched in *Discipleship* and *Letters and Papers from Prison*. Apart from these books and *Life Together*, his two doctoral dissertations, as well as lectures on Creation and Christology were also produced as books. He was working on his *Ethics* when he was arrested. After his death, friends published his letters and poems – 'Resistance and Submission' (*Widerstand und Ergebung*) – and parts of a drama and novel, 'Fragments from Tegel: Drama and Novel' (*Fragmente aus Tegel: Drama und Roman*).

Bonhoeffer's friend, Eberhard Bethge, divided Bonhoeffer's life into three stages, and noted that each stage was marked by a particular theological preoccupation. During the first phase of Bonhoeffer's university teaching he was primarily concerned to promote the understanding that the Church is essentially a community. In the second, while he was struggling in the Confessing Church, he was transfixed by costly discipleship. In the third stage, while he was working against Hitler, he was concerned with 'worldly holiness'.[33]

The *Letters and Papers from Prison* contain Bonhoeffer's most mature reflections on God and Jesus Christ. His understanding of God is inseparable from his fondness for Jesus: 'All we might rightly expect from God, and ask him for, is to be found in Jesus Christ. ... If we are to learn what God promises, and what he fulfils, we must persevere in quiet meditation on the life, sayings, deeds, sufferings, and death of Jesus.'[34]

These words were written in Tegel prison on 21 August 1944. Bonhoeffer's theology was so focused on Jesus that he could say: 'If Jesus had not lived, then our life would be meaningless, in spite of all the other people whom we know and honour and love.'[35]

Linking the identity of God so closely with the historical career of Jesus led Bonhoeffer, at the height of

George Bell (1883–1958)
Lord Bishop of Chichester

the Second World War, to espouse the notion that God suffers, and that only a God who suffers in the light of people's anguish is of any help to them: 'Here is the decisive difference between Christianity and all religions. Man's religiosity makes him look in his distress to the power of God in the world: God is the *deus ex machina*. The Bible directs man to God's powerlessness and suffering; only the suffering God can help.'[36]

the world's coming of age

In Tegel prison during June of 1944, Bonhoeffer toyed with the notion of the 'world coming of age'. He means by the concept that the world of human beings has reached an age in which it is less reliant on God. Bonhoeffer traces the beginning of humanity's movement towards greater autonomy from about the thirteenth century, and links it with the discovery of laws by which the world works in areas such as science, political and social concerns, as well as religion, art and ethics: 'Man has learnt', opines Bonhoeffer, 'to deal with himself in all questions of importance without recourse to the "working hypothesis" called "God".' And again: 'As in the scientific field, so in human affairs generally, "God" is being pushed more and more out of life, losing more and more ground.'[37]

religionless christianity

Bonhoeffer's notion of a world coming of age is associated with his inchoate ideas on religionless Christianity. Immured in Tegel prison, he asked in April of 1944, 'Are there religionless Christians?', and 'What do a church, a community, a sermon, a liturgy, a Christian life mean in a religionless world?'[38] These questions stem from Bonhoeffer's observation that for 19 centuries Christianity had assumed the form of 'religion'. It occurred to him that the structure of religion may not be essential to Christianity, but is 'a historically conditioned and transient form of human self-expression ...'.[39] It follows for Bonhoeffer that neither God nor Jesus is tied to a religion's language: 'In that case Christ is no longer an object of religion, but something quite different, really the Lord of the world.'[40]

At this stage of his life, Bonhoeffer was troubled by the issue of 'what Christianity really is, or indeed what Christ really is, for us today'. He had the sense that 'We are moving towards a completely religionless time; people as they are now simply cannot be religious any more.'[41]

Related ideas were sketched in Bonhoeffer's *Ethics* as he wrestled to find a secular way of talking about God for a world that had come of age and for people who were living without religion: 'The separation of the sacred from the secular denies the unity of God and the world achieved in the revelation and work of Jesus Christ. There is no God apart from the world, no supernatural apart from the natural, no sacred apart from the profane. Christ is the ultimate reality and the world is part of that reality.'[42]

the cost of discipleship

The driving intellectual engine of Dietrich Bonhoeffer's life and work is captured in one word – discipleship. In the first paragraph of his most influential book, *Discipleship*, he asks:

> What did Jesus want to say to us? What does he want from us today? How does he
> help us to be faithful Christians today? It is not ultimately important to us what this
> or that church leader wants. Rather, we want to know what Jesus wants. When we
> go to a sermon, his own word is what we want to hear. This matters to us not only
> for our own sakes, but for all those who have become estranged from the church and
> its message.[43]

It is as well to note at this stage that Bonhoeffer evinces a concern for 'those who have become estranged from the church and its message'. For Barth, theology is a work of the Church for the Church. Bonhoeffer demurs from such a view and affirms that theology must speak to a world that has come of age. It must address the preoccupations of a sophisticated, secularized modern culture:

> Today there are a great number of people who come to our preaching, want to hear
> it, and then repeatedly have to admit sadly that we have made it too difficult for
> them to get to know Jesus. Do we really want to deny being in community with
> these people? They believe that it is not the word of Jesus itself that they wish to
> evade, but that too much of what comes between them and Jesus is merely human,
> institutional, or doctrinaire.[44]

Karl Barth insisted that God is revealed to human beings heteronomously from a transcendent realm. In *Letters and Papers from Prison*, Bonhoeffer calls Barth's view of revelation 'positivist': it is simply laid down as a non-negotiable given (Latin:

positum, 'a given'). Bonhoeffer contended that Barth's view of revelation effectively said to a person, '"Like it or lump it": virgin birth, Trinity, or anything else; each is an equally significant and necessary part of the whole, which must simply be swallowed as a whole or not at all.' Bonhoeffer could not accept such a stance because, as he said of it, 'That isn't biblical.'[45]

Returning to the subject of discipleship, when Bonhoeffer was but 31, he depicted the cost that discipleship of Jesus Christ exacts on a person in an extremely startling way: 'Whenever Christ calls us, his call leads us to death.'[46] In Bonhoeffer's case, discipleship led to physical extinction. He alerted other Christians to expect suffering if they set upon a path of imitating Jesus Christ: 'Discipleship is being bound to the suffering of Christ.'[47] As such, it can take different forms: 'Whether we, like the first disciples, must leave house and vocation to follow him, or whether, with Luther, we leave the monastery for a secular vocation, in both cases the same death awaits us, namely, death in Jesus Christ, the death of our old self caused by the call of Jesus.'[48]

Above all, Bonhoeffer railed against what he called 'cheap grace'. In *Discipleship* he trumpets:

> Cheap grace is the mortal enemy of the church. Our struggle today is for costly grace. Cheap grace means grace as bargain-basement goods. ... Cheap grace is preaching forgiveness without repentance, it is baptism without the discipline of community; it is the Lord's Supper without the confession of sin; it is absolution without personal confession. Cheap grace is grace without discipleship, grace without the cross, grace without the living, incarnate Christ.[49]

conclusion

The calamity of Dietrich Bonhoeffer's life is that his attempts to live as a twentieth-century disciple of Jesus Christ led him directly to an executioner's noose. That is his worth, not his shame. Those who killed him, and all who kill wantonly, are often dominant for a while, but hardly victorious in the end. Villainy is never ultimately strong because it always falls. Even so, while particular villainies eventually collapse in human history, only to mutate into other forms, they and their progeny last long enough to plague peaceful people. Bonhoeffer is a shrill alarm for anyone who imagines blithely that a following of Jesus Christ in a mean and murderous world comes without deadly cost. As both discovered, a person who directly opposes a deadly political power in the name of a just God can expect but one fate – annihilation.

Bonhoeffer's brother-in-law, Hans von Dohnanyi, was executed at Sachsenausen camp on the same day he was – 9 April 1945. His older brother, Klaus, with whom he had happily travelled as a very young man to Rome in 1924, was shot by the Gestapo on 23 April, together with Rüdiger Schleicher.[50] Will God ever vindicate victims of the world's violent bullies?

8

Paul Tillich: 1886–1965

> Faced with the Inexpressible the West has tried to describe it in
> absurdly concrete terms: the whole traditional theology is a case of
> the misplaced concrete.
>
> *Philip Toynbee*

Two of the most accomplished and learned Protestant theologians of the twentieth century were born in the same year. Karl Barth and Paul Tillich were both
born in 1886. They died within a mere three years of each other: the former in
1968, and the latter in 1965 – the final year of the deliberations of the Second
Vatican Council, and the year in which the USA began regular bombing of North

Vietnam. Their lives were thus lived in parallel, although they produced markedly different types of theology. Barth stood primarily in a Calvinist theological tradition, while Tillich, like Bonhoeffer, was a Lutheran. Barth became a theologian of diastasis ('to stand apart'). He sought to elucidate Christian faith over, against and apart from the surrounding culture in which he found himself. He regarded the Bible as both a revelation from God and a sword of judgement over the vanities and inanities of human behaviour in the twentieth century. Tillich shared many theological interests with Barth, such as the identity of God and the nature of Jesus Christ, but he was more a theologian of synthesis than diastasis. His theology strived to interrelate or correlate Christian faith with the culture and philosophy of the societies in which Christian churches found themselves last century. Barth was the most prominent Protestant theologian of diastasis in the twentieth century. His Catholic counterpart was another Swiss, Hans Urs von Balthasar (1905–88). For Barth and von Balthasar, theology focuses on the Church.[1] Other theologians to be encountered later in this book took a different view, a perspective that is voiced in the writings of Paul Tillich. For these thinkers, theology is not simply an exercise of and for the Church, but a reflection on human experiences in the history of their world that is correlated with articulated experiences of past generations.

a professorial theologian

Paul Tillich was a professor of theology for most of this life. He began lecturing shortly after the outbreak of the First World War, and continued to do so until his death in 1965. When he died he was the Nuveen Professor of Theology (named after bankers) in the Divinity School of the University of Chicago. In some other American universities of the time he would have had to retire a decade earlier. His professorial career straddled two continents. He was born in Germany and died in the USA. The Nazis were the catalysts for him to move from one to the other. He did not have a command of English when he arrived to teach in New York in late 1933. His experience of two starkly diverse cultures, one Germanic, the other North American, helps to explain why he was fascinated by human culture and theology's engagement with it.[2]

Paul Tillich was born on 20 August 1886 in the village of Starzeddel, which lay close to Berlin in the district of Guben in the Province of Brandenburg – a name made famous by Johann Sebastian Bach (1685–1750) with his *Brandenburg Concertos* (1721). Starzeddel has been part of Poland since 1945, and is now called

Starosiedle. Paul's father, Johannes Oskar Tillich, was a Lutheran who served as the village pastor for the Evangelical Church of Prussia. 'Evangelical' here stems from the Greek word, *evangelion*, meaning 'good news' or 'gospel'. Paul was the oldest of three children, with two sisters, Johanna and Elisabeth. He was extremely fond of his mother from whom he received, as he later recalled, a 'zest for life, love of the concrete, mobility, rationality, and democracy'.[3]

Four years after Paul's birth, his family moved to Schönfliess, a small medieval town surrounded by farms and with a lake nearby.[4] Paul spent most of his boyhood here in rustic beauty, where it was not difficult for him to be enthralled by the flora and fauna of his natural environment. He also began his schooling here. Paul's youth in Schönfliess bred in him a romantic love of nature – romantic in the sense of a yearning for ultimate aesthetic and emotional fulfilment.

In 1898, the Tillich family moved to Berlin. Paul was sent to boarding school in Königsberg in East Prussia (now called Kaliningrad and in Russia). He moved back to Berlin in 1901 where he attended the Friedrich Wilhelm Gymnasium. He successfully completed his studies there in 1904.[5]

When he was 17, his mother died of cancer. He was left bereft, to the extent that he refused to speak of her to anyone or even mention her name. Some have explained his stark reaction as a psychological repression of his love for her, which later emerged in erotic encounters with other women.[6]

At the age of 18 he decided to study for ordained ministry in the Lutheran Church. He pursued theological studies in Berlin, Tübingen and Halle. He only spent one semester in Tübingen. After that time he lived for two years in Halle, where he first discovered the writings of the philosopher, Friedrich Wilhelm Joseph von Schelling (1775–1854).[7] He was also taught theology by Martin Kähler (1835–1912), who was critical of attempts to base interpretations of the significance of Jesus Christ on historical data. Kähler drew a distinction between the historical Jesus and the historic Christ of faith. By 'historical' he referred to the Jesus who lived and died in first-century Palestine. By 'historic' he meant the individual who influenced the lives of centuries of later Christians:

> The real Christ, that is, the Christ who has exercised an influence in history, with
> whom millions have communed in childlike faith, and with whom the great
> witnesses of faith have been in communion – while striving, apprehending,
> triumphing, and proclaiming – *this real Christ is the Christ who is preached*. The Christ
> who is preached, however, is precisely the Christ of faith.[8]

Kähler argued that Jesus Christ is significant for Christians, not because of what can be ascertained of his historical career, but on account of his death, and as early Christians proclaimed, his triumphant resurrection.[9] All this was to shape Tillich's later published interpretations of Jesus.

Tillich passed his initial theological examination in 1909. The following year, when he was 24, he was awarded a doctorate in philosophy in the University of Breslau on the basis of a thesis devoted to the philosophy of Schelling, who was an early associate of Hegel and an exponent of philosophical idealism. This was the first of two theses attending to Schelling's thought. His doctoral dissertation was titled 'The Conception of the History of Religions in Schelling's Positive Philosophy: Its Presuppositions and Principles'.[10]

In 1911, Tillich was awarded a licentiate degree in theology at the University of Halle. For the second time in his life he received a degree for a thesis on Schelling: 'Mysticism and Guilt-Consciousness in Schelling's Philosophical Development'. He then completed an *Habilitationsscrift* that would qualify him to teach in universities as a *Privatdozent* (unsalaried lecturer). His qualifying thesis was called, 'The Concept of the Supernatural, Its Dialectic Meaning and the Principle of Identity, in the Supra-naturalistic Theology prior to Schleiermacher'.[11]

> **idealism, philosophical**   Idealism was a form of philosophy that flourished in the eighteenth and nineteenth centuries, particularly in Germany. It is not an aspiration to noble human ideals. It takes its name from 'ideas', not 'ideals'. Idealism is not an existential quest for an ideal life, but a metaphysical world-view. That is, it is a particular understanding of reality. In a counter-intuitive or counter-commonsensical fashion, it concludes that reality is constituted by ideas. It distinguishes between the real and the appearance of reality. On this basis, it avers that ideas, or the conceptual contents of the human mind, are the primary realities which human beings are able to know. Modern philosophical idealism was espoused by Descartes and George Berkeley (1685–1753). Among German-speakers, it was championed by Kant, Hegel and Schelling.

Tillich passed his final examination in theology in July 1912. The following month in Berlin he was ordained in the Evangelical Church of the Prussian Union. It had taken him eight years of philosophical and theological study to reach that stage. As sophisticated and instructive as all of his university studies were, they were not to have as decisive an impact in his life as historical events that were about to unfurl.

Tillich's plans to combine a life of university teaching and ministry in the Church were disrupted by the commencement of the First World War. He married Grethi (Margarethe) Wever in September 1914, but their plans to live together were disrupted by the war. Tillich began military service as a chaplain to the German Army. Service in the army exposed him to the full horrors of trench warfare. He was sent for six months to the front lines of battles, where he encountered the sick and dying in trenches. He worked as both a pastor and a gravedigger.[12]

In 1919, he began lecturing as a *Privatdozent* in the University of Berlin. Thus commenced a distinguished academic career leading to appointments in a string of universities: Marburg, Dresden, Leipzig and Frankfurt.[13] He also joined the Social Democratic Party.

The immediate post-war years for Tillich were both academically promising and personally tumultuous. His academic career advanced, but his wife Margarethe left him to have an affair with a man who was one of Tillich's friends. Thus began in his life a phase of experimenting with new social and sexual encounters. He met Hannah Werner Gottschow in the socially non-conformist circles in which he mixed. They married in 1924.[14]

By the mid-1920s, Tillich was very familiar with the neo-orthodoxy of Karl Barth and his circle. It was a style of theology that he did not embrace whole-heartedly. Far from it. He was wary of its disinclination to include an analysis of contemporary culture and experiences in the task of theology. The most signifi-cant flaw of the theologies of Barth and von Balthasar is that they chain theology to the Church – past and present. The Church is a small dimension of historical existence. If God engages with humans and their experiences, there is nothing a theologian can do limit to God's encounters to members of the Church, in forget-fulness of the masses of suffering people outside the Church whom God is said to have created.

Before the First World War, Tillich tried to convey the meaning of Christianity to people he encountered in Berlin's Moabite workers' district.[15] There he became well acquainted with the struggles and travails of poor labourers. While engaging with these workers, Tillich came to the conclusion that the traditional theological language so often employed in the Church of his day did not effectively communi-cate the sense of Christian faith to twentieth-century urban labourers.[16] While studying with Martin Kähler in Halle he had become familiar with the work of European theologians of mediation. These were nineteenth-century thinkers, like Schleiermacher, who attempted to mediate or link traditional Christian language with newly emergent modern world-views and cultures.[17] Tillich's experiences as a young pastor in Berlin set him on his own life-long course to formulate a theol-ogy that more effectively conveyed than conventional orthodox approaches the sense of Christian faith for contemporary cultures.

The Great War destroyed in Tillich the notion that Germany was a unified nation. He concluded that it was riven by an entrenched class-consciousness. This awareness, coupled with his encounters with poor workers spawned within him an interest in socialism. Two of his earlier published books broach his twofold interest: conveying Christian thought in modern cultures and linking Christianity with socialism. The books were called *The Religious Situation of the Present*, which deals with his sketch of Christianity's predicament in his time, and *The Socialist Decision*.[18]

After the First World War, Tillich joined a group of German socialists who were keen to promote radical social change in Germany. This group, 'The Kairos Circle', labelled their movement for comprehensive social transformation as 'Religious Socialism'. Tillich became a prominent member of this group, and for ten years, from 1923 to 1933, most of his publications formulated principles for advancing Christian socialism.[19]

The kind of socialism envisioned by Tillich was inimical to the political vision of Germany's National Socialists under Hitler. When they came to power in Germany in 1933, they promptly dismissed Tillich from his professorship in Frankfurt.

emigration to america

The North American theologian, Reinhold Niebuhr, came to Tillich's aid, and arranged for him to teach at New York's Union Theological Seminary and Columbia University on the Upper West Side of Manhattan. Tillich emigrated to the USA in 1933. It was not an effortless task. He had to begin a new life and second academic career in an English-speaking country, while working in a Christian seminary preparing students for ministry.

In Germany, Tillich had enjoyed professorships in state universities. His lectures focused principally on philosophy rather than theology. He maintained lively friendships with writers, poets and artists. His life in New York was starkly different. He arrived at Union Theological Seminary in November of 1933 to teach as a visiting professor. Before long he was appointed as a professor of the philosophy of religion and systematic theology. His lectures began to address theological topics more comprehensively. The routine of lectures and classes at the Seminary was punctuated by chapel services and meetings for prayer every day. At Columbia University, Tillich joined the Philosophy Club. His first book in English was published in 1936 and called, *On the Boundary; An Autobiographical Sketch*.[20]

Tillich was due to retire from lecturing in Union Theological Seminary in 1955, but the year before he accepted a professorship in Harvard. From there he moved in 1962 to the University of Chicago, where he continued to teach until he died of heart failure on 22 October 1965, at the age of 79.[21]

tillich's systematic theology

Tillich was a prolific author. The collected German edition of his writings includes 14 principal volumes and eight supplements.[22] The work for which he is mostly known is his *Systematic Theology*, published in three volumes towards the end of his life. It is the most sustained exposition of his theology and benefits from the many intellectual, religious and cultural influences that impinged upon him. The first volume was published in 1951 as he was about to move from New York to Harvard. The final instalment appeared in 1963 while he was in Chicago, two years before his death. It is the principal resource for studying his theology even if only because it was the culmination of a project that engaged his energies for most of his professorial life.

There are five major subdivisions in the trilogy. The first volume addresses the themes of 'Reason and Revelation' (Part 1) and 'Being and God' (II). The second volume is shorter than the other two and has the subtitle of 'Existence and the Christ' (III). The final tome discusses 'Life and the Spirit' (IV), as well as 'History and the Kingdom of God' (V).[23]

Tillich opens his *Systematic Theology* in an arresting way. In plain terms he announces his understanding of the task of theologians: 'Theology, as a function of the Christian church, must serve the needs of the church.' This sounds very Barthian at first sight, but Tillich continues: 'A theological system is supposed to satisfy two basic needs: the statement of the truth of the Christian message and the interpretation of this truth for every new generation. Theology moves back and forth between two poles, the eternal truth of its foundation and the temporal situation in which the eternal truth must be received' (*ST*, 1: 3).

In trying to address his generation, Barth turned to the language of the Bible. Here is where Tillich differs. He relies on biblical traditions and relates them to new forms of philosophy and culture peculiar to his own generation. He concludes that most theological systems are not able to balance the twin poles of articulating truth and interpreting Christianity for each new generation. He is wary of theologies that are incapable of speaking to a contemporary situation. The more he elaborates, the clearer the difference between Barth and himself becomes. Referring to theologies that do not manage to balance the two poles of theology just mentioned, Tillich observes: 'Afraid of missing the eternal truth, they identify it with some previous theological work, with traditional concepts and solutions, and try to impose these on a new, different situation. They confuse the eternal truth with a temporal expression of this truth' (*ST*, 1: 3).

theonomy

The first part of the initial volume of Tillich's *Systematic Theology* ('Reason and Revelation') adumbrates Tillich's understanding of theology and describes his theological method. Several outstanding Christian thinkers have made their mark by expounding a single cardinal idea, and then reworking it in diverse variations throughout their writings. Barth's seminal idea was the sovereignty of God who is revealed to humanity. Bonhoeffer's work all relates to the notion of an exacting discipleship. Albert Schweitzer expounded the idea of reverence for life. A distinctive and original overriding idea also stands at the heart of Paul Tillich's theology. It sounds strange since it is a concept of his own coinage – theonomy. This word is a neologism in English and is formed by joining two Greek terms *theos* ('God') and *nomos*.

Tillich explains the odd term theonomy by relating it to two others – autonomy (from *nomos*/'law' and *autos*/'self') and heteronomy (*heteros*/'strange, other' and *nomos*/'law'). Autonomy means 'the obedience of the individual to the law of reason', while heteronomy imposes a strange law on 'one or all of the functions of reason' (*ST*, 1: 84). By contrast, theonomy means 'autonomous reason united with its own depth':

> In a theonomous situation reason actualizes itself in obedience to its structural laws and in the power of its own inexhaustible round. Since God (*theos*) is the law (*nomos*) for both the structure and the ground of reason, they are united in him, and their unity is manifest in a theonomous situation. But there is no complete theonomy under the conditions of existence (*ST*, 1: 85).

This way of talking may seem to be a farrago of nonsense. It can be explained in different terms. Tillich first elaborated what he meant by theonomy in a lecture he gave in Berlin at the end of the First World War. The presentation was given on 16 April 1919 to the Kant Society and was called, 'On the Idea of a Theology of Culture'. This was a revealing title. So too was the first course Tillich taught as a *Privatdozent*, called 'Christianity and the Present Social Problems'. Both titles belie an interest that Tillich harboured for the rest of his life – to relate religion to its surrounding culture.

The lecture, 'On the Idea of a Theology of Culture', shows Tillich's struggle to link religion and culture in a new way. He called this relation 'theonomy'. After the First World War and the social dilemmas it provoked, Tillich was spurred on to find a novel theological language that would simultaneously explain faithfully the thrust of Christian faith and address social problems that had not previously been encountered by human beings. Thus, at the heart of his career stood a tension between being both a theologian of and for culture, and a theologian for and of the Church.

In formulating his new theological vocabulary, Tillich criticized what he called the 'heteronomy' of much Christian discourse. By this he intended that the Church too often imposes on culture a set of alien words and laws that violate the ways of thinking and living of the Church's public audience. If the Church practised heteronomy, Tillich also concluded that society practises autonomy, that is, it celebrates its independence from Churches which speak in culturally foreign tongues. Over and against both heteronomy and autonomy, Tillich proposed a theonomy, a situation in which sociocultural structures are valued in themselves while at the same time being explicitly related to divine life.

Tillich, as a theologian of synthesis rather than diastasis, strove energetically to marry theology with prevailing thought forms of his day. To his end, his writings use philosophy, art, natural science, psychology and any other cultural expressions he thought would communicate the sense of Christianity to his war-ravaged generation. His attempt to articulate a theology of culture influenced a host of later North American theologians.

the theological method of correlation

Tillich's idea of theonomy is closely linked to his understanding of theological method. He was convinced that choosing the correct method for constructing a theology is as crucial as selecting the right materials for constructing a building. If theonomy describes his vision of the task of theology, correlation designates his preferred method for theologizing.[24]

He defines a method as 'a tool, literally a way around, which must be adequate to its subject matter' (*ST*, 1: 60). The method he prefers helps him to maintain a tension between a theology addressed to the Church, and a theology formulated according to the world-view of his culture. A correlation is a relation between two or more things. Tillich's correlational method establishes a cycle of relations between questions and answers. For him, people today formulate questions about their existence in the world in relation to God, while the Bible and Christian traditions are a reservoir which furnishes answers to the questions of today: 'Symbolically speaking, God answers man's questions, and under the impact of God's answers man asks them' (*ST*, 1: 61). In this way, Christian faith and contemporary culture are set in a mutual interdependence wherein culture raises existential queries and faith provides theological responses.

Tillich's correlational method proceeds in two steps. First it engages philosophy and other investigative disciplines such as sociology and anthropology to analyse a given human condition, in order to specify the most troubling existential questions that arise from it. In a second step the Christian Gospel is articulated in such a way as to address the problems uncovered through existential analysis (*ST*, 1: 62). Within this method, theology and philosophy work hand in hand.

Tillich relies on three sources when employing a method of correlation: the Bible; the history of the Christian Church; and the history of religion and cultures. In Tillich's theological system, it is important that theologians use the material provided by his three preferred sources because 'Culture is primarily the source of the existential questions that theology attempts to answer, thereby determining the form of every theological answer derived from the Bible and church history.'[25]

The object of theological discourse and Christian faith is what Tillich calls an ultimate concern: '*The object of theology is what concerns us ultimately. Only those propositions are theological which deal with their object in so far as it can become a matter of ultimate concern for us*' (*ST*, 1: 12; italicized in the original). The phrase 'ultimate concern' is simply an abstraction which Tillich uses to translate a command found in Mark's Gospel: 'the Lord our God, the Lord is one; you shall love the Lord your God with all your heart, and with all your soul, and with all your mind, and with all your strength' (Mk 12: 29b-30; see *ST*, 1: 11).

god as being-itself

As a philosophically educated theologian, Tillich was fascinated by ontology – the investigation of being.[26] Ontology forms the basis of his language about God. He stands in a long philosophical and theological tradition that refuses to depict God as *a* being, not even a supreme being. He distinguishes between God as being and finite beings (such as humans). 'The being of God', he says, 'is being-itself. The being of God cannot be understood as the existence of a being alongside others or above others. If God is *a* being, he is subject to the categories of finitude, especially to space and substance' (*ST*, 1: 235).

In the first volume of Tillich's *Systematic Theology*, he makes no mention of the medieval Islamic thinker, Avicenna (980–1037). Yet Tillich's way of refusing to call God a being (*ST*, 1: 235) ultimately derives from him. Avicenna drew a distinction between essence and existence.[27] This was later used by Thomas Aquinas to teach that there is no distinction between essence and existence in God. God is existence, or being, itself. The distinction can only be made with regard to finite beings such as humans. Their essence is to be human, and they are also able to exist. To say that God has essence and existence relegates God to the status of a finite entity.

It is extraordinarily common for God to be called a divine person, a supreme being, a mighty force, a powerful judge, or a loving father. As odd as it may seem, if Avicenna is to be followed, God is not anything, that is, God is not a thing that can be located or counted. On this atheists and theists can agree: God is not anything!

jesus christ as the new being

The second volume of Tillich's *Systematic Theology* was published in 1957, six years after the first. It grapples with the exigencies of human existence considered in relation to Jesus Christ. It outlines what amounts to Tillich's Christology.

With regard to the human predicament, Tillich meditates on the biblical story of Adam and Eve in the primordial Garden of Eden. Tillich does not regard the story of their gradual estrangement from God (Gen 3) as a record of an historical event. It is a myth. Rather, he interprets it as an expression of human beings' anxiety generated by their sins and estrangement from what they could be (free from sin). One of Tillich's best known publications is *The Courage to Be*. It deals with people's struggles in coping with anxiety produced by estrangement from what they could realize.[28]

Tillich's reading of Genesis sets the scene for his depiction of Jesus Christ as the New Being. Because humans are alienated from an ideal state of being, the only way for them to be saved from their anxious state in Tillich's eyes is by a divine initiative. This Tillich sees manifested in history of the life of Jesus. The New Being in the Person of Jesus Christ is not interpreted by Tillich in a mythical way according to which God mutates into a human being, but as the manifestation of God in Jesus' life: 'This is not a myth of transmutation but the assertion that God is manifest in a personal life-process as a saving participant in the human predicament' (*ST*, 2: 95). Jesus Christ construed as the New Being can be related to what Paul of Tarsus calls the New Creation (2 Cor, 5: 17).

Tillich studied the nineteenth-century quest for the historical Jesus and came to the same conclusion as his former teacher, Martin Kähler: 'the attempt of historical criticism to find the empirical truth about Jesus of Nazareth was a failure' (*ST*, 2: 102). The quest was a failure in his eyes because it searched for a body of historically reliable facts about Jesus, when all that can be ascertained factually about his life are probabilities of a higher or lower degree (*ST*, 2: 105). What matters for Tillich's Christology are the writings Christians call The New Testament. Tillich concludes that these provide 'a picture of Jesus as the Christ' (*ST*, 2: 117).

Tillich does not interpret the picture of Jesus provided in Christian Scriptures in an historically literal way. He regards the stories of Jesus' life, such as those dealing with his death and resurrection, as symbols of his New Being.[29] In other words, he accepted that modern historical-critical criticism of the Bible can legitimately distinguish between biblical stories that are mythical, symbolic, legendary or historically probable to a greater or lesser degree. In any case, Tillich's Christology avers that human estrangement from God is overcome in the New Being actualized in Jesus Christ. As the New Being, Jesus saves people from their anxious alienated predicament. The words, actions and final suffering of Jesus all express his New Being (*ST*, 2: 121–3).

theology as symbolic language

The classical Christian paradigm for explaining the identity of Jesus Christ is that of an incarnation: in Jesus, the Son of the Father-Creator of the world assumed human flesh. Tillich interprets this metaphorically. 'Flesh' refers to historical existence, while 'God becoming' flesh signifies that God participates in a reality that is estranged from God.[30]

The recognition that Christological and theological terms are symbolic is a lynchpin of Tillich's thought. Some would say it is an unacceptably controversial pivot, because Christians of the past have normally regarded the Bible and its manifold stories about God and Jesus as literally descriptive.

To assert that all theological language is metaphorical or symbolic easily gives rise to the protest among traditionally minded Christians, that theology is being vitiated because symbols are unreal. Such a protest labours under the misapprehension that symbols are secondary to empirically demonstrable facts. Symbols are real, not fictive.

Late in the twentieth century, the British theologian Maurice Wiles advanced the view that the primary themes of Christian faith and theology are best understood as symbols: 'Stressing the symbolic nature of the language of faith saves us from treating it as if it were on a par with ordinary, everyday, factual language and the misunderstandings of it to which that can give rise.'[31] For liberal theologians of the nineteenth and twentieth centuries, it becomes difficult if not impossible for people to regard Christian teachings as true and credible if they are regarded as facts on a par with empirically demonstrable evidences.

signs and symbols Signs are things that refer to other things. As such, they are arbitrary. For example, the red road sign, 'Stop', refers to the command for motorists and cyclists not to proceed. It is not necessary for road signs to command 'Stop', or be painted red. They could easily be green images saying 'Halt'. Symbols, by contrast, are not arbitrary. A symbol is a thing or sign that, while referring to another thing, also mediates within it the reality of that thing. To illustrate, a woman away from home on an international business trip might carry with her a photo of her beloved husband, partner or friend. The photo is a symbol. It refers to her beloved, who is not bodily present with her, but whose reality is mediated to her by the image of the photo, and thus becomes present to her. The photo is not arbitrary because it is necessarily the case that its image must really be that of the beloved, and not of someone else.

Symbols can be of two kinds – conceptual or concrete. Any word, phrase or sentence is a conceptual symbol. Statues, flags, paintings and photos are all concrete symbols.

Religious symbols are like all others, either conceptual or concrete. The expression, 'Jesus is the Incarnation of God', is an instance of the former. Velázquez's oil paintings of Jesus crucified, housed in Madrid's Prado Museum, are all concrete religious symbols. Religious symbols are unique in that they are not focused on trivialities.

The final volume of Tillich's trilogy on systematic theology (1963) continues the analysis of the ambiguities inherent in humans that he broaches in the previous volumes, and discusses such topics as the Trinity, the Kingdom of God, human history and its end.

As philosophically refined as Tillich's theology and Christology are, a residual difficulty with his interpretation of Jesus is that few people would want to give their lives, devote their energies, use their resources or sacrifice themselves for a figure as abstractly conceived, and eviscerated of human warmth, as a New Being!

the protestant principle

Suffusing Tillich's theology is the recognition that God is an impenetrable mystery because God is not a being, but Being-Itself. He frequently refers to 'the Protestant Principle' in counterpoise to a 'Catholic substance'. The latter signifies the tendency of the Catholic Church to maintain itself throughout history with a hierarchical government and a reliance on sacraments, which are concrete religious symbols in the form of rituals. The Protestant Principle is the recognition that all forms of religion are finite and transitory.[32]

At Union Theological Seminary, Tillich delivered lectures on the history of Christian thought that were eventually published. They reveal his undisguised enthusiasm for Protestantism and the Reformation. As a Lutheran, it is no surprise to discover him teaching his students:

> The turning point of the Reformation and of church history in general is the experience of an Augustinian monk in his monastic cell – Martin Luther. Martin Luther did not merely teach different doctrines; others had done that also, such as Wycliff. But none of the others who protested against the Roman system were able to break through it. The only man who really made a breakthrough, and whose breakthrough has transformed the surface of the earth, was Martin Luther. This is his greatness.[33]

conclusion

The significance of Paul Tillich in the course of twentieth-century theology was that he began to relate biblical and Christian traditions with the previously unseen human cultures that emerged in the wake of two world wars. He achieved this by stressing the indispensability for theology of attending to its addressees. All theologies are addressed to particular audiences. Some theologians write to refute their colleagues. Others publish to help students. There are theologians who devote their energies to promoting the papacy or the World Council of Churches. Quite a few engage in discussion with philosophers and sociologists. Many argue with atheists. Some wish to police the sexual activities of others and produce vast tomes on moral theology, often assuming to know precisely what God likes or hates.

Barth and his followers have been largely disdainful of attempts to relate the language of the Bible with modern cultures and their scientific and philosophical discourses. Barth's world was biblical; his addressees were mostly devotees of the Church. Tillich yokes two worlds together – past and present – and speaks to the Church and the cultures in which it is found.

Tillich's legacy of correlating the Church's theological legacy with modern politics, philosophy, sociology and science was continued later in the twentieth century by a host of theologians working in exceptionally diverse settings.[34] Such theologians might not call themselves Tillichians, but their bifocal interest in culture and the Church finds clear expression as it does in the works of Tillich. They include David Tracy, Sallie McFague, Langdon Gilkey, John B. Cobb, Gregory Baum and Gordon Kaufman.[35]

When Tillich died in 1965, new worlds and cultures, characterized as globalized, digitized, postmodern, feminist, pluricentric, terrorized and religiously pluralistic, had only begun to hatch. Much more of the story of twentieth-century theology remained to be told.

9

Dorothy Day: 1897–1980

The greatest of evils and the worst of crimes is poverty.

George Bernard Shaw

It is always a sad situation when fathers denigrate their daughters. Here is a case in point: 'Dorothy, the oldest girl, is the nut of the family. When she came out of the university she was a communist. Now she's a Catholic crusader. She owns and runs a Catholic paper and is separated from her husband. ... I wouldn't have her around me.' Thus, Dorothy Day's father, John, describing her unkindly in a letter to one of his friends.[1]

Despite John Day's dismissive characterization of his daughter, she was one of the most radically consistent Christian thinkers and political activists of the twentieth century. She was radical in the etymological sense of the term (Latin: *radix, radicis*, 'root'): keen to anchor her life on a life-giving root of Christianity, instead of becoming superficially preoccupied – as multitudes do – with ephemeral matters such as ecclesiastical political intrigues and sexual mores. She was consistent, in that her Christian radicalness, or integrity, was not whimsical. She sustained it from her initiation into the Catholic Church in 1927 until her death in 1980. Like Feuerbach and Harnack before her, she mused at length about the essence of the Christian religion – the *essentia Christianae religionis*. Unlike the former, she decided that the point of Christianity was to love in such a way as daily to feed, house, wash and serve the putridly poor and smelly destitute people she encountered throughout her adult life. Upon her death, she was lauded as 'the most significant, interesting, influential person in the history of American Catholicism'.[2]

Dorothy Day lances the boil of the centuries-long conceit that theology is the preserve of monastic, priestly or professorial men. She was a woman who divorced her husband after a year of marriage, who gave birth to a child after living with another man to whom she was never married, and who felt compelled to have a six-month-old foetus aborted that she had conceived with a third man. She was well acquainted with the travails of trying to establish and maintain sexually expressive intimacy with other human beings.

She also stands as a profound, challenging and unceasingly unsettling theologian of the twentieth century. Risible for some, unthinkable for others, it is still the case that women produced penetrating theological discourses from the beginning of the twentieth century, and long before that. That they have been ignored for so long is not a just commentary on their abilities, but an exposure of a male pretence – often with female acquiescence – that generally debarred them until the twentieth century from advanced levels of theological education. All of which suggests forcefully that academic education is not inevitably the exclusive or most ideal formation for a theologian. Indeed not. Dorothy Day's school of theology was the poor house, not the lecture theatre. That is why she was an accomplished theologian.

There are three primary records of Dorothy Day's theology: articles she wrote as a journalist over five decades; her autobiography; and her diaries, which were published for the first time in 2008.[3] She ordered that they were not to be released until 25 years after her death. Her wishes were respected. The diaries now constitute a new and enticing entry into her theological world-view. They run into nearly 700 pages, and have not as yet been closely studied by university students of theology and their teachers. Would that they were! Another revealing repository of her theological thinking is unveiled in her autobiography, *The Long Loneliness* (1952). Still more of her godly reflections are voiced in articles she wrote over more than four decades for the magazine, *The Catholic Worker*, which she helped to establish in New York in 1933. By the end of her life she had published seven books and about 1,500 articles, reviews and essays.[4] Exceptionally scant are the pages of her printed thoughts that do not discuss God, Jesus Christ or the Church in relation to bodies and bed lice, homelessness, death, disease, war and unrelenting poverty.

None of the theologians broached thus far in this book daily lived over several decades with grit and grime while fending off pestilential insects. Not one of them tried to feed soup and bread to homeless street people on a regular basis. Dorothy Day did just that for most of her life. Fighting vermin is a common and regular task for the dirtiest and poorest of the world. Dishing out soup can be done by anyone who has the will, strength and means to do so. Such activities in themselves do not produce a worthy theologian. Dorothy Day's strength as a theologian was twofold. First, she strove to speak about God in relation to human misery. Her theology was not theoretical speculation, but directed to specific paupers in concrete circumstances. The second facet of her integrity as a theologian concerns consistency. A harmony between belief and behaviour obtained in her daily dealings with others. Few people repel more quickly than double-dealers who verbally profess beliefs, and in mundane activities contradict them. Conversely, people who doubt or deny Christian beliefs also invite disdain if their demeanour tries to convince others that they are sincere believers. Generations of Christians in the modern era have known full well that Jesus is remembered in the Bible as someone who had no time for the acquisition of money or property. That did not stop them projecting themselves as faithful disciples of Jesus, while they simultaneously craved capital for comfort.

Dorothy Day's greatest ability was this – in her life and arduous work there was no ugly divorce between her religious passions, and the way she lived in conformity with those convictions. As a young woman she read the life of Jesus as it is painted in the Bible. She believed what she read. From that springboard she practised what she professed until the day she died.

the beginnings

Dorothy Day was born in Brooklyn, New York, on 8 November 1897. Her parents were John Day (mentioned above) and Grace Satterlee. John's family came from

Tennessee. He was a journalist by profession and wrote mostly about horse racing. Grace was born in Marlboro, New York. Dorothy was one of five children. She had two older brothers, Donald and Sam, a younger sister called Della, and a younger brother called John, of whom she became extremely fond. She often had to help her mother care for him when he was an infant. In her autobiography, *The Long Loneliness*, she says of him: 'I had never loved anyone or anything as I loved him, with a love that was open and unreserved, entailing hardship but also bringing peace and joy.'[5]

Dorothy's father was not demonstrably affectionate with his children. With regard to religion he was sceptical, although he liked to quote from the Bible.[6] He met Grace Satterlee while they were studying at a business school in New York. Grace had been brought up as an Episcopalian. She and John married in an Episcopal church in New York's Greenwich Village.[7] All of their children became journalists, with the exception of Della. Later in her life, Dorothy was the only one of the family regularly to be arrested for social activism that involved fighting poverty, unjust working conditions, warfare and military conscription.

The Day family moved to San Francisco in 1904 so that John Day, the father, could work there as a sports writer for a newspaper. Dorothy was seven at the time. In 1907, the building housing the paper's production was destroyed in a massive earthquake, which killed 700 people in San Francisco and left 250,000 of the city's inhabitants homeless.[8]

> **episcopal church**   The word 'episcopal' designates that which relates to bishops. The Episcopal Church is a North American denomination of Christians that accepts government by bishops. It is an analogue of the Church of England – the Anglican Church. The historical origins of the Church date from the sixteenth century with the arrival of Anglicans in North America. The first Episcopal congregations were established in the North and South Carolinas, Maryland and Virginia. They submitted to the jurisdiction of the Church of England. In 2005, Katherine Jefferts Schori was elected the Presiding Bishop of the Protestant Episcopal Church in the USA. She is the first woman to act as the Presiding Bishop.

Now lacking a job, John Day moved his family to Chicago. They lived in dingy accommodation until he found a new position as a sports editor for the paper, *The Inter Ocean*. Thereafter they were able to live in a more comfortable house.

As an adolescent in Chicago, Dorothy read Upton Sinclair's novel, *The Jungle*, which is set amid the appalling squalor of Chicago's stockyards and slaughterhouses. She began to take her baby brother, John, for long walks in his carriage so that she could see for herself the depredations endured by impoverished workers. She was greatly distressed by the sight of people struggling to fend for themselves:

Disabled men, without arms and legs, blind men, consumptive men, exhausted men with all the manhood drained from them by industrialism; farmers gaunt and harried with debt; mothers weighed down with children at their skirts, in their arms, in their wombs, children ailing and rickety – all this long procession of desperate people called to me. Where were the saints to try to change the social order, not just to minister to slaves but to do away with slavery?[9]

The question that vexed her for the rest of her life was germinating within her: what must be done to eradicate the causes of injustice and poverty? She noticed even as an adolescent that the Church's way of responding to poverty and injustice 'was to be kind to the poor but not to open its doors to them. If it shed occasional tears for their tragedies, it did not raise a cry against those who piled up fortunes at their expense.'[10]

Dorothy attended the Waller High School and demonstrated an aptitude for studying languages. She studied Greek and Latin in optional classes held after school. She was so successful at school that she was awarded a scholarship of $300 when she completed her studies. This sum enabled her to attend university. At the age of 16 she left home and enrolled in the University of Illinois in Urbana. There she studied English literature, biology, European history and Latin. She also joined the Socialist Party, which helped her to find expression for her interest in redressing social injustices. She discontinued her studies after two years and never completed a degree. In 1916 her father accepted a position with the *Morning Telegraph* in New York. Dorothy decided to move there as well so that she could be closer to her family.[11]

life in new york

Dorothy was 18 when she moved to New York. Initially, she lived with her parents and Della, as well as the four-year-old John. The poverty she saw in New York was worse than Chicago's.[12] Jobless men wandered the streets throughout New York.

The socialist daily paper, *The Call*, employed Dorothy as a reporter. Thus began her life-long career as a journalist. Her brief with *The Call* was to report on strikes, union meetings, police violence against picketers, demonstrations against the First World War, and social tragedies such as children being burnt to death in tenement fires.[13] With independent means of support, she moved into her own lodgings. She spent her early 20s living in Greenwich Village and mixing with its radical socialist set. She became a very close friend of the playwright Eugene O'Neill.

There was much for her to report in 1917. The First World War had been flaring for three years. The USA finally entered the fray, declaring war on Germany on 6 April. Dorothy and her friends in Greenwich Village were adamantly opposed to

the conscription of soldiers. 1917 was also a year in which women actively sought equal status with men in political affairs. On 10 November, Dorothy travelled to Washington, DC, to join a suffragette demonstration. She was promptly arrested and held in gaol until 28 November.[14] This was her first experience of being locked up in a police cell. It was repeated often for the rest of her life.

Dorothy was 20 at this stage of her life and attracted to people who wanted to change her country.[15] On her return to New York she became curious about Christianity. She regularly visited a local Catholic church and occasionally attended Mass. All this she kept a secret from her socialist friends.[16] Catholicism began to intrigue her. She frequently visited immigrant churches in lower Manhattan.[17] She had not been taken to

Dorothy Day in a police cell

church as a child, even though she had been baptized in the Episcopalian Church and taught to pray. Of her childhood, Dorothy commented in later life: 'We did not search for God when we were children. We took Him for granted.'[18]

Dorothy Day was not a perfect person. She struggled to establish and maintain intimate relations with men and, with three of them, met with a mixture of happiness, frustration and failure. The next phase of her life was difficult in terms of her experiences with men. She began to tire of late-night carousing with her friends in Greenwich Village, and decided to train as a nurse. She enrolled in a nursing course with her sister Della at Kings County Hospital in Brooklyn. Instruction began in January 1918. At the hospital she met an orderly called Lionel Moise. She was attracted to him and began to live with him in a rented apartment on 35th Street. She became pregnant, but Lionel declared he would not marry her. She agreed to have an abortion, which was illegal at the time. The operation took place on the Upper East Side of New York. She had been pregnant for six months. Lionel promised he would meet her after the procedure, but he abandoned her while it was taking place. When she returned home she found money he had left her as well as a letter. His text reminded her that the experience she had just endured was shared by millions of women. He also expressed his hope that she would marry a rich man.[19] Dorothy never mentions either Lionel Moise or the abortion in her autobiography.

Nor does she mention the next man who became important to her. She trained as a nurse for a year and then did precisely what Lionel Moise had hoped for her. She married a rich man – Barkeley Tobey. In total, Barkeley married eight women on separate occasions.[20] He was 20 years older than Dorothy.[21] She explains why she did not want to talk about either Lionel or Barkeley in her autobiography. Commenting on the time when she finished as a nurse, she noted: 'I cannot write too intimately of the next few years, because I do not want to write about other people with whom I was intimately associated.'[22]

In 1920, Dorothy and Barkeley went to Europe, where they travelled for a year. Dorothy was drinking heavily at this stage of her life. Their marriage ended when they returned.[23] Dorothy moved back to Chicago. She worked as a reporter for the City News Bureau and rented a room in a house which was home to three Catholic women of her own age. She noticed how attending Mass was an important part of their lives. She felt attracted to the Catholic Church. Lionel Moise was still living and working in Chicago. She had remained in love with him even while she was married to Barkeley. By 1923 she had moved to New Orleans to work as a reporter for *The New Orleans Item*. The following year her first book was published. It was an autobiographical novel called *The Eleventh Virgin*. Later in life she reviled it.[24] Happily for her, she was paid $5,000 dollars for its Hollywood film rights. She moved back to New York and bought a small beach-front cottage on Staten Island, across the river from Manhattan.

staten island and manhattan

During 1925 in New York, Dorothy met and fell in love with Forster Batterham. They began to live together. She regarded him as her common-law husband.[25] Forster was born in North Carolina. As an adult he was an atheist anarchist, with no time for religious observances. He became the father of Dorothy's only child. She was born on 4 March 1927 and given the name Tamar Teresa. Dorothy Day was 29 at the time.

She and Tamar lived on Staten Island and Forster joined them from New York at weekends. On Staten Island, Dorothy met a nun called Sister Aloysia. The latter helped to run a soup kitchen for poor and homeless people. The two struck up a friendship and Dorothy began to peel vegetables and cook for the needy with Sister Aloysia, while Forster was in New York. The nun began to explain Catholic beliefs to Dorothy.

In July 1927, Tamar was baptized according to the rites of the Catholic Church, much to the irritation of Forster. Dorothy was now torn between the man she loved and the Church to which she was increasingly drawn. As she noted after giving birth:

> A woman does not want to be alone at such a time. Even the most hardened, the
> most irreverent, is awed by the stupendous fact of creation. Becoming a Catholic
> would mean facing life alone and I clung to family. It was hard to contemplate giving
> up a mate in order that my child and I could become members of the Church.
> Forster would have nothing to do with religion or with me if I embraced it. So I
> waited.[26]

However, after much argument with Forster, Dorothy decided to join the Catholic Church. She was baptized into the Church on 28 December 1927, even though she had already been baptized as an Episcopalian when she was a child. There were no friends at her baptism in 1927, except her godparent Sister Aloysia. Forster left her. She could not face the thought of living as a single mother on Staten Island, so she moved back to New York.[27]

She lived in Manhattan during winter months, but returned to her cottage on Staten Island for summers. It was at this time that the Great Depression took hold of the USA, massively increasing the plight and numbers of hungry, unemployed, and homeless people.[28] The Depression threw into sharp relief the social disparities between wealthy and poor people in the US.

In November of 1932, Dorothy heard of a march on Washington by unemployed citizens. About 600 jobless marchers assembled at a departure point in New York's Union Square. Dorothy went to Washington to report on the event for the magazines *Commonweal* and *America*. She was appalled by the sight of a phalanx of hungry people pleading for food on Union Square. The sight of the marchers changed Dorothy Day's life.[29] On 8 December 1932, she visited the Catholic University of America to pray in its National Shrine of the Immaculate Conception. There she 'offered up a special prayer', she later recalled, 'a prayer which came with tears and with anguish, that some way would open up for me to use what talents I possessed for my fellow workers, for the poor.'[30]

great depression   The Great Depression was the worst and most debilitating international economic turmoil of the twentieth century. Its beginning is normally associated with the collapse of the American Stock Market, localized at the New York Stock Exchange, on 24 October 1929 – a day remembered with dread as Black Tuesday. The Depression rapidly spread to other countries of the world, many of which had borrowed extensively from American banks to eradicate massive debts they had accumulated during and after the First World War. On the eve of the Great Depression, the USA was the world's most significant lender of financial capital to other nations. When unstable governments and investors failed to repay large loans, the Federal Reserve in the USA augmented lending interest rates. Thereafter, banks began to collapse, first in Europe, and later around the world. Manufacturing companies, governments and individual workers soon found themselves shackled by ineradicable debts. International trade began to diminish, as did the value of foodstuffs produced by primary production. Manufacturers reduced their scale of building goods and sacked large numbers of their workers. Unemployment increased drastically in the industrialized nations as the Great Depression took hold.[31] The USA began to recover from the Great Depression at the end of the 1930s as international manufacturing increased on the eve of the Second World War.

peter maurin

The next day, Dorothy returned to her home in New York and met the solution to her anguished quest to find a way to help poor people. His name was Peter Maurin. In New York, Dorothy lived in rented accommodation on East 15th Street with Tamar, her brother John, his wife, Tessa, and their baby. When she returned from her trip to Washington she found Peter Maurin waiting for her in her apartment. Tamar had welcomed him in. Peter had come to the attention of George Schuster, the editor of the magazine, *Commonweal*. Schuster had previously pub- lished Dorothy's articles, and he recognized that she shared with Maurin a desire to work as a social activist by combining religion and politics. Schuster suggested to Maurin that he might like to meet Day, hence the purpose of his unannounced visit to her apartment. She recorded her first impressions of him: 'When I walked into my apartment, I found waiting for me a short, stocky man in his mid-fifties, as ragged and rugged as any of the marchers I had left.'[32]

Peter Maurin

Peter Maurin was French and spoke English with a thick accent. He had been born in the southern Languedoc region of France into a family of peasant workers. He was the eldest of 23 children. When he was 16 he joined the Saint Jean-Baptiste de La Salle brotherhood of Catholic teachers, but parted company with them nine years later. He admired Pope Leo XIII's encyclical, *Rerum Novarum* ('Of New Things'), which was proclaimed on 15 May 1891. Leo's text focused on the social conditions of workers. He wanted to promote social justice for them, and he called powerful and wealthy people to share more of their assets with the needy.[33] Leo was particularly concerned to challenge mistreatment of workers. As he says: 'If we turn now to things exterior and corporal, the first concern of all is to save workers from the cruelty of grasping speculators, who use human beings as mere instruments for making money. It is neither justice nor humanity so to grind men down with excessive labor as to stupefy their minds and wear out their bodies.'[34]

Peter Maurin was a pacifist to such an extent that he left France rather than undertake military service. He moved to Canada in 1909 and lived a simple, unencumbered life as a wanderer and manual worker.[35] His meandering led him to New York. The reason he had sought out Dorothy Day was to explain his vision for a better society. He was confident she could help him. He was not interested in possessions, property or acquiring money, but in encouraging people to live in communities whose members would care for one another materially and spiritually.

When Peter and Dorothy met, he explained his vision for improving society in terms of a three-point strategy. First, he wanted to conduct round-table discussions with people who were prepared to help him. The point of these would be to clarify a Catholic social philosophy dedicated to the pursuit of justice. Second, he yearned for houses of hospitality to be established in every parish in which the poor, homeless and unemployed could be fed and even housed. Finally, he hoped to build what he called 'agronomic universities' – farms on which people could support themselves by working and producing food:

> In a world offering the promise of wars, revolution, and the empty struggle for economic security, Peter held that what people really desired was community, meaningful work, some sense of purpose, something to reverence and honour, some measure of control over the fundamental issues affecting their lives. The present system could not provide such things.[36]

the catholic worker

Peter and Dorothy began to collaborate. To disseminate their ideas they decided to publish a radical Catholic newspaper, *The Catholic Worker*. Dorothy was ever keen to identify with workers. The Paulist Press agreed to set in type and print 2,500 copies of an eight-page tabloid newspaper for $57. The first issue was distributed in Union Square on 1 May 1933.

By then the Great Depression was well under way and there were hordes of homeless hungry people needing help on New York's streets. When reading about houses of hospitality in *The Catholic Worker*, some naturally sought to find them. Dorothy's response was to start renting properties that could house communities dedicated to feeding and caring for the homeless. She opened her own apartment on 15th Street to anyone who wanted to come. 436 East 15th Street became the Catholic Worker office. 'Catholic Worker' served as a title for both the newspaper as well as the hospitality houses. Dorothy rented another property on 7th Street. A priest told her about an old house on Charles Street in Greenwich Village that was available for rent with enough space for staff and their guests to live, as well as for an office.[37] This became a primary base for Dorothy's work. *The Catholic Worker* paper moved to 144 Charles Street in March 1935. By the following May, 100,000 copies of the paper were being printed each month. The headquarters of the Catholic Worker Movement moved in April 1936 and was established on 115 Mott Street. It remained there for the following 14 years.

The start of the third part of Peter Maurin's strategy for improving an unjust society was realized in 1936 when the movement bought a farm outside Euston in Pennsylvania. Editions of *The Catholic Worker* frequently published appeals for money to fund works for the poor. Generous donations arrived from around the country. By 1943 there were 15 houses of hospitality and six farms operating for the Catholic Worker.[38] From Dorothy Day's apartment on 15th Street, houses and hospices sprang up

Serving soup to friars

Dorothy Day reading on the farm in Pennsylvania around 1937

in slums and tenements in Washington, Baltimore, Philadelphia, Harrisburg, Pittsburgh, New York, Rochester, Boston, Worcester, Buffalo, Troy, Detroit, Cleveland, Toledo, Akron, St Louis, Chicago, Milwaukee, Minneapolis, Seattle, San Francisco, Los Angeles, Oakland and Houma in Louisiana.[39] All of these houses were open to any person in need, regardless of ethnicity, gender, political commitment, religion or hue of skin. The houses operated according to a recognition of a common good for a common humanity, and not along lines of racial or religious demarcations.

For the rest of her life Dorothy lived among and with poor homeless people. She kept her daughter Tamar close to her and raised her in hospitality houses. Tamar married David Henessey in 1944 when she turned 18. They moved into a house on the Pennsylvania farm and raised a family of eight children. David became overwhelmed by the problems of caring for his family and abandoned them.

While living in hospitality houses, Dorothy wrote regularly for *The Catholic Worker*. The movement's houses used to collect second-hand clothing for poor street inhabitants. Dorothy always wore these clothes. For a decade she wore used stockings she obtained from a hospital. An elderly friend darned and patched them for her.[40] This was one of her ways of avoiding spending money on herself so that she could provide for the poor. Another was that she usually travelled on buses because this was the way impecunious people had to travel long distances, if they could afford to undertake journeys at all.

dorothy day's theology

The theology of Dorothy Day is not confined to print. It was displayed in the way she lived from 1933 to 1980. Theological themes that were printed are contained mostly in her articles for *The Catholic Worker* and in her diaries, which date from 1934. Previous entries have never been found.

Dorothy Day's theology was based on a daily imitation of the life of Jesus Christ as it is depicted in the Bible. She read Thomas à Kempis' book, *The*

Imitation of Christ, and kept its theme – following Jesus Christ – at the centre of her life. Her thought was untroubled by doubts as to whether Jesus was God incarnate. In her diaries she records a sadness occasioned by meeting a nun in July 1969. The nun told Dorothy that she had been attending daily Mass for 14 years, but now regarded it as an unnecessary routine. Dorothy's theological outlook is expressed in her reaction. It is a conservative, straightforward and literal acceptance of traditional Christian doctrine, according to which Jesus Christ is human and divine, and who sacrificed his life for sinful people. Reacting to the nun, Day records:

> One could only point out that breathing was routine, and eating was routine, and many a time we had no appetite, food even seemed disgusting to us. We go to eat of this fruit of the tree of life because Jesus told us to. 'Do this in remembrance of me.' When we take to heart literally the humanity of Jesus as well as his divinity, and remember how he died for us, laid down his life for us, took upon himself our sins, then we should simply obey his commands. He took upon himself our humanity that we might share in his divinity. We are nourished by his flesh that we may grow to be other Christs. I believe this literally, just as I believe the child is nourished by the milk from his mother's breast.[41]

The primary source of Dorothy's Day's theology was the Bible and, in particular, the Gospels. For her, their fundamental and unifying theme is love. She interpreted human love expressed in giving to others as like the love of God and Jesus. Thus in her eyes, the most important, theologically motivated task of the Catholic Worker houses is love. As she declared, '"Love" is the reason for it all.' In her diaries she observes:

> It seems to me that one of the happiest lessons in the gospel is that of love. That we are told to love one another and to show that love by giving. And that love becomes more like that of God when we see Jesus Himself in those around us, as the apostles did on Mt. Tabor, when the celestial light faded, and 'they saw only Jesus', most loveable. ...
>
> He taught them about love, about loving. The prodigal son, the sick, the leprous, the privileged, the tax-gatherers, the sinners, those in prison – in other words, loving the unloveable, naturally speaking.[42]

Dorothy's understanding of love was not a sentimental romanticism, but fully realistic about the frequently unlovely task of loving. As she notes in her diaries: 'Love in practice is a harsh and dreadful thing compared to love in dreams.'[43]

This is actually a reference to the character Father Zossima, in Dostoevsky's novel, *The Brothers Karamazov*. Dorothy was often oppressed by the harsh conditions in which she forced herself to live amid the poor. She refers to and comments on some of her hardships: 'Going to bed at night with the foul smell of unwashed bodies in my nostrils. Lack of privacy. But Christ was born in a stable and a stable is apt to be unclean and odorous.'[44] Elsewhere she notes: 'The dirt, the garbage heaped in the gutters, the flies, the hopelessness of the human beings around me, all oppress me.'[45]

She referred to God as the 'Living God' and was clear that 'The thing to remember is not to read so much or talk so much about God, but to talk to God.'[46]

One of her favourite observations about God was 'There is no time with God.' This related to her thoughts about the efficacy of praying, of addressing God and asking God for help. What is the point of praying for a child who has committed suicide? Very little from a human perspective. 'There is no time in God' was Dorothy's way of saying that God is not constrained in a space-time continuum as humans are, and could well respond to prayers in ways humans could only hope for and imagine.[47] She did not write details or accounts of why anyone should believe and hope in God. She regarded God's presence to humanity as straightforwardly evident: 'God wishes us to feel His Immanence. He is near as the breath we draw. We have Him present in the Blessed Sacrament of the altar, and if our faith were as a grain of mustard seed, we would be prostrate as we entered His presence. We take His presence so much for granted!'[48]

In the Catholic Worker houses in which she lived she followed, almost invariably, a daily routine of attending Mass early in the morning, followed by reading and writing letters, all preceding work in the kitchen, preparing food to be distributed to queues of hungry people in the street waiting to be fed and clothed.

Reading was important for her throughout her life. She read novels, philosophers, the lives of saints and the works of theological masters like Augustine and Aquinas. One of the works which had a direct bearing on her life was Thérèse of Lisieux's journal, in which the latter describes her efforts to cope with the trials of living in a community.

Dorothy Day's understanding of the demands and the commands incumbent on a Christian, after reading of Jesus' life and love of the poor, was such that she struggled to comprehend why so many of the priests and bishops she regularly encountered lived lives of untroubled privilege. *The Catholic Worker* drew national and international attention to her, and she was frequently asked to meet archbishops and to travel around the USA giving talks in universities and churches. Once, while eating in a Catholic Worker home, she recalled a previous meal with an archbishop: '… while I ate this noon I remembered the set up at the Archbishop's palace, the delicate wines, the delicious food, the abundance of delicacies and exquisite service. And I wished the princes of the church were living voluntarily down in a place like this where the food is scarce and often bad.'[49] She could be even more biting. Writing on 10 September 1938, she spoke of walking down the street after attending Mass:

> As I came down the street afterward a well dressed priest drove by in a big car. Then I passed another – also well dressed, comfortable. Then still another out in front of a most luxurious mansion, the parish house, playing with a dog on a leash. All of them well fed, well housed, comfortable, caring for the safe people like themselves. And where are the priests for the poor, the down and out, the sick in city hospitals, in jails. It is the little of God's children who do not get cared for. God help them and God help the priest who is caught in the bourgeois system and cannot get out.[50]

political pacifism and activism

Dorothy Day's understanding of God, Jesus, Christianity and Catholicism addressed public political issues as well as individuals' suffering. Her writings for *The Catholic Worker* tried to marry conservative, traditional theology and radical political involvement. The latter alarmed many of her Christian contemporaries.[51] *The Catholic Worker* was consistently opposed to war, and Dorothy Day frequently took to the streets to protest against war and military conscription and was regularly arrested.

A Japanese fleet attacked Pearl Harbor on 7 December 1941, and as a result the USA declared war with Japan. The first issue of *The Catholic Worker* after the declaration was published in January 1942. It bore the headline, 'Our Country Passes from Undeclared War to Declared War. We Continue Our Christian Pacifist Stand.' The following

Demonstrating against war

January, Dorothy wrote an editorial for the paper and declared with reference to the possibility of conscription for women: 'I shall not register because I believe modern war to be murder, incompatible with a religion of love.'[52]

In September 1945, she responded in the pages of *The Catholic Worker* to the dropping of an atomic bomb on Hiroshima:

> Mr Truman was jubilant. President Truman. True man; what a strange name, come to think of it. We refer to Jesus Christ as true God and true Man. Truman is a true man of his time in that he was jubilant. He was not a son of God, brother of Christ, brother of the Japanese, jubilating as he did. He went from table to table on the cruiser which was bringing him home from the Big Three conference, telling the great news; 'jubilant' the newspapers said. Jubilate Deo. We have killed 318,000.[53]

The remainder of Dorothy Day's life was dedicated to a daily round of reading, praying, writing, seeking money, food, clothing and housing for the poor, marching against war, and confronting politicians and Church leaders with the urgent tasks involved in building a more just society. She travelled to Rome during the final session of the Second Vatican Council, hoping that her pacifism would be noticed. It was. The Council's *Constitution on the Church in the Modern World*, as noted previously in this book, unequivocally condemned as crimes against God and humanity acts of war that indiscriminately destroy entire cities or large areas together with their inhabitants.

Dorothy Day died on 29 November 1980, and is buried on Staten Island. She was acknowledged by the Vatican in 2000 as a 'Servant of God', the first title accorded by the Vatican to anyone it is considering canonizing as a saint. Day reacted sharply while she was alive to the suggestion that she was a saint. Her motive was not false modesty. It was a direct challenge to those who wish to absolve themselves from a love that is a 'harsh and dreadful thing'. Saying, 'You are a saint who can cope with the putrid poor', is also a statement to the effect: 'I could not possibly do that because I am not a saint. I am just a normal person.' It is a self-absolution from trying to redress debilitating poverty and injustice.[54]

In not wishing to be called a saint, Dorothy Day is a constant irritant to those who still wish publicly to be regarded as godly, while comfortably living sequestered from any sight or smell of the poor.

IO

Karl Rahner: 1904–84

> … Real speculative knowledge can encounter no object anywhere
> except that of experience … .
>
> *Immanuel Kant*

Studying theologians of the twentieth century is an exercise in linguistic comparison. This is so because they work with starkly disparate and occasionally odd
verbal styles. Those writing mainly in the earlier part of the century by no means
used the same terminology as those who were active at the century's end. There
is no assurance that words and phrases favoured by theologians during the Middle
Ages and the Renaissance were still in vogue during the last century. Who nowadays loves to talk at length about hell, angels and demons, as was much more the
custom in Europe during the Reformation? There are theologians currently who
describe Jesus' mother, Mary (or Miriam), as the Co-Redemptrix and Mediatrix
of all graces. What might that mean? Others say she was an impoverished peasant

struggling to survive in Lower Galilee. The prose of some theologians is liberally peppered with philosophical terminology like praxis, phenomenology, epistemology, and modal logic. Others prefer the earthy language of Jesus' parables – foxes, birds in the air, mustard seeds, loaves, wine and fig trees. Karl Rahner was a major theologian of the twentieth century who developed a way of speaking about God that is peculiar to him. He frequently speaks of grace – a word with an ancient provenance and a long theological history, but not always prominent in the language of contemporary theologians and their audiences. Scantily clad kids gyrating and flirting in night clubs to the pulsating sound of overly loud hi-fi generated beats, while illuminated kaleidoscopically with the beams of flashing strobe lights, do not normally discuss divine grace!

In the course of Rahner's longish life, he produced about 4,000 written works, mostly in the form of essays and articles, but also including lengthy and highly erudite monographs.[1] Throughout all of these texts is operative a single concept, whether expressed overtly or not, which is unique to Rahner. It encapsulates the core of his theology and is called the supernatural existential. This term is laden with meaning, and will need to be explored below. For the moment, suffice it to register that in Rahnerian terms the supernatural existential is a God-implanted constitutive dimension of human beings that impels them to make contact with God. The supernatural existential is the motor that drove Rahner's life and work. The language of a supernatural existential is ultimately a theory of grace. The theology of Karl Rahner, from his first work to the last, is a theory grace. The purpose of this chapter is to discuss his theology by looking at his life, considered in its historical setting.

Rahner was a theologian who always remained convinced that human beings and God are able to encounter each other. That explains why the activity of prayer was indispensable for him. Prayer is an odd activity for a religious sceptic. What is the point of it? Does it actually address anyone? Can it produce any effective results? Prayer can assume many forms, including individuals praising God, thanking God, asking God for favours, or even cursing God in believing, yet anguished and distressed frustration. Whatever its form, prayer could generally be described as the attempt of persons to become more aware of God's presence in their lives.

A vignette from Karl Rahner's life clearly illustrates the ineluctability of prayer for him. In February 1984, only six weeks before his death, he attended an academic celebration of his 80th birthday at London's Heythrop College. The Anglican theologian, John Macquarrie, was the principal guest lecturer at the celebration, and sat with Rahner and other theological luminaries on a podium.[2] Rahner spent nearly all his life in a German-speaking world, and was never entirely at ease speaking or listening to English. Understandably fatigued after travelling, he became listless during Professor Macquarrie's lecture. At which point he stopped listening with his full attention, and began to handle a string of rosary beads. For everyone to see, he was obviously praying.[3]

rahner's early life

Why Germany produced so many outstanding theologians in the twentieth century is a topic worthy of detailed study, but beyond the scope of this book. Rahner is the fifth German, and the sixth German-speaker, to be considered in these pages – after Harnack, Schweitzer, Barth (a Swiss), Bonhoeffer and Tillich.

He was born on 5 March 1904, in the southern regions of Germany in the city of Freiburg-im-Breisgau. The place of his birth is occasionally confused with the Swiss city of Freiburg in der Schweitz. The latter is a bilingual town, also known in French as Fribourg. Rahner grew up in Freiburg-im-Breisgau on the edge of the Black Forest, in a family of two sisters and four brothers. Later in life he described his upbringing:

> I grew up, I must say, in a normal, middle-class, Christian family. My father was
> what is called today an assistant principal; then known as 'Baden professors'. For
> most of his life he was a professor at the teachers' college in Freiburg. My mother
> came from an innkeepers' family. My grandparents had a small hotel ('Zur
> Kybburg') on the outskirts of Freiburg. And there were seven children in my
> immediate family .... So one could say that I grew up in a middle to lower-middle
> class family. There was always something to eat.[4]

Two of Karl's brothers became medical doctors. Another taught at a business school. His older brother, Hugo (1900–68), became a Jesuit priest and spent most of his life as a missionary in India. One of his sisters married a lawyer; another married a mathematician. His father, also called Karl (1868–1934), had to undertake teaching outside of his college in order to help support his family.[5] The mother of the family, Luise Trescher (1868–1976), also assumed additional responsibilities to support the family by baby-sitting. She lived to a very advanced age.

Unlike Dorothy Day or Thomas Merton (1915–68), Karl Rahner was not given to keeping personal diaries and talking at length about his feelings. He refused to write an autobiography. Later in his life he gave a series of interviews that were published as books and contain revealing accounts of his life and education.[6]

Between 1908 and 1922, Rahner lived in Freiburg. From 1910 to 1913 he attended the city's Knabenburg School, and continued his schooling between 1913 and 1922 in the Realgymnasium. The first year of his education (1910) coincided with the invention of neon lighting, the annexation of Korea by Japan, the invasion of Tibet by China, and political revolutions in Portugal and Mexico. His final year of schooling (1922) witnessed Herbert Kalmus' invention of technicolour cinema film, the first BBC radio broadcast, and the birth of the English philosopher-theologian, John Hick. The strange new world that Rahner was later taxed to address theologically was beginning to gestate. While Germany went to war between 1914 and 1918, Rahner continued to study at school.

His schooldays were spent in a liberal, humanitarian and tolerant atmosphere. He shared his classrooms with Catholics, Jews and Protestants. At school he often found his studies tedious. His teachers regarded him as moderately talented. A religious disposition was evident in his character while he was a schoolboy. He liked to translate hymns by Thomas Aquinas from Latin into German.[7]

life and education as a jesuit

Three weeks after he passed the examination that allowed him to leave school, he entered the Society of Jesus and began to live in the Jesuit noviciate of the Upper

society of jesus   The Catholic Church includes a large variety of religious institutes, congregations and societies that are conventionally known as religious orders. The members of these organizations make different kinds of public vows or promises to structure their lives. The Society of Jesus was founded by Ignatius of Loyola (1491–1556), a Basque, and nine of his companions in 1540. That was the year in which it received the approval of Pope Paul III ([1468] 1534–49). The members of the Society are generally known as Jesuits. They were founded in the wake of the Reformation and often engaged in theological debates with Reformed theologians. Since their origin their mandate has been to propagate Christian faith and to care for Christians by means of preaching and teaching. During their centuries-long existence they have also been involved in missionary work throughout the world.

Since their founding, they have proved to be skilled educators in schools and universities. The adjective, 'Jesuitical', was coined to deride Jesuits, whose detractors accused them of being equivocating or dissembling in argument. *The Spiritual Exercises*, written by Ignatius of Loyala (and completed around 1541), outlines a complex programme of meditation that lasts for about a month. This programme forms a major part of a Jesuit's life of prayer.

Province of the Jesuits, which was located in Feldkirch in Austria. He joined the Jesuits on 20 April 1922.[8] He was 18.

Rahner remained at Feldkirch from 1922 to 1925. He was a Jesuit novice during his first two years there. On 27 April 1924, he made his first profession of religious vows. He then set to work studying philosophy. Catholic students in religious orders at this time were not permitted to study theology without having previously studied philosophy and the history of philosophy. At Feldkirch, Rahner was introduced to the writings of the scholastic Doctors of the Church, Thomas Aquinas and Bonaventure. He also began to study Kant's theory of knowledge. Crucial for the evolution of his thought was his reading of the French Jesuit, Pierre Rousselot (1878–1915), and the Belgian Jesuit philosopher, Joseph Maréchal (1878–1944). Rousselot and Maréchal were born in the same year, but as in the case of Bonhoeffer, the inhabitants of the twentieth century were robbed of the talents of a promising theologian by war. Rousselot was killed during the First World War. Before that he was a professor of theology at the Institut Catholique in Paris, where he was appointed in 1909. He built upon Aquinas' teaching regarding the *lumen fidei* ('the light of faith') by emphasizing that faith has an experiential dimension, and is not purely conceptual, or the intellectual assent to propositions.[9] Maréchal helped Rahner to interpret Aquinas in liaison with Kantian philosophy.

When Rahner was 22, and still living in Austria, he published for the first time. The text he wrote was devoted to the necessity of prayer, and signals what was to become an ever-present conviction in his thought, namely, that humans can contact God in the course of their lives. If they are not able to do so, prayer is pointless, apart perhaps from psychologically calming or comforting the person who prays. Rahner's initial published reflection on prayer is called, 'Why We Need to Pray'. As a youthful Jesuit, he asserts:

> You must pray. We must pray!
>
> If we don't pray, we remain attached to earthly things, we become small like them, narrow like them, we get pressured by them, we sell ourselves to them – because we give our love and our heart to them.
>
> We must pray!
>
> Then we are far away from the petty everyday that makes us small and narrow. Then we draw near to God and become capable 'of touching our Creator and Lord'.[10]

This is not the polished writing of a German Jesuit professor of theology. Even so, it is the first recorded exposition of a leitmotif that is rearticulated and

modulated throughout Rahner's writings. The leitmotif centres on the verb of
'touching' and evinces Rahner's assurance that God may be encountered by
humans. The theme of touching (as in contacting God) uncoverers the young
Rahner as a mystical thinker: 'a particular mystical tradition in fact speaks of
thigganein, the Greek word for "touch, contact".'[11]

Rahner continued the philosophical studies he began at Feldkirch at
Berchmanskolleg in Pullach, which is near Munich, the capital of Bavaria. He
remained there from 1925 to 1927. The Jesuit period of study after the noviciate is
called the scholasticate. It is followed by a regency period – a time of practical
work such as instructing students. Rahner spent his regency back in Feldkirch
teaching Latin.[12] He was not much older than his pupils. One of his students
was the novice Alfred Delp, who was later arrested and hanged on a charge of
conspiring against Hitler. Rahner later regarded Delp to be in 'the front ranks
of those witnesses who were motivated by Christianity to resist the Evils of
Nazism'.[13]

theological studies

In 1929, Rahner moved to the Netherlands to study theology in Valkenburg, with
other Jesuit students. His first encounter with theological studies in a Catholic
institute was strictly controlled by decrees from the Vatican in the aftermath of
the Modernist crisis. All of Rahner's theology professors in the Netherlands, as
elsewhere, had to take the Oath Against Modernism, promulgated originally on
1 September 1910. It forced them to declare: 'with due reverence, I submit and
adhere with my whole heart to the condemnations, declarations, and all the
prescripts contained in the Encyclical *Pascendi* and in the decree *Lamentabili*,
especially those concerning what is known as the history of dogmas.'[14]

Rahner was not about to be lobotomized by anti-Modernist witch-hunts, or to
be chained to manualistic neo-scholastic rehashes of medieval thought. In
Valkenburg he investigated patristic mysticism, the history of piety, spiritual
theology and the thought of Bonaventure.[15] Between 1932 and 1933 he published
studies on figures such as Origen, Evagrius Ponticus (346–99) and Bonaventure.
He could use his studies in the Netherlands to build on his previously acquired
acquaintance with the creative attempt by Joseph Maréchal to interpret Aquinas'
theory of knowledge in dialogue with Kantian philosophy.

On 26 July 1932 – the year before he left the Netherlands – he was ordained a
priest in Munich by Cardinal Faulhaber. He then returned to the Netherlands to
complete his theological studies. Thereafter he spent a year (1933–4) in St Andrä,

Austria, undertaking his Tertianship – a year-long retreat in which he was to concentrate on his spiritual or religious development.

doctoral studies in germany

The priests in charge of Rahner's intellectual development decided that he should be prepared to teach the history of philosophy. With that ambition he was sent to the University of Freiburg-im-Breisgau to begin doctoral studies in philosophy. At the time he enrolled, Martin Heidegger (1889–1976), an initial supporter of Nazism, was the rector of the university. Rahner attended Heidegger's seminars on philosophy, but chose another professor, Martin Honecker, to direct his studies. Honecker proved to be a difficult taskmaster to please.

Rahner chose as the topic of his research Thomas Aquinas' understanding of knowledge. Aquinas argues that human beings cannot know anything without their senses, or sense intuition.[16] Rahner interpreted Aquinas with reference to the philosophies of Kant and Heidegger. After two years of work, Rahner produced an exceptionally complicated thesis that was later published as *Geist in Welt* ('Spirit in the World').[17] The text in which Aquinas explains his theory of knowledge is only 700 words long, but Rahner's dissertation on it extends for 400 pages.[18]

Both Kant and Heidegger recoiled from the suggestion that human beings enjoy rational knowledge of God. In his thesis, Rahner argued against them. He asserted that the human mind is dynamic in its apprehension of reality. Its dynamism is inspired by God. Otherwise stated, God has implanted a restlessness in human beings which attracts them to God.[19]

Rahner's thesis failed in examination. His director of studies, Martin Honecker, rejected the dissertation, thus terminating Rahner's doctoral candidacy in Freiburg. In referring later in life to his failure, Rahner simply commented: 'I was flunked by the Catholic Honecker for being too inspired by Heidegger.'[20] Karl then moved on to Innsbruck where he successfully completed a doctorate in theology with the cumbersome title of 'The Origin of the Church as Second Eve from the Side of Christ the Second Adam: An Investigation of the Typological Significance of John 19: 34.' Rahner was later disdainful of this working in saying, 'I had also written a small, lousy, but at least according to the standards of the time, adequate theological dissertation.'[21] He was named a doctor at the end of 1936.

life as a theologian

The initial plan to have Rahner prepared so that he could teach the history of philosophy was altered on 1 July 1937, when he was appointed as *Privatdozent* in Dogmatic Theology in the theology faculty of the University of Innsbruck in Austria. He began to lecture on the 'Foundations of a Philosophy of Religion'. The lectures became Rahner's second significant book, and were published as *Hörer des Wortes* ('Hearers of the Word') in 1941.[22]

Rahner's appointment to Innsbruck began his prolific university career as a teacher that lasted for 34 years until his retirement in 1971. In retirement he continued to write, publish and lecture.

The Nazis marched into Austria in March of 1938. They closed the Faculty of Theology in Innsbruck in July of the same year. Rahner moved to a Jesuit College in the Stillgasse, and from there to Vienna. Between July 1944 and August 1945 he worked as the parish priest of the village of Mariakirchen in Bavaria. He returned to the University of Innsbruck in 1948. There he was promoted on 30 June 1949, to the status of Ordinary Professor of Dogma and the History of Dogma. He remained in Innsbruck until 1964, when he took up a professorship in Munich. After three years there he went to Münster in Westphalia. On 1 April 1967, he began work at Münster as the University Professor of Dogma and the History of Dogma. He went back to Innsbruck in 1981, where he died on 30 March 1984.

theological works

The scale of Karl Rahner's theological output is immense. To begin with, he edited and co-edited huge multi-volume compendia and encyclopedia of theology. The process of having to read, write, compile, collate and correct these volumes equipped Rahner with a vast and detailed knowledge of the history of Christian thought, ancient and modern. A simple listing of the works he edited, and in which substantial sections were composed by him, gives an impression of his productivity. Rahner edited the 28th and 31st editions of a compendium of theology known as the *Enchiridion symbolorum definitionum et declarationum* ('Handbook of creeds, definitions, and declarations'). It is commonly referred to as 'Denzinger', after one of its original compilers. Rahner coedited the *Lexikon für Theologie und Kirke* ('Lexicon for Theology and Church', 1957–68). The *Lexikon* has 13 volumes. Between 1958 and 1984 he co-edited a work of 101 volumes – *Quaestiones Disputatae* ('Disputed Questions'). Other publications he co-edited were the four-volume encyclopedia, *Sacramentum Mundi* ('Sacrament of the World', 1967–9), followed by the edition in five volumes of *Handbuch der Pastoraltheologie* ('Handbook of Pastoral Theology', 1964–9); *Mysterium Salutis* ('The Mystery of Salvation', five volumes, 1965–76); and the encyclopedia of 31 volumes, *Christian Faith in Modern Society* (1980–3). In 1965 he was one of the founders of the international theological journal, *Concilium* (related to the Latin term, *consilium*, meaning a group of advisors). Between 1968 and 1974, Rahner collaborated with Herbert Vorgrimler to edit the international journal, *Dialog*. Again working with Vorgrimler, he wrote a single-volume theological dictionary (1961) that appeared in English in 1965 as the *Concise Theological Dictionary*. Despite this massive production of published material, Rahner regarded himself as a person who went to bed early and who was not very industrious![23]

To all these publications Rahner added another, entirely written by himself, and which ended up on shelves in libraries and the studies of theologians around the world. In its German edition it is called *Schriften zur Theologie* ('Writings on Theology'). It includes 16 volumes. It was translated into English as *Theological Investigations*. The English version is printed in 23 volumes. The first German instalment of this massive work was published in 1954 and the last in 1984, the year of Rahner's death. The entire set of volumes leaves virtually no theme in Christian theology untouched. The first volume in English, for instance, has the subtitle: *God, Christ, Mary and Grace*. The sixth volume has the subtitle *Concerning Vatican Council II*, while the final one is designated as *Humane Society and the Church of Tomorrow*.

Rahner published many other, briefer books which he called 'devotional works'. These include *The Eternal Year, Encounters with Silence, On Prayer*, and *Spiritual Exercises*.[24] In all of these works, Rahner invested the full extent of his erudition. 'I believe', he commented, 'that in some chapters of *On Prayer* there is at least as much theology tucked in – painstaking, thoughtful theology – as in my so-called scholarly or scientific works'.[25]

the second vatican council, 1962–5

By far the most significant event of Rahner's life in its last quarter was his involvement with the Second Vatican Council. When it opened in 1962 he was 60 years of age. In 1961, Pope John XXII appointed him as an advisor to assist Cardinal König of Vienna in preparing for the Council. In 1962, the Pope appointed him as a *peritus* (expert adviser) to the Council. While the Council sat, Rahner collaborated with theologians such as Henri de Lubac, Yves Congar, Hans Küng and Edward Schillebeeckx to bring to an end the Catholic Church's antipathy to the Enlightenment and the modern world that grew in its wake, and to organize the life of the Church in less Tridentine, or clerical and hierarchical, ways. Vatican II will be discussed in more detail in subsequent chapters.

Rahner devoted the remainder of his life in Austria and Germany to promoting and writing on the reforming programme of the Council. He was a major theological architect of many of the Council's promulgations. Because he could lecture and converse fluently in Latin, he communicated his ideas with ease while in Rome attending the Council. Before Vatican II, he was not well-known outside the German-speaking zone. Afterwards he achieved international renown and respect. In the last year of Rahner's life he commented ruefully on what had happened in the years following the Council's deliberations: 'Actually that ecumenical Council has not really been put into practice in the Church, either according to its letter or according to its spirit. In general, we are living through a "wintry season", as I have often said.'[26]

His work became more familiar to a generation of English-speaking students of theology after 1976, the year in which he published a masterly summary of his thought called unassumingly in German, *Grundkurs des Glaubens* ('Basic Course on Faith'). This was translated into English as *Foundations of Christianity: An Introduction to the Idea of Christianity*.[27]

the supernatural existential

The theology of Karl Rahner has three principal themes – God, Jesus Christ and Grace, or the Supernatural Existential. Considered as a whole, his theological output is a vast, multidimensional commentary on the ancient theological theme of grace.

The distinctiveness of Rahner's understanding of grace is that he refuses to acknowledge that it can be entirely separated from a human nature that may stand by itself in contradistinction to God. Before Rahner's work, such an understanding of the human person was often designated by theologians as a *natura pura* – a pure nature. Rahner spurns the notion that grace and human nature can neatly be separated:

> My basic theological conviction, if you will, is in opposition to this. What we call grace is obviously a reality which is God-given, unmerited, free, dialogical – in other words – supernatural. But for me grace is at the same time a reality which is so much a part of the innermost core of human existence in decision and freedom, *always* and above all given in the form of an offer that is either accepted or rejected,

that the human being cannot step out of this transcendental peculiarity of his being at all.[28]

The word 'transcendental' occurs often in Rahner's writings. He does not understand it in terms of the spatial metaphor that one thing lies beyond ('transcends') another, but as a condition that makes something possible. To illuminate: eggs are transcendental to omelettes. They are the prerequisite that makes the cooking of omelettes possible. Chickens are transcendental to eggs. Food is transcendental to excrement! A bomb is transcendental to an explosion. Somewhat similarly, for Rahner, grace is a necessary condition that enables humans to be human. They could not be human were it not for grace.

The phrase, 'supernatural existential', is another way of saying all this. In Heidegger's philosophy, an existential is a constitutive dimension of a human being. Rahner adopts and adapts the idea of an anthropological existential to

> **grace**   The English word 'grace' was originally a Christian theological term that translates the Latin *gratia* and the Greek *charis*. In the Christian Sciptures (often called the New Testament), *charis* means divine favour, or an unmerited gift. Paul's Letter to the Romans captures the central notion of a theology of grace: 'God's love has been poured into our hearts through the Holy Spirit that has been given to us' (Rom 5: 5b). In Christian theology grace refers to the generous way in which God relates to people. God (the Holy Spirit, as Paul says) is present as love in people, and they may be changed so as to become more like God's love. The Council of Orange in 529 CE addressed the question of the way in which divine grace relates to human freedom. It taught that human beings are free to reject or accept what Augustine of Hippo called 'prevenient grace', a phrase that designates God's generous initiate to relate to people. While people are free, the Council of Orange insisted that prevenient grace needs to be accepted if people are to benefit from God's initiative to save or help them.

say that a dynamic thrust towards, or graced relationship with, God is an indispensable part of human nature: 'grace has always been given, and this supernatural formal object is always at work somewhere in the total of human consciousness.'[29]

Rahner regarded his concept of the supernatural existential to be a faithful reflection of the thought of Thomas Aquinas. He even chides a Baroque form of Jesuit theology that attempted to separate divine grace and human nature: 'The failure to understand the teaching of Saint Thomas led to a strict separation between the human and the graced supernatural by a modern, seemingly humanistic real distinction between them. I believe the original and mortal sin of Jesuit theology lies right here.'[30]

Rahner used his understanding of a supernatural existential to develop a theory of 'anonymous Christianity', by which he meant that he considered 'no religion – it's immaterial which one – ungraced, although this grace may be suppressed, or expressed in a depraved way'.[31] In other terms, Rahner accepted that God's initiative to relate to human beings in their history is not confined to Christians, because all human beings have as part of their makeup a restless searching for God.

Rahner's theology of grace has an anthropological starting point: humans are able to experience and know God because their nature impels them to respond to God's approach to them.

The God of whom Rahner speaks so often is understood by him in Trinitarian terms. He wrote a chapter of 85 pages devoted to the Trinity for *Mysterium Salutis*. It was called 'Der dreifaltige Gott als transzender Urgrund der Heisgeschichte' ('The Threefold God as Transcendental Ground of Salvation History'). He published another tract on the Trinity in 1967, which was translated into English as *The Trinity*.[32]

An aspect of Rahner's Trinitarian theologian that became influential among other theologians was his refusal to differentiate between an *immanent* and *economic* Trinity. The former refers to God as God is in Godself without reference to anyone or anything. The latter designates God as God graciously relates to human history to save human beings from all that imperils them. Rahner taught that the Immanent Trinity *is* the Economic Trinity. That is, in relating to human beings, God as God is manifest.

Rahner's Christology does not depart from a traditional doctrine according to which Jesus Christ is truly God and truly a human being. Towards the end of his life his preferred way of interpreting the significance of Jesus was to say: 'I would prefer to say that in Jesus, the Crucified and Risen One, I know whereof I should live and die.'[33]

conclusion: rahner as a dilettante

Throughout his long career, Rahner never adopted an historically-critical method in his investigation of the works of theologians in the past. He acknowledges the importance of that method, but asserted a right 'not to do such research, or to reflect less on it'.[34]

Rahner was both disarmingly modest and candidly honest about the limited achievements any single theologian, including himself, could accomplish. He went so far as (playfully) to accuse himself of dilettantism:

> I would also say, mischievously but earnestly, that in a certain sense I always wanted
> to be a dilettante in theology. I claim the right to this dilettantism, fully aware that

there are vast numbers of technical problems which cannot be mastered today, either methodologically or practically. I recently said to some colleagues in Munich who aren't theologians that if one added up what a scholarly theologian must ideally know today, after forty years of my theological work I have become ten times dumber. Forty years ago the ratio between what I knew, and the problems, available information, and methods, was maybe 1:4; today it's more like 1:400. That gives me the right to be a dilettante, and to say I am.[35]

Karl Rahner was the last great Jesuit theologian of the twentieth century. For all his superlativeness as a theologian, he was not able to incorporate into his work the accumulated findings of historically-critical biblical scholarship, with the result that his Christology remained in the mould of Greek metaphysics. Nor did he have an opportunity to explore at length the implication of the suggestion that arose especially among South American theologians in the latter half of the twentieth century, according to which orthopraxis ('correct action') takes precedence over orthodoxy ('correct teaching') in the life of a Christian. As he intimated, he could not be expected to accomplish or know everything.

Rahner's theology exerted an enormous influence on other Catholic theologians, notably in North America. A highly plausible explanation of why he proved to be so prominent among Catholic thinkers is captured in the following quotation: 'His importance perdures as decades pass, partly because an age distinguished by important theologians, artists, or scientists is not followed immediately by equally imposing figures, and partly because the pontificate of John Paul II encouraged an intellectually superficial Catholicism of past devotions.'[36]

As the twenty-first century transpires falteringly, no one has begun to emerge showing signs of either matching the extent or variety of Rahner's publications, or of surpassing his detailed knowledge of the vast and varied flux of Christian tradition. Perhaps it is too early to tell whether his kind of theologian – a prayerful priestly celibate, educated philosophically, respectful of papal authority, fluent conversationally in Latin, and deferential to the Christian theologian tradition – will ever be a paradigm for aspiring theologians again.

The intellectual and religious protein of Rahner's elephantine body of theological writings is as simple, profound or deluded – according to his contemporary judges' points of view – as this: a person hungers for God because God has formed that individual in such a way as to lunge beyond human limitation in search of God. Yet this hunger is primarily a pining of the individual self. Later in the twentieth century, other theologians decided that God is best discovered in the activity of helping enfeebled others.

II

Yves Congar: 1904–95

No bishop should be installed against the will of the people.

Pope Celestine I, ca. 425 CE

Since the Reformation, relations between Christian denominations have not merely been difficult. They have also been deadly. The memory of the Thirty Years War (1618–48) between Catholics and Protestants is a chilling reminder of the ferocity of which Christians are capable when they fall out with each other. Before the French Revolution and the Enlightenment, hounding and persecution of Protestants by Catholics, and of Catholics by Protestants, was common in Europe. Movements for increased religious tolerance only gained significant momentum during the nineteenth century.[1] The long and baneful history of acrimony among Christians has not entirely dissipated, but relations between different denominations has improved since the revolutionary years of the Second Vatican Council (1962–5). Above all else, Vatican II was a convocation of Catholic bishops that attempted to reform their Church and to improve its rapport with its surrounding cultures. Before Vatican II, the leadership of the Catholic Church had normally been aggressively dismissive of modern cultures and philosophies. In the 200 years since the French Revolution the Church's leaders, most notably its popes, had been sternly and illiberally anti-modern, anti-Reformation, anti-Enlightenment, and anti-democratic. Vatican II theoretically brought to an end the Tridentine or Baroque era of the Catholic Church, which prized an absolute papal monarchy, a triumphalist hierarchical dominance of the Church, and a refusal to re-examine doctrines in the light of modern science and higher biblical criticism. One of the principal architects of the Council was the unassuming French scholar, Yves Congar. He was the most important and effective ecclesiologist of the twentieth century. This is so because, on the eve of the Council, the principal ways in which he wanted the Church to be changed were set in motion once the Council was under way.

Why bother with Vatican II in a book devoted to twentieth-century theologians? Because, in historical terms, the Second Vatican Council was the most significant religious and theological event of the twentieth century. It was the largest and most representative Council in the Church's history. Its 2,540 delegates came from around the globe.[2] It transformed the lives of Catholics, who formed the largest of all Christian denominations at the time; revolutionized the self-understanding of the Catholic Church; drastically improved relations with other Christian Churches; ended the 400-year-long period of the Counter-Reformation; recognized the legitimacy of religious liberty and the value of religions apart from Christianity; purged language offensive to Jews from its public worship; and began to dialogue with modern cultures and philosophies:

> **ecclesiology** Ecclesiology is a discourse on the Church. It involves the theological and historical investigation of the Church's origins, nature, purpose, variety and mission. The word 'ecclesiology' comes from the Greek term *ekklesia*, which designates a group or assembly of people. *Ekklesia* translates the Hebrew word *gahal*, which refers to a convened assembly. The word **ecclesial** refers to the Church considered as a theological mystery constituted as the People of God or the Body of Christ. **Ecclesiastical** designates the institutional structures of a Church. An **ecclesiastic** is a Church official or leader.

By the time it had finished, on December 8, 1965, the Council had turned the Church on its head. To name but a few examples: as a result of the Council, the Roman Catholic Church relinquished its claim to be the one true church, and with it, abdicated claims to power in relation to nation-states, by declaring that the only just form of government was one under which people were free to worship as they pleased. The Council relaxed dietary restrictions and requirements regarding confession and attire for the laity, eliminated the Latin mass, and forever changed the character and identities of Roman Catholic nuns and brothers – and their orders. Most importantly, Vatican II changed the way the Church understood itself, as its identity went from being a hierarchical authority to a church conceived as the people of God.[3]

the people of god

Yves Congar was the principal intellectual architect of the theological revolution wrought by Vatican II. In 1958 he published a book called *Le Mystère du Temple* ('The Mystery of the Temple'). The text refers to the Church as God's People. It contains a passage that interprets Jesus' death in sacrificial terms with reference to the Jewish commemoration of the Pasch – an annual recollection of the Jewish passing over from Egyptian slavery to freedom: 'after Our Lord's Pasch, each accomplishes and offers his own pasch to the best of his ability, but all these paschs in the end form one single Pasch, the Pasch of the People of God, the People which has become the Body of Christ ... .'[4]

Congar's characterization of the Church in terms of its people set in relation to God might appear innocuous. In effect it was ground-breaking, and was to have an enormous impact on the theology of the Second Vatican Council. Since the Reformation, the idea that the Church is a community of God's People was absent from ecclesiologies sanctioned by the Vatican. Congar's book anticipated the most important and radically revisionary ecclesiological conclusion of the Second Vatican Council, which is the dogmatic proclamation that the Church, as a mystery, is the People of God.

The notion of God's People is biblical. Its recovery as an ecclesiological theme took place in the 1940s and 1950s thanks to the work of the two Catholic scholars, Domenikus Koster and Lucien Cerfaux. Congar helped them to draw attention to the theme.[5]

At Vatican II, Congar did not work as a soloist. He joined a creative cluster of like-minded theologians and bishops who ardently hoped that the rigid structures of the post-Reformation Catholic Church could be changed, so that believers could actively participate in the Church's manifold activities, instead of being the passive recipients of instructions from hierarchs. Amid all the cooperation to advance reform at Vatican II, 'no theologian's influence was greater than Congar's'.[6]

Congar's writings presaged other major themes of the Second Vatican Council apart from the ecclesiology that the Church is primordially the People of God. The Council's calling for lay people in the Church to participate fully in the Church's mission to a wider world finds clear expression in Congar's book, *Lay People in the Church* (1953). His earlier book, *Divided Christendom* (1937), reminds its readers that the Church is more than the Church governed by Rome, and ends hopefully by referring to a time when Catholicism and Protestantism will be reunited: 'Of reunion, as of the second Coming of the Lord, we can only know that God alone knows the time, and it is vain for us to try to determine the day or the means.'[7] In Congar's later book, *True and False Reform in the Church* (1950), he observes that the Church always stands in need of reform. The same idea was later voiced at Vatican II.[8]

Congar's life-long ambition was to participate in the reform and renewal of the Catholic Church so that unity could be restored among Christians, and that Christian faith would be less repugnant to modern audiences repelled by the Church and tempted to atheism.

life as a dominican

Yves Congar was born on 13 April in the same year as Rahner – 1904. Two other major theologians of the twentieth century were born in 1904 – Bernard Lonergan (1904–84), a Canadian Jesuit, best known for his book, *Method in Theology* (1972), and the North American Jesuit, John Courtney Murray (1904–67), who inspired much of Vatican II's teaching on religious freedom.

Congar was born in Sedan in north-west France, and said of himself: 'Je suis un Celte des Ardennes' ('I am a Celt of the Ardennes').[9] As a boy he witnessed the travails of the First World War. His father was taken hostage and deported. He became particularly close to his mother. During his boyhood he mixed freely with Protestants and Jews. This experience fed his adult desire to advance ecumenism. His local Catholic community worshipped in a Protestant church because their own building had been burned by Germans.[10]

Between 1921 and 1924, Congar studied scholastic philosophy in Paris at the Institut Catholique. During these years he met the Dominican theologian Réginald Garrigou-Lagrange, but did not feel at ease with the latter's antipathy to the work of modern philosophers such as Maurice Blondel (1861–1949), Lucien Laberthonnière (1860–1932) and Joseph Maréchal (1878–1944). Congar never regarded himself as a philosopher.

After his philosophical studies he decided to join the Dominican Order. He began his long career as a Dominican in 1925 when he became a novice in the Order's French province. From 1926 to 1931 he studied at a French Dominican centre for higher theological studies, L'Ecole du Saulchoir ('The School of the Saulchoir'), or Le Saulchoir, for short. The word *Saulchoir* refers to a willow tree (French: *un saule*). Le Saulchoir was established by French Dominicans in 1904 at Kain-la-Tombe in south-west Belgium. It was

ecumenism   The twentieth century can rightly be regarded as the ecumenical century. The noun 'ecumenism', and the adjective 'ecumenical', stem from the Greek, *oikoumene*, meaning 'the inhabited world'. It designates the belief and practice that relations between Christian denominations need to be improved and maintained. Ecumenism is not the same phenomenon as inter-faith or inter-religious dialogue. The latter entails discussions between adherents of different religions, whereas ecumenism involves Christians. The World Missionary Conference of Edinburgh in 1910, the formation of the World Council of Churches in 1948, and the Second Vatican Council, are all milestones of the twentieth-century ecumenical movement.

the dominicans   The Dominicans are a Catholic religious order of friars (from Latin: *fratres*, 'brothers'), founded by a Castilian cleric called Dominic – hence the name 'Dominicans'. Dominic established the order early in the thirteenth century. Dominicans since their beginnings have always included women in their ranks. The women participate in the mission of the order, but live apart from friars, in convents or monasteries. The Dominicans are formally known in the Catholic Church as the *Ordo Praedicatorum* ('The Order of Preachers'), a title that captures their primary purpose, which is preaching. In the English-speaking world Dominicans are also known as Blackfriars, after the black mantle they wear over their white habits during the winter and while preaching. Orders of friars such as the Franciscans, Dominicans, Carmelites and Augustinians, are neither monks nor canons. A monk normally lives in one monastery for a lifetime. A canon assumes liturgical responsibility in a major church, cathedral or basilica. A friar, by contrast, is meant to be mobile and to be able to be sent to preach or serve the poor wherever an urgent need is perceived. By the early twentieth century, Dominican theology had become sclerotic because of its rigid preoccupation with orthodoxy, and reliance on Baroque commentaries on Aquinas. The School of the Saulchoir was a major centre for rejuvenating Dominican theology in the middle of the twentieth century on the basis of historical research and engagement with contemporary political and social problems.

here that Congar first studied theology. The school could not be based in France because of anti-clerical legislation there. Its faculty and students moved to France in the late 1930s and settled just outside Paris, in what became known as Le Saulchoir d'Etiolles, after the locality in which it was built.

the new theology

The Saulchoir was a powerhouse of intellectual instruction and research. Several of its professors became *periti* (advisors) to bishops at Vatican II. Its teachers developed what came to be known in general terms as the new theology (*la nouvelle théologie*). The centre of the new theology was the Jesuit faculty of theology based at Lyon, Fourvière. Henri de Lubac and Jean Daniélou were two if its distinguished professors. The novelty of the new theology was its method. The promoters of the new theology wanted to reinvigorate theology through a method of *ressourcement* – going back to venerable sources. Bypassing neo-scholastic interpretations, they wished to base their writings on much earlier sources. The Dominicans at the Saulchoir turned to medieval theologies and especially to Aquinas. The Jesuits concentrated more on patristics.

One of Congar's teachers at the Saulchoir was Marie-Dominique Chenu, an historian of the Middle Ages. Chenu was not an intellectual obscurantist. He used his vast knowledge of medieval history not only to interpret Aquinas by explaining his writings with reference to their historical contexts, but also to relate theology to his contemporary setting in France. Chenu's *ressoucement* was inspired by the Dominican biblical scholar Marie-Joseph Lagrange (not to be confused with Garrigou-Lagrange). Marie-Joseph Lagrange was the pioneering founder of the Dominican school for biblical studies and archaeology in Jerusalem – the École Biblique. Just as Lagrange applied an historical-critical method to the analysis of biblical texts, Chenu wanted to do the same with medieval texts to ferret out insights that might enlighten his contemporaries. In 1937, Chenu elaborated his vision for the Saulchoir, of which he was the director between 1932 and 1942, in a manifesto called *Une école de théologie: le Saulchoir* ('A School of Theology: The Saulchoir').[11] Chenu also inspired the French worker-priest movement, which promoted the idea that priests would communicate better with workers if they laboured like workers. Chenu sent Dominican students to work as miners in 1933.[12]

Congar was ordained a priest on 25 July 1930. He taught as a professor at the Saulchoir between 1931 and 1939 and from 1945 to 1954. During the Second World War he was captured and interned as a prisoner of war in Germany.

Problems began to emerge for French Dominicans in 1950 when Pope Pius XII published his encyclical *Humani Generis* ('The Human Race'). This document severely criticized theological initiatives favoured by exponents of the new theology, and insisted that students for the priesthood were to study philosophy according to Aquinas (thereby bypassing modern post-Enlightenment philosophies).

congar's exile

For all Congar's innovative contribution during the Second Vatican Council, it did not come without considerable personal cost and suffering. He was regularly hounded and harassed by officials in the Vatican. The Master of the Dominican Order summoned him to Paris in February 1954. Under pressure from Rome, he was informed by the Master that he was dismissed from his post at the Saulchoir, along with three of his colleagues – Chenu, Henri-Marie Féret and Pierre Boisselot. Congar had been a Dominican for 29 years at this stage. Congar went into exile and began to live in Jerusalem. In November 1954, he moved to live in the Dominican house of Blackfriars, Cambridge. He was forbidden to have any contact with students of theology. The Bishop of Strasbourg kindly intervened and arranged for Congar to return to France in December of 1955.[13]

pope john xxiii

The course of Congar's life changed unexpectedly on 28 October 1958. On that day the Patriarch of Venice, Angelo Giuseppe Roncalli, was elected Pope. Duly elected, he immediately sent signals that he was going to be an innovator. He took the name of John XXIII, the first Pope to be called John since the fourteenth century.

After three months as the new bishop of Rome, John made an announcement that took the Vatican completely by surprise. He had been elected as Pope at the age of 77 with the hope that his papacy would be short and uneventful, following the long reign of Pope Pius XII. It was indeed a short papacy of five years, but anything but uneventful. On 25 January 1959, John held a consistory with a small group of cardinals in Rome's Basilica of St Paul Outside the Walls. Addressing the assembled cardinals, he informed them: 'Trembling a little with emotion but at the same time humbly resolute in my purpose, I announce to you a double celebration which I propose to undertake: a diocesan synod for the City and a general Council for the universal Church.' He went on to say that he was motivated 'solely by a concern for the "good of souls" and in order that the new pontificate may come to grips, in a clear and well-defined way, with the spiritual needs of the present time.'[14]

John XXIII was extraordinarily well experienced with international affairs. He had served as a papal diplomat for 31 years. When he was the apostolic delegate (a papal envoy) to Turkey during the Second World War, he saved the lives of thousands of Romanian and Bulgarian Jews, especially children, by issuing them with baptismal certificates which, although blank, prevented them from being killed.[15]

When John first announced his plan to convoke a general Council of bishops, he was not *consulting* the assembled cardinals but *informing* them of a resolute decision he had made as the Patriarch of the Latin West. It is difficult to overestimate how completely unforeseen his announcement was. General Councils of bishops have been extremely rare over the course of the past 2,000 years. There was only one such Council during the twentieth century and one during the nineteenth – the First Vatican Council of 1869–70. Vatican I had been the first Council since the Council of Trent, which was held over three periods: 1545–8, 1551–2 and 1562–3.

On the eve of Vatican II, the Catholic Church was governed by the Roman Curia, which itself operated according to instructions from the pope. The Curia (an ancient name for the house of the Roman senate) involved several bureaucratic departments in the Vatican which directed all aspects of finance, education,

---

conservatives and progressives   The blanket labelling of people as conservatives and progressives is risky, because a conservative thinker can be tolerant and open-minded, while a progressive can be rigidly intolerant of the views of others. In this book, the label 'conservative' simply refers to a person who wants to preserve or conserve the status quo of a given situation, and is opposed to change. By a 'progressive' is intended an individual who is convinced that a situation is not legitimate, and needs to be reformed. It does not follow that a progressive is an anti-traditional figure. While conservatives may style themselves as traditional, the traditions to which they are allied can be of quite recent historical provenance. A progressive, in turn, can be squarely traditional by working for the reform of a current situation along the pattern of an ancient state of affairs. In the same way a radical can be traditional by wishing to dispense with epiphenomenal matters by focusing on a root problem. At Vatican II one of the most daringly progressive of bishops was Maximos IV Saigh, who constantly referred to conservative, ancient practices in the Church to challenge the status quo of his age.[16]

doctrinal policies and punitive actions within the Catholic Church. When Angelo Ronacalli became John XXIII, the Roman Curia was firmly in the control of conservative clerics.

It is easy to see why Curial officials would be upset and disturbed, as they were, by John XXIII's convocation of a general Council of bishops. The last Council, Vatican I, had bequeathed a doctrine of papal infallibility to the Catholic Church. Why consult a Council, when a potentially infallible pope is at hand? Yet papal power was not what bothered the Curialists most. By their very nature, Councils are designed to allow bishops to discuss what is of concern to them. A free discussion or vote by bishops has the clear potential to frustrate or impede the best-laid plans, plots and ambitions of a bureaucratic department in the Vatican.

Congar's long period of ostracization at the hands of the Curia ended on 20 July 1960, when he was appointed as a Consultor to the theological Commission established by the Pope to prepare for the Council. He served as a *peritus* (official expert) once the Council began.

Congar kept a meticulous and long diary throughout the proceedings of the Council. He instructed that these notes were not to be published until the year 2000. His wishes were respected. They were published in two volumes in 2002. It is now clear why their publication was delayed. They are replete with candid and occasionally ascerbic comments. Of the man in the Curia who condemned Chenu, Congar declares: 'le fasciste, le monophysite' ('the fascist, the monophysite'). By 'monophysite' Congar meant someone who denies the human nature of Jesus.[17] Elsewhere he speaks of 'l'effroyable satrapisme de Pie XII' ('the dreadful satrapism of Pius XII').[18] He noted that a large number of bishops at Vatican II were incapable of having a comprehensive view of questions because they had lost the habit of studying and deciding for themselves.[19] He reports an encounter at the Council with Karol Wojtyla, who later became Pope John Paul II. Bishop Wojtyla gave Congar texts he had edited. Congar found them fairly confused, full of imprecisions, errors or defects. Yet he was glad to make contact with the Polish episcopate.[20]

the drama of the council's first day

During the first session of the Second Vatican Council an attempt by Curial conservatives to control the Council's proceedings and outcome was thwarted. The Curia was made to submit to the authority of the bishops. Radical change in the Catholic Church finally became a possibility after centuries of unbending anti-modernism.

Three years of preparations elapsed between John XXIII's convocation of the Council and its first session. On 13 October 1962, roughly 2,500 bishops, theologians and observers gathered in Rome's St Peter's Basilica, presided over by the Pope. The bishops needed to elect members for ten groups or commissions which would draft and revise the Council's published documents. The daily proceedings of the Council were directed by a small group of Cardinals called the Council of Presidents. Cardinal Felici, the General Secretary of the Roman Curia, also acted as the General Secretary of the Council. At the beginning of the first session he asked the bishops to cast their votes. At this stage they had come from the five continents of the world, some from far-flung places, and did not know each other well, if at all. It was impossible for them to vote in an informed way. Away from Rome the bishops were isolated from each other and could easily be dominated by the Curia. Such was not the case when they were together. The Curia had every reason to fear the convocation of an assembly of bishops.

One of the Council Presidents, Cardinal Liénart, a progressive French cardinal, could see that the bishops were bewildered when asked to vote. He turned to the person chairing the Council of Presidents, Cardinal Tisserant, who was also French, and said he would like to speak to the assembly. Tisserant refused to give permission, indicating that time for discussion had not been placed on the agenda for the day's proceedings. Liénart stood up anyway in full view of the bishops, grabbed a microphone, and asked in Latin that the voting be postponed so that the bishops could come to know each other over the course of a few days. His proposal met with prolonged applause from the bishops, and was supported by three other Council Presidents – Cardinals Frings (of Germany), Döpfner (Germany) and König (Austria).[21] The voting was postponed for three days. The Curia had been prevented from dictating the course of events.

the displacement of latin

The Second Vatican Council took three chronological years to complete, beginning in October 1962 and ending in December 1965. Its bishops and theologians did not stay in Rome for all of that time, but could travel back and forth between their homes and Rome. The Council sat in four sessions: October 1962–June 1963; September 1963–June 1964; September 1964–February 1965; and September–December 1965. It ended on 8 December 1965.

John XXIII did not live until the end of the Council. He died of cancer at the age of 81 on 3 June 1963. He was succeeded by a much more cautious figure, Pope Paul VI. Paul thrice stymied the free interchange of views between bishops. He intervened to stop any discussion of contraception and compulsory celibacy for clerics. He also suffocated attempts to make the government of the Catholic Church more collegial or democratic.

By its end, Vatican II had promulgated four constitutions, two of which were styled as dogmatic, and 12 decrees and declarations. The first constitution was devoted to liturgy and was easily passed by a majority of bishops.[22] It did not seem at the time that many bishops of the twentieth century wished to continue requiring their people to worship in the defunct language of Latin. How many individuals in the twentieth century could converse and understand fluently in Latin? Not as many who thought in terms of new supermarkets, fast cars and television sets. In Vatican II's second session there was clear agreement among bishops to reform the liturgy, and to allow it to be celebrated in languages other than Latin. All this transpired 400 years after the Council of Trent which, in response to the Reformation, had resolutely refused to allow liturgies to be conducted in the vernacular.

By the Third Session of Vatican II (1964–5), Catholics around the world were able to worship in the languages of their childhood. This innovation alone illustrates how radically progressive Vatican II was: 'On November 29, 1964, the first Sunday of Advent, Roman Catholics walked into their parishes around the globe and, for the first time since the fall of the Roman Empire, participated in a mass that was given largely in their native tongue.'[23]

collegiality

The progressive cogs of Vatican II did not stop there. The second constitution of the Council, *The Dogmatic Constitution on the Church*, was proclaimed on 21 November 1964. The preparatory schema for discussion on the Church that had been drawn up by the Curia began by referring to the Church as a hierarchy. It was thrown out in debate on the Council floor. The approved version opens with a chapter called 'The Mystery of the Church'. It is followed by the seismically significant chapter, 'The People of God'. Only then, in an ensuing chapter, does the Council affirm that 'The Church is Hierarchical'.[24] The effect of a reordering and rewriting of chapters is that Congar's primary image of the Church as the People of God was placed above and instead of a long-entrenched and far more hierarchical picture. From then on, the Catholic Church taught in principle that its hierarchy came forth from God's People, and is not placed above it as an unaccountable norm. Subsequent papal practice has proved to be monarchical.

The chapter on the Church's hierarchy affirmed the principle of collegiality, that is, the affirmation that bishops constitute a college that exercises an authority that is equal to the Pope's. By far the overwhelming majority (81 per cent) of bishops at Vatican II voted for collegiality.[25] The timorous Paul VI was disturbed by their conclusion and intervened unilaterally once again, in opposition to the clear wish of voters. He appended an infamous note (*Nota Praevia*) to the Constitution asserting the Pope's privilege to rule the Church without consulting the college of bishops. His intervention gave sanction to attempts by later popes to rule as monarchs – hence Karl Rahner's lament in the year before he died that he was then living in a 'wintry season'.

scripture and tradition

A major dissipation in strained relations between Catholic and Protestants was achieved with the next constitution to be proclaimed – the *Dogmatic Constitution on Divine Revelation* (18 November 1965). At issue during the Reformation was a dispute about the status of the Bible considered as a divine revelation. Reformers stated that God is revealed primarily in the Bible. In response, the official teaching of the Catholic Church insisted that there are two sources of revelation: the Bible and the tradition of the Church.

Vatican II tried to address and redress this stand-off by teaching that the Church 'has always regarded and continues to regard the scriptures, taken together with sacred scriptures, as the supreme rule of its faith'. And again, 'The sacred scriptures contain the word of God, and because they are inspired, they truly are the word of God; therefore, the study of the sacred page should be the very soul of sacred theology.'[26]

On ecclesiastical tradition, Congar was a theological master. Of Vatican II's decision regarding the disputed sources of revelation (Scripture alone, or Scripture and tradition), he observed:

As is known, the expression 'two sources of Revelation' was rejected by a near two-thirds majority at the Second Vatican Council. This decision is of considerable importance for the future of the dialogue on this question between Protestants and ourselves. As a well-informed commentator noted on his subject: 'With this vote of November 20th (1962), it may be said that the period of the Counter-Reformation is at an end, and that Christianity is entering a new era whose consequences are as yet unpredictable.'[27]

Congar often addressed the point of contention between Catholic and Protestants as to whether there is a source for knowledge of God apart from the Bible. He pointed out that many post-biblical ecclesial traditions, like infant baptism, praying for the dead and prayer facing the East are 'secondary points relating to some main reality itself clearly mentioned in Scripture'.[28]

'Tradition' is a word often discussed in ecclesiology. It can bear a negative connotation in everyday use. To be called traditional is not always and everywhere regarded as a compliment. Congar regarded tradition as a dynamic reality that simply transferred a reality from one generation to another:

> 'Tradition' comes from the Latin *traditio*, the noun of the verb *tradere*, 'to transmit', 'to deliver'. … *Tradere* implied giving over and surrendering something to someone, passing an object from the possession of the donor to the receiver. In Greek, *paradidonai*, aorist *paradounai*, had the same meaning. An equally good simile would be that of a relay race, where the runners, spaced at intervals, pass an object from one to the other, a baton, for example, or a torch.[29]

There are four clearly discernible phases in Congar's career. He lived and worked for another three decades after Vatican II. The first phase lasted from 1904 until 1939. The second was a period of turmoil during the Second World War, lasting from 1939 to 1945. The third encompasses the period 1945–65. This was Congar's most prolific period of publishing. In 1950 he published a book called *True and False Reform in the Church*. This was followed in 1952 by *Christ, Mary and the Church*. In 1953 he published *First Steps for a Theology of the Laity*. Thereafter he wrote *The Tradition and Traditions* (2 volumes, 1960 and 1963), *Christians in Dialogue* (1964). Then came his Christology – *Jesus Christ* (1965).

The final phase of his life unfolded after the end of Vatican II until his death. During that time he continued to promote the major preoccupations of his third period – tradition, the reform of the Church, ecumenism and lay involvement in the Church's mission to the world. He published several books after the Council, including a three-volume study of the Holy Spirit.[30] He was able to produce a multitude of publications in his life because for 35 years of his adult life he worked every day from seven in the morning until ten at night.[31]

In the decade before Congar died, he reflected on the situation of Christians then. After all his work seeking to advance the cause of unity among them, he remained starkly realistic about what had and had not been achieved, and could say of himself, 'I feel very small and very inadequate'.[32] By the late twentieth century, Christians were not neatly united, but 'side by side': 'No church or communion has succeeded in convincing the rest that it is in the possession of *the* truth. ... We are still in a position of being face to face or side by side, though to some degree we are also together and even incorporated.'[33]

the church and the poor

For all Congar wrote, he never managed to produce a systematic account of his understanding of the Church. Scanning his publications it becomes clear that he regarded the Church as God's People in history, guided by the Holy Spirit of God, standing always in need of reform, while passing on faith and practices it inherited from earlier generations. His primary legacy for the history of theology in the twentieth century was his insistence that of all the images that may be used to describe the Church, like communion, mystical body or messianic people, the most apt is the People of God.

For all Congar's mention of the Church, he was not a purely ecclesiocentric thinker. Everything he said about the Church he related to the problems of the world in which he lived. He used the fundamental theme of his ecclesiology – the motif of the People of God – as a reminder to Christians that they are obliged to work to eliminate poverty. Vatican II's 'Dogmatic Constitution on the Church' twice calls the People of God the 'messianic people of God', a phrase indebted to Congar. The significance of calling the Church messianic is that it reminds humanity of a hope for future release from suffering. Without a commitment to help the poor, Congar concluded that the Church in all it said and did would not be credible: 'People will only believe us if our practical works bear witness to our faith and our charity. The spiritual or evangelical poverty of which God speaks in our hearts today is by itself a religious value. It is also meant to allow and sustain an effective service of the poor.'[34]

The year before Congar's death in Paris, and four decades after he was dismissed from his professorship at the Saulchoir, John Paul II recognized his achievements in ecclesiology. In 1994, Congar was named and created a cardinal.

12

Edward Schillebeeckx: b.1914

After mocking him, they stripped him of the purple cloak
and put his own clothes on him.
Then they led him out to crucify him.

Mark 15: 20

Jesus remains a figure of fascination 20 centuries after he was executed by the Roman Prefect, Pontius Pilate. As each year elapses since his death by torture, the more difficult it becomes for anyone to imagine who he was and what he did. Unlike the theologians discussed in this book, Jesus did not bequeath any writings to anyone. Frustratingly, for an image-bedazzled world of the Houses of Dior, Chanel, Armani and Abercrombie and Fitch, no one even knows what Jesus looked like. He is disarmingly distant from people living in the twenty-first century. He is far removed spatially, temporally and experientially from anyone currently seeking to depict his identity and historical significance.

His remoteness in time and culture has not stemmed a modern avalanche of publications about him. The twentieth century generated a massive industry of journal and book production devoted to investigating and specifying why the name of Jesus is one of the most mentioned, discussed and worshipped in the chaotic flux of human history. So voluminous was the academic commentary on Jesus last century that an adroit guide is needed to navigate it. Few are as adept at doing so as the Flemish theologian, Edward Schillebeeckx.

None of the theologians discussed thus far in the book, and none hereinafter, articulated theological studies of Jesus as long and as detailed as those of Schillebeeckx. Crucially, his intense interest in Jesus was neither arbitrary nor academic: he wanted to retrieve a vivid portrait of Jesus from an alien past, in order to focus the minds and hearts of his contemporaries on what ought to matter most among humans this world – the service of utterly debased poor people. He sought an antidote to the cruel neglect of down-and-out individuals, crushed by the machinery of political tyranny and economic exploitation. He found it lucidly outlined in the Bible's account of the life of Jesus.

Schillebeeckx began his career as a dogmatic theologian. In 1963, one of his earlier works was published in English as *Christ the Sacrament of the Encounter with God*. His account of Jesus Christ therein is reverentially traditional:

> The dogmatic definition of Chalcedon, according to which Christ is 'one person in two natures', implies that one and the same person, the Son of God, also took on a visible human form. Even in his humanity Christ is the Son of God. The second person of the most holy Trinity is personally man; and this man is personally God. Therefore Christ is God in a human way, and man in a divine way.[1]

This book brought Schillebeeckx to international attention. In the aftermath of two global wars, he adopted what seemed to be the warm existential category of human encounter to describe the relation between God, Jesus Christ and humanity. All this he links to the ecclesiastical category of sacraments. 'A sacrament', he explains, 'is a divine bestowal of salvation in an outwardly perceptible form which makes the bestowal manifest; a bestowal of salvation in historical visibility.'[2]

At this point in Schillebeeckx's life he interprets Jesus as the primordial sacrament of God in human history, and a manifestation of divine salvation for people: 'The man Jesus, as the personal visible realization of the divine grace of redemption, is the sacrament, the primordial sacrament, because this man, the Son of

God himself, is intended by the Father to be in his humanity the only way to the actuality of redemption.'[3]

By the 1980s, Schillebeeckx's language about Jesus was decidedly different. It was much less ecclesiastical in style (grace, sacrament, Church, redemption), and far more concentrated on poverty and suffering: 'For Jesus God is not the guarantor of society, or prosperity and the family. Jesus' image of God was shaped by the thirsty, the stranger, the prisoner, the sick, the outcast: he sees God in them' (Mt 25).[4] This is a strikingly divergent way of talking about Jesus, as is this: 'If Jesus becomes your way, then any fellow human being whom you encounter is a challenge and a call; in him or her Jesus stands before you as someone who needs you. To follow the life of Jesus in this way is to seek God.'[5] And again: 'The most obvious, modern way to God is that of welcoming fellow human beings, both interpersonally and by changing structures that enslave them.'[6]

Schillebeeckx re-examined his Christology of the 1950s and 1960s early in the 1970s. By that stage he was less likely to speak of Jesus with honorific titles like 'the Son of God'. Instead he focused on suffering in Jesus' life:

> Jesus, who had come blessing and healing, opening up communication from Palestine to Jerusalem, would within a few days bleed to death outside the gates of Jerusalem on a Roman cross.
>
> Christ is not a myth but a living person who (according to the Greek version of the creed) *'was crucified under Pontius Pilate'*. That is not there for nothing. Tyrannical power exterminated Jesus in a corner of the world; powerful men did away with him. … Only a constant falling back on Jesus' concrete, historical career can avoid the abstract domination of confessional titles of honour, demoting the vulnerable man Jesus to an outmoded religious or cultural myth.[7]

Schillebeeckx could not disagree more with Karl Barth and Paul Tillich that the historical unfolding of Jesus' life in Palestine is less significant for theology than the Church's proclamation of faith in a Christ figure because inattention to Jesus' historical career breeds docetic theories about him as if he were not really human, but a supernatural visitor from outer space. What accounts for the modulation in style from Schillebeeckx's earlier dogmatic language about Jesus, and his later terminology that speaks so much of suffering, poverty, injustice or the misery and degradation of outcasts? An answer to that question may be found in the story of Schillebeeckx's own life.

schillebeeckx's origins

For an English-speaker, the first hurdle to straddle in attending to the life and thought of Edward Schillebeeckx is his family name! It is Flemish, and in the Kingdom of Belgium, very few people indeed bear the name Schillebeeckx. It is pronounced in three syllables with a primary accent on the first: *Skill*-a-Bakes. The initial syllable is more guttural that the English 'skill'. The second resembles the vowel ending the word 'Chin*a*'. The third is pronounced with a long open 'a', as in 'bay'. The meaning of the name is uncertain, but may mean in Flemish, 'those who come from the place where the stream divides'.

Edward Cornelis Florentius Alfons (Schillebeeckx's first four names) entered a world at war, in ravaged times of economic, political and social chaos. He was born in the port city of Antwerp in the upper north-west region of Belgium on 12 November 1914. A German army had invaded Belgium only weeks before his birth – on 4 August 1914. German occupation lasted until 11 November 1918. Edward's father, Constant Johannes Maria Schillebeeckx (1882–1978), and his mother, Johanna Petronella Calis (1888–1974), both came from Geel in north-central Belgium. Constant worked for the Belgian Ministry of Finance.

Edward's family moved to and settled in Kortenberg in 1914. Kortenberg then was a small town lying midway between Louvain (Flemish: Leuven) and Brussels. Edward spent his infancy in Kortenberg. He was the sixth child to be born in a family of 14 children, with five girls and nine boys.[8]

The culture into which he was first initiated as a boy was markedly Catholic. His parents regularly attended early morning Mass in their town church. Looking back in 1983 on this stage of his life, Schillebeeckx recalled: 'I served at Mass regularly from the age of six or seven onwards and then Christ was, as far as I was concerned, the host elevated after the consecration. I have no emotional reaction at all now at the moment of elevation, but I did then.'[9] Edward's childhood experiences at Mass instilled an ambition in him. The idea came to him at Mass: 'One day I shall be a priest.'[10] The idea later became a reality.

Edward was sent to a Jesuit boarding school in Turnhout after he finished his primary schooling in Kortenberg. While completing his studies in Kortenberg he decided to become a Dominican.

When he was 20 (1934), Edward began life as a novice with the Dominicans in the city of Ghent in north-western Belgium. In 1935, after a year as a novice, he started life as a student of philosophy and theology. After three years of philosophy (the *philosophicum*) he progressed to four years of theology (the *theologicum*). Like all students in Catholic educational institutions of the time, his studies were intensely focused on the works of Thomas Aquinas – with an unexpected difference. His principal teacher of philosophy in Ghent, Dominic De Petter (1905–71), ignored the intellectual restrictions imposed on Catholics by the Roman Curia, and encouraged his students to investigate modern and contemporary philosophies as a complement to their immersion in medieval theology. Noticeably absent from Schillebeeckx's programme of studies in this phase of his life was a detailed initiation into historical-critical analyses of biblical texts. He was a student only 20 years after the Modernist crisis and during the time of what Congar called the 'dreadful satrapism' or despotism of Pius XII, whose pontificate lasted from 1939 until 1958.

De Petter was intimately familiar with twentieth-century phenomenology, a form of philosophy that analyses human experience and the structures of consciousness, and is exemplified in the thought of Edmund Husserl (1859–1938). Under De Petter's tutelage, Schillebeeckx set to work studying philosophers such as Kant, Hegel, Husserl, and Maurice Merleau-Ponty (1908–61). These studies were formative. Schillebeeckx is not accurately described as a Thomistic or neo-scholastic theologian. Thomas Aquinas is indeed a major theological resource for him, but he has always developed his knowledge of Aquinas in dialogue with contemporary patterns of thought.

can god be known?

Like most theologians, Schillebeeckx has long been motivated to make sense of the ancient idea that humans and their divine Creator are able to contact each other. The enigma which each theologian faces is how is a divine-human encounter to be explained rationally in terms that are intelligible and credible to those who cannot see how it is possible for the universal to meet the particular, the atemporal to engage the temporal, the transcendent to be immanent, or the infinite to emerge in the finite? This intellectual conundrum is captured in the simple question, 'Can God be known?' Some would declare yes, because the Bible says so, or because reason can demonstrate there is a God to whom humans can pray. Others would say: 'Prove it.'

In Ghent, Schillebeeckx began to investigate whether human cognition is essentially conceptual, or whether it might include non-conceptual elements (like intuition or emotion). He came to the conclusion, like De Petter, that it is both, but also that human beings apprehend God cognitively mainly because of the non-conceptual factor.[11]

Later in his life, Schillebeeckx changed his way of explaining the nexus of divine-human encounter. By then it was no longer a matter to be understood in terms of the structure of consciousness, but of action. God is known primarily, for the mature Schillebeeckx, in a particular kind of action, called praxis (an activity determined by a theory). After the late 1960s, it is difficult if not impossible to read a book by Schillebeeckx that does not talk about praxis, especially the praxis of siding with debased poor people, and fighting to overcome the forces that render their lives a dreadful dreary misery. Hence the Schillebeeckx of 1990:

> What is at stake here is not simply the ethical consequences of the religious or theologal life; rather, ethical praxis becomes an essential component of a life directed to God, or the 'true knowledge of God': 'He judged the cause of the poor and needy; then it was well. Is not this to know me? Says the Lord' (Jer 22: 16). God is accessible above all in the praxis of justice and love. 'No one has seen God; if we love one another, God abides in us and his love is perfected in us' (1 Jn 4: 12).[12]

Schillebeeckx finished his three-year course in philosophy in 1938. Then (after a period of compulsory military service) he went to study theology in Leuven, a city in the province of Brabant, which has boasted a Catholic university since 1432. Schillebeeckx lived in Leuven's Dominican *Studium Generale* ('general house of studies'). Schillebeeckx's course involved an almost exclusive reading of Thomas Aquinas. The method of his teaching did not examine Thomas' thought (alluring in itself, for Schillebeeckx) with reference to its medieval historical context. Nor did it relate theology and medieval concepts to the experiences of Schillebeeckx's contemporaries. A good while after Schillebeeckx left Leuven, he described his first studies of theology as perfectly 'fruitless and useless' ('vaines et inutiles').[13]

advanced studies and teaching

Schillebeeckx's frustrations with theology were not to last for long. He was sent to France for advanced theological studies. He was based at the Saulchoir d'Etiolles. He arrived there in 1946. He combined his time at the Saulchoir with frequent visits to Paris. There he attended classes at the Université de la Sorbonne, the École des Hautes Études and the Collège de France. His classes in the latter two institutions were devoted to philosophy.

In Paris, where Merleau-Ponty was teaching, Schillebeeckx was able to advance his familiarity with phenomenological philosophy. At the Saulchoir he was taught by Chenu and Congar, and was finally able to investigate theological texts with historical-critical methods.

While De Petter was the dominant intellectual mentor in Schillebeeckx's life in Belgium, the equivalent figure in France was Marie-Dominique Chenu. When Schillebeeckx studied with him, Chenu was actively involved in supporting priest-workers (*prêtres-ouvriers*), in addition to his burden of teaching at the Saulchoir.[14] The priest-worker movement eventually incurred the wrath of the Roman Curia. As mentioned in the last chapter, Chenu and Congar were removed from their professorships at the Saulchoir in 1954. By that time Schillebeeckx was back in Leuven, but when he left Paris in 1947, he took with him an abiding memory of Chenu's ability to bring detailed theological and historical research to bear on the problems vexing the world of the mid-twentieth century. Chenu directed Schillebeeckx's doctoral dissertation at the Saulchoir, which was devoted to a study of sacraments.

teaching as a dogmatic theologian

Schillebeeckx was appointed a professor of theology at the Dominican's General House of Studies in Leuven during 1947. He taught there for a decade, during which his life was hectic. He was appointed to take charge of caring for the overall well-being of Dominican students. He combined that duty with regular visits to the local prison, lecturing and publishing. His lecturing concentrated on five principal areas of theology: theological propaedeutics (an introduction to theology); the theology of creation; sacraments; Christology; and eschatology. He used the research he undertook to prepare his lectures to publish articles on the subjects he was teaching.

Apart from lecturing, Schillebeeckx completed writing the doctoral thesis which he had begun with Chenu in France. It was published in the form of a lengthy book in 1952, and is called in Flemish/Dutch, *De sacramentele heilseconomie* ('The Sacramental Economy of Salvation').[15] It has been translated into French, but not English. It is a detailed study of Aquinas' understanding of sacraments in light of tradition and present-day difficulties regarding the understanding of sacraments. The much shorter book, *Christ the Sacrament of the Encounter with God*, first published in Dutch in 1959, is a digest of some of the sacramental theory outlined in the dissertation.

Schillebeeckx's doctoral dissertation was his first major publication. It deploys a masterly command of patristic and medieval theology, and especially of the thought of Aquinas. He first began to publish in 1945. Between then and 1952 his writings took the form of journal articles devoted to topics such as spirituality, the consideration of religious experiences, sacraments, or the relation between Christianity and the cultures of post-Second World War Europe.

---

sacraments   A sacrament is a concrete religious symbol (as opposed to a conceptual symbol). It is a ritual – a form of behaviour that follows a pre-established pattern of actions that is repeated each time the ritual is performed. Nowadays, sacraments are Christian, whereas a ritual need not be. The term 'sacrament' derives from the Latin, *sacramentum*, an ancient word meaning a 'promise', 'public pledge' or 'oath'. Two of the earliest Christian rituals were baptism, which symbolized a person's initiation into the Church, and the eucharist, a commemoration of Jesus' Last Supper. 'Eucharist' means 'thanksgiving', from the Greek *eucharistein*, 'to give thanks'.

A complex theology of sacraments (sacramentology) developed during the Middle Ages. Peter Lombard (c. 1100–60) enumerated seven primary Christian rituals that have been regarded in the western Catholic theological tradition ever since as seven sacraments: baptism, confirmation, penance, eucharist, marriage, holy orders (ordination to the diaconate [deacon], presbyterate [priest] or episcopate [bishop]) and the anointing of the sick, otherwise known (before Vatican II) as extreme unction, and popularly referred to as the Last Rites.

At this juncture in his life, Schillebeeckx's theological vocabulary was drawn mainly from the Christian dogmatic tradition. It is at ease talking about the Church, sacraments, the rosary, cloistered religious life, Holy Communion, the Mass and Mariology – discourse about the theological significance of Jesus' mother, Mary or Miriam. He published a book in 1955 called *Maria, moeder van der verlossing* ('Mary, Mother of the Redemption'). It is a revised edition of a book he published the previous year as *Maria Christus' mooiste wonderschepping* ('Mary, Christ's Most Beautiful Creation').[16] Such titles could easily be off-putting to Protestants, many of whom in the past have been suspicious that Catholic piety venerates Mary inappropriately, and sentimentalizes her significance repugnantly. This suspicion was not eased during the Second Vatican Council when some bishops militated for the Council to proclaim Mary as Co-Redemptrix, that is, as cooperating with Jesus Christ, and sharing his status, as the redeemer of the world. Vatican II made no such proclamation. Schillebeeckx's second book on Mary, despite its conventional Catholic devotion to her, is clear that Mary is not a redeemer: 'At the level of the Redemption, Mary is Christ's most beautiful creation. She has her own individual and irreplaceable function to fulfil within the plan of salvation, but this in no way adds to Christ's redemptive work.'[17]

Schillebeeckx returned to the question of Mariology almost 40 years later. By then he interpreted Mary on the basis of what the Bible says about her and what can be known historically of her. He regards her as a Jew (not the first Christian), who is a model for Christians today because of her confidence and faith in her son. All contemporary forms of admiration for Mary in Schillebeeckx's later terms stem from the fact that she was Jesus' mother, a point acceptable to Protestants and Catholics alike:

> No sensible person can historically deny the fundamental fact that Mary was the mother of Jesus. That is the historical foundation of everything that can be said critically about Mary in a meaningful way. She is thus the mother of someone who was later confessed by Christians as the liberator, the redeemer, the one who bears the sin of the world, but was done away with by human beings because his disarming love seemed dangerously threatening above all to those who were put in authority.[18]

signs of the times

A great deal had transpired in the world and in Schillebeeckx's life between the publication of his first book on Mary in 1954, and his second (co-authored) study of 1992. One of the greatest lessons Chenu and Congar confirmed in Schillebeeckx was the importance of what they styled as *presence au monde* ('presence to the world'), by which they meant the inescapable necessity of Dominicans and theologians constantly to strive to relate their activities to a world far broader than the Church. Related to this theme was the notion of 'the signs of the times', the cultural and intellectual indicators that major social change is afoot.

In the late 1950s there were two symbolic signs of hope indicating that the second half of the twentieth century was to be very different from what preceded it. The first of these hope-engendering signs of the times was Expo 58, also known as the Universal Exhibition, or the World Trade Fair, held in Brussels from 17 April to 19 October 1958. This exhibition paraded newly available gadgets for a generation regaining economic strength and emotional confidence after the debacle of two world wars. The sight of washing and calculating machines had a mesmeric affect on the millions of visitors to the fair. An age of confident consumerism was gathering pace. The second symbol of hope followed in 1959 – the summoning by John XXIII of a new Council of bishops (Vatican II) to consider seriously the concerns and needs of the age.

the netherlands

By 1958 and 1959, Schillebeeckx was no longer living in Belgium. In 1957 he had gone to live in the Netherlands, in the city of Nijmegen. He began work and a new life there as the Professor of Dogmatic Theology and the History of Theology in the Catholic University of Nijmegen, since renamed Radboud University. Nijmegen is the oldest city in the Netherlands, having been settled by ancient Romans. Its cathedral was consecrated by Albert the Great, the teacher of Thomas Aquinas. It lies on the River Waal in the south-eastern plains of the Netherlands, close to Germany.

When Schillebeeckx first moved there he later remarked that he thought he had returned to the Middle Ages.[19] This was not because the Netherlands was a feudal country, but because the Catholicism he encountered was strict in its practice and resolutely traditional. In the Netherlands, Catholics formed a minority of the population, the obverse of the situation obtained in Belgium, which was overwhelmingly Catholic in its culture. The Netherlands was dominated by Calvinism, and had been for 400 years. Whereas Catholics in Belgium tended to define their religious identity in counterpoise to post-Enlightenment humanism, those in the Netherlands ordered their lives in contradistinction to Calvinism.[20] This situation changed swiftly in the late 1960s and 1970s, as Dutch Catholics and their leaders reconfigured their churches according to the teachings of the Second Vatican Council.[21]

In Nijmegen's university, Schillebeeckx could lecture to both men and women for the first time in his life. In Belgium he had taught Dominican friars. His moving from a Dominican house of studies to a university also opened him to influences from the vast variety of subjects investigated in universities.

vatican ii's dead end

Throughout the first half of the 1960s, Schillebeeckx became intensely involved in the preparations for, and deliberations of, the Second Vatican Council. The Dutch Catholic bishops began preparing for it in 1961. Schillebeeckx remained in Rome for each session of the Council as the personal theologian to Cardinal Alfrink, the Primate of the Dutch Catholic Bishops.

The trouble with Vatican II is that it did not work. It came to a dead end. After 200 years of slighting and fighting modernity, the hierarchy of the Catholic Church at the Second Vatican Council finally acknowledged that the modern world of sophisticated science, democracy and personal freedoms was not intrinsically inimical to Christianity. While the voters at the Council were trying to catch up with cultures that had formed over the previous 300 or so years ('Modernity'), the world they wished to engage proved largely unresponsive. It was a new beast. It now had no need of Christianity, and the majority of its citizens were not Christians. An entirely unexpected result of the reforming Second Vatican Council, whose participants had so ardently sought to make the Church much more of a religious magnet to its contemporaries, was that even its own members left it in droves. Priests and nuns resigned their commitments in tens of thousands, while younger generations proved reluctant to live lives as celibates, repulsed by the very thought, as they socialized in sexually supercharged nightclubs, or simply listened to the Beatles. Coupled with the indifference of later-twentieth-century societies to the preoccupations of the participants at Vatican II was the election in its aftermath of two popes – John Paul II (Karol Wojtyla) and Benedict XVI (Joseph Ratzinger), who proved less than enthusiastic about a collegiate vision of the Church. During the Council, Karol Wojtyla did not distinguish himself with a radically reforming zeal. Subsequently and fatefully, he came to great power in the Church and appointed a soulmate, Joseph Ratzinger, as the Cardinal Prefect of the Vatican's Sacred Congregation for the Doctrine of the Faith (CDF).

Karol Wojtyla was elected Pope in 1978. The following year the CDF began a relentless hounding of theologians who had been enthusiastic for change in the Church. The first to be removed from his teaching post in 1979 was Jacques Pohier, a former Dean of the Saulchoir. When Joseph Ratzinger became Cardinal Prefect he cooperated with the Pope to suppress or police the voices of many other theologians, including Hans Küng, Charles Curran, Uta Ranke-Heinemann, Leonardo Boff, Gustavo Gutiérrez, André Guindon, Paul Collins, Tissa Balasuriya, Jon Sobrino, Jacques Dupuis and Schillebeeckx.[22]

'an almost feverish urge': the quest for a new theological language

After the Council, Schillebeeckx threw himself into actively promoting change in the Church so that it would become less hierarchically conceived and more ecumenical. His experiences of lecturing, travelling around the Netherlands speaking to Church groups, and journeying abroad, convinced him that traditional theological discourses were not making much sense, if any, to his contemporaries.

Schillebeeckx's writings began to reflect his quest to find a new theological language that would be more intelligible to his audiences, who voiced marked dissatisfaction with the terminological categories of dogma.

In the 1960s he continued to publish on sacramental theology with a book on marriage and another called *The Eucharist*.[23] The main body of his writings in the 1960s reveals his attempt to relate theology to society, the Church to the world, and the gospel to people. The very titles of his books in this decade indicate his double interest: first, to formulate a new theological nomenclature; and second, to relate theology to its surrounding cultures. The results of his interest appeared in his books *God and Man* (1965), *World and Church* (1966), *God the Future of Man* (1968) and *The Mission of the Church* (1968).

By the end of Vatican II, Schillebeeckx had never left Europe. Then in 1966 he was invited to give lectures in major universities in North America. His trip to the States shocked him to the core. This was his first visit to a highly secularized culture. When Schillebeeckx landed in America, he arrived in a world of hippy-dom, growing student unrest and pop music. In the USA, Schillebeeckx ran into what he later regarded as a pervasive crisis of faith among Christians. A major component of this convulsion concerned Christology. He records that he was frequently asked during his visits to universities, 'Is Christ really God?' After his time in the USA he spoke of having 'an almost feverish urge' ('een bijna koortsachtige aandrang') to respond to the difficulties he diagnosed contemporary Christians were experiencing in a secularized world.[24] His writings of the late 1960s bristle with references to 'crises' and 'newness'. By 1968 he had developed a novel eschatological concept of God as 'the God who is to come' ('de komende God'), or a God who is humankind's future.[25] In 1967 he asserted that God needs to be spoken of in a way quite different from the manner in which God was discussed in the past.[26] By 1969 he commented that he had the impression that former Christian theology was mummified in ideology.[27]

Schillebeeckx set to work trying to formulate a fresh theological language for his times. He began to lecture on hermeneutics in Nijmegen in 1966. This led him to examine critical theory (a multi-disciplinary philosophy that analyses societies) as exemplified in the works of the German philosophers Max Horkheimer and Jürgen Habermas. Based on a study of hermeneutics and critical theory, he began to talk about God in relation to people with two master-concepts: orthopraxis and negative contrast experiences.

orthopraxis

Since the first Christian centuries, theologians have often seen as one of their primary duties the defence and interpretation of correct teachings – orthodoxy (*ortho*, 'right'; *doxa*, 'doctrine'). In 1966 a new word entered Schillebeeckx's theological terminology – 'orthopraxy', also rendered in English as 'orthopraxis', meaning 'correct action'. In that year, Schillebeeckx criticized Christian believers who are more concerned with ideological orthodoxy than with Christian ortho-praxy, and argued that 'right-doing' is the best guarantee for 'right-thinking'.[28]

From then on, Schillebeeckx's theology was formulated on four bases: hermeneutics, a philosophy of praxis, historical-critical biblical studies and human experience, or more specifically, experiences of suffering that contrast negatively with human flourishing.

jesus the eschatological prophet of praxis

During the late 1960s and early 1970s, Schillebeeckx lectured frequently in Germany, Belgium, and the Netherlands. Everywhere he went, he recalls, people complained to him that they had no idea what the language of Chalcedon could possibly mean for them in their own time and place.

Schillebeeckx was stung into action. For four years he searched frenetically for a new way of talking about Jesus, a way that would be intelligible for people living with different understandings of time, space and causality, from the bishops of fifth-century Chalcedon. After four years of studying biblical critics, he decided that Jesus was, in historical terms, an eschatological prophet who demonstrated in his praxis siding with paupers that he anticipated that God would imminently inaugurate a kingdom of justice as history concluded.

What Schillebeeckx was searching for during these years was a launching from which he could talk about Jesus to any interested party. The foundation he chose on which to construct a new Christology is a particular kind of experience – an experience of suffering. All humans suffer in one way or another. Hence, to speak of Jesus in the context of suffering might well be a way of finding a Christological language that is comprehensible to all people:

> The reality of suffering and threatened humanity is, in my view, the central
> problem for us as we enter the third millennium. People suffer from disease, from
> social injustice, from the evil that they do to one another, and especially in massive
> numbers from the incomprehensible evils of the Holocaust and murderous forms
> of genocide.[29]

From 1974 to 1989, Schillebeeckx worked on a three-volume investigation of the identity and significance of Jesus Christ. The volumes are called, in English, *Jesus*,[30] *Christ*[31] and *Church*.[32] They were originally published in Dutch with very different titles. The English translations actually misconstrue what Schillebeeckx was trying to accomplish with his trilogy, which is to offer a new method for articulating a unique Christology. This method is basically the narration of a story. His trilogy constitutes the lengthiest and most detailed Christology produced in the entire course of the twentieth century (*Jesus*, 767 pp.; *Christ*, 925 pp.; *Church*, 268 pp.). No twentieth-century *theologian* engaged with historical-critical investigations of the Bible as resolutely as Schillebeeckx. The first part of his book, *Jesus*, remains the best current explanation of why critical historical research into the life of Jesus is indispensable for Christology. Without that research, Jesus is all too easily portrayed as a deity in disguise wandering among hapless humans.

The starting point of Schillebeeckx's entire Christological output is the suffering that bedevils the lives of human beings today.[33] He remains adamant that 'the problem of evil, concretised most disturbingly in the suffering of the innocent, is both the primary issue that has preoccupied religions and philosophies of the past and present, and the most urgent challenge faced by Christianity.'[34]

Evil is not a philosophical puzzle for Schillebeeckx. He concludes there is no intellectual solution to the tension between belief in a loving God and the prevalence of suffering among innocent people. In his understanding, the only adequate response to suffering is 'via a practical exercise of resistance to evil, not a theory about it'.[35]

How might people be galvanized practically to resist the evil of suffering? By telling the stories, the dangerous subversive tales of people in the past who, in their lives and work, sought to undermine anyone or anything that inflicted suffering on people. All of which led Schillebeeckx to turn to the life and career of Jesus. Rather than theorize about suffering for his contemporaries, Schillebeeckx opted to give them hope in the midst of suffering by telling the story of Jesus interpreted as the story of God manifest in human history. In short, Schillebeeckx provides his readers with a narrative Christology. His method for interpreting the identity and significance of Jesus is to narrate the experiences of Jesus himself, and the experiences of the first people who become enraptured by him. Hence the title of the first volume of Schillebeeckx's trilogy, *Jezus, het verhaal van een levende* – *Jesus: The Story of the Living One*.

The first instalment of Schillebeeckx's trilogy seeks to discover who Jesus was in historical terms and the processes by which people came to believe in him. The second examines biblical testimonies about him in relation to modern experiences of suffering, while the third discusses God's relation to human beings, the Church and revelation. It also contains a large section on Jesus.

It ought not escape unnoticed that the dogma of Chalcedon says nothing about Jesus' way of living, his sufferings, evolving sense of self-understanding, or his public execution. Instead it talks in ontological terms of *the being* of Jesus. He is truly God and truly a human being united in the person of the pre-existent Logos.

The novelty of Schillebeeckx's book, *Jesus*, is that it does not talk about its subject mainly in metaphysical or formulaic terms. It does not seek to define Jesus with the formula of Chalcedon. Instead, Schillebeeckx argues that the way a person lives is integral to his or her identity. To neglect or ignore the way Jesus spent his life is to ignore who he actually was. Books and sermons on Jesus frequently attempt to pin-point his identity with recourse to dogmatic formulations, or by proclaiming Jesus' death and reported resurrection in isolation from his life. For Schillebeeckx, Jesus was executed because of the way he lived – not because God wanted him to die on a cross. According to Schillebeeckx, it is not possible to glimpse the identity of Jesus without scrutinizing the way in which he lived.

In this Schillebeeckx is entirely correct. A person's behaviour, not words, reveals identity. An individual can talk endlessly about believing in God, the importance of orthodoxy, and the evils of atheists, while treating others as doormats.

the kingdom of god

According to Schillebeeckx, the key term in Jesus' discourse to others was 'the Kingdom of God', which is 'the presence of God among men and women, affirmed or made welcome, active and encouraging, a presence which is made concrete above all in just and peaceful relations among individuals and peoples.'[36] Schillebeeckx's entire late twentieth-century portrait of Jesus conforms entirely with what the first chapter of Mark's Gospel remembers of Jesus' preaching: 'The time is fulfilled, and the kingdom of God has come near; repent, and believe in the good news' (Mk 1: 15).

For Schillebeeckx, it is particularly striking that there was no cleavage in Jesus between what he said about God's kingdom and the way he behaved towards others. He proclaimed that God loved the poor, and he demonstrated that love by his actions: 'Jesus does not defend immoral or anarchic people, he goes and stands next to them.'[37]

Schillebeeckx's narrative Christology was produced by the exhilaration of a discovery. It is the outcome of a dogmatic theologian's awakening to the powerfully subversive story of a prophet proclaiming the impending rule of God in a world of bullies, tyrants and ruthless overlords.

13

Mary Daly: b.1928

Frankly I do not understand why Epicurus prefers to say
that gods are like men, rather than men are like gods.

Cicero

Woman was God's second blunder.

Friedrich Nietzsche

Christianity occasionally repels its own devotees. Some of the Christian theologians of the twentieth century renounced their initiation into traditional forms of Christian life and thought, because they decided that the religion of their youth was a riot of sexist, misogynist patriarchy, and was, as such, morally repugnant, humanly enslaving and intellectually decrepit. The North American philosopher and theologian, Mary Daly, is a case in point. She was raised a Catholic, but eventually ridiculed that tradition. As a young woman at the beginning of the 1960s, she aspired to become a philosopher and theologian. After making enquiries, she discovered that precisely because she was a woman, she was ineligible to prepare for a doctorate in theology in an American Catholic faculty. She trumped her initial frustration by enrolling at the Swiss University of Fribourg. It is a unique educational institution in Switzerland in a threefold way. First, its instruction is entirely bilingual. Lectures are delivered in French and German. Second, its student population in its Faculty of Theology is the most international of any Swiss university. Third, and importantly for the young Mary Daly, as a state university, its degrees are accorded pontifical recognition. Because the university was an organ of the state, it could not refuse to admit a female doctoral candidate. Mary Daly thus began her studies there, in a city of medieval origins. That was not all which was medieval about the place. The professors who directed the two doctorates she eventually earned – in theology and philosophy – instructed her with a primary emphasis on the philosophical mind, and theological method, of Thomas Aquinas. While lectures are now delivered in French and German, when Daly was a student there she was taught in Latin.

Like Karl Rahner, Yves Congar and Edward Schillebeeckx, Mary Daly's life was decisively changed by the Second Vatican Council, but unlike them, her visit to Rome during the Council led her adversely to revise her previous theological and philosophical patterns of thought. Her off-putting experience in Rome, of seeing women excluded from the official debates and voting of the Council, led to her publishing one of the first significant texts of feminist theology in the twentieth century – *The Church and the Second Sex*. Feminist theology is not the same as feminism. The latter found an eloquent voice in Simone de Beauvoir's book, *The Second Sex*, which is fundamentally preoccupied with the denigration of females. Its title obviously served as the main inspiration of Mary Daly's attempt to relate the Church of her upbringing to women of her times.

One of the more prominent features of Christian theology in the second half of the twentieth century was the proliferation of studies devoted to feminism and the status of women in the Church. Feminism is the belief and intellectual conviction that females are humanly equal to males. It also involves the active promotion of that conviction. Feminist theology is a discourse about God that complements a centuries-long tradition of theology articulated mostly by men, by using the experiences of girls and women – peculiar to them – to devise language about God that is neither sexist, androcentric nor patriarchal.

Mary Daly was among a vanguard of Christian theologians developing such a discourse. Her renunciation of traditional forms of Christianity does not detract from the innovative ways in which she exposed the ways orthodox theology can misrepresent God – by relying on patriarchal theological terms – and demean female human beings.

---

feminism

Feminism is a belief that males and females are fundamentally equal in their status as humans. It can involve the exposure of social and econnomic structures that exploit females, and the advocacy of their rights and privileges wherever and whenever they are denied. **Sexism** is the belief that one sex is biologically, intellectually or culturally superior to another, and the practical discrimination against one sex on the basis of that belief. Men and women can both be sexist in their thought and behaviour. Sexism also involves the stereotyping of genders with men ordered above women. It can spark an attempt to overturn the social hegemony of males over females. **Patriarchy** is a system of organizing human societies in such a way that men, normally elderly men, govern younger men, women and children. The word *patriarchy* means 'rule by a father'. A *patriarch* is 'a father who rules'. In ancient Roman law, a *paterfamilias* ('father of the family') ruled everyone and everything belonging to a *familia* ('family'), including enslaved people, land and animals. **Androcentrism** is the belief that the male human being is the paradigm of the human species. Whereas patriarchy is a form of social structuring, androcentrism is a way of thinking. Both men and women can be androcentric in their understanding of humanity. **Misogyny** is the hatred of women. **Gynophobia** is the irrational fear of women.

Mary Daly's life was altered by a distressing experience – her first-hand view of massive institutional patriarchy at the Second Vatican Council. It is not uncommon for pious people who have been brought up in a religious tradition to undergo distraught experiences within in it. The French philosopher, Maurice Merleau-Ponty, speaks of the way a disturbing experience can generate an indignation in people that leads them to become revolutionaries.[1] Great psychological stress can result when people realize that they no longer believe what the authorities of their religious traditions prescribe they must: 'Whether individuals become irrational seems to depend on what they do when they become aware of a conflict between what they themselves believe, or have been told to believe by their religion, and what they know, or suspect they know if they thought rationally and empirically.'[2] Such individuals have at least two options. Either they can harbour doubts privately and continue to give to others the impression they are content with the religion of their upbringing, or they can publicly disavow, challenge or radically revise the tenets of that religion. Mary Daly chose the latter option, well aware that she would be ridiculed as a religious deviant.

The startling transformation of her thought following her forays into feminism can easily by illustrated by quoting from her early and later work. In 1965 she wrote like this: 'The superiority of experiential over theological knowledge of

God is because in the former the mode of knowing itself is supernatural. It operates out of "divine instinct", rather than proceeding from the judgement of reason. It attains God more closely, through a certain union of the soul to Him.'[3] Notice that God is designated reverentially with the capitalized pronoun, 'Him'. Fourteen years later, her style of talking about God was – for some – shockingly different. Commenting on the Christian doctrine that God is a Trinity of divine persons, Father, Son and Spirit, she states:

> This triune god is one act of eternal self-absorption/self-love. The term *person* is derived from the Latin *persona* meaning actor's mask, or character in a play. 'The Procession of Divine Persons' is the most sensational one-act play of the centuries, the original Love Story, performed by the Supreme All Male Cast. Here we have the epitome of male bonding, beyond the 'best,' i.e., worst dreams of Lionel Tiger. It is 'sublime' (and therefore disguised) erotic male homosexual *mythos*, the perfect all-male marriage, the ideal all-male family, the best boys' club, the model monastery, the supreme Men's Association, the mold for all varieties of male monogender mating. To the timid objections voiced by Christian women, the classic answer has been: 'You're included under the Holy Spirit. He's feminine.' The point is, of course, that male made-up femininity has nothing to do with women. Drag queens, whether divine or human, belong to the Men's Association.[4]

Presented with such prose, an easy temptation for her detractors has been to denounce her as a Lesbian Witch. The challenge her radical feminist language offers her readers is for them to discern whether she is making a profound and accurate point with the deliberately crafted jolting words she deploys. One of her interpreters judges that trying to understand Mary Daly is well worth the effort:

> If the creative rage inscribing Daly's work mars the image of serene timelessness connoted by the 'classical,' nonetheless the conceptual density, the linguistic originality, and the sheer prophetic impact of her writing will place her among the great religious authors of Western civilization – truly, from her perspective – a case of dubious honor.[5]

The outrage and indignation animating Daly's writings is the product of, and reaction to, the nemesis of her life – patriarchal religion. As with every other theologian addressed in this book, the way Mary Daly wrote about God, women and the Church since the late 1960s is best understood in view of what happened to her in the historical circumstances in which she lived. She was once more than happy to regard herself as a Catholic. What happened to that allegiance?

a catholic education

Mary Daly was born in 1928, and was therefore a child of the Great Depression. She was born in the town of Schenectady in New York State. She was an only child. Her parents, Frank and Anna, were working-class Catholics. Her grandparents were Irish. Her grandmother, Joanna Favley, left Ireland because of the potato famine, and settled in the state of New York. Mary attended St John the Evangelist School in Schenectady for her primary education before moving to St Joseph's Academy in the same town. St Joseph's was run by the Sisters of St Joseph of Carondelet, one of the manifold religious orders staffing Catholic Schools around the USA.

The Great Depression took its toll on Mary's family. A bank claimed ownership of their house. Her parents had no option but to pay rent to live on the first floor of the home.[6]

Upon leaving High School, Mary enrolled in the College of St Rose in Albany, New York. It was a university exclusively for the education of women. By this stage of her life Mary had decided that she wanted to study philosophy, but it was not possible for her to major in philosophy at the college. So she focused on English instead, well aware that she wanted to be a writer. Equipped with a Bachelor of Arts and a scholarship, she enrolled to study for a Master of Arts in the Catholic University of America in Washington, DC. The terms of her scholarship restricted her to the study of English. Once more she was not able to explore philosophy in depth.

She was awarded an MA. A few months beforehand she was travelling by train from Schenectady to Washington, DC. On the way she passed through New York's Grand Central Station. Pausing at the station, she picked up a liberal Catholic magazine at a news-stand and noticed an advertisement in it mentioning 'A School of Sacred Theology', which was about to begin a doctoral programme of studies for women on religion. Mary applied and was accepted to begin the course, which was based at St Mary's College, Notre Dame, Indiana. Here she was taught by Dominican priest professors who introduced her to the work of Thomas Aquinas. She was enthralled: 'Through studying his work', she said, 'I learned to use my mind in an intellectually systematic way. I now could finally begin to acquire a philosophical *habitus* – a habit of thinking philosophically in a rigorously logical manner. I say *philosophical*, because Aquinas's *Summa Theologiae*, was ninety per cent philosophy. ... So I was studying philosophy, after all, and under excellent conditions.'[7]

It was at St Mary's that Daly developed a fascination for the Trinity, later recalling: 'I was carried away with the theological doctrine of the "Blessed

Trinity" as expounded by Aquinas. In fact I was so happy studying the stuff that I felt something like pity for people who did not understand the theology of "the Trinity".[8]

After Daly successfully completed her doctoral research on religion she decided that she would study for what she called 'the highest of higher degrees in theology', by which she meant a doctorate from a Pontifical Faculty of Sacred Theology. There was only one university in the USA in the 1950s that was licensed to confer such a degree – the Catholic University of America in Washington, DC. Repeatedly and over a long period of time, Daly wrote to the dean of its faculty of theology to lodge an application. Eventually she received a curt rejection, which she remembered by saying:

> I had studied Latin, Greek, Hebrew, as well as German and French. I had more than an equivalent of an M.A. in philosophy, and a Ph.D. in religion, but they could not bring themselves to reply. The crude bigotry of that wretched institution was blatant in this case. The only 'problem' was that I was a woman, and they didn't even have the courage to say that with minimal courtesy.
>
> I was very lucky that they rejected my application, because I had to turn my attention to bigger and better things.[9]

Thinking of 'better things' led her to consider studying in Europe, and more particularly either in Germany or Switzerland, where both Catholic and Protestant theological faculties are fully incorporated into state universities. Neither the German nor Swiss government prevented women from entering these faculties on the basis of sex.

In the second half of 1959, Mary Daly was admitted to the Faculty of Theology in the University of Fribourg. She obtained the degree of a Baccalaureate in Sacred Theology at the end of her first academic year in Fribourg. In 1963 she was awarded a doctorate in theology, her sixth university degree. Her quest for academic recognition did not end there. She began working for a doctorate in philosophy, which she successfully completed in 1965 with a thesis entitled 'Natural Knowledge of God in the Philosophy of Jacques Maritain'.[10]

voices for change

1963 was a turning point in Mary Daly's life. In December of that year the North American magazine, *Commonweal*, published an article by a professor of philosophy at St John's University in New York. The professor was Rosemary Lauer. Her article, 'Women and the Church', argued that women should be regarded as equal to men in the Catholic Church, an argument that stung Mary Daly as she recorded: 'That article was magical in its effect. It awakened in me the power to speak out and to Name women's oppression.'[11]

Spurred on by the initiative of Rosemary Lauer, in 1965, Day published her first two feminist studies, called 'Catholic Women and the Modern Era' and 'A Built-in Bias'.[12] These followed and accompanied books written by Catholic women the previous year. One was penned by Gertrude Heinzelman and called *We are Silent No Longer: Women Express Themselves About the Second Vatican Council*. It argues for church law and university faculties to be changed in favour of women. Another was by Catherina Halkes in the Netherlands, called *Storm after Quiet*. It addresses the place of women in the Church, which in 1964 was far from ideal.[13]

The 1960s was the decade in which feminist theology was born. Theologians in Europe joined voices and published books calling for far-reaching change in the way women are treated in the Catholic and other Christian Churches. Innovative works of this time include Elisabeth Gössmann's *Woman and Her Mission* (1961), Elisabeth Schlüssler Fiorenza's *The Forgotten Partner – Foundations, Facts and Possibilities as to the Professional Participation of Women in the Salvific Work of the Church* (1964), Maria de Leebeeck's *Being Woman: Fate or Choice?* (1967) and Kari Børresen's *Subordination and Equivalence* (1968).

cardinals in red dresses

During Mary Daly's seven years of study in Fribourg, she travelled frequently during holiday times and managed to visit France, Spain, England, the Irish Republic and Italy. No trip was more consequential for her later philosophical and technological development than a visit to Rome during the late stages of the Second Vatican Council in the second half of 1965. After arriving in Rome by train she stayed there for a month. She had not been invited to go, and had no official role to play. That did not prevent her from meeting students, feminists and journalists. 'My visit to Rome', she recalls, 'was packed with intense, multi-colored, multileveled experiences. I saw and heard the pompous cardinals, who seemed like silly old men in red dresses, droning their eternal platitudes. I engaged in intense conversations with catholic thinkers and advocates of social change. We shared an exhilarating sense of hope, an impassioned belief in the possibility of change.'[14]

During the sessions of Vatican II in St Peter's Basilica, the bishops and cardinals present were required to dress formally – bishops with floor-length purple and lace attire, cardinals with red and lace. There could be up to 2,500 men dressed thus during any session of the Council. The scene of so many prelates assembled and formally attired seared itself into Daly's consciousness on a day during which she borrowed a journalist's pass and gained entry to the Basilica to observe a session. A few women were present as observers. They were mostly veiled nuns in long black habits. They were not permitted to speak. Daly recounts her impressions: 'The contrast between the arrogant bearing and the colorful attire of the "princes of the church" and the humble, self-deprecating manner and somber clothing of the very few women was appalling.'[15]

The image of the contrast between the splendidly colourful robes of the prelates and the dark clothing of the women marinated in Mary Daly's mind when she returned to Fribourg. Her imagination in Rome had been sparked as she later recounted a stunning array of visual experiences. One impression in particular spurred her on to write a book about women and the Church. One day during the Council she was just outside St Peter's Basilica when she noticed she was in close proximity to a cardinal. She recounts her image of him as follows:

> ... I suddenly found myself within a few feet of a pathologically weighty cardinal in
> his flaming red attire literally being lifted out of his limousine by two sturdy
> members of the Swiss Guard who apparently had been assigned to get him to the
> council on time. His eminence saw me gaping and gave me a look of pure hate. I
> would never forget those dark beady eyes and that look of utter misogyny. Indeed,
> one could say that this was, in a certain way, a Moment of Inspiration.[16]

the church and the second sex

Indeed it was. When she returned to Fribourg she wrote the first five chapters of her first major book, *The Church and the Second Sex*. She completed and published the book in 1968. She returned to the USA in 1966, and began to teach in Boston at the Jesuit university of Boston College. She admits that she might never have written *The Church and the Second Sex* if there had never been 'one great carnival of an event, the Second Vatican Council of the Roman Catholic Church' and 'the crimson and black of the Roman circus in Saint Peter's basilica'.[17]

Her first book is an analysis of, and theological response to, Simone de Beauvoir's earlier book, *Le deuxième sexe* ('The Second Sex'), which appeared in French in 1949, and was first translated into English in 1953.[18]

Simone de Beauvoir was born in Paris in 1908, and died there in 1986. Among the earliest of feminist thinkers in the twentieth century, she was also a moral, social and existential philosopher. She was educated at the Sorbonne and the École Normale Supérieure. She taught in various schools until dismissed by authorities of the German government in 1943. Thereafter she supported herself by writing and giving lectures. She cooperated with Jean-Paul Sartre in editing the journal, *Les Temps Modernes* ('Modern Times'), which promoted the cause of feminism and left-wing political concerns in France.

Her published works were strongly influenced by Sartre's existential philosophy, and *The Second Sex* is no exception. Existentialism was a broad movement in philosophy during the twentieth century and was most popular in France during the 1960s. Heideggar and Sartre and the early de Beauvoir were among its principal exponents. The primary question it explored was what it might mean for people to exist as human beings embodied in the world. Simone de Beauvoir develops precisely this question in *The Second Sex* with particular reference to the way women have been treated by men in past history, and the ways they have been expected to consider themselves. It is a complex work in two volumes that is based on a wealth of research in the fields of history, psychology, anthropology, biology, philosophy and theology. It is organized around the existentialist category of the Otherness, or the Other – the designation of people as distinct, foreign, apart, alien or subordinate. De Beauvoir argues that men in past history have demoted women socially to the status of non-essential Otherness, while regarding themselves as indispensable to the proper functioning of societies.

De Beauvoir was not a Christian. *The Second Sex* is not particularly concerned with the ways the Church might have designated women as peripheral Others in the past. That was the task Mary Daly set herself in *The Church and the Second Sex*. What de Beauvoir does undertake throughout her text is a 'vigorous criticism of catholic ideology and practice'.[19]

Daly begins her book by explaining five of de Beauvoir's principal themes with regard to Christianity, the first of which is oppression and deception. De Beauvoir asserts that Christianity over time has been an oppressive force in the lives of women. She illustrates this oppression with reference to the Middle Ages: '... the canon law admitted no other matrimonial regime than the dowry scheme, which made woman legally incompetent and powerless. Not only did the masculine occupations remain closed to her, but she was forbidden to make depositions in court, and her testimony was not recognized as having weight.'[20] The oppression which de Beauvoir seeks to illustrate is tied to deception. She alleges that women have been deceived by and distracted from their unjust circumstances by the promise of recompense in an afterlife.[21]

De Beauvoir's second thematic objection to Christianity is that its doctrines convey the notion that women are inferior to men. She regards the religious cult of the Virgin Mother of God as it is found within Catholicism as a symbolic expression of the enslavement of women to men: 'For the first time in human history the mother kneels before her son; she freely accepts her inferiority. This is the supreme masculine victory, consummated in the cult of the Virgin – it is the rehabilitation of woman through the accomplishment of her defeat.'[22]

A third criticism which de Beauvoir makes deals with what she regards as harmful Catholic moral teaching according to which women have inferior natures to men and are especially sinful because they tempt men into sin: 'since woman remains always the Other, it is not held that reciprocally male and female are both flesh; the flesh that is for the Christian the hostile *Other* is precisely woman. In her the Christian finds incarnated the temptations of the world, the flesh and the devil. All the Fathers of the Church insist on the idea that she led Adam into sin.'[23] Fourthly, de Beauvoir charges that the Church, by which she primarily intents the Catholic Church, inculcates feelings of inferiority in women by excluding them from the Church's hierarchy: 'God's representatives on earth: the pope, the bishop (whose ring one kisses), the priest who says Mass, he who preaches, he before whom one kneels in the secrecy of the confessional – all these are men. ... The Catholic religion among others exerts a most confused influence upon the young girl.'[24]

The fifth of de Beauvoir's major topics in her assessment of women in relation to Christianity is surprisingly positive in view of the previous four. She observes that women can transcend or rise above the harmful features of religion, and she points to the Spanish mystic Teresa of Avila (1515–82) as an example of someone who was able to transcend limitations placed on her because of her sex.[25]

Mary Daly's first book-length attempt to redress the subjugation of women in and by the Catholic Church is still reverential to that Church. The root problem which she diagnoses with regard to the denigration of women and antifeminism are faulty conceptualizations of God as 'masculine'.[26]

While Simone de Beauvoir rejected Christianity, Daly at this juncture of her life did not. She ended her book by expressing a hope that the Church would change: 'Men and women, using their best talents, forgetful of self and intent upon the work, will with God's help mount together toward a higher order of consciousness and being, in which the alienating projections will have been defeated and wholeness, psychic integrity achieved.'[27]

preaching at harvard

By 1971, Mary Daly had lost patience with patriarchal religion. This was in the space of three years of having written *The Church and the Second Sex*. In 1971 she accepted an invitation to preach on Sunday in Harvard's Memorial Church. She became the first woman ever to preach there.

Before she rose to preach, two passages were read from the Bible. One included the verse of 1 Sam 15: 23, 'For rebellion is no less a sin than divination', which can also be translated from Hebrew as 'For rebellion is as the sin of witchraft'. Rebellion was precisely what Mary had in mind after preaching. The second passage included the verse of 1 Tim 2: 11–12: 'Let a woman learn in silence with full submission. I permit no woman to teach or to have authority over a man; she is to keep silent.'

When Mary Daly mounted the steps to enter a large pulpit from which to preach, she had formed the intention of inviting her listeners symbolically to abandon Christianity by following her in marching out of the chapel. This is part of what she said and did:

> We cannot really belong to institutional religion as it exists. ...
>
> The women's movement is an exodus community. Its basis is not merely in the promise given to our fathers thousands of years ago. Rather its source is in the unfulfilled promise of our mothers' lives, whose history was never recorded. Its source is in the promise of our sisters whose voices have been robbed from them, and in our own promise, our latent creativity. We can affirm *now* our promise and our exodus as we walk into a future that will be our *own* future.
>
> Sisters – and brothers if there are any here:
>
> Our time has come. We will take our place in the sun. We will leave behind centuries of silence and darkness. Let us affirm our faith in ourselves and our will to transcendence by rising and walking out together.[28]

beyond god the father

Hundreds of people walked out of the church that day with Mary Daly. The rest of her career was dedicated to articulating a radical feminist theology and philosophy. The designation of her as a 'Lesbian Witch' is not as silly as it first sounds. She was awakened to her lesbian identity in 1972, and playfully toyed with the language of 'Be-witching actions' and 'the Witches of Boston' in her later writings.[29] 'WITCH' is also an acronym for radical feminist groups, and in one usage of 1969 in New York stands for 'Women's International Terrorist Conspiracy from Hell'.[30] Daly is not, of course, a witch in a mythical magical sense.

Mary Daly's second book, *Beyond God the Father*, was published in 1975. It develops the problem she diagnosed in the final stages of *The Church and the Second Sex*, which was the misconception of God's identity through a reliance on false images of God. *Beyond God the Father* confronts the problem of the deleterious effects an exclusive reliance on masculine concepts of God can have on people in general, and women in particular.

In the early phases of her book, Daly observes that an image of God as a great patriarch in heaven, who punishes people according to *his* mysterious will, '... has dominated the imagination of millions over thousands of years'.[31] Daly rejects the image of God as a supreme heavenly Father on the basis of an aphorism she coined that has subsequently become one of the more famous one-line observations of feminist theology: '... if God is male then the male is God'.[32]

Beyond God the Father is the last of Daly's publications in which she speaks of God in a way that is easily familiar to Christians. With this text she expunged from her writings the image of God as a divine patriarch, on the grounds that such an image '... castrates women as long as he is allowed to live on in the divine imagination. The process of cutting away the Supreme Phallus can hardly be a merely "rational" affair. The problem is one of transforming the collective imagination so that this distortion of the human aspiration to transcendence loses its credibility.'[33] By the end of her book, language about God, or that which is ultimate, had modulated so as to refer to 'the creative drawing power of the Good Who is self-communicating Be-ing, Who is the Verb from whom, in whom, and with whom all true movements move.'[34]

Daly continued to teach, write and lecture throughout the 1970s, 1980s, and 1990s. The main focus of lecturing at Boston College was feminist ethics. She continued to publish books whose very titles and subtitles reveal her ambition to formulate an ever more radical voice for feminism: *Gyn/Ecology: The Metaethics of Radical Feminism* (1979); *Pure Lust: Elemental Feminist Philosophy* (1984); and *Quintessence ... Realizing the Archaic Future: A Radical Feminist Manifesto* (1998).

Mary Daly's writings after the 1970s became increasingly peppered by neologisms, to such an extent that it can be difficult to divine the meaning of prose such as this: 'When a Seeker Sees, Names, and Acts in accordance with the Cronelogical connections among her Moments/Movements across time, her knowing of the Fourth Dimension is enlivened, and she herSelf becomes more Alive. She is filled with Gynergy and is moved by a Lust to leap forward.'[35]

conclusion

The back cover of Mary Daly's recent book, *Amazon Grace: Re-Calling the Courage to Sin Big*, describes her in these terms: 'This Pirate/Voyager Craftily pursues her own Intellectual Quest and disturbs the peace by lecturing around the United States, Canada, and Europe. She is a Nag-Gnostic philosopher, Positively Revolting Hag, and author who holds doctorates from the University of Fribourg in Switzerland.'[36]

She left Fribourg four decades before her publisher described her playfully as a 'Positively Revolting Hag'. In the years between the time in Fribourg and the first decade of the twenty-first century, she never lost traces of Aristotle's and Aquinas' constant reference to Being. Throughout her career she remained as fascinated by the Trinity as she had been as a doctoral student in Indiana in the late 1950s. She was still writing about it in 1998: 'The paradigm of the trinity is a product of Christian culture, but it is expressive of all patriarchal patterning. Human males are eternally putting on the masks and playing the roles of "Divine Persons".'[37]

Patriarchy, or rather drawing attention to its omnipresence in theology and Christian practice, is one of Mary Daly's significant contributions to the history of theology in the twentieth century.

Yet patriarchy has not only led to the formulation of deceptive images of God as a Sky-Patriarch-Punisher. It has been, and is, also responsible for the relegation of millions of women and girls in the world to struggle to work and stay alive in wretchedly impoverished conditions. In the indexes of the original editions of all of the books by Mary Daly mentioned in this chapter, the word 'poverty' is not to be found. It was left to other feminist women and men in the twentieth century, working and living outside the wealthy world of the West, to talk about God in relation to the dangerously and materially impoverished females of this planet.

I4

Jürgen Moltmann: b.1926

Nil desperandum – Never despair.
Horace

Horrific war not only slaughters bodies. It also kills hope, maims minds, strangles love and stymies faith. That anyone exposed to the excruciatingly traumatic suffering engineered by war can manage to live on in its aftermath is stupefying. Also startling is the case that the very misery endured by individuals embroiled in war can ignite hope, elicit love and produce faith within them. Such was the case with Jürgen Moltmann, who was enlisted in the German army during the Second World War, and suffered horribly as a result. He was on duty in Hamburg in 1943 at an anti-aircraft battery when the Royal Air Force began to bomb the city. As bombs fell one hellish night, Jürgen was standing near a comrade. A bomb landed and exploded too close to them. The comrade's head was torn off from the rest of his body. Jürgen survived. Before then, he had not been a pious or religious boy, but his exposure to violent death at such proximate quarters when his soldier-friend was killed, and subsequent terrifying experiences during the war, fermented in him a religious faith that impelled him to become a theologian. By the end of the twentieth century his name and his theology were known around the world. His theology that attracted international attention in a fractured world is captured in one word – hope. Moltmann is a utopian thinker. His writings are a cleverly crafted corpus animated by hope for a much better world that is not plagued by pandemic suffering.

Moltmann's blown-apart friend was called Gerhard Schopper. The RAF code-name for the attack on Hamburg was 'Operation Gomorrah' – a biblical reference to two ancient cities (Sodom and Gomorrah) deemed to be incorrigibly wicked. The bombing began on 24 July 1943. The tactics of the RAF involved the calculated destruction of densely populated working-class areas in East Hamburg. The practice of killing large numbers of civilians was later condemned unambiguously by the Second Vatican Council as a crime against God and humanity – as mentioned previously in this book. The bombers first dropped explosives, followed by incendiaries devised to set buildings ablaze. The explosives and incendiaries created a firestorm that reached a temperature of around 1000°C. It was so lethal that it killed people below ground who were hiding in air raid shelters. The bombing lasted for nine successive nights. More than 40,000 people, mostly women and children, were killed during Operation Gomorroh. The reason most of the casualties were children and women is that the majority of the able-bodied men of the city had been sent to battle elsewhere.[1]

The night Gerhard Schopper was annihilated, and whose head was never found, Moltmann underwent what Schillebeeckx calls a negative contrast experience – an ordeal of personal suffering that is negative in that it contrasts so starkly with a situation of human happiness, love and joy. The very bleakness of the experience can produce its opposite: a pining and searching not only for release from suffering, but for human fulfilment in joy and hope.

After his friend was killed, Moltmann could have become insane or paralysed by depression. His negative contrast experience created in him just the contrary – a desire for God. Moltmann describes the life-changing consequences of that dark event:

During that night I cried out to God for the first time in my life and put my life in his hands. I was as if dead, and ever after received life every day as a new gift. My question was not, 'Why does God allow this to happen?' but, 'My God, where are you?' And there was the other question, the answer to which I am still looking for today: Why am I alive and not dead, too, like the friend on my side? I felt the guilt of survival and searched for the meaning of continued life. I knew that there had to be some reason why I was still alive. During that night I became a seeker after God.[2]

It ought not pass notice that Moltmann refers to himself having become 'a seeker after God'. His theology that stemmed from that night has always been since a series of questions, invitations to discussion, soundings and probings, rather than unilateral dogmatic pronouncements that are untroubled by uncertainties.

Jürgen Moltmann is before all else a theologian of hope. The source of his hope is a conviction that Christian faith is eschatological – it is directed in hope to the promise that God will bring human history to a blissful conclusion at an end of human history. In October 1964 he published a book to that effect called *Theologie der Hoffnung*. It appeared in English in 1967 as *Theology of Hope: On the Ground and the Implications of a Christian Eschatology*.[3] *Theology of Hope* was Moltmann's first major work in exploring the eschatological dimensions of Christianity. It quickly drew him into an international limelight and was translated into many languages.

To understand more of Moltmann's theology requires an attention to his biography, for, as he himself recognizes, 'the biographical dimension is an essential dimension of theological insight'.[4] He, like any other theologian of the twentieth century, writes and speaks the way he does because of what transpired in his life.

moltmann's origins

Jürgen Moltmann was born in Hamburg on 8 April 1926. His father was a teacher there and had married Jürgen's mother in 1923. She came from Schwerin. Jürgen was one of four children. He had an older brother, Hartwig, and two younger siblings: a brother, Eckhart, and sister, Elisabeth. Hartwig was stuck down by meningitis the day after he was born. He died of pneumonia in 1940.

In the late 1920s, Jürgen's parents grew tired of metropolitan life and moved to settle in the country. They were in search of a simpler, less encumbered life. So they joined a commune of like-minded people in the countryside at Wulfsdorferweg. The commune consisted of a small group of houses with gardens that shared a communal playground, hall, poultry farm, water supply and cesspit.

Jürgen's parents moved there in 1929 and built a family house, known as 'Im Berge 4'. Their relatives thought they were mad and would not support them.

Jürgen's childhood was somewhat wild. He regularly played with a group of boys close to his own age, at least four of whom bore the name Jürgen. Of this group he later said: 'We were country boys, and accordingly unkempt.'[5] Jürgen's childhood among the boys and girls of the commune was not especially happy. All the children were required regularly to work in gardens and to cultivate vegetables. They attended a local primary school. Jürgen did not relate well with his teachers and at this stage in his life, as might be expected, he was unsure as to what he wanted to do. His father was enlisted in the German army in 1939, after which Jürgen had to assume many more responsibilities in the home.

His life at home was not markedly religious. While his father was still at home the family attended a church service once a year in the school hall. The service they attended was Lutheran and conducted on Christmas Eve. In 1948, Jürgen became disgruntled with the Lutheran Church and left it to join a Reformed congregation. Of his youth he later commented: 'During my youth, religion and the church remained completely alien, and I would never have dreamt that I would find my calling there.'[6]

soldier and prisoner of war

When he was 14 he joined the mounted section of the Hitler Youth, which was more interested in horses than in Hitler. In February 1943 his school class was conscripted into the army. The boys were stationed in Schwanenwieck with the Alster anti-aircraft battery, which was positioned on stilts in Hamburg's lake. Five months later, Operation Gomorrah began. After it ended, Jürgen spent the rest of 1943 and all of 1944 moving between Germany, the Netherlands and Belgium, with occasional close encounters with enemy soldiers. He suffered the normal depredations of soldiers. He was often cold and hungry. He contracted lice, and frequently had to sleep in trenches, dugouts and ditches.

In February 1945 he was captured by British soldiers and interned as a prisoner of war in a Belgian camp. His nights in the camp were marred by mental and spiritual torment as he was locked in dark huts with 200 other men. As a boy he had wanted to study mathematics, but that ambition was now lost to him. As he remarked:

What was the point of it all? Then there were those sleepless nights when the tormenting memories rose up, and I woke up soaked in sweat – when the faces of the dead appeared and looked at me with their sequenced eyes. It was a long time before

I found a degree of healing for these memories. In those nights one was alone and,
like Jacob at the Brook Jabbok, exposed to the sinister powers and destructive forces
of darkness.[7]

The war ended on 8 May 1945. Moltmann was sent to Scotland as a prisoner, and
was housed in Camp 22 in Kilmarnock on the Ayrshire coast of Scotland. The
prisoners were not subject to criticism or reproaches by the local people, but
were treated kindly and humanely. In September 1945 the prisoners were shown
pictures of the Belsen and Buchenwald concentration camps, revealing the
horrors of the Nazi regime.

Then came a turning point in Moltmann's life. One day an army chaplain visited the camp and distributed Bibles. Moltmann began to read his copy and came
across a text in Mark's Gospel which recounts a cry from Jesus when he was crucified on a Roman cross: 'My God, why have you forsaken me?' This text set
Moltmann thinking about the forsakenness and abandonment of Jesus in his final
hour, and felt that in Jesus he had encountered a fellow-sufferer, an understanding
companion in his own suffering. By his own account this experience never left
him:

This early companionship with Jesus, the brother in suffering and the companion on
the road to the land of freedom, has never left me since, and I became more and
more assured of it. I have never decided for Christ once and for all, as is often
demanded of us. I have decided again and again in specific terms for the discipleship
of Christ when situations were serious and it was necessary. But right down to the
present day, after almost 60 years, I am certain that then in 1945, and there, in the
Scottish prisoner of war camp, in the dark pit of my soul, Jesus sought me and
found me.[8]

Moltmann's life as a Christian seeking God had begun. Still a prisoner, he was
transferred to England to Camp 174 in Cuckney, which is near Mansfield in
Nottinghamshire. The camp was normally known as Norton Camp, and was situated in parkland belonging to the Duke of Portland.[9] An extraordinary feature of
the camp was that it conducted a school of theology. Distinguished scholars visited the camp to conduct classes. In this setting, Moltmann began an intense
study of Hebrew, Christian ethics, Church history, biblical studies, systematic
theology and twentieth-century literature. The studies were so engaging that
Moltmann could later say: 'I have never again lived so intensive an intellectual
life as I did in Norton Camp.' Moltmann made this remark after retiring from a
long career as a professor of theology in diverse German universities.

university studies in theology

He was set free and sent home in April of 1948. He was discharged from military service on 19 April. His five years as a soldier, living in camps, dugouts, bunkers and barracks determined the course of the rest of his life. At Norton Camp he had decided to become a theologian.

Back in Hamburg he began to study theology more, but soon moved to Göttingen, where he enrolled in its university. There he studied the Book of Genesis with Gerhard von Rad, the Synoptic Gospels with Günter Bornkamm, and Luther's early writings in Latin with Hans Joachim Iwand. Göttingen's theological faculty at this stage included eminent figures in their fields. Apart from those already mentioned it could also boast the biblical critic, Joachim Jeremias, who became famous for his study of Jesus' parables, and the theologian Friedrich Gogarten. With Iwand, Moltmann studied Luther's Heidelberg Disputation of 1518, and was taken by Luther's reflections on the cross (that is, the cross on which Jesus hung). Moltmann's ruminations over Luther resulted in the publication of his second major theological study in 1972 – *The Crucified God*.

During 1949, Moltmann travelled to Copenhagen with other students from Göttingen for discussions with Danish students. One of the German students in his group was Elisabeth Wendel. In her he found the love of his life. Back in Göttingen, Elisabeth was a doctoral student of the theologian Otto Weber. Moltmann joined Weber's stable of doctoral students, and began preparing a thesis on Moyse Amyrut, a seventeenth-century Calvinist theologian. Elisabeth passed her doctoral examinations in 1951. Moltmann passed his in 1952, though not without a hiccup. During an oral examination, Professor Zimmerli asked him what the fifth commandment was. Moltmann was unable to give the correct answer.[10]

He and Elisabeth married in Basle on 17 March 1952. As a new Doctor of Theology, he did not have a home among German Protestant Churches. So he aligned himself with Elisabeth in the United Church of Prussia. The two moved to West Berlin. Moltmann began to train as a pastor in the Hubertus Hospital in Schlactensee. Thereafter, the Westphalian Church accepted him to train as a curate at Erndterbrück in the area of Wittgenstein (a region, as distinct from the philosopher of the same name). In 1953 he was admitted to the Reformed Preachers' Seminary in Wuppertal-Elberfeld. Late in the same year he became a village pastor in Bremen-Wasserhorst.

One of Moltmann's biographers has noted that once Moltmann finished being a prisoner of war, he did not align himself with the Lutheran Church, 'but all his life stood apart from the established church groups in Germany'.[11] This may well be so in the sense that Moltmann was always at ease during his career associating with Christians of all allegiances. Even so, in 1954 he was ordained a minister by the Reformed Regional superintendent of the Bremen Protestant Church.[12] Thereafter, Moltmann has been a Reformed theologian of the Reformed Church with lively links to many other Churches.

His life was still not free of grief. The first child of Elisabeth and Jürgen died at birth. Their daughter, Susanne, was born the following year. Late in 1956 another daughter, Anne-Ruth, was born.

Moltmann passed his post-doctoral thesis (*Habilitation*) in Göttingen on 27 February 1957, and was thereby qualified to teach in a German institution of higher learning. In January of the following year he accepted an invitation to begin teaching in the Kirchliche Hochschule (Church Seminary) in Wuppertal. During his first two semesters he began to concentrate on the architectonic theme of his career, which is hope. His lecture course in those semesters was called 'The History of Hope for the Kingdom of God'. He later began to lecture on 'A Comparison between the Theology of the Reformers (Luther – Zwingli – Calvin)'. During 1963–4 he focused more on formulating a theology of hope.

ernst bloch

In addition to lectures, Moltmann also conducted classes for discussion. From 1959 his classes attended to Bonhoeffer's theology, and philosophies associated with Feuerbach, Marx and Ernst Bloch – a thinker who was to become an incalculably significant influence in his life.

Bloch was a German philosopher born in Lugwigshafen in 1885. He died in Stuttgart. He was a Marxist thinker, but did not follow Marx slavishly. He was educated in psychology, philosophy, physics and music in the universities of Munich, Wurzburg and Berlin. He lived in Switzerland during the First World War, before returning to Leipzig where he worked during the 1920s as a freelance writer. He left Germany for the USA once the Nazis came to power. He returned to Leipzig in 1955 and began to teach philosophy. He defected to the West from the German Democratic Republic in 1961 and began a professorial career in Tübingen.[13]

The work by which Bloch is most known, and which exerted a profound influence on Moltmann, is his three-volume *Das Prinzip Hoffnung* ('The Principle of Hope'). It was published in Germany in 1959, but it was not until 1986 that it was translated into English. Bloch was a utopian thinker. He understood religion as the expression of hope for a better future, and human beings as individuals who dream for a more ideal existence. The governing leitmotif of his entire philosophy is captured by the notion of a dream, of which he speaks when begining one of his essays: 'With this do we wish to begin, namely with the simple affirmation that it is not only at night do we dream.'[14]

The first part of the first volume of *The Principle of Hope* is called 'Little Daydreams', and underscores the significance of dreams for Bloch:

> When someone dreams, they never remain rooted to the spot. They move almost at will away from the place or the state in which they find themselves. Around the thirteenth year, a fellow-travelling ego is discovered. That is the reason why dreams of a better life grow so luxuriantly around this time. They stir the fermenting day, fly beyond school and home, take with them what is good for and dear to us. ...
> Girls play around with their first name, just like they do with their hairstyles, they make it more piquant than it is, and in doing so they reach the beginning of a dreamed existence that is different. Young boys aspire to a nobler life than their father might lead, to tremendous deeds. They try their luck, it tastes forbidden and makes everything new.[15]

Dreaming about a better life, aspiring for a happier existence and hoping for a future realization are all aspects of a utopian craving. Bloch took the theme of a utopia from Thomas More's book, *Utopia* (1516). In ancient Rome, the term *topia* stood for gardens and stories about them. A *topia* is a pleasant place. Thomas More (1478–1535) used the word 'u-topia' (*ou* plus *topos*) both to designate the current non-existence (*ou*) of an imaginary ideal place, and the where or elsewhere of such places. A utopia, like a garden, is an open, ideal space, in which it would be nice to be.[16]

Bloch was born into a Jewish family. He is unique among twentieth-century philosophers in his ability to quote copiously from the Bible. He regarded the Bible as a markedly utopian collection of writings.[17] The Tanakh, for instance, speaks of an Exodus: with God's help, the enslaved Hebrews escaped from Egyptian tutelage and sought a Promised Land. In the latter parts of the Bible, Jesus speaks apocalyptically of a Kingdom of God that is at hand.

Karl Marx had another kind of pleasant kingdom in mind. He referred to religion as opium, implying narcosis, a blissful escape from reality. Bloch creatively interprets Marx's maxim that religion is the people's opium as an acknowledgement that religion can refer to hopes or aspirations beyond itself.[18]

theology of hope

In May 1961, Bloch was invited to speak in Wuppertal to a group of like-minded friends, with Moltmann among them. This was Moltmann's first meeting with Bloch; the two and their wives dined together after Bloch had spoken to the group which had invited him. The year before this meeting Moltmann had read Bloch's *The Principle of Hope*. Moltmann was impressed by the way Bloch highlighted eschatological thought in the Bible, and began to formulate a Christian eschatology which he called, as mentioned above, *Theologie Hoffnung* ('Theology of Hope').[19]

Moltmann's *Theology of Hope* interprets Christianity as an eschatological religion, that is, as a hope for a better future. He announces the book's principal theme in its opening pages:

> From first to last, and not merely in the epilogue, Christianity is eschatology, is
> hope, forward looking and forward moving, and therefore also revolutionizing and
> transforming the present. The eschatological is not only one element *of* Christianity,
> but it is the medium of Christian faith as such, the key in which everything in it is
> set, the glow that suffuses everything here in the dawn of an expected new day.[20]

The heart of Moltmann's book is its third chapter, which deals with Christian belief in Jesus' resurrection. 'Christianity', says Moltmann, 'stands or falls with the reality of the raising of Jesus from the dead by God'.[21]

Moltmann bases his theology of hope on belief in the resurrection to affirm that 'the raising of the crucified Christ means that he has a future towards which faith in the risen Christ must be directed … '.[22] In Moltmann's terms, because Jesus Christ has a future, people living today have a basis to hope for a similar future: all statements and judgements about Jesus 'must at once imply something about the future which is expected from him'.[23]

Moltmann's assertion that Christian faith stands or falls with the reality of the resurrection could be challenged. People followed Jesus, and believed in him, well before he died. Quite apart from a resurrection, it is possible to be intrigued by him, to believe in him, and to emulate him, because of the way he lived and what he said.

resurrection of jesus   Christians and Muslims believe that Jesus' death on a cross was not the end of his life. They accept the testimony of the Bible that three days after his death God raised him to a new form of existence (see the Acts of the Apostles: 2: 22–4; 3: 15; and 4: 10). The Bible observes that Jesus did not rise himself from death, but *was raised* by God (Gal 1: 1). The resurrection is understood as God's reaction to what human beings did to Jesus in killing him.

The word 'resurrection' is one of a cluster of terms used in the Bible to address the issue of what happened to Jesus after his death. Other terms are 'exaltation', 'glorification' and 'ascension'. There is no historical witness for the resurrection. Nowhere in the Bible is it stated that anyone saw such an event. There are two types of biblical stories that talk about events *after* the resurrection. One type narrates how Jesus' tomb was found empty after his body had been laid there. The second form tells of Jesus appearing to former disciples after his death.

'Resurrection' is an eschatological concept: it does not designate the resuscitation of a cadaver, as in the story of Jesus bringing his friend Lazarus back to life (Jn 11: 43–4), or the raising of the daughter of Jairus (Mk 5: 41–2). It assumes that God transformed Jesus' body into a new mode of existence, which humans are unable to understand because they have no experience of such existence. They live with the hope that they too will eventually be transformed from death by God into an unimaginably wonderful new form of bodily and thoughtful life after their demise in this world.

In the twentieth century the biblical critic Rudolf Bultmann interpreted faith in Jesus' resurrection to be an affirmation that Jesus' spirit survives in the memories of those who believe in him.

political theology

The 1960s were an eventful time for Moltmann. In 1963 he left Wuppertal with his family and moved to Bonn, where he began work in the city's university as a professor for systematic and social ethics. Between 1965 and 1967 he participated in conferences devoted to encouraging intellectual dialogue among the Christian and Marxist professors who attended. The conferences were held in Austria, Czechoslovakia and Germany. In 1967, Moltmann accepted an invitation to become the Professor of Systematic Theology in the Protestant theology faculty of Tübingen's Eberhardt-Karls University.[24] In Tübingen, Moltmann began to develop a political theology in close association with the Catholic theologian Johann-Baptist Metz, who was then a professor of fundamental theology in Münster.

A political theology is not a rival to a political party. Much less does it seek to control the state. It is a way of talking about God that relates concepts of God and the Church to the ways societies operate, especially if they function to exploit the poor. A political theology is concerned for the welfare of the people (*polis*). It does not regard religion as a bourgeois, private affair. The stimulus for Metz and Moltmann to formulate a political theology was shock: an appalling silence reigned among many Christian churches and theologians at this stage with regard to the murder of Jews in concentration camps under the Nazis.[25]

Moltmann was not in Tübingen for long before he interrupted his work to undertake a trip to the USA. Between 1967 and 1968 he went to live in Durham, North Carolina. There he noticed that 'white and blacks' (his terms) were segregated into different districts of the city.[26] From Durham, he was able to visit cities such as New York, Atlanta, Santa Barbara and Chicago to deliver lectures.

By 1968, the American public had become deeply troubled by the Vietnam War. Aware of social unrest and protests, Moltmann also noticed other worrying aspects of life in the States, especially racism and poverty. 'The racism' he observes, 'under which the blacks chafe, and the capitalism under which the poor and the people "who haven't made it" suffer, belong together to this downside of America.'[27]

the crucified god

Moltmann returned to Tübingen in 1968, where the university was gripped by student unrest. He continued to lecture at home and abroad, but his mind remained troubled by the problem that had so vexed him as a soldier – the apparent godforsakenness of the world's social, political and economic victims. His *Theology of Hope* has as its pivot the resurrection of the forsaken and executed Jesus, and the hope which that resurrection might instil in poor, imprisoned, undernourished people today. The theme of hope for the poor is continued in Moltmann's reflections on suffering, which were published in German in 1972 as *Der gekreuzigte Gott*. Two years later they were translated into English as *The Crucified God*.[28]

This book is one of the most discussed tracts in the history of twentieth century theology. Its central thesis is that God suffers in response to human suffering – an assertion that starkly contrasts with a centuries-long theological tradition which insists that God is impassible – incapable of suffering. In this tradition, creatures suffer, but their creator does not.

Since the patristic age, theologians have attempted to relate God to humanity with a theory that Jesus Christ has two natures – one divine, the other human.

According to this theory, on the cross Jesus suffered in his human nature, but not in his divine nature. The theory thereby upheld a doctrine of divine impassibility.

In the twentieth century, many Catholic and Protestant theologians began to experiment with Christologies known as kenotic theories – from the Greek term, *kenosis*, which means 'emptying' or 'humbling'. These theologians included Karl Rahner, Hans Küng, Hans Urs von Balthasar, Karl Barth, Eberhard Jüngel and Moltmann. Each in their own way drew attention in their Christologies to the biblical text of The Letter of Paul to the Philippians, Chapter 2.[29] This text addresses the theme of Jesus' self-emptying on the cross:

> Let the same mind be in you that was in Christ Jesus, who, though he was in the
> form of God, did not regard equality with God as something to be exploited, but
> emptied himself, taking the form of a slave, being born in human likeness. And
> being found in human form, he humbled himself and became obedient to the point
> of death – even death on a cross (Phil 2: 5–8).

If a Christology becomes kenotic, it is difficult if not impossible to maintain a classical two-nature interpretation of Jesus. For the latter, Jesus suffers in his humanity on the cross, but appears to be utterly abandoned by God who in no way suffers through such an event.

Moltmann is well aware that traditional Christian theology has for many centuries taught that God is impassible. Moltmann transforms this doctrine to conclude that although God does not suffer as creatures do, God suffers in response to the suffering of creatures. Yet if God as manifested in the divine nature of Jesus humbled Godself unto death on a cross, God entered into the dereliction of the human Jesus on the cross.

Attempting to relate a classical two-nature interpretation of Jesus with a kenotic one is the pivotal theological dilemma which Moltmann addresses in the *The Crucified God*. He concludes that traditional Christology, which is based on a theory of two natures, 'came very near to docetism, according to which Jesus only appeared to suffer and only appeared to die abandoned by God: this did not happen in reality.'[30]

Moltmann is thus confronted by a paradox: 'How can the almighty God be in a helpless man? How can the righteous God be in a man who has been condemned in accordance with the law? How can God himself be in one who has been forsaken by God?'[31] Moltmann resolves this paradox by concluding that God suffers:

> The Son of God is not first at work in his exaltation and glory, but in his
> humiliation and lowliness. The 'Son of God' is here the representative and revealer

of God in a godless and godforsaken world. That means that God represents and reveals himself in the surrender of Jesus and in his passion and death on the cross. But where God represents and reveals himself, he also identifies and defines himself. Therefore Paul can say: 'God (himself) was in Christ' (2 Cor 5: 19). **Logically this means that God (himself) suffered in Jesus, God himself died in Jesus for us.**[32]

Having arrived at the conclusion that God suffered in the crucifixion, Moltmann proceeds to develop his conclusion in the context of a Trinitarian theology of the cross: God is Father, Son (Jesus) and Spirit. In the event of the crucifixion the Son 'suffers dying', while the Father 'suffers the death of the Son'. The Son thereby becomes Fatherless and the Father Sonless, and 'if God has constituted himself as the Father of Jesus Christ, then he also suffers the death of his Fatherhood in the death of the Son.'[33] From this event between Father and Son flows the Spirit who fills forsaken people with love.[34]

Such language has the potential to baffle and repel anyone thinking about Jesus' death. His crucifixion was, first and foremost, an execution by torture: a cruel and harrowing ordeal. Moltmann is aware of this, and so uses his theology of the cross to advance a political theology: the authority of God, in his terms, is no longer represented in the world after the crucifixion 'by those in high positions, the powerful and the rich, but by the outcast Son of Man who died between two wretches.' From this observation, Moltmann draws the conclusion that the consequence for Christian theology 'is that it must adopt a critical attitude towards political religions in society and in the churches. The political theology of the cross must liberate the state from the political service of idols, and must liberate men from political alienation and loss of rights.'[35]

At the outset of the *Crucified God*, Moltmann speaks of inquiring into 'the revolution needed in the concept of God'.[36] He clothed such a revolution in the language of suffering – of God and human victims.

a european theology of liberation

With the *Theology of Hope* and *The Crucified God*, the rudiments of Moltmann's theology were set in place. He has never abandoned the cardinal themes and conclusions of these two books. He continued to develop these themes during the 1970s, 1980s and 1990s in a series of books. Cumulatively, these works constitute Moltmann's most significant contribution to the twentieth-century, which is the development of a European theology of liberation, that is: (1) a theology addressed to the European context in which Moltmann has lived and worked; and

(2) a way of talking about God that seeks to liberate people in that setting from all that subjugates them.

The lineaments of this kind of theology were evident in the next major book he wrote after *The Crucified God*. It was called *The Church in the Power of the Spirit* (1997). It is an ecclesiology couched in terms of a liberation theology.

conclusion

Having returned to Tübingen in 1968, Moltmann remained there for the rest of his academic career. He retired from professorial duties in 1994. His search for God began with the sight of his friend's head being blown off during a bombardment. It reached a climax in the notion that God suffered like Moltmann's friend, in the crucifixion of Jesus. Whether such an idea is risible or reasonable remains a matter of deepest dispute.

15

Gordon Kaufman: b.1925

Nature, and Nature's laws lay hid in night.
God said, *Let Newton be!* and all was light.

Alexander Pope

The twentieth century was a time of ceaseless scientific discovery. In theory and practice, scientists around the globe accumulated a vast reservoir of new information about the universe and entities within it. More is now known about the constitution of reality at micro-, meso- and macroscopic levels than in any previous age. Humans today find themselves on a little planet in a cosmos of about 100,000 million galaxies. In each of these are roughly 100,000 million stars. The universe (all there is) has a history. It began as many as 13.7 billion years ago. Planet Earth is younger, having been formed around 4.5 billion years in the past. No one living before the twentieth century knew that the universe is so vast, and that it is expanding. All theologies penned before the last century assume the existence of a smaller, more static cosmos, with humans occupying an important place within it. Theologians throughout the twentieth century encountered a daunting conundrum as scientifically informed views about the world changed extensively, rapidly and breathtakingly. Some ignored new science. Others decided it was irrelevant to theology, which only needs faithfully to repeat traditional concepts and rehearse biblical passages. Gordon Kaufman followed a different path. He is a theologian who was born at the end of the first quarter of the twentieth century, and lived throughout the rest of the century. His theology came to be dominated by an overarching problem – the problem of God, that is, the questionableness of all talking and thinking about God in the light of new scientifically generated knowledge. For Kaufman, the concept of God needs to be radically reconceived and reconstructed, while methods for talking about God that are based on the notion of divine revelation are no longer intellectually viable.

The now-known puny position of humans in the universe is overwhelmingly humbling for them – or ought to be! Their world is in flux as a dynamic and evolutionary process. It is also frightening, violent and riddled with death. Even stars die. While there is much that humans know about their cosmos, there is a great deal too that baffles, unnerves and distresses them. Naturally they wonder and hope whether there is any purpose to their existence. Are they aimlessly adrift in a universe devoid of sanity and symmetry? Are they the soulless by-products of the interaction of atoms, or the creatures of God? Are they governed by genes or directed by God? If they have any ground for relating themselves to God, and hope for a divinely guided destiny, how is God best thought of and talked about by them? To address this last question, Gordon Kaufman has dedicated his entire career as a theologian.

a century of discovery

Kaufman is a North American professorial theologian who spent the longest stage of his academic career teaching and writing in Harvard's Divinity School. To appreciate more of why he has been so impelled to formulate a new theological language, it is only necessary to consider a little more the dazzling array of scientific discoveries and inventions throughout the twentieth century that were hitherto obscured from humankind.

The twentieth century began with most of its Western inhabitants thinking that the atom is the smallest constitutive and indivisible part of reality. Such a view was not to last long. In 1900, Max Planck began to articulate a quantum theory of mechanics, which envisaged particles smaller than an atom. From 1897–99, Joseph Thomson isolated the electron. The ultraviolet lamp was invented in 1904 as the photo-electric cell was devised. In 1905, Albert Einstein's special theory of relativity united space and time in one mathematical description, dealing with the dynamical relations between objects moving at constant speeds in straight lines. In 1919, Ernest Rutherford identified the proton. In 1923, Niels Bohr developed a theory of atomic structure and Louis de Boglie conceived of the idea of a particle-wave duality. Carl David Armstrong discovered positive electrons in 1932.

During the 1920s, Edwin Hubble showed the Milky Way is just one of several galaxies and that galaxies are moving away from each other as the universe expands. Pluto was found in 1930. By the end of the twentieth century, Fermat's last theorem had been solved, pulsars and brown dwarfs discovered, and the Hubble Space Telescope launched.[1]

a pacifist's upbringing

The USA was home to many of the world-transforming discoveries of the twentieth century, and most of its inhabitants were able to enjoy the benefits of technologies devised on the basis of new science. The continent of North America is now criss-crossed by jet lanes for rapid national and international flights. It is also the launching pad for rockets to explore outer space, and for satellites to manage information around the globe and to spy on enemies. It houses gigantic telescopes to explore stellar atmospheres.

Gordon Dester Kaufman was born and grew to maturity on this capacious continent. He was born in 1925 in Kansas, and raised in a Mennonite family.

Gordon grew up in a Mennonite home community that was part of the tradition of the General Conference of the Mennonite Church. He lived with his parents on the campus of Bethel College in Kansas. The College is a Mennonite institution, and Gordon's father was its president for many years. As a Mennonite, one of Gordon's lifelong convictions was that relations between human beings should always be loving in character, even towards those regarded as enemies. His parents emphasized the importance of Jesus' commands as they are recorded in Matthew's Gospel:

> But I say to you, Do not resist an evildoer. But if anyone strikes you on the right
> cheek, turn the other also; and if anyone wants to sue you and take your coat, give
> your cloak as well; and if anyone forces you to go one mile, go also the second mile.
> Give to everyone who begs from you, and do not refuse anyone who wants to borrow
> from you (Matthew 5: 39–42).

---

mennonites and anabaptists   Two of the more religiously radical
Protestant groups that appeared during the course of the sixteenth-century
Reformation were the Anabaptists and Mennonites. Anabaptists were distinctive
among their contemporaries in refusing to recognize the validity of infant baptism. If
they had been baptized as infants, they would undergo baptism once more as adults,
hence the name of 'Anabaptists' or 'Rebaptizers'. They grouped principally in
Switzerland, the Netherlands and Germany. They were critical of Martin Luther and
Ulrich Zwingli for not seeking a sufficiently radical reform of the Church. They
insisted that the Church and State ought to be kept separate. Mennonites are
offshoots of Swiss Anabaptism. They derive their name from the Dutch religious
reformer Menno Simons (1496–1561). He was a Catholic priest in Dutch Friesland
before joining the Anabaptists. His own followers, Mennonites, became an influential
religious community in the Netherlands in the seventeenth and eighteenth centuries.
Mennonites were established in North America in 1683. There they now form 12
different, though related, traditions. In the past, Mennonites internationally tended
to be more organized than Anabaptists. One of the more distinctive features of
Mennonite religiosity is resistance to violence in human affairs. Menno Simons
refused to takes oaths, accept public office or undertake military service. He was more
strictly pacifist than Anabaptists and more willing to cooperate with civic leaders.

Mennonites very seriously tried to conform their lives to these instructions,
which were certainly emphasized in the Kaufman home. Gordon found them
particularly well exemplified in the way his mother behaved at home and among
others.[2] He needed the example of his parents when he was a teenager during the
1940s. At his local high school in Newton, Kansas, patriotic fervour was intensify-
ing as the USA prepared for, and eventually entered, the Second World War.

Four months after Gordon turned 18, in October 1943, he was drafted. Because
of his Mennonite convictions he was a conscientious objector throughout the war.
That he was thus, signals that he was capable of articulating quite different
thoughts about God and Christianity, while standing apart from bishops who
bless battleships, chaplains who wear warriors' uniforms and priests who accept
military ranks. As an objector he was dispatched to Civilian Public Service Camp
Number 5 in Colorado Springs. From there he was sent to the State Mental
Hospital in Ypsilanti in the state of Michigan. Then he was moved to Gulfport in
Mississippi.

He spent a year in Colorado Springs. While there, and unusually for his age as
an 18-year-old, he read for the first time Immanuel Kant's *Critique of Pure Reason*,

one of the three most difficult works in the corpus of Western philosophical literature. Two others are Hegel's *Phenomenology of Spirit* and Theodor Adorno's *Negative Dialectics*. By the young Kaufman's own account, he understood very little of Kant's intricate treatise, but he returned to it many times during the later course of his life.[3] His reading of Kant when he was 18 influenced all of his subsequent thinking.[4]

At this stage he also began to explore mysticism, but struggled with the notion of religious experience. 'I seem to be "tone deaf"', he candidly recounts, 'with respect to so-called religious experience. When others speak of their "experience of God" or of "God's presence," or the profound experience of "the holy" or of "sacredness", I simply do not know what they are talking about. Perhaps that is one reason why the problem of God has been, throughout my life, so baffling and difficult.'[5]

university education

After the war ended, Kaufman returned to Kansas to complete a Bachelor's degree in Arts. When he graduated (1947), he went to Northwestern University in Evanston, Illinois, to study for a Master's degree in Sociology. While there, his intellectual development was profoundly shaped by his study of two books: George Herbert Mead's *Mind, Self, and Society* (1934), and Lugwig Feuerbach's *The Essence of Christianity* (1841).

Mead's book was a revolutionary study of the human mind. It was avant-garde, in the sense that it reverses a then common view that language is created by mind. Mead argued contrariwise that mentality and a person's idea of selfhood are created through the evolution of language. Mead thereby offered his readers an evolutionary explanation for the way human mind emerged on this planet. Kaufman was also impressed by Feuerbach's thesis that Christian doctrines about God are unconscious articulations of human features that are unwittingly projected onto a cosmic reality (God) that is non-existent.[6]

Kaufman earned his Master's degree in 1948. In the same year, when he was 23, he enrolled in the Divinity School of Yale University in Connecticut to study for the degree of Bachelor of Divinity. This course of studies was at the time intended to prepare students for Christian ministry, but Kaufman had no intention of becoming a minister. After his initial studies at Yale he embarked on doctoral studies in philosophical theology. He worked under the supervision of H. Richard Niebuhr (1894–1962). Yale in the late 1940s was dominated by the neo-orthodox theology of Karl Barth. Niebuhr aligned his thought with Barth

and opposed liberal Protestant theology. Kaufman successfully completed his doctorate with Niebuhr in 1955 with a dissertation titled 'The Problem of Relativism
and the Possibility of Metaphysics: A Constructive Development of Certain Ideas
in R.G. Collingwood, Wilhelm Dilthey, and Paul Tillich.' It was published in 1960
with the shorter title of *Relativism, Knowledge, and Faith*. This book explores the
problems which human limitation (finitude and contingency) generates for
knowledge. It concludes that humans do not enjoy a contact with reality, either
cognitive or experiential, that is unvarnished by their personal, perspectival
interpretations. Humans only enjoy concepts of reality that are coloured by their
imaginations.[7] As the title of Kaufman's first book intimates, human knowledge is
relative to the limited perspective of the knower, and never apprehends reality
directly or comprehensively.

While Kaufman was preparing his doctorate he began in 1953 to teach at
Pomona College in California. From 1955 to 1958 he lectured there as an Assistant
Professor of Religion. During 1958–63 he worked in Nashville, Tennessee, as an
Associate Professor of theology at Vanderbilt University. From there he moved to
the Harvard University Divinity School, based in Cambridge, Massachusetts. He
has remained there ever since. He began teaching in Harvard as a Professor of
theology in 1963. In 1969 he became the Divinity School's Edward Mallinckrodt,
Jr Professor of Divinity, and remained in that post until 1995. He became an
Emeritus Professor in 1995.

five major influences

During Gordon Kaufman's life, at least five primary influences have proved decisive in his attempts to elaborate a theology. First, his Mennonite upbringing
taught him to value correct living over correct doctrine, just as liberation theologians champion orthopraxis over orthodoxy (to be discussed in the next chapter).
Second, his early studies of neo-orthodox theology led him to describe God
initially as the 'Wholly Other', a view that is found in his early book, *Systematic
Theology: A Historicist Perspective* (1968). He later dispensed with the concept as the
principal notion of his theology. Third, his ingestion of Kant's philosophy and
ethics led him to recognize the thoroughly human provenance of theological
speech, and confirmed his predilection for practice over theory or doctrine.
Fourth, through a study of Paul Tillich he became more aware of what it means
to confirm that human existence is inescapably historical, constrained and finite.
Finally, from 1976 to 1991 he regularly travelled to Asia. Between those years, he
taught at the United Theological College in Bangalore, India; Doshisha

University in Kyoto, Japan; and at the University of South Africa in Pretoria. During 1986 he undertook research in England at Oxford. In 1991 he taught at the Chinese University of Hong Kong; Beijing University; Shanghai's Fudan University; and Nanjing Theological Seminary in China. These intense years of travel and lecturing brought Kaufman face to face with the manifest plurality of world religions and with the daunting task of attempting to elaborate the distinctiveness of Christianity in relation to other religions.[8]

god the problem

In many of his writings, Gordon Kaufman frequently talks of God as a problem. In 1972 he published a collection of essays gathered together with the title, *God the Problem*. This book contains the seeds of the distinctive understanding of theology that Kaufman formulated during the last three decades of the twentieth century. From the mid-1970s, Kaufman began to regard theology as a continually evolving human exercise in the imaginative construction of concepts about God.

His book, *God the Problem*, contains residues of a neo-orthodox influence in that it retains 'the notion of God as *agent*, as one who *acts*'.[9] It also has indications that Kaufman was in a process of moving away from any attachment to Barth's understanding of God as Wholly Other.

Kaufman introduces his book by saying: 'All the essays included here are directly concerned with the meaning of talking about God, with understanding how God is related to the world, with the significance and foundations of belief in God, or with defining the human task of thinking about God – theology.'[10] He then makes an observation, the significance of which could easily be overlooked. He reminds his readers that theology is not narrowly confined to thinking about God, 'but involves a full-blown interpretation of man and the world as well'.[11] Here in a nutshell is the fulcrum of an understanding of theology that Kaufman developed and defended for the rest of his career. Simply expressed, theology is not a human response to a divine revelation as Barth had supposed, but a creative and imaginative formulation of ideas about God that are rooted in people's experiences of humankind (or 'man', as Kaufman says in 1972) and the world. In the *Problem of God*, Kaufman refers to God as a symbol (Chapter 5) and construct: 'The available God – the God spoken of in scripture and tradition, worshipped in church and synagogue, conceived in the minds of the faith – is ... a cultural construct.'[12]

The problem of God of which Kaufman so regularly speaks is this: '"God" raises special problems of meaning because it is a noun which by definition refers to a reality transcendent of, and thus not locatable within, experience.' Yet if absolutely nothing in people's experience 'can be directly identified as that to which the term "God" properly refers, what meaning does or can the word have?'[13] If God is the Creator of the Universe, God and humans cannot directly encounter each other because, as Creator, God is the source of all being and is not identifiable with particular human beings.[14] With *God the Problem*, Kaufman begins to distance himself from the centuries-long tradition that the starting point of theology is the human recognition of (or encounter with) divine revelation.

the problem of revelation

Each and every theology has a starting point. It would not be inaccurate to observe that most theology of the past, and the majority of the theologians discussed in this book, assume that theology begins with a recognition and interpretation of God's revelation to humanity. Theologians have disagreed about the primary historical loci of God's revelations, but the ones most often appealed to are the history of Israel, the Bible, Jesus Christ, human experience and the traditions of the Church. Some theologians, mystics and generally religious individuals have insisted they have enjoyed personal one-to-one revelations from God – special revelations as distinct from general revelation.

Gordon Kaufman is a careful and subtle thinker. He neither prescribes nor proscribes what God could or could not achieve in relation to humans. His originality in the history of twentieth-century theologians lies in an argument, developed over four decades, that the recognition of a divine revelation is not a legitimate starting point for theology. His objection to revelation is methodological.

theological method

Kaufman explained his objection to the concept of revelation serving as the initiating point for theology in a programmatic essay that he published in 1975. It is called *An Essay of Theological Method*. References to it in this chapter are to its third edition.[15]

The essay is the overture to the rest of Kaufman's theological compositions. Its 'Preface' announces the leitmotif of all Kaufman's subsequent works: theology is an activity of the *construction* (and reconstruction) of concepts about God. It is not an exercise in *description* or *exposition*.[16] Theology is a thoroughly human *creation.* In this view, even the words 'God' and 'revelation' were created by human beings.

Apart from Kaufman's argument that theology is a work of conceptual construction, a second theme is announced in the *Essay* that has remained a permanent feature of his theology ever since. The theme is a refusal to recognize that theology proceeds from a starting point that acknowledges a pre-established authority such as revelation, scripture or dogma.

Kaufman stands apart from a long tradition of theology by describing reliance on revelation as 'very misleading'. He calls into question the commonly accepted view that 'the theologian must work with what has been given – given by God, of course – and proceed to explicate and interpret that.'[17] For Kaufman, this view involves the questionable presupposition of faith that God has revealed Godself: 'and this faith is not itself subject to theological questioning or doubt'.[18] Such, of course, was the way Karl Barth understood theology.

Kaufman finds this perspective wanting and misleading because it assumes 'as evident and clear and already given concepts that surely must be established and explained'.[19] To assert that theology should begin by accepting 'God's revelation' as evident and pre-given before any work of human interpretation is unwittingly to presuppose that people know explicitly what they mean when they say 'God' and 'revelation', and that these terms are not problematical. Kaufman argues in counterpoint that the terms 'God' and 'revelation' were created by people and developed over time through people's reflections on their lives and interpretations of their experiences. Theological concepts are like any other: people construct them; they are not given by God. Humans have no divine concepts of the divine; only human ones: 'It is only because some persons at certain times and places found it useful and meaningful and perhaps even necessary to speak of "God's revelation", in order to make sense of the life and history which they were undergoing, that these terms and concepts and concepts were developed and employed within the human sphere at all.'[20]

Kaufman is here quite rightly taking to task: first, the view that theology is a faith-driven work of the Church for the Church; and second, the idea that a theologian enjoys the ability to speak on behalf of God and declare what God wants, hates, wills or likes.[21] The first view reduces theology to a ghettoized, parochial exercise, and is logically unconvincing. It evinces a parochial understanding of theology because it overlooks that, sociologically speaking, the Church's linguistic terms are rooted in the wider context of the experiences and histories of human cultures. The Church's vocabulary is the vocabulary of every human being – ordinary words in everyday language: words like 'faith', 'love', 'death', 'hope', 'virtue', and 'belief'. The meanings of these and other terms are not determined by the Church in a sectarian understanding of theology as designed by and for the Church, because their meanings stem from the wider cultures in which the Church is embedded. To say that theology begins by accepting divine revelation is logically self-policing because it assumes as evident a premise ('God has revealed Godself') that stands in need of demonstration to any interested inquirer.

Kaufman humbles the theologian who aspires to be God's ventriloquist in history:

> Theology is and always has been a human work: it emerges out of and interprets human historical events and experiences; it utilizes humanly created and shaped terms and concepts; it is carried out by human processes of mediation, reflection, ratiocination, speaking, writing and reading. We as theologians can perform only these human activities; we cannot in any way do God's speaking, acting, inspiring, or providential guiding.[22]

the theological imagination

Kaufman's *Essay* did not make much of the role that imagination plays in the conceptually constructive task of theology as he sees it. That undertaking fell to his next book: *The Theological Imagination: Constructing the Concept of God*.[23] The influence of Immanuel Kant is evident in this book as Kaufman draws attention to the mental power of imagination and begins to talk of 'the theological imagination'.[24] He reminds his readers that ever since Kant it has been acknowledged that human experiences of objects are rendered possible by 'the elaborate synthesizing powers of the mind: these bring together and hold together in enduring conceptual unities what is given to us only piecemeal and in separate moments of experience.'[25] For Kaufman, following Kant, the mind creates unified concepts from the particular impressions of experiences. The point to which he is leading is this: the idea of God 'is in many ways the mind's supreme imaginative construct'.[26]

Kaufman's largest and most significant book, *In Face of Mystery*, was published in 1993. It is the capstone of his works and is complemented by a later volume called *God-Mystery-Diversity: Christian Theology in a Pluralistic World* (1996). In the decade before these two books appeared he wrote a brief text called *Theology for a Nuclear Age*. It underscores the implications for theology of the bomb dropped on Hiroshima, one of which might be that it is foolhardy for Christians to pray for God to deliver them from peril while they simultaneously possess the means to destroy the biological conditions necessary for human survival. The book is driven by the concern that the most profound problem for humankind nowadays is not alienation from God, 'but the steady undermining of the conditions that make meaningful and fruitful human life possible, through our pollution and poisoning of the ecosystem, on the one hand, and through social and political and economic arrangements that are oppressive and dehumanising, on the other.'[27]

creativity

Before the publication of *In Face of Mystery*, Kaufman's books progressively built up a cluster of concepts concerning the ways humans talk about God. His *Essay on Theological Method* revolves around the idea of construction: theology is not description or exposition but construction. With *The Theological Imagination*, Kaufman grafted the notion of the imagination onto the idea of construction. Theology is now understood as an exercise in imaginative conceptual construction: theology begins in the human imagination. A major new concept, creativity, is emphasized and developed with *In Face of Mystery*: theology here becomes the creative, imaginative construction of concepts about God.

The word 'creativity' is not employed regularly in the writings of scientists. That is one reason why Kaufman sets upon its potential to assist him in his attempt to create a concept of God that complements what is known through science. The concept of creativity for him refers to 'a very significant feature of life and the world, namely that novel realities continuously come into being in time …'.[28]

the question of/about god

In the early stages of *In Face of Mystery*, Kaufman explains what he means by 'the question about God':

> Are we humans responsible simply to ourselves for the shape we give our lives and our society, and for what we do to the environment that surrounds and sustains us and which has brought us forth? Or must we understand our existence in terms of norms and values and realities that do not derive from us and to which we will be held accountable willy-nilly. The question about God is the question whether there is some extra-human reality in relationship to which human existence gains its being and its fulfilment, some ultimate point of reference in terms of which our human life and its problems and possibilities must be understood.[29]

In these terms, the question of God is eminently functional or pragmatic. Human beings daily live by choices regarding what to eat, wear, do, believe or say. Their lives are not dress rehearsals. They only have one life to live, and it cannot be repeated. At some stage they need to decide whether to live as if they are only accountable to themselves, or whether they are ultimately answerable to some kind of extra-human reality, commonly called God in the English-speaking West. A life lived without reference to God will obviously in some ways be fundamentally different from one organized as if God is an ultimate point of orientation for human beings. Kaufman may surprise his readers by saying that theology's central question is not merely, nor pre-eminently, concerned with what or who God is. Nor is it a speculative or epistemological question; can God be known? Most fundamentally, the question of God is 'a *practical* question: How are we to live?'[30]

humanity-world-god

In Face of Mystery is a long and complex work divided into five parts. The first discusses the idea that theology is a constructive exercise. The fifth ponders faith and life in today's world. The middle three parts explain in detail Kaufman's comprehension of *how* people construct concepts of God. His explanation hinges on a threefold categorical schema involving three cardinal concepts – Humanity, the World and God. Part II of the book is called 'Constructing a Concept of the Human'; Part III is 'Constructing a Concept of the Context of Human Existence: The World'; and Part IV is entitled 'Constructing a Concept of an Ultimate Point of Reference: God'.

Kaufman's strategy in this book is deceptively simple. He argues that everything human beings can experience and know can be explained in terms of this threefold conceptual schema. If people do not believe in God, they still refer their lives to an ultimate point of reference with another name, like sport, the making of money, or the enjoyment of life. Kaufman's point is that each and every human being lives with some kind of understanding (concept) of what being human entails, and everyone has a comprehension of what the world in which they find themselves is like. To the concepts of humanity and the world, humans orient their lives to someone or something they consider to be supereminently desirable.

Crucially for Kaufman, the notions of God (ultimacy), the human and the world are interconnected.[31] He is clear that the word 'God' 'is a human word and a human idea'.[32] As such, it is imbricated with understandings of cosmology (the world) and anthropology (humanity). Human beings have always created concepts of God on the basis of what they perceive to be the constitution of the world and of people, or such is the principal argument of Kaufman's later work. Diagrammatically depicted, Kaufman's tripartite conceptual schema becomes:

GOD

WORLD   HUMANITY

If this argument is sound, it becomes evident that all pre-modern theologies have crafted words about God that are linked to cosmologies and anthropologies which have largely been discounted by modern science. Traditional theologies are cast in a language which assumes that humans have a fixed nature and are passive (God directs their lives and the course of history), while the world has three tiers – heaven *above*, earth in the *middle* and hell *below*. Hence the language of Jesus *ascending* to heaven, being *sent* by God (from heaven) and *descending* to hell.

Kaufman wishes to convince his audience that if cosmologies and anthropologies change as human cultures develop and gain new knowledge, traditional concepts of God stand in urgent need of correction or abandonment.

In Kaufman's later theology he abandons the traditional idea that God is a Father-Lord-Creator who is transcendent to the world, and replaces it with a concept that God is a serendipitous creativity *in* the world.[33]

the history of 'god'

To grasp what Kaufman means by conceiving of God as a serendipitous or constantly surprising creative force in the world, it helps to consider previous concepts of God. It is easily assumed that human beings have always spoken about God, which is not the case. Because the English word 'God' is a human artefact it has an identifiable history of about 4,000 years old. Gordon Kaufman is adept at illustrating this history.

There has never been a single standard understanding of the meaning of 'God' in human history, but a vast, constantly changing spectrum. The term 'God' normally functions in English as either a common noun (God as a species of deity) or a proper noun (God as a name). It is most often used as a proper name: 'God is the one on whom humans can call in a time of desperate need; God is the creator of the world and of all that is in it … .'[34] 'God' is the name ordinarily employed to nominate 'that reality (whatever it might be) that grounds and undergirds all that exists …'.[35] God has most often been envisioned in the past a superhuman supreme being or spirit who created the world, rules over it, and is worthy of worship.

The oldest images of God in Western theism (Judaism, Christianity and Islam) are found in the Bible, a collection of texts, the earliest of which was composed about 4,000 years ago. The Bible itself was written over a period of about 2,000 years. The variety of images in the Bible is striking. Some are anthropomorphic, with God envisaged as someone with arms, legs and a larynx. In the Bible, God is depicted as a King, Ruler, Judge, Creator, Mighty Warrior, Punisher, who is jealous, can turn to anger, tried to drown the entire human race with a great Flood, and who parted the Sea of Reeds so that the Hebrews could escape from the Egyptians. God is an all-knowing supremely powerful moral agent who acts in history to smite the enemies of Israel.

These anthropomorphic concepts are accompanied in the Bible by abstract metaphors: God is Light; Love; 'the first and the last' (Isa 44: 6, Rev 1: 17); the reality in which people move and have their being (Acts 17: 28); and an omnipresent reality (Ps 139: 8).[36]

All the images of God in the Bible presuppose that the world is three-tiered and that the earth is the centre of the known world.

The term 'God' is like the stem of a sapling that grows. As a sapling is nourished and grows taller, branches begin to shoot out from the stem. So too with the concept of God. From the basic stem of the biblical concept of God as a transcendent Lord and Creator, a branch grew which conceived of God in Christian Trinitarian terms as a Father, Son and Spirit. Yet another branch developed after the Bible was written according to which nothing meaningful can be said about God. In this view, God is a *Deus Fugitivus*, a fugitive God who always takes flight from human attempts to depict God with concepts.

twentieth-century cosmology

Kaufman's later theology develops an abstract concept of God which he concludes chimes with what is known about the world and humanity according to a contemporary cosmology (often called 'Big Bang' theory). This cosmology instructs that the universe began with a cosmic explosion about 13.7 billion years ago, and has been expanding ever since.[37]

According to this view, all things – humans, planets, stars, gases and atoms – are not only interrelated, but have evolved over time from the initial singularity of hot condensed matter that exploded and expanded. Reality is thus dynamic, in process, constantly changing, and in some sense improving. There has been a direction, a progression from a primeval cosmic sludge of gases and dust to the emergence of self-conscious human mind. For Kaufman, a startlingly creative force is at work in the world, progressively driving the evolution of all realities.

god as serendipitous creativity

What is this elemental thrust, élan, vivacity and energy driving the universe onward and outward? Why not call it God? This is precisely what Kaufman does. As stated above, his favoured abstract metaphor for God is serendipitous creativity.

The use of the word 'metaphor' is important here. Again relying on Kant, Kaufman warns against the tendency humans have had to reify concepts of God. In Kantian terms, reification is the process by which people regard thoughts as things (from the Latin, *res*, 'thing'). Conceptual symbols for God, such as 'creator', 'father' and 'lord' are reified when their users take them to mean that in reality God *is* a creator/father/lord. By contrast, a metaphor such as 'serendipitous creativity' refers to a reality in the hope that the reality might be related to the metaphor's imagery.[38]

It is clear that Kaufman's idea of God is discordant with traditional Christian doctrinal orthodoxy. He is well aware of that. The reason he has distanced himself from orthodoxy is because he charges that it is metaphysically dualistic: it posits a supernatural world over and above a natural realm. It also paints a cosmic division between heaven and earth. Humans are on one side of the division; God is on the other. If this is so, the supernatural world is inaccessible to humans because they have no experience of it. Thus, metaphysical dualism is incoherent for Kaufman.[39]

jesus christ

Gordon Kaufman works expressly as a Christian theologian.[40] The conceptual symbol, 'Christ', operates as a fourth major pole in his integrative schema of God-World-Humanity. For Christians, Jesus Christ is a manifestation of God, of the destiny of the world, and of human nature. Christian theology thereby becomes a conceptual interplay between four symbols:[41]

GOD	CHRIST
WORLD	HUMANITY

Yet just as Kaufman is critical of a traditional Christian understanding of God, he also calls into question the viability of classical Christology. He points out that 'in traditional Christian faith and theology "Christ" is said to be of absolutely decisive significance for understanding both who or what God is and what human life is all about.'[42] Chalcedonian Christology teaches that Jesus Christ is perfect in Godhead and perfect in humanity, leaving Kaufman facing the question of deciding what to make of this double-sided claim today. He concludes that it focuses too narrowly on the idea that God became incarnate at a particular point in history in a particular man, Jesus. He argues for what he calls a wider Christology. By this he means that Jesus should be interpreted in relation to others around him: 'On this view it is the appearance of a new communal ethos in history, rather than a metaphysically unique individual, that is the matter of central importance.'[43]

The Gospel According to John depicts Jesus declaring 'The Father and I are one' (Jn 10: 30). Kaufman asserts that this statement was '"put in Jesus' mouth"' by the Gospel's author, and goes on to opine: 'This is remarkably strong language: it claims that God had actually been basically inaccessible to men and women through most of human history, but had become accessible through Jesus, that is through the complex of events surrounding and following upon the ministry and death of Jesus.'[44]

---

anthropomorphism, andromorphism, anthropocentricism   These clumsy terms serve to designate regularly recurring temptations in history for those who seek to speak about God. **Anthropomorphism** is the belief that God resembles a human being: God is an active moral agent; a person who loves, wills and hates, and who can communicate with people. **Andromorphism** is the belief that the *male* human being is an image of God, and therefore that God is most appropriately spoken of as He, Him and Father. **Anthropocentrism** is the belief that human beings are the centrally most significant inhabitants of the world, and the assumption that God with all animals and things must be valued according to their relation to humans.

Kaufman's central objection to this way of speaking about Jesus, and the very idea that God became incarnate in a man, is that God is conceived in an anthropomorphic and anthropocentric manner.

In Kaufman's work, the notion of incarnation is anthropomorphic because it presupposes the idea of an agent-God in history; it is anthropocentric because it assumes that God has *a special love* for humankind.[45]

conclusion

Once Gordon Kaufman's works have been read and studied, he teases the mind: what if he is right? If he is correct in his account of the history of the term 'God', and the way theological concepts are formulated, a great deal of theology is exposed as an absurdly delusional riot of anthropocentrism and anthropomorphism.

The significant strengths of his theology are at least threefold. First, he rightly recognizes that traditional theologies are based on defunct anthropologies and cosmologies that need to be replaced or revised by theologies that take account of knowledge established by modern sciences. Second, he uncovers the logical circularity, and hence untenableness, of traditional theological work which assumes, but cannot demonstrate, that it is already known by theologians: (a) what or who God is; (b) that God is self-revealing and worthy of trust; and (c) that God has chosen to reveal Godself in the Bible and Jesus Christ.[46] Third, he deftly explains why theological concepts have an entirely human provenance. Hence their fallibility and provisionality.

Kaufman's proposal that God is a Great Creative Serendipity is clever, but not unassailable. A God imagined as a Cosmic Creativity impelling forth the evolutionary expansion of the universe is worthy of wonder, and admiration, but so too is a supernova, the complexity of a crystal, the Megellanic Clouds (two galaxies nearest to the Milky Way galaxy) and quarks. If God is in the world, God will die, because everyone and everything in the world is finite, as the Second Law of Thermodynamics instructs.

As ingenious as Kaufman's works are, it will probably prove difficult for people to love, worship and take as the ultimate focus of their lives, the abstract metaphor of Serendipitous Creativity.

16

Gustavo Gutiérrez: b.1928

Tyranny is always better organized than freedom.

Charles Péguy

Here is a story of a missionary who went missing, presumed tortured and murdered, in Honduras during the early 1980s. By then, liberation theology was well developed in South America. The purpose of this chapter is to introduce liberation theology, the most significant theological initiative in the second half of the twentieth century, especially as it is exemplified in the life of the Peruvian theologian, Gustavo Gutiérrez. The missing missionary was an enthusiast of liberation theology, and tried to live according to its vision and principles. His downfall followed as a consequence.

His name was James Carney, known to his friends as Jim. He was born into a Catholic family of seven children in Chicago on 28 October 1924. After serving as a soldier in the US army during the Second World War, he joined the Society of

Jesus to train as a priest. After his ordination, and once he obtained a degree in theology, he left the USA, and during 1964 began to work in Honduras as a missionary among *campesinos* – poor peasants. Amid his needy villagers he was known as Padre Guadalupe Carney.

His career as an outpost priest lasted for about 20 years. Halfway through, he briefly visited his family, friends and fellow Jesuits back home. His stay there irked him. So much so, that when he returned to Honduras he composed, signed and sent 'An Open Letter' to the people he had visited. The year was 1971. His tract began in this way:

> My dear American friends, Jesuits and non-Jesuits:
>
> I love all of you, and I think you're wonderful loving persons, but I can't stand living with any of you. I was raised like all of you, as a middle-class, Catholic white American. But right from high school age on, I've had a deep impression that most middle-class Catholics are phony Christians, just as materialistic and self-seeking, and as liable to go along with others, as any non-Christian, and often more so.[1]

What made him write in such a way – and for his friends, such a rude way? He had discovered liberation theology in the late 1960s. South American bishops met in Medellín, Colombia, in 1968 to put into place in their countries the hope of Pope John XXIII that the Church would become a Church *of* poor people. One of the theologians advising the bishops was Gustavo Gutiérrez. The bishops spoke of an urgent duty incumbent on Christians to help the poor. After the bishops met, Jim Carney attended a course in Honduras conducted by Jesuit priests explaining liberation theology. He deepened his study of the subject by reading Gutiérrez's book, *A Theology of Liberation*. The bishops, the course and the book electrified him religiously. He became alive to a text in Luke's Gospel that recounts an incident when Jesus, while teaching in a synagogue, read a passage from a scroll of the prophet Isaiah, which states: 'The Spirit of the Lord is upon me, because he has anointed me to bring good news to the poor. He has sent me to proclaim release to the captives and recovery of sight to the blind, to let the oppressed go free, to proclaim the year of the Lord's favour' (Lk 4: 18–19).

'To bring good news to the poor'? 'To let the oppressed go free'? How many Christians now really find their daily purpose in such verses? Carney could not escape the obvious conclusion of Luke's text: what was good enough for Isaiah and for Jesus ought to be sufficient as a programme of life for him and anyone else aspiring to become a Christian. Ruminating on the new ideas he had encountered he was led to conclude: 'The basic tenet of liberation theology is that one can only reflect under the light of the gospel on the liberation, the salvation, that

Christ brought (that is, do theology), when one is involved in the praxis, the practice of the political struggle for the liberation of the oppressed in this world.'[2]

Into a political struggle he leapt, and since 1983 has never been seen again. The Christian Human Rights Organization of Honduras filed a report on his fate in October 1983: 'These North Americans participated directly in the tortures and interrogations that ended with the cowardly assassination of the priest James Carney (Padre Guadalupe), also of other revolutionary leaders. These acts took place in the middle of September in two hidden basements at El Aguacate ... .'[3]

toward a theology of liberation

Fifteen years earlier, in July 1968, Gustavo Gutiérrez gave a talk to a group of priests meeting in Chimbote, Peru. His talk was called: 'Toward a Theology of Liberation'. He began his discourse by offering an etymological explanation of the meaning of the word *theology*. He noted that 'theology is a treatise or discourse about God – which really does not tell us very much'.[4] He was uneasy with this classical definition of theology because it offers an *intellectual* understanding of faith. His aim in the talk was to link Christian faith and theology to practical commitment. He proceeded to explain a concept of theology to his listeners that involves three main points. First, theology is a progressive understanding of *commitment* in history. Second, theology is a reflection that follows action. The central component of the action concerned is charity, or love. Third, theology is an intellectual understanding of a commitment that must continuously *be linked with* the commitment: 'Every action of ours', Gutiérrez told his audience, 'must be accompanied by a reflection to orient it, to order it, to make it coherent, so that it does not lapse into a sterile and superficial activism'.[5] His principal point follows: 'If faith is a commitment to God and human beings, it is not possible to live in today's world without a commitment to the process of liberation.'[6]

In speaking in such a fashion, Gutiérrez indicated he was aware that he was blazing a trail in twentieth-century theology when he commented: 'A genuine theology of liberation can only be a team effort, a task which has not yet been attempted.'[7] Perhaps theology is not an individual's isolated cogitations penned in a solitary professorial study after all!

By this stage of his talk to the priests gathered in Chimbote, he had not yet explained what he meant by liberation. It soon became clear in his exposition that liberation is a kindred term for the much more ecclesiastical-sounding word 'salvation'. He acknowledges that 'The gospel is primarily a message of salvation.'[8] The trouble with the word 'salvation', if a scrutiny of its usage among Christians over centuries in the past is any test, is that it can all too easily connote divinely offered forgiveness for an individual's sins. For Gutiérrez, 'If we understand salvation as something with merely "religious" or "spiritual" value for the soul, then it would not have much to contribute to concrete human life.'[9] 'Contributing to concrete human life' is precisely what is meant by 'liberation'. It is 'the suppression of oppression' and the overcoming of injustice. All of which Gutiérrez illustrates with reference to messianic promises and expectations in the Bible: 'The elimination of misery and exploitation is a sign of the coming of the messiah.'[10] He warms to his theme by commenting on exactly the same text that enthused the ill-starred Jesuit, Jim Carney – Luke's Gospel, Chapter 4. The passage concerned, to recall, speaks of God's Spirit being upon the One anointed 'to bring good news to the poor', 'to proclaim release to the captives', 'recovery of sight to the blind' and to 'let the oppressed go free'.

Gutiérrez shows how this very plain text has been interpreted among Christians in a spiritual, not practical, way:

> Thus we translate 'to preach good news to the poor' as meaning that we should tell the poor in spirit that they should hope in God. 'To preach liberation to captives' means to speak to the captives about sin. 'The recuperation of sight by the blind' means that they do not see God. 'Freedom to the oppressed' means those oppressed by Satan.
> In reality all these expressions have a meaning that is direct and clear.[11]

theology as biography

To grasp why Gutiérrez came to speak of theology as linked to a practical liberation, which is the 'suppression of oppression', it is necessary to attend to the details of his life. The entire methodology of this book has been determined by the conclusion that theologians speak the way they do about God because of events and people in their lives. The methodology is guided by a book written by the German theologian Johann Baptist Metz in 1977. It contains a section called 'Theology as biography'.[12] Therein he decries the way dogmatic or neo-scholastic theology separated doctrines from personal histories and biographies. Gutiérrez's warning not to separate 'salvation' from 'concrete human life' is not unrelated. What happened in his own life to lead him to formulate a theology of liberation?

Gustavo Gutiérrez Merino is the first theologian broached in this book who was born in the Southern hemisphere, where the majority of Christians now live, and where most of them are poor. He was born in Arco Street in the Monserrat barrio (city district) of Lima, Peru, on 8 June 1928.[13] He is a *mestizo*: someone descended from both Hispanic and Indian, or Quechuan, ancestors. Such a person is frequently labelled as a 'half-caste' or 'half-breed', by those who still subscribe to the racial ideology of full-bloods or blue-bloods. Mestizos in Peru during the 1920s were among the poorest and most socially oppressed people in the nation. Apart from his parents, he also had two sisters in his immediate family.

Gustavo's childhood was blighted by physical suffering. From the ages of 12 to 18, he was afflicted by an acute case of osteomyelitis which wrought havoc with his teenage skeleton. During these years he was confined either to bed or a wheel-chair. The illness left him with an abiding limp.

He spent his childhood in three different barrios of Lima with his family: Monserrat, Rímac and Barranco. He was intellectually gifted, to the extent that he learnt to speak five main languages – Quechua, Spanish, French, German and English. Having suffered a debilitating illness for six years, he decided to study medicine, with a preference for psychiatry. Between 1947 and 1950 he studied for and earned a medical science degree (BSc) in San Marcos University in Lima. Even at this stage of his life he began a study of Karl Marx and joined a political group that publicly protested against Peruvian economic and social inequalities.

Upon graduation, Gustavo changed his mind about medicine and decided instead to become a priest. His decision set him on a long and arduous academic safari in South America and Europe. He began his theological studies in 1951 at the University of Santiago in Chile. Thereafter he studied philosophy in the Catholic University of Lima.

At the time, a view was still widely held among Catholic bishops that anyone aspiring to be a theologian needed to be educated in Europe. Gutiérrez was duti-fully dispatched to the Catholic University of Leuven, or Louvain, in Belgium. There he completed a Master's degree in philosophy and psychology with his thesis, 'The Psychic Conflict in Freud' (1955). Following his Belgian studies, he spent the time between 1955 and 1959 studying at an even more advanced level in the theological faculty of the Catholic University of Lyons, France, completing a Master's degree in theology with a thesis on 'Religious Liberty' (1959). Much later in his life, in 1986, the same faculty conferred a doctorate in theology on him. His experience in Lyon exposed him to 'the new theology' (*la nouvelle théologie*) of French theologians trying to interpret Christian faith with direct ref-erence to historical events in the twentieth century. Between 1959 and 1960, he studied at the Gregorian University in Rome. He was in Rome in 1959 when John XXIII announced that he would convene the Second Vatican Council.

poverty in peru

Gutiérrez was ordained to the order of the presbyterate in the Catholic Church of the Roman Rite on 6 January 1959. He then returned to Lima in the early 1960s and began working as a parish priest. He opted to live in a tiny apartment in Rímac barrio, and he began to teach theology in Lima's Catholic University.[14] There his psyche was seared by the unremitting reality of his people's poverty, hopelessness and misery. How is it possible to tell such people that God providentially loves them and cares for them, when they are forced to feed stewed rat to their children, and compete with feral dogs to find food?

Poverty in Peru is the proximate fountainhead and catalyst for Gutiérrez's formulation of a new method for theology, now known, and occasionally defamed, internationally as liberation theology.

In 1992, only 10 per cent of Peru's working population was gainfully employed. Since 1950, the country's population more than trebled, from 7.6 to 25 million in 1998. Lima, the country's capital, had a population of 6 million in 1990. Of these, only 5.3 per cent were employed; 8.3 per cent were officially declared to be unemployed, while 86.4 per cent were underemployed, in the sense that they worked for themselves in order to survive. Roughly 60 per cent of the city live in slums and shanty towns, and lack basic facilities such as running water, sewerage and a constant supply of electricity.[15] The nation as a whole over the past two decades has been plagued by four destructive forces – poverty, drugs, corruption and terrorism. Peru's problems have been compounded by a massive migration of rural dwellers to its cities, which have become dysfunctional because they do not have the resources to house many more inhabitants. The present population of Lima is nine times greater than it was in 1940. Between 1940 and 1990, the rural population of Peru grew from 4.5 to 6.7 million, whereas the urban population augmented from 1.7 to 15.6 million.[16]

medellín: 1968 in south america

When Gutiérrez gave his talk to priests during July of 1968, South America was a deeply troubled continent. In that year, an aggressive dictatorship held sway in the massively populous country of Brazil. A military government in Argentina was ruthlessly subduing its people. Mexico witnessed the massacre of Tlaltelolco. Governments in Peru and Chile offered little solace to impoverished citizens. Corrupt and oppressive overlords controlled Nicaragua, Paraguay and Haiti.[17]

All was not lost. An event transpired in 1968 that has marked Christian life and thought in Latin America ever since. It was a conference of South American bishops, held between 26 August and 6 September in Medellín, Colombia. The meeting was called the Second General Conference of Latin America Bishops, also known as CELAM II, which in Spanish stands for the second gathering of the Episcopal Council of Latin America. The first CELAM was held in Rio de Janeiro in 1955.

The bishops of CELAM II had only recently returned from the Second Vatican Council, and they sought to introduce its reforms into South America, a continent that had been plundered and ravaged by rapacious colonizing conquerors since 1492. South America by the latter twentieth century had endured five centuries of imperialistic Christendom, with the Catholic Church structurally aligned with wealthy and militaristically armed governments.

The charge has been made, not just in relation to South America, but elsewhere as well, that

> ... the Christian church and its theology consistently buttressed the expansion of empires. The majority of the church, regardless of where it stood in the conflict with modernity, blessed colonialism, neo-colonialism, extreme stratification of wealth, centuries of genocide of Amerindians, blacks, Jews, the subordination of women, the persecution of the sexual other, and the social exclusion of the pagan. During the last five centuries theology has glorified all these historical projects as divine constructions of reality.[18]

This is a damning indictment. It is also far from being false or inaccurate. The bishops gathered at Medellín wanted to unshackle the Church's traditional links with conquerors, so that the Church could help alleviate the economic and political oppression of growing masses of poor people in their respective countries. To do this they focused on the theme of liberation.[19] Gutiérrez was in their midst as a theological adviser.

the preferential option for the poor

The bishops used a term in their published conclusions that was to become a shibboleth for liberation theologians. It was the word 'preference'. They taught that:

> The Lord's distinct commandment to 'evangelize the poor' ought to bring us to a distribution of resources and apostolic personnel that effectively **gives preference to the poorest and most needy** sectors and to those segregated for any cause

whatsoever, animating and accelerating the initiatives and studies that are already being made with that goal in mind.[20]

CELAM III, held at Puebla de los Angeles, Mexico, during January and February of 1979, took up Medellín's theme of giving precedence to the poor. The bishops at Puebla spoke of a 'preferential option for the poor', and decried people trying to vitiate the spirit of Medellín: 'We affirm the need for conversion on the part of the whole church to **a preferential option for the poor**, an option aimed at their **integral liberation**.'[21]

It is crucial to note that liberation theologians who subsequently adopted the idea of a preferential option for the poor were not motivated, as so many of their detractors charge, by a neo-Marxist desire to slaughter the rich. They were emboldened by what they believed about Jesus Christ, a poor person who spent himself trying to urge others to help destitute street people. The bishops of Medellín were clear about the Christological basis of their conclusions: 'The poverty of so many brothers and sisters cries out for justice, solidarity, open witness, commitment, strength, and exertion directed to the fulfilment of the redeeming mission to which it is committed by Christ.'[22]

a theology of liberation

When Gutiérrez returned to Lima after advising the bishops at Medellín, he mulled over what the bishops had said, and contemplated the dreadful increase in suffering inflicted on a massively increased population in South America by dictatorships and poverty. It was time for him to talk about God in a way that bore little resemblance to the theological style of the theological masters who had taught him in Belgium, France and Italy. The people he wanted to address and help were not frequenters of Parisian salons, shoppers on New York's Fifth Avenue, curial officials in Rome, or the glitterati of Monaco's beaches.

He found his theological voice and a new addressee for theology in a book he produced in 1971 called, in Spanish, *Teología de la liberación, Perspectivas* ('Theology of Liberation, Perspectives'). It was published in English in 1973 as *A Theology of Liberation: History, Politics, and Salvation*. This is one of the five most significant books in the mountain of volumes included in twentieth-century theology.

Why? Partly because it is not an abstruse philosophical discussion about whether or not there is a God, but a treatise about what kind of deity God is. In the book, God is not depicted as the guarantor of the privileges of politicians, aristocrats, company directors, prelates, playboys and bejewelled socialites. Nor is the God envisioned by Gutiérrez in the first place the enjoyer of enviable attributes – omnipotence, omniscience, omnibenevolence, impassibility and immutability – that philosophers of religion love to debate at international conferences held in ivy clad universities or five-star hotels.

A Theology of Liberation is not a treatise for the sated, but the suffering. It advances the view that God is by nature One who loves urchins, widows, orphans, vagabonds, layabouts, penniless street kids, and the unclean and the unnoticed who die at an early age without nutrition to survive. Introducing a second edition of the book, Gutiérrez spoke of 'the irruption of the poor'.[23] This is one of his favourite themes. The huge increase in the human population in the second half of the twentieth century involved a vast expansion of the world's poorest people. Are they irrelevant to theology? This is Gutiérrez's germinal question.

In the early stages of *A Theology of Liberation*, Gutiérrez quotes approvingly from the work of Edward Schillebeeckx, who stated in 1970, the year before Gutiérrez's book was published: 'It is evident that thought is also necessary for action. But the Church has for many centuries devoted its attention to formulating truths and meanwhile did nothing to better the world. In other words, the Church focused on orthodoxy and left orthopraxis in the hands of nonmembers and nonbelievers.'[24]

With Schillebeeckx in mind, Gutiérrez had decided that the function of theology is best described as 'critical reflection on praxis'.[25] More specifically, it is a critical reflection on praxis conducted in light of the Bible.[26]

---

praxis   The term 'praxis' has an ancient Greek provenance and is a neologism in English. Its basic meaning is that of an action which is guided by a theory, belief or idea. In this way it is distinguished from the more common noun, 'practice', which can imply an action that is not the fruit of intense contemplation, like turning on a light switch. Aristotle seems to have been the first philosopher to speak of praxis. He employs it to mean almost any type of activity that a free person is likely to perform, but more particularly activity associated with business and politics. He does not use the term to specify bodily labour. In Aristotle's usage, praxis is often opposed to poeisis, which can be rendered in English as 'doing' or making', and is understood as a mundane, routine, activity.[27]

Karl Marx produced a philosophy of praxis in the nineteenth century, and quipped in his Eleventh Thesis on Feuerbach, to paraphrase, that 'hitherto philosophers have only interpreted the world, whereas the point is to change it'. In the hands of liberation theologians this effectively became: 'before now theologians have chatted about the world, whereas the point is to transform it to reduce suffering'.

Gutiérrez's newly found understanding of theology has three terms. First, it is a 'critical reflection'. It is not brute, mindless activity. Second, it is a thoughtfulness consequent upon an action (praxis). Herein lies the originality of liberation theology as typified by Gutiérrez. It is a theology like any other in that it is a discourse about God. It differs from other theologies in terms of its method. It begins with an ethical step: action to obliterate poverty. Yet this action is not blind. As praxis, it is directed by a theory. The belief or theory that guides praxis leads to the third term involved in Gutiérrez's understanding of theology, which is the Bible. He speaks of God's preference for the poor because the Bible does, and this preference is the lifeblood of liberation theology: 'The entire Bible, beginning with the story of Cain and Abel, mirrors God's predilection for the weak and abused of human history.'[28] Even the word 'praxis' is biblical. The Greek word for 'Acts' in the biblical book, 'The Acts of the Apostles', is 'Praxes'.

For Gutiérrez, a statement in the Bible's First Letter of John is indispensable for an understanding of who God is and how people should relate to one another: 'Whoever does not love does not know God, for God is love' (1 Jn 4: 8). Gutiérrez declares that the statement 'God is love' 'sums up the biblical revelation about God'.[29]

Speaking of God's predilection for the poor, and of a preferential option for the poor, does not mean in Gutiérrez's terms that people who are not poor are excluded from God's love. It simply means that the poor are in must urgent need of solidarity from those who believe that God is love.[30]

One of the more frequent charges levelled against liberation theologians is that they are only concerned with material poverty and political liberation. Gutiérrez has been careful to explain that he distinguishes between three levels of meaning of both poverty and liberation. Poverty can be regarded as an evil, as something not wanted by God; or as spiritual poverty, in the sense of a person's readiness to seek God's will; or solidarity with and joining in the life of poor people. Liberation can be a viewed as expressing the aspiration of oppressed people to escape their plight; or as an understanding according to which humankind assumes responsibility for its destiny; or as a release from sin brought about by Jesus Christ.[31]

critical consciousness of conditions of poverty

It is all very well to talk about liberating poor people from all that oppresses them, but how is this to be done? Mere chatting about poverty by those who are not poor is a constant peril:

If the term 'poverty' carries with it the implication and moral imperative that something should be done about it, then the study of poverty is only ultimately justifiable if it influences individual and social attitudes and actions. This must be borne in mind constantly if discussion on the definition of poverty is to avoid becoming an academic debate worthy of Nero – a semantic and statistical squabble that is parasitic, voyeuristic and utterly unconstructive and which treats 'the poor' as passive objects for attention, whether benign or malevolent – a discussion that is part of the problem rather than part of the solution.[32]

After the Conferences of Medellín and Puebla, liberation theologians around South America began to implement in their localities a new ecclesiology, called Basic Ecclesial Communities (BECs). Clodovis Boff was one of the first to do so among the Amazonian Indians in Arce, in the far west of Brazil.[33] These communities were often led by people who were not priests. Their primary function was to hold meetings, have stories read from the Bible, to see how the local people would react, and to pray.

A major inspiration in the efforts of these communities and their leaders to extract people from poverty was the work of the Brazilian pedagogue, Paulo Freire. In 1971 he published a short but carefully argued book, *Pedagogy of the Oppressed*. He dedicated the book 'To the oppressed, and to those who suffer with them and fight at their side.'[34]

Freire became a significant influence in Gutiérrez's attempts to formulate a theology of liberation. He decried what he called 'verbalism': 'When a word is deprived of its dimension of action, reflection automatically suffers as well; and the word is changed into idle chatter, into *verbalism*, into an alienated and alienating "Blah".'[35] In Gutiérrez's hands, this stance becomes: 'What is to be done away with it the intellectualizing of the intellectual who has no ties with the life and struggle of the poor – the theology of the theologian who reflects upon the faith precisely from the point of view of those from whom the Father has hidden his revelation: the "learned and clever" (Mt 11: 25).'[36]

As a first step towards liberating oppressed people from poverty, Freire formulated a pedagogy for helping people to become aware of the conditions and structures that exploited them and rendered them poor. In Portuguese, he called this strategy *conscientização*, which can be rendered in English as *conscientization*.[37] It was a way of making people become critically aware of the causes of their suffering.

Freire would go into a village and invite its inhabitants to take pictures of their surroundings. He would then call a community meeting and ask the villagers to examine the images of their region. In this way they could see that neighbouring wealthy farmers had fertile fields yielding healthy crops, while their own were tired or barren. Through discussion the villagers could perceive graphically that the wealthy farmers could afford fertilizers for the crops, whereas they could not.[38] Becoming aware of their predicament (*conscientization*) was the initial move towards practical improvement, and this was the method adopted by liberation theologians involved with BECs.

bartolomé de las casas

It is no accident that twentieth-century liberation theology had its origins in South America, a continent blighted by rapacious invaders since the fifteenth century. *A Theology of Liberation* thrust Gutiérrez into an international limelight, which brought him both admiration and denigration, but it is not his *chef-d'œuvre*. The labour of love in his life was a long-standing project which he published in 1992 as *En Busca de los Pobres de Jesucristo*. It was translated into English the following year as *Las Casas: In Search of the Poor Jesus Christ*.

This is by far Gutiérrez's largest and most detailed work. It tells of a small band of Dominican friars who arrived in Hispaniola in 1510, led by Antón Montesino. The friars saw immediately how the Spanish conquerors in the Americas were killing off Indian peoples and publicly denounced the practice. A Spanish slave-owning priest, Bartolomé de las Casas, joined the cause and order of the friars, and spent the rest of his life defending economically crushed people. Las Casas became aware of a constant problem in human history – a fateful link between greed and death. He suffered pangs of conscience, as someone who kept people in slavery, when he came across the biblical text which states: 'The Bread of the needy is the life of the poor; whoever deprives them of it is a murderer. To take away a neighbour's living is to commit murder; to deprive an employee of wages is to shed blood' (Sirach 34: 25). Las Casas realized that the absence of justice among oppressed people 'entails the death of the poor': 'The crust of bread – symbol of human nourishment, as its minimal expression – is the life of the poor. To deprive them of it is to kill them.'[39]

leonardo boff

Gustavo Gutiérrez did not work as a soloist in formulating a theology of liberation. From the late 1950s onwards, a community of friends who were theologians laboured to bring public, political attention to the plight of the poor in South America. One of the first to do so was Juan Luis Segundo, who in 1959 sketched a liberation theology in lectures he delivered in Montevideo, Uruguay.[40] Another was the Brazilian theologian, Leonardo Boff. He and his brother Clodovis worked tirelessly to link Christian faith with struggles to keep the poor alive. Anyone who suspects that liberation theology is intellectually shallow need only attempt to read and comprehend Clodovis Boff's monograph, *Theology and Praxis*.[41]

In 1981, Leonardo Boff published a book that was subsequently translated from Portuguese into English as *Church: Charism and Power*. With this text, Boff is astringently critical of authoritarian abuses of power in the Catholic Church. Commenting on the power of a bishop, he notes:

> A bishop may decide to halt a project that affects priests, religious, pastoral leaders, and dozens of communities. Without any previous discussion, he may literally expel religious from his diocese and dismiss lay leaders, leaving the faith community confused. There is no one to whom they can appeal because they are dealing with the final judge. In cases like this, many are often led into crises of faith provoked by the actions of their cardinals, bishops, and pastors.
>
> Does this have anything to do with power as service described in the Gospel?[42]

Of course not, but Boff was writing in the third year of a new and extremely authoritarian papacy – that of John Paul II, who became Bishop of Rome in 1978. One of the Pope's closest associates in the Curia, Cardinal Joseph Ratzinger, proved in action the central thesis of Boff's book that deals with the use and abuse of hierarchical power in the Church. Ratzinger, as Cardinal Prefect of the Vatican's Congregation for the Doctrine of the Faith, did not enter into sustained discussion with Boff, but muzzled him. He ordered the Brazilian liberation theologian to remain silent for an unspecified period, which turned out to be ten months in duration. Boff received the order as a Franciscan friar and priest on 9 May 1985. In doing so, the Cardinal gagged a voice who alerted his reading public to this: '40 percent of all Brazilians live, work, and sleep with chronic hunger; there are 10 million who are mentally retarded due to malnutrition; 6 million suffer from malaria; 650,000 have tuberculosis and 25,000 suffer from leprosy.'[43] Hounded and harassed, Boff eventually left the Franciscans and the priesthood to marry. His case is important because the Vatican's move against him was not purely personal: it was targeted against all liberation theologians, including Gutiérrez.[44]

deus caritas est

The slighting of liberation theologians has not halted. Joseph Ratzinger became Pope Benedict XVI in 2005. His first encyclical letter, primarily addressed to bishops, was called *Deus Caritas Est* ('God is Love'). Tell that to a mother whose three fly-infested children are starving to death in the Sudanese desert! The new Pope's letter comments on the importance of sexual relations between men and women, and was welcomed for doing so in a positive way. In public commentary on his text, a passage went virtually unnoticed. It comes near the end of his encyclical. While it could easily be overlooked, it cries for contradiction. While speaking about justice and charity, the new Pope declares: 'A just society must be the achievement of politics, not of the Church.'[45]

This statement is not just an observation about the Church, justice and politics. It is also a politely worded papal slap in the face for liberation theologians. Though carefully expressed, it is a theological smack nonetheless. Ultimately, it is unconvincing. What if a political body is gassing Jews in their millions? Ought the Church be mute? What if a state is executing children? Ought the Church turn away? What if a nation practises genocide? Ought bishops pray in solitude? What if politicians tax their people heavily, hoard loot in banks and build luxurious palaces, while their citizens starve? Ought theologians forget about the Bible and its depictions of a God who wants justice to reign in God's kingdom?

Joseph Ratzinger is mistaken on the question of the pursuit of justice by politics rather than the Church, because he espouses a dichotomized view of reality: there is a sacred, ecclesiastical, supernaturally guaranteed realm, and a mundane space that is the preserve of politics. Fortunately, no God is confined by humans to any space.

Liberation theology is not an ethical charter for social do-goodism in competition with politics. It is a biblically based, prophetic reminder that God by nature, if Jesus was correct in what he said and did, loves the poor by preference.

conclusion

Liberation theology in its South American form is not without its faults. Its practitioners during the 1970s did not attend sufficiently to the plight of embattled women, nor did they speak overly about people who were not Christians. That said, the most arresting feature of liberation theology is that it mirrors the passions of Jesus as they are recorded in the Bible. Perhaps this is why liberation theologians and their supporters have frequently met with shockingly violent deaths.

A case in point was Oscar Romero, the Archbishop of El Salvador in the 1970s. He was killed by an assassin's bullet while presiding at Mass in San Salvador on 24 March 1980.[46] He had previously asked soldiers in the army of El Salvador not to shoot their own citizens, and was a fearless champion promoting justice for peasants. The façade of Westminster Abbey in London is graced by a newly crafted statue of Romero. Would that he and his liberating clan be mimicked elsewhere, not just in stone, but in praxis!

As for Gustavo Gutiérrez, he was made a member of France's Legion of Honour in 1993. He was appointed the John Cardinal O'Hara Professor of Theology in Notre Dame University, Indiana, in 2003. During 2001, he joined his kindred spirit, Bartolomé de las Casas, by becoming a Dominican friar. With them, protected from the reaches of the Opus Dei Archbishop of Lima, he could at least preach about the poor Jesus Christ.

17

Uta Ranke-Heinemann: b.1928

I have never met anyone whose desire to build up his moral power
was as strong as sexual desire.

Confucius

It is not a frequent occurrence that a book on sexuality written by a German feminist theologian attracts the attention of a Cardinal Archbishop of New York.
The late 1980s provided the setting for such an event. By then, a pervasive
cultural revolution in attitudes to sex and human interactions had taken hold
of Western cultures. It was a significant upheaval for theologians because it
questioned and rejected many conventional Christian attitudes to marriage, par-
enting, sex apart from marriage, same-sex relations, abortion and contraception.

Language about God is often coloured by attitudes to sexuality. A transformation in attitudes can invite new ways of talking about God, for example, as if God were not male. In 1988, the German biblical scholar and theologian, Uta Ranke-Heinemann, published a book addressing many aspects of changed approaches to sexuality in the twentieth century. It was called *Eunuchen für das Himmelreich*, and translated into English as *Eunuchs for Heaven: The Catholic Church and Sexuality*. It was described by the then Archbishop of New York, Cardinal O'Connor, as graffiti written on the walls of a public toilet.[1]

Ranke-Heinemann's work is significant because it is a comprehensive overview of Christian teachings on sexuality over 20 centuries, and the ways these teachings have often been profoundly deleterious in people's lives, especially the lives of women. There were many other noteworthy books on sexual subjects and the Church published in the twentieth century. Two in particular come to mind. One is John T. Noonan's *Contraception: A History of Its Treatment by the Catholic Theologians and Canonists* (1969). Another is by Jean Delumeau, *Le péché et la peur: La Culpabilisation en Occident. xiiie-xviiie Siècles* ('Sin and Fear: Culpabilization in the Occident. The Thirteenth to the Eighteenth Centuries', 1983). Neither treatise covers as many topics as Ranke-Heinemann's book. Her primary quarry is a traditional body of Catholic teachings and laws dealing with sexuality. It is not surprising that she upset the Archbishop of New York as she observed:

> Catholic moral theology has lost much of its reputation in very recent times, and its elaborate antisexual edifice lies in ruins. Many a human conscience has been warped by its insane demands, with their claims to religious validity and divine authority. It has burdened people with idiotic sophistries and sought to turn them into moral acrobats instead of making them more human and philanthropic.[2]

a protestant beginning

Uta Ranke-Heinemann was born in 1928, and raised in a Protestant home in Essen. Her mother studied theology with Rudolf Bultmann in Marburg during the 1920s. Her father, Gustav Heinemann, was the President of Germany from 1969 to 1974. Her uncle was the Minister of the Interior in the time of Konrad Adenauer, the first Chancellor of Germany after the Second World War.[3]

Even as a young child, Uta was perplexed by theological issues. She was particularly preoccupied by the question as to whether there is a life after death. Occasionally she would lie awake for lengthy periods, before she fell asleep imagining herself 'lying in a coffin: for ever and ever and ever'.[4]

In 1944, the city of Essen was mostly razed by bombs roughly six months before the war ended. Her family home and local school were destroyed. Her parents took her to live in Winterberg, where there was no school for her to attend. So her mother took her on a trip to Marburg to visit Rudolf Bultmann in his home. Uta's mother asked Professor Bultmann whether her daughter could stay in his home and continue her studies in Marburg. Uta was 17 at the time. Bultmann responded graciously and benignly, and assured Uta's mother that he, his wife, and daughters looked forward to having Uta in their home.[5]

Bultmann achieved notoriety during the 1940s by arguing that myths in the parts of the Bible peculiar to Christians need not be regarded as essential to Christian faith. When it became known that Uta was going to stay in his home, one of her father's closest friends, Friedrich Graber, wrote to her advising: 'Professor Bultmann doesn't believe in the resurrection: Don't let yourself be influenced by him.'[6] As mentioned in a previous chapter, Bultmann had argued that the resurrection is best understood as an event in the life of a believer rather than as an event in Jesus' life:

> The event of Easter, insofar as it can be referred to as a historical event alongside the cross, is nothing other than the emergence of faith in the risen one in which the proclamation has its origin. The event of Easter as the resurrection of Christ is not a historical event; the only thing that can be comprehended as a historical event is the Easter faith of the first disciples.[7]

Uta was keen to learn from Bultmann. Every Tuesday and Friday afternoon she studied the works of Plato with him in Greek. She also studied Protestant theology in Marburg. She changed the course of her life in 1954 by becoming a Catholic.[8]

She eventually became the first woman in Europe to become a professor of Catholic theology. That is not a slight achievement, and that is partly why she is worth considering in this book. Her appointment was in the University of Essen, but was interrupted in 1987 when the Vatican removed her licence to teach in a Catholic faculty. In that year she publicly questioned the historical verisimilitude of the doctrine that Jesus was born of a virgin mother.

eunuchs for heaven

Stung by her fate, she responded by publishing *Eunuchs for Heaven* the following year. The book takes its title from a teaching attributed to Jesus in Matthew's

Gospel: 'For there are eunuchs who have been so from birth, and there are eunuchs who have been made eunuchs by others, and there are eunuchs who have made themselves eunuchs for the sake of the kingdom of heaven. Let anyone accept this who can' (Mt 19: 12). There has been a long tradition among Christians of interpreting this verse figuratively as a summons by Jesus for his followers to assume a life of celibacy. Ranke-Heinemann argues against this tradition by noting that the verse's first word, the conjunction 'For', links the verse to the preceding one, in which Jesus urges people to renounce adultery. Both verses are concerned with avoiding adultery, not with a duty to undertake celibacy.[9]

Religion and sex were closely intertwined in most ancient cultures. The earliest extant religious writings, from Sumeria, describe in sacral terms an erotic love between the Goddess Inana and her partner Dumuzi.[10] Relating the sacred and the sensual has normally proved a taxing task for Christian theologians in the past. One of the more unmistakeable marks of Christianity is that many of its lodestars are portrayed in its lore and legend as asexual: Jesus has no sexual intimate; his mother is a virgin – before and after his birth; his apostles are emboldened to follow him and, by implication, to dump their wives; his putative foster father, Joseph, is portrayed in Christian iconography as too old and decrepit sexually to delight his much younger spouse; Augustine abandoned his concubine; Aquinas refused to be lured by the temptress his brothers delivered to him; and most of the canonized saints of the Catholic tradition are celibate popes, bishops, priests, canons, nuns and monks. Mary Magdalen, a contemporary of Jesus and suspected of sexual activity by later male ecclesiastics, is usually and traditionally maligned as a sexually wanton, though reformed, woman. In 2001, Pope John Paul II beatified Luigi and Maria Quattrocchi, thereby preparing the way for them eventually to be declared saints. On the advice of their spiritual director, Luigi and Maria spent the last 25 years of their married life in separate beds.[11] Their beatification dispatches an unhelpful signal to most couples that closeness to God requires distance from bodies.

christian sexual pessimism

Very little is known of Jesus' attitudes to what is now called sexuality. He is not remembered as a person who was squeamish about pleasure and sensuality. The Gospels of Matthew and Luke record that his opponents vilified him as a glutton and a winebibber (Mt 11: 19; Lk 7: 34). Ranke-Heinemann begins *Eunuchs for Heaven* by slighting views that present Jesus as a joyless decrier of pleasure. The primary purpose of her book is to take issue with what she regards as 20 centuries of Christian pessimism about sexual activity.[12]

Christianity has a very long and, for some, utterly overbearing theological tradition that insists that intimacy with God requires abstinence from sexual relations with people. Since 1139 CE, it has normally been required of men seeking to be ordained in the Catholic Church of the Roman Rite that they be celibates. The Council of Trent (1545–63) precluded married men from the priesthood at a time when Protestant reformers were reminding their public that a life of celibacy was not required by what Christians call the New Testament. In 1979, the year after Pope John Paul II became Bishop of Rome, he published a letter addressed to the priests of the Catholic Church. In it he taught that compulsory celibacy for Catholic priests is an 'apostolic' doctrine.[13] If he means by 'apostolic' a reality 'related to Jesus' apostles', his case is disingenuous, because most if not all of the Twelve Apostles were married men, and they were not priests in either an ancient Jewish cultic sense, or in a post-Theodosian Christian sense.

The papal court has long been a breeding ground for strongly expressed views on sexuality. Pope Siricius dispatched a letter to a bishop called Anysius in 392. It declared: 'Jesus would not have been chosen to be born of a virgin had he been compelled to regard her as so incontinent that the womb in which the body of the Lord took shape, that hall of the Everlasting King, would be defiled by the presence of male seed.'[14]

So entrenched is sexual pessimism in the Christian theological tradition that one of its greatest theologians, Thomas Aquinas, used a panoply of terms to deride copulation within marriage. He variously described it as *immunditia* ('filth'), *macula* ('a stain'), *foeditas* ('foulness'), *turpitudo* ('vileness'), *ignominia* ('disgrace'), *deformitas* ('degeneracy'), *morbus* ('disease') and *curruptio integritatis* ('a corruption of the inviolate').[15]

Aquinas' understanding of sexuality was so bizarre that he described the process of begetting devils' children through copulation. His understanding relied on a theory of semen-transmission: 'one and the same devil could procure semen by copulating with a man in female guise (as a succubus) and then, after assuming male form, transfer that semen to a women (as an incubus).'[16]

By and large, the Christian theological tradition is an elaborate anti-sexual edifice. That said, its suspicious attitudes to sexual engagement should not automatically be judged by contemporary sensibilities. Modern fastidiousness about health and cleanliness might help anyone understand 'why sex might appear degraded in an age when many men and women did not choose their own spouses, and when bathing was rare, disease rampant, pregnancies, infant and maternal mortality frequent, and scientific medicine unknown.'[17]

Moreover, the women of the Christian tradition who become consecrated virgins were not always motivated by a loathing of sex. Very often, entering monasteries was the only way for some women to escape the repressive control of men in feudal societies:

> Extreme fasting, akin to today's anorexia, was employed by Saint Catherine of Siena and Saint Clare of Assisi, among hundreds of others, as their only way of escaping male clerical control and establishing some autonomy of their own. Dominated by the male church in every other way, they could defy and frustrate their own eating habits, their own bodies, in reflection of a familiar contemporary claim. Beneath the surface accidents, the struggle for individuality, for breaking the male ordering of their existences, was the true story of their lives.[18]

paul and augustine

Two of the most significant influences on Christian attitudes to sex were Paul of Tarsus and Augustine of Hippo, and both of these men vehemently opposed sexual practices that subsequently became widespread in contemporary societies. It is unlikely that Paul ever met Jesus, in whom he became an ardent believer. The core of his preaching about Jesus was a proclamation of the latter's death and resurrection. Paul apparently expected Jesus to return to earth very soon after his glorious resurrection. Thus, virginal living was highly esteemed by Paul: there was no point doing anything if a forthcoming messiah would obliterate current human customs. If people could not control themselves, says Paul, 'it is better to marry than to be aflame with passion' (1 Cor 7: 9). Paul opposed divorce, denounced all forms of extramarital sex, condemned adulterers and male prostitutes, together with drunkards and thieves – all slighted as people unfit for heaven (1 Cor 6: 9). He clearly denounced sexual activity between males (Rom 1: 27). He slighted women who 'exchanged natural intercourse for unnatural' (Rom 1: 26), without specifying precisely what activity he had in mind. The Hebrew Bible, by the way, is entirely silent on the matter of female homosexuality.

Paul's letters were not intended to be read by people in Los Angeles or Moscow today. They were occasional texts, written to and for particular ancient local communities in cities like Corinth and Rome. They were composed to address specific individuals in the communities, to correct perceived vices, to offer a personal theological vision, and to call into question customs he disliked. They subsequently exerted a far-reaching influence in the formation of a traditional Christian attitude to sexual relations that relegates women to an inferior status to men, that renounces divorce, adultery, masturbation, male-male sex, and which confines copulation to marriage.

In the middle of the twentieth century, Paul's Letter to the Romans was described as 'the most important theological work ever written'.[19] Commentaries were written on it by Origen, Ambrose, Augustine and Karl Barth. For homosexuals, 'this pre-eminence has been tragic, for it has enshrined an intemperate diatribe at the very heart, if not of Christianity, then at least of Christian theology.'[20]

Almost as towering as Paul in the edifice of traditional Christian theology is the figure of Augustine. At a time when the Roman Empire in the West was gradually waning, Augustine served as the Bishop of Hippo, a city in North Africa. He had not always been a Christian. He converted to Christianity after living as a Manichean, that is, as a disciple of the Persian prophet Mani (216–77 CE). Manicheans espoused an eclectic religious world-view that combined elements of Platonism, Gnosticism and Christianity. Portentously for the development of Christian theology, Manicheans taught that sexual desire and activity were intrinsically evil since they lead to souls being trapped in bodies. Those of their members who could renounce sexual activity and thoughts were called adepts.[21] Augustine never became an adept because for many years he could not abandon his concubine, with whom he raised a son.

When Augustine became a Christian he was not able to discard a pessimistic view of human nature and sexual desire that he professed as a Manichean. His theology establishes a direct link between the Fall of Adam and Eve, sin and sex. More explicitly, he taught that original sin, the sin inherited by all human beings because of the Fall in the Garden of Eden, was transmitted to all human beings through semen emitted in sexual encounters.[22] Augustine was the greatest of the Church Fathers. It is Augustine, Ranke-Heinemann concludes, who is also primarily responsible

for welding Christianity and hostility to sexual pleasure into a systematic whole. His influence on the development of the Christian Sexual Ethic is undisputed, and the papal condemnations of the Pill by Paul VI (1968) and John Paul II (1981) were heavily coloured by it. To speak of sexual hostility, therefore, is to speak of Augustine. He was the theological thinker who blazed a trail for ensuing centuries – indeed, for the ensuing millennium-and-a-half. The history of the Christian sexual ethic was shaped by him.[23]

For most of Christianity's history, its bishops taught their communities that the primary purpose of sex is the generation of children. The teaching of the bishops was highly effective in Christian countries. In the early decades of the nineteenth century in England, the average woman had nearly eight children, whereas in the seventeenth century, English women bore on average four to five children.[24] During the twentieth century the reproductive labour of women declined drastically around the Western world, and not just in England.

the twentieth century's sexual revolution

Birth rates continued to decline in the West during the twentieth century. One reason for the decrease was a revolution in sexual behaviour that is symbolized by a socially pervasive use of birth control. The revolution involved a growing repudiation of Christianity's age-old derogation of the physical and its teaching that sex is for generating children and no other purpose. It is more widely recognized now that sexual activity has multiple purposes and results: to relish pleasure; to relax the body; to conceive offspring and, most difficult of all, to establish *and maintain* human intimacy. The contemporary sexual sea change in the West is at root a cultural rejection of the theology of Augustine, which in itself defers to the legacy of Paul.

Since the 1960s, Western societies have become more sexually enthused and libidinously supercharged. The catalyst for a more blatantly freewheeling approach to sexual interchanges is modern: the technological uncoupling of sexual engagement from the production of children. In the 1920s, 'the first publications intended specifically to inform men and women about birth control appeared'.[25] In England, Francis Place (1771–1854) produced the first handbills in 1820 to inform people about birth control. In the two centuries between 1770 and 1970, the two most significant direct methods for controlling birth were abortion and self-restraint. From the 1840s to the 1930s, new technologies greatly facilitated the manufacture of condoms. The vulcanization of rubber was developed in the 1840s and was used for condoms by the 1870s. Liquid latex was used as a substitute in America in the early 1930s.[26] The Pill was available to be prescribed in 1961, thus granting women another way to sunder sexual coupling from conception.

Christian tradition restricted sexual activity to marriage, and several denominations require their adolescent members to remain sexually disengaged until marriage. The modern age brought with it improved nutrition, antibiotics and drug therapies that have led to an earlier onset of puberty in children in regions benefiting from the goods of the West. The net result is that very young teenagers are sexually developed, but not financially solvent enough to cohabit with a partner or partners in a home of their own. To insist on sexual abstinence before marriage can create an enormous sexual tension and frustration in young physiologically developed people. Contraceptive methods devised over the last 200 years are relied upon by young people currently if they have no intention of either marrying or rearing children. They represent yet another aspect of a major sexual revolution that has transpired in the West, especially since the 1960s.

Readily available and widely diverse means of birth control only date from the twentieth century. The North American moral theologian, Charles Curran, draws attention to the way contraception became popular during the last century:

> The widespread acceptance of contraception is recent and has taken place well within the twentieth century. Individuals do not make human moral judgements in the abstract but in the concrete situation. A number of very significant social factors have influenced the near unanimous acceptance of contraceptive practices within marriage – the increased life expectancy of all human beings; massive improvements in infant and child health care; the realities of an increasingly urbanized and industrialized society; the changing role and function of women in society; the wider and more accurate understanding of the physiology of human reproduction; the recognition of the population explosion and the need to limit population; the development, and the ready availability, and active promotion of newer, more effective forms of contraception.[27]

While Charles Curran summarizes well why so many have readily concluded that contraception aids human well-being, it needs to be noted that much of what he says about recent social factors does not apply at all to vast masses of wretchedly poor people today. Their life expectancy has not been increased as it has been for the inhabitants of Japan. They enjoy no massive improvements in infant and child health care; and they are not offered readily available and more effective forms of contraception.

The principal challenge for theologians and theists today is to uncouple sexuality and divine desires. Marriage, celibacy, sexuality, cohabiting, masturbation and all forms of sexual expression are, strictly speaking, theologically neutral. They are of consequence for humans, not God. Too often they are discussed by theologians who presume they know what God desires and dislikes, commends or offends. Humans are animals. As such, they often need to control their impulses, but their desires, loves and attractions are, in the first place, purely human, not religious. People can certainly behave very badly in their sexual encounters with others, and the sexual revolution is faithfully accompanied by a galaxy of sexually transmitted infections. Yet the mistake of the Christian tradition has often been to transfer natural, animalistic desires and behaviour into a sacral realm. Whether a person marries, or remains celibate, or lives with a partner, is a human option based on human influences with human consequences.

condemning what is not understood

The sexual revolution has rejected the Augustinian pleasure-fearing understanding of human relations. Many would agree that Augustine was right to be wary of desire:

> One-night stands, child sex abuse, Internet porn, date rape, compulsive masturbation, raunchy bachelor parties, adults-only strip clubs, or any sexual encounter in which one person is left feeling used and abused would all be instances of what Augustine (and most Christian churches today) would call a hideous corruption of the God-given gift of human sexuality.[28]

Others charge that Augustine's coupling of original sin with sexual engagement induced a sense of morbid and unnecessary guilt in a countless number of Christians over the ages. The sexual revolution is a very recent phenomenon in terms of the span of human history. It is impelled by modern knowledge of biology, physiology and psychology. Even so, there are many aspects of the way people relate to each other sexually that are still not adequately understood. There is no scientifically agreed explanation, for instance, of why people of the same sex can be attracted to each other; why some adults are sexually drawn to very young children; why some people are excited by the prospect of sexual connection with a horse; why others can only masturbate with shoplifted women's underwear; and why still more seek sexual thrills through torture.

The study of animals' sexual behaviour is still in its infancy. In the late twentieth century, zoologists and biologists identified and documented sexual encounters between members of the same sex in at least 450 animal species, including primates, marine and hoofed mammals, carnivores, marsupials, rodents, insectivores, as well as waterfowl, aquatic, wading, perching and shore birds.[29] Sexual identity and behaviour is still not entirely comprehended among all animals, including humans. This has not inhibited many moralists from condemning specific practices in the starkest of terms. In 50 years' time, if not sooner, Christianity's leaders may well be impelled to admit that their tradition has been as skewed on matters sexual as it was to condemn Galileo, tolerate slavery, launch crusades and burn witches.

conclusion

The contemporary sexual revolution in the West is not an exercise in wantonness and self-indulgent licence. Like other cultural evolutions in the modern age, it is based on knowledge and insight. Augustine, and those who followed him for over 1,000 years, did not acknowledge that sexuality is an intrinsic part of authentic humanity.[30] Sexuality is not a thing a person possesses. It is a mode of being in the world that is indispensable to any person's fundamental identity.

The sexual revolution is not yet over. It has not even begun in many parts of the world where women are routinely subjugated to men, worn down by child-bearing, have no access to contraceptive means, and are vulnerable to infection by HIV. The sexual revolution has not begun in places where homosexuals are buried alive (the practice is still current); where children are routinely sexually abused; and where prostitutes are enslaved to pimps. The sexual revolution has certainly not taken the Vatican by storm. The authority of the latter, or more particularly of the papacy, suffered its greatest blow in the latter half of the twentieth century when Catholics, by a huge majority, totally ignored Pope Paul VI's prohibition of so-called artificial contraception in his encyclical of 1968, *Humanae Vitae* ('Of Human Life'). His teaching, perpetuated by John Paul II, is a clear example of a moral doctrine that Catholics have refused to receive. To those within and without the Catholic Church, it can appear perfectly absurd for aging celibates housed in the oligarchy of the Vatican, who forsook and forswore sexual relations before they had experienced them, subsequently to police the sexual activities of others not so constrained.

The sexual revolution of the twentieth century was in part a scientifically informed debunking and rejection of Christianity's creed of sexual pessimism. Human beings now know much more about the function of their bodies and have a better understanding of mental ill health than 200 years ago. The revolution was also an exposure of Christianity's most famous theologians' fetishistic focus on sex, and especially of Augustine's dire doctrine of original sin's transmission through semen. Libraries of Christian moral dissertations on bodies and bodily effluvia give the clear though false impression that the bedroom, rather than the battlefield, is the primary site of sin and suffering. Current cultures may well involve too much self-aggrandizement, individualism, hedonism and dandyish dilettantism, but their inhabitants can at least normally see that sex in itself is neither depraved nor degraded.

18

John Hick: b. 1922

It is a mistake to suppose that God is only, or even
chiefly, concerned with religion.

William Temple

Religious beliefs have practical consequences. If the devotees of a religion believe
their doctrines and practices are uniquely true, and other religions are shams,
they can easily behave intolerantly and violently towards others. The belief that
Jesus was a deity, sent by the Creator of the world to begin the Christian religion, and to establish a Church, has often led Christians in the past to force or
invite others to become Christians. Normally, people initiated into a religion

know very little about other religions. This ignorance, too, can feed irrational fear and bigotry towards unmet religious strangers. When theologies produced in the first half of the twentieth century are compared with those emanating from the second, it soon becomes apparent that the former are often much more introverted than the latter. They show little interest in, or explicit knowledge of, religions apart from Christianity, and their authors frequently assume that because Christianity is exclusively legitimated by God, other religions are pretences or pale shadows. This situation began to change slowly after the Second World War. One of the philosophers and theologians involved in engineering that change was John Hick, a retired Presbyterian minister and a philosopher, who used his training to reinterpret Christian teachings in the light of the world's religions.

John Hick published an autobiography in 2002. He observes therein that:

> A great deal of contemporary British (and also German) theology continues to be depressingly inward looking, a continuation of traditional Church Dogmatics. Within the churches there is today a great concern and effort to contribute to solving the problems of British society and of the world. But theology itself remains basically as it was several generations ago. The more outward-looking theologians have grappled with the reality of secularism, have absorbed the insights of feminism, and are facing the challenge of modern science – in the latter area in particular much excellent work is being done – but few have faced more than superficially the issues raised by the fact that Christianity is only one of the great world faiths, and does not seem, when viewed throughout history and around the world, to be spiritually, intellectually or morally superior to all other religions, as however its theology implicitly claims.[1]

Hick's work is a challenge to theologians to take their heads out of the ecclesiastical sand, and to think again about those dogmas that assume and imply Christianity's peerless superiority over other religions. It may be the case that 'in the twenty-first century Hick will best be remembered as the most significant advocate of a philosophy of religious pluralism that challenges the soteriological hegemony of Christianity.'[2]

England in the last quarter of the twentieth century was a fertile incubator for the study of religions. Ninian Smart (1927–2001) promoted that study in Birmingham, and then at Lancaster, while in early 1991, Keith Ward (b. 1938) moved from King's College, London, to Christ Church in Oxford, where he began work as Oxford's Regius Professor of Divinity.[3] In that Chair he introduced undergraduate and postgraduate courses in Oxford's Theology Faculty, and began to publish a series of books comparing themes, practices and theologies of major world religions.[4] Unlike John Hick, Keith Ward's first university studies were in music. Like Hick, he later trained primarily as a philosopher and uses his familiarity with philosophy to expound theology (Christian and otherwise), the history of theology, and similarities as well as divergences among religions.

Interest in the academic investigation of religions flourished in the latter half of the twentieth century under multiple stimuli. Large-scale transmigrations of peoples after the Second World War brought adherents of different religions into close proximity to each other in religiously mixed societies. Comparatively inexpensive air travel on an international scale enabled millions of people to encounter religious cultures unknown to them, and as a result they could see at first hand that there are vast nations and cultures whose citizens are as happy as human beings can be, without having any contact with Christianity. Television and the Worldwide Web enabled people in any corner of the planet to see images of, and study texts about, religious strangers in any other corner. Because of enhanced contact between people, and an increased interest in religions, university faculties and departments were established around the world over the last three decades of the twentieth century. In these students, who had no particular fondness for the Church, or interest in theology, could investigate the difficult intellectual problem of what constitutes any religion, and become familiar with beliefs and practices of particular religions. Doing so they could avail themselves of the insights of the philosophy of religion, the sociology of religion, the anthropology of religion and the psychology of religion.

a boy philosopher

John Harwood Hick was born in the port town of Scarborough, England, on 20 January 1922.[5] He had a brother, Pem (Pentland), who was two years older, and eventually a sister, Shirley, who was born two years after he. His relations with his mother, Aileen, were good: 'She was a wonderful mother, always loving and understanding, devoting herself utterly to the interests of her children and later also her grandchildren.'[6] John's dealings with his father, Mark, were strained. Mark was politically conservative. During the First World War he worked as a lieutenant commanding a howitzer battery. By contrast, John as a young man was a socialist and a conscientious objector during the Second World War. Mark Hick was also upset that John abandoned the study of law to prepare for Presbyterian ministry.[7]

presbyterian churches   Protestant Churches that are governed by elders have since the sixteenth century been called 'Presbyterian', from the word 'presbyter', which in Greek means 'elder'. Leaders of churches in the early centuries of Christianity's existence were often called 'presbyters'. Presbyterian government in churches involves the members of congregations cooperating with each other to resolve arguments, approve the appointment of ministers, and to establish rules for the community. Particular Presbyterian congregations are led by a group of elders. Different groups in a geographical region unite to establish a presbytery. Presbyteries are not governed by bishops, but by representatives of clergy and lay people. Presbyterianism first emerged in Scotland under the leadership of John Knox (1514–72). In contemporary terms, the polity of Presbyterian churches could be called democratic.

John Hick's education in primary school was unpleasant. He attended a private school called Lisvane, whose headmaster was mentally unbalanced and was later imprisoned for pretending to be an army colonel. Under his direction, bullying thrived in the school, and the boys were regularly shouted at and caned by the masters. On one occasion a master forced Hick to cover his head with a waste-paper basket and stand in a cupboard.

By his own reckoning, Hick was a painfully shy child. He showed signs of being philosophically precocious as a teenager. At the age of 17 he was reading Friedrich Nietzsche's *Zarathustra*, Leibniz's *Monadology*, John Stuart Mill's *Utilitarianism*, as well as Schopenhauer, Freud, Russell, Plato, Descartes, John Locke, George Berkeley, David Hume and Kant.

After primary school, Hick was educated privately at home before being sent as a boarder to Bootham School in York. He stayed there for two years (1937 and 1938). The school was a Quaker establishment, and the students were encouraged to fulfil their potential. When Hick left the school he became an articled clerk at a law firm called Hick & Hands. Twice a week he travelled by train to Hull to train in the city's University College. He stopped commuting during his second term in Hull and begun to live in Cottingham in a student's hostel. By this time the country was again at war and Hull had begun to be bombed by the Germans.

As a child, Hick attended a local (Anglican) parish church. At Hull he 'experienced a powerful evangelical conversion to fundamentalist Christianity'.[8]

His closest friends in Hull were members of an evangelical Protestant group called the Inter-Varsity Group. They were Christian fundamentalists, and Hick adopted their creed, which involved believing that the Bible was verbally inspired by God, that Jesus was God the Son incarnate, born of a virgin and who redeemed the world from sin and guilt by shedding his blood. Enthused by his companions, he decided to switch from studying law to begin training to become a Christian minister. Because his friends were Presbyterians, he decided to become a member of the Presbyterian Church of England. That Church later united with the Congregational Union of England and is now known in England as the United Reformed Church.[9]

Before Hick's ministerial training he enrolled in the University of Edinburgh to study philosophy. He was there between 1941 and 1942, but the Second World War interrupted his studies. Because he was a conscientious objector, between 1942 and 1945 he served in the Friends' Ambulance Unit. He then returned to Edinburgh and graduated as a Master of Arts in 1948. After that, he moved to Oriel College in Oxford, where he stayed for two years and successfully completed a doctorate in philosophy. From there he moved to Westminster Theological College in Cambridge. After three years of preparation (1950–3) he was inducted as the minister of the Bedford Presbyterian church (August 1953). In the same month as being inducted he married Hazel Bowers in the church to which he was minister. They had met at Westminster College.[10]

His stay in Bedford was interrupted in 1954 when he was approached by the philosophy department of Cornell University, which is based in Ithaca, New York. He was invited by the department to apply for a position as an assistant professor with responsibility for teaching the philosophy of religion. He and Hazel moved to Cornell in 1955. In 1957, Cornell University Press published Hick's first major work, *Faith and Knowledge*, which is a study in religious epistemology, and was the published form of his doctoral thesis.[11]

doctrinal doubts

The Hicks moved to Princeton, New Jersey, in 1959, where John began teaching as the Stuart Professor of Christian Philosophy. According to custom, once Hick had arrived in Princeton, he applied to join the local Presbytery. The chair of the committee that reviewed such cases was Clyde Henry, an enthusiast of the work of J. Gresham Machen, an illiberal theological thinker and author of *The Virgin Birth of Christ* (1930). Machen had broken away from Princeton Theological Seminary in 1929 to establish his own seminary.

Reviewing Hick's application, Clyde Henry asked Hick whether he took exception to anything in the *Westminster Confession* (a Presbyterian creed dating from 1647). Hick was honest, declaring that he regarded the Confession as 'completely out of date'. He went on to indicate his reservations about the literal interpretation of the first two chapters of Genesis, which speak of the creation of the world in six days and a Garden of Eden. He neither affirmed nor denied the virgin birth of Jesus, but did not regard it as essential to the doctrine of the incarnation.

That last caveat landed Hick in trouble. His initial reception into his local Presbytery was rescinded by the Presbyterian synod of New Jersey. Had Hick not appealed against this decision he would have been removed from his professorship. Hick's appeal, involving lawyers, was successful. The synod's decision was overturned by a Judicial Commission, which ruled that the synod had made procedural errors.[12]

Hick left Princeton in 1964 and became a lecturer in divinity back in England at Cambridge University.

birmingham's cornucopia of religions

Hick's life took a major turn in 1967 when he became the H.G. Wood Professor of Theology in the University of Birmingham.[13] He found himself working in a city starkly different from Princeton. He was no longer teaching in a seminary, surrounded daily by Protestants, but in a university. Birmingham in the late 1960s was a city that enjoyed a lively mix of different ethnicities and religions, and Hick began to associate regularly with Muslims, Sikhs, Hindus, Buddhists, Taoists, Jains, Bahai's, Vaishnavites and Shaivites. He visited local mosques, synagogues, gurudwaras and temples.

His experiences with all these groups changed his life, and helped him formulate the idea which became his intellectual trademark in the study of religions. He explains this idea in his autobiography:

> ... it seemed evident to me that essentially the same thing was going on in all these different places of worship, namely men and women were coming together under the auspices of some ancient, highly developed tradition which enables them to open their minds and hearts 'upwards' towards a higher divine reality which makes a claim on the living of their lives. They are called in the words of the Hebrew prophet, 'to do justice, to love mercy, and to walk humbly before their God'. At this basic level the religions are at one. In my favourite words of the Sufi Jalaluldin Rumi; 'The lamps are different, but the Light is the same: it comes from Beyond.'[14]

the pluralistic hypothesis

Hick later formulated his central notion as the pluralistic hypothesis: despite external discrepancies between religions, at their core they all refer to what Hick calls 'the Real'. He explained his hypothesis in detail in a book he published in 1989, called *An Interpretation of Religion: Human Responses to the Transcendent*. With this work he relied on Kant's theory of knowledge, according to which people do not know things in themselves but only the appearances of things to them, to explain religious diversity. Since no religion attains knowledge of 'the Real', it is only to be expected that there will be an abundance of interpretations (religions) of the way the Real appears to people. The reason Hick prefers the term, 'the Real', is because he is aware that some religions do not envisage a personal deity as theists do, but have as their focus an impersonal Ultimate Reality.[15] Hick sustained his pluralistic hypothesis throughout the rest of his career with works such as *The Rainbow of Faiths* (1995) and *The Fifth Dimension* (1995).[16]

the myth of god incarnate

In Hick's terms, if all religions share the same fundament (focus on the Real), none is more estimable than another. Arguing thus led him to concentrate on Christology and, more particularly, on rethinking the consequences for all religions of Christianity's doctrine of the incarnation. The fruit of his attention to Christology was the publication of a work, which he wrote in collaboration with others and was published in 1977 with the title, *The Myth of God Incarnate*. Mainly because of its provocative title, this book caused theological pandemonium in England and remains one of the most controversial books of twentieth-century English-language theology. No matter how carefully scholars explain to a general reading public that the word myth means 'a story', and not a concocted fairy tale, the use of the term suggested to many in 1977 that the authors of *The Myth of God Incarnate* were asserting that the doctrine of the incarnation had the same truth value as a narrative about Donald and Daffy Duck.

Seven authors contributed to the book: Hick, Frances Young, Michael Goulder, Leslie Houlden, Dennis Nineham, Don Cupitt and Maurice Wiles, the then Regius Professor of Divinity in Oxford. Hick wrote on 'Jesus and the World Religions', while Maurice Wiles contributed a pivotal and carefully worded chapter called 'Myth in Theology'. He explains that the term 'myth' has only been used in theology since the nineteenth century in the wake of David Friedrich

Strauss' massive tome, *The Life of Jesus Critically Examined* (1835). Wiles concludes that 'myths may be historical in origin but their historical basis may be either very slight or entirely non-existent'.[17]

Hick conceived of editing a book that was eventually issued as *The Myth of God Incarnate*, after his experiences in Birmingham, and following visits to India and Sri Lanka. He later explained the train of his thought:

> I came fairly soon to see that for Christianity the problem of religious plurality
> hinged on the central doctrine of the incarnation. If Jesus was God incarnate,
> Christianity alone among the world religions was founded by God in person and
> must therefore be uniquely superior to all others. This made me look again at the
> traditional doctrine and its history.[18]

the metaphor of god incarnate

Hick pondered the problem which the doctrine of the incarnation generates for Christianity's relations with other religions during the 1980s. In 1993 he published a book-length investigation of the matter called *The Metaphor of God Incarnate*. He had arrived at the stage of preferring to call the incarnation a metaphor, or figure of speech. The book begins with a pithy summary of Christian belief: 'The traditional understanding of Jesus is that he was God incarnate, who became a man to die for the sins of the world and who founded the church to proclaim this.'[19] Hick is primarily vexed by the implications of this understanding: if Jesus was an incarnate God, Christianity must be superior to other religions because its founder was divine. There is nothing, of course, to stop God from establishing several religions, but this thought is not addressed overtly in the opening pages of *The Metaphor of God Incarnate*.

Hick's primary intention with this book is to argue against the dogma of the Council of Chalcedon. That council not only taught a theory of Jesus' two natures, human and divine. It also stated that 'our Lord Jesus Christ himself' taught this theory.[20] Hick takes issue with this, and argues that Jesus did not teach what later became Christological dogma about him, and that the doctrine of the incarnation is aptly regarded as a metaphor rather than as a literal description of Jesus' identity and status. He also argues that 'historically the traditional dogma has been used to justify great human evils'.[21] Indeed it has propelled crusades, witch-burnings, inquisitorial torture and the slaughter of Jews, but it does not follow from the dogma's manifest misuse that it is false. The issue of whether the dogma is true is related though distinct from the question of people using it to inflict suffering and death on others. Not everyone in the past who believed the teaching of Chalcedon was a homicidal maniac!

conclusion

Returning to the matter of whether Jesus taught others about himself in terms of two natures, Hick is right. There is no biblical, empirical or historical indication that Jesus ever taught others he enjoyed divine and human natures. That theory and its terminology date from the fifth century, not the first. The seven authors of *The Myth of God Incarnate* were openly honest: they dared to explain forthrightly to a general public what had been known to academic theologians for well over 100 years. Jesus could not possibly have regarded himself as a deity because he was a strictly monotheistic Jew who venerated the Temple in Jerusalem and its cult, which was certainly not centred on him. The daring authors were charged with upsetting 'the faithful', but they could easily rebound by showing that believers need not be afraid of what is true and accurate, and do not like being deceived and fed religious nonsense.

As intriguing as it is, at least two major problems remain unsolved by Hick's theory of religious pluralism. First, what Westerners call religions advance different, contradictory pictures of the world. Because they are contradictory, they cannot all be equally true. If the terms 'reincarnation' and 'resurrection' are regarded literally, either a person can be reincarnated in another life, or not; either Jesus was raised from death, or not. Second, some religions, *because* of religious tenets, are brutish and bigoted towards groups in their societies. There is no reason why anyone should therefore hold them as valuable. Religions, after all, are made on Earth, not in paradise. They are born in people's minds. That is why, despite any wisdom and love, they can display the stupidities, cruelties, superstitions and fallacies of which human beings are more than capable. None of them deserves to be esteemed as absolute.

19

Tissa Balasuriya: b.1924

In all mothers conception does not take place without sin.

Pope Leo I

South American liberation theologians initially spoke of poor people as such, without devoting much attention to the worst off among the poor, who very often are home-bound women, struggling to feed malnourished children. Tissa Balasuriya, a Sri Lankan, could also be described as the first Asian theologian of liberation who drew attention to the masses of impoverished women and girls in Asia. He did this in the final decade of the twentieth century by publishing a book on Jesus' mother, called *Mary and Human Liberation*.[1]

Mary is a volatile subject for twentieth-century theologians. To recall, Uta Ranke-Heinemann was removed from her professorship in Essen for questioning the truthfulness of the teaching that Jesus was born to a virginal mother, who remained a virgin perpetually. The Bible mentions Jesus' brothers and sisters, who need to be regarded as removed relatives rather than immediate siblings if his mother always remained a virgin. John Hick too encountered difficulties with his appointment in Princeton Theological Seminary when he indicated that he did not regard the story of a virgin birth as an essential component of the Christian doctrine of the incarnation. Tissa Balasuriya encountered even more ominous trouble. Because of his book on Mary he was excommunicated by the Vatican in 1997. He was the first theologian to be excommunicated from the Catholic Church *as a heretic*, or teacher of falsehoods, since the Second Vatican Council. After an outcry that he had been unjustly dealt with by the Vatican, his excommunication was rescinded. The French archbishop, Marcel Lefebvre (1906–91), incurred excommunication in 1988, shortly before his death. He was excommunicated for ordaining four priests as bishops without the consent of the Holy See (the Pope's seat of power and jurisdiction). Hence, he attracted excommunication for a schismatic action, not for heresy or apostasy.

After Vatican II, Catholicism of the Latin Rite experienced a good deal of acrimonious doctrinal squabbling among and between its leaders, theologians and believers. Amid a slew of controversies as to how the Council's decisions ought to be implemented, opposing parties lampooned each other as saboteurs of faith, hard-nosed know-nothings, or atavistic fundamentalists. That a protracted period of intellectual ferment and debate never produced a doctrinal excommunication before 1997 is, at least, an indicator of considerable mutual tolerance among Catholics. Theologians such as Hans Küng, Edward Schillebeeckx, Jean-Marie Roger Tillard, Charles Curran, Jacques Pohier and Leonardo Boff, all endured demeaning hermeneutical skirmishes with curial officials after Vatican II, though none was ever excommunicated as a heretic, apostate or schismatic. It becomes all the more intriguing, if not deeply disquieting, that Tissa Balasuriya's fate was declared more than three decades after Vatican II and its disputatious aftermath. Why him? Why then? On what evidence?

an oblate of mary immaculate

At first sight, Balasuriya seemed an unlikely candidate for excommunication because of his views on Mary, because he was a member of the Catholic religious institute, the Oblates of Mary Immaculate. An oblate (from the Latin, *oblatus*, 'offered') is a person devoted to leading a religious life. The Oblates of Mary Immaculate were founded in 1816. It was precisely over the topic of Mary being venerated as 'immaculate' that led to Balasuriya's skirmish with the Vatican. Traditional language about Mary adulates her as pure, spotless and virginal.

Balasuriya came to the conclusion that such language denigrates women who have borne children. If Mary is immaculate because she was a virgin, women who have reared children are the opposite: dirty, spotty, stained, spoiled and unclean. A *macula*, after all, is a dark spot, and forms the root of 'immaculate'.

Sirimevan Tissa Balasuriya was born on 29 August 1924, in the village of Kahatagasdigiliyain, which lies in a central province of what was then known as Ceylon, and is now called Sri Lanka. He was educated in three different schools: Stella College in Negombo, St Patrick's College in Faffna and St Joseph's College, Colombo.[2] He still lives in Sri Lanka and works mainly as a liberation theologian, while regularly lecturing internationally.[3] 'Sri Lanka' is shorthand. The official name for this tropical island, which lies in the Indian Ocean to the south-east of India, is Sri Lanka Prajathanthrika Samajavadi Janarajaya, that is, the Democratic Socialist Republic of Sri Lanka. The country is renowned for exporting textiles, tea and rubber. It has a long history of dealing with colonizers. It became a Portuguese settlement in 1505. It was taken over by the Dutch around 1650 and became a British colony in 1802, and was called Ceylon. It became an independent British dominion in 1948, and finally a socialist republic in 1972. Its official language is Sinhalese, and its main ethnolinguistic peoples are Sinhalese (Singhalese) and Tamil.[4]

After finishing secondary school, Balasuriya embarked on a long course of study in different parts of the world. In 1945 he received a bachelor of arts degree, in economics and political science, from the University of Ceylon. The upshot of his studies at the university was an awakening to the systematic exploitation of poor people throughout Asia. Asians form the largest sector of humankind today. An overwhelming majority of them are dogged by the degradation of chronic poverty. It is for such people that Balasuriya writes and works.

After graduating, his next stage of study took him to Rome and its Jesuit-run Gregorian University. Graduating there in theology, he was ordained a priest in Rome during 1952. In 1953, he returned to Sri Lanka to labour as a priest. After ten years of work, in 1962 he left for England to study economics in the University of Oxford. Becoming deeply disenthralled by what he perceived as Oxford's extolment of capitalism at the time, he discontinued his post-graduate course there and moved to Paris, where he conducted research at the Institut Catholique and studied sociology in the University of Paris. In 1965, just as Vatican II was drawing to a close, he joined the religious institute of the Oblates of Mary Immaculate.

The 1960s were decisive for his subsequent life. By the early 1960s he had rejected both the Aristotelian philosophy and Thomistic theology that marked the writings of many of his Catholic colleagues. By the end of Vatican II, he had become preoccupied by two problems: the situation of economically debased and enfeebled Asians; and the perplexing theological conundrum of trying to specify Christianity's superlativeness in relation to other major religions. The Sinhalese account for about 70 per cent of the Sri Lankan population. Most of them are devotees of Theravada or Hinayana Buddhism. Balasuriya is the first theologian noted in this book to work in a country without a dominant Christian culture. He is accompanied in his labours in Sri Lanka by the Jesuit theologian, Aloysius Pieris, who has explored the relevance of Christianity in Asia, where by far the majority of people have nothing to do with Christianity.[5]

From 1964 to 1971, Balasuriya served as the Rector of Colombo's Aquinas University. There his new theological ideas about the plight of social victims met resistance from Sri Lankin capitalists. He also drew suspicion from the Catholic hierarchy. So in 1971 he resigned as Rector, convinced that he needed to reconsider the function of theology in relation to ubiquitous poverty. He abandoned large urban life and moved to the village of Talahena, eight miles from Colombo, to establish a Centre for Society and Religion.

Over the years since, he has published a number of noteworthy monographs, including: *Jesus Christ and Human Liberation* (1976); *Eucharist and Human Liberation* (1977); *Sri Lanka Economy in Crisis* (1981); and *Indicators of Social Justice* (1990).

With the publication of *Mary and Human Liberation* in 1990, he continued to develop the driving intellectual passion of his life, which is to theologize for destitute people in terms of God's liberating power manifested in Jesus, and proclaimed by Mary in the Bible in a joyful declaration traditionally called the Magnificat. That title comes from the word 'magnifies' in the first verse of her manifesto:

> My soul magnifies the Lord, and my spirit rejoices in God my Saviour, for he has looked with favour on the lowliness of his servant. ... He has shown strength with his arms; he has scattered the proud in the thoughts of their hearts. He has brought down the powerful from their thrones, and lifted up the lowly; he has filled the hungry with good things, and sent the rich away empty (Lk 1: 46–8a, 51–3).

The idea of God 'lifting up the lowly' in Mary's proclamation helped to focus Balasuriya on the urgent need for him to work for the poor.

mary and injustice

Balasuriya's aim in *Mary and Human Liberation* is clear (subsequent numbers in parentheses refer to its pages, unless otherwise indicated). His purpose is to reflect on Mary's current theological meaning in the context of a brutally unjust contemporary world (ii). In the text's very first paragraph its author sounds a controversial note: 'Mary has been interpreted in favour of male domination and of conformism to the prevailing social inequality' (i). For Balasuriya, 'the social radical significance of the Magnificat attributed to her was bypassed during many centuries' (i).

Having charged that traditional theologies of Mary have often occluded the way she is portrayed in the Gospels, Balasuriya sets out to enquire how Mary came to be so misunderstood. He divides his inquiry into nine chapters. The first considers Mary's place in traditional Catholic devotion. It is followed by an analysis of conventional theologies of Mary. Subsequent chapters ponder the need for Marian theology (Mariology) to be renewed, the role of presuppositions in theology, Mary considered as a mature adult woman, and Mary viewed in relation to her society. The sixth chapter is axial because it explores the doctrine of original sin that serves as a basic presupposition of traditional theology (64–86). It sets the scene for the eighth chapter which reflects on orthodox Marian doctrines such as the Immaculate Conception (which affirms that Mary was conceived without original sin), Mary's Virginity and Divine Motherhood.

In Balasuriya's 'Preface' to his book he indicates he is aware that he is treading on delicate theological ground and is careful to articulate his purpose: '*My intention is not to dilute Marian devotion but to help make it more meaningful and truly fulfilling for everyone*' (19; italicized in the original).

To render this devotion more meaningful he declares that traditional Mariological dogmas are not entirely sufficient for understanding Mary in relation to societies past and present: 'In many ways they have been used to domesticate Mary, women, religion and spirituality' (79). The starting point for his interpretation is not a probing of the dogmas of the Immaculate Conception or Perpetual Virginity of Mary, but the life of Jesus: 'We should, rather begin with Jesus and his work for, more than anyone else, Mary lived for Jesus. Her life was linked to his' (79).

This is a decisive link for Balasuriya because 'Jesus promoted social liberation. The wealth of society was to be for all. He was in favour of resource-sharing' (83). The key to Balasuriya's case is his view that Mary, like Jesus, stands for liberation, and that Marian devotion, or spirituality 'which takes seriously the Magnificat must involve an approach which declares that the goods of the earth are for everyone' (98–9). Balasuriya is here presenting 'a Mariology in which the human Mary is seen as participating in the mission of Jesus, a mission characterized by openness to all humanity' (89), whereas a traditional Marian devotion, and Marian theology, have been associated with, and partly responsible for, the oppression of women. The image of Mary was made to fit into the stereotype of a dominated, patient women, and this Marian model itself fostered a concept of holiness linked to the subordination of women to men, and of the poor and weak to the wealthy and strong (88).

It is easy to see now why Balasuriya would encounter trouble with the Roman Curia, which had been at work since the 1970s to straitjacket liberation theologians. In addition, 1994 was the year in which Pope John Paul II forbade Catholic theologians from arguing that women could be ordained to the priesthood. Balasuriya was undaunted: 'Since women participated fully in the Jesus community there is no reason why they cannot share in the leadership patterns, including the priesthood' (92). Congar, Schillebeeckx, Rahner and Küng all agreed for related reasons, but High Officials in the Curia have been unable to cope with the suggestion of ordained women. It is their loss and that of their Church.

mary and original sin

In the opening chapter of *Mary and Human Liberation*, Balasuriya meditates on Marian hymns sung by English-speaking congregations in Sri Lanka. The hymns praise Mary as a humble virgin mother who is a 'gentle, chaste and spotless maid' (26). She is 'Virgin of all Virgins', 'Lily of the Valley' and 'Mystic Rose' (26). Motifs of sexuality, chastity and virginity are clearly apparent.

Balasuriya is quick to point out that, in contrast to Mary, other humans are portrayed as sinful by these hymns. He argues that classical theology, including its Mariology, is built on the hypothesis of 'humanity's fall in original sin, and our inability, as a consequence, to help ourselves. It is a negative view of humans without the original blessing of God. Mary, on the other hand, is portrayed as the rarest virgin, insulated from having to face the normal trials and temptations of life' (26).

With mention of original sin, Balasuriya goes to the pivot of his book. Traditional dogmatic theology in the West before the Enlightenment tended to interpret the Genesis story of the Fall in literal terms with allegorical embellishments.[6] The Doctrine of the Fall, interpreted literally as if humans were aboriginally fallen because a primordial Adam and Eve fell out of favour with God, serves as the dogmatic basis for three major dogmas of Marian theology: the Immaculate Conception, the Virgin Birth and the Divine Motherhood (Mary as the God-bearer).

All three correspond to sex, sin and virtue. They portray Mary as bodily and sexual. Simultaneously, they subtly underscore a link between human sex and divine redemption. From there it is all too easy to assume that humans are in danger of perdition simply by virtue of their sexual natures and predispositions. In Balasuriya's eyes, to propagate a spirituality (or religious life) centred on Mary's sexual virtue can lead to a preoccupation with sexual sin and defilement, and a forgetfulness of major sins such as social injustice and exploitative male domination: 'This Marian Spirituality makes for less socially concerned women and men in the Church' (27).

After discussing Marian hymns, Balasuriya turns his attention to Marian shrines. He draws attention to Mary championed as a 'Lady of Victories', who sided with Christians against Turks at the Battle of Lepanto. He raises the suspicion that a Mary construed thus is actually a European or Christian Goddess, rather than Jesus' mother who cared for all (32), and certainly did not assist armies.

Having examined traditional Marian devotion, Balasuriya's conclusion is stark: the Mary of theology, spirituality and popular devotions is 'portrayed as one who does not understand the social world, nor the suffering imposed by countries that called themselves Christians in Asia, Africa and the Americas – now called the Third World. This traditional Mary is a Mary of the capitalist patriarchal, colonialist, First World of Christendom' (32).[7]

That stated, Balasuriya moves closer to dwelling on the doctrine of original sin. In his seventh chapter he is careful to clarify that he does not deny original sin 'in the sense of human proneness to evil' (132). What he questions is traditional theology's hypothesis that 'human beings are born into a situation of helpless alienation from God, because of the primary original sin of the first parents' (132). He interrogates the traditional doctrine of original sin in terms of its sources; its incompatibility with God's goodness; and its consequences. He asserts that: (a) it does not come directly from the Bible; (b) it was never taught by Jesus; and (c) it did not come from Saint Paul (132–3). Moreover, Balasuriya contends that the doctrine 'discriminates against females' (141) and people 'of other religions or no religion' (142).

In sum, Balasuriya argues that the doctrine of original sin 'is based on unproved and unprovable assumptions, as for instance concerning the conditions in the Garden of Eden' (140). One could well comprehend John Paul II's displeasure with this text, since Balasuriya charges that both John Paul II and Vatican II speak of Eve as though she had been a virgin in the Garden of Eden. To speak thus obviously assumes what the Bible does not state, and connects the idea of original sin with sexuality (140). The entire theology of original sin in this setting stems from the mistaken tendency to read the Genesis creation stories as historical descriptions of actual past events.

It should not escape notice that the doctrine of original sin was a prime target for many Enlightenment *philosophes*. Because of its intrinsically pessimistic anthropology, it is 'the common opponent against which all the different trends of the philosophy of the Enlightenment join forces'.[8] Balasuriya concludes that the concept of original sin is not found in the gospels and that it evolved during a long history from Augustine to the Council of Trent. The point is: the history of its evolution was Western and Latin, not Eastern or Asian. So why should a pessimistic Western view of a fallen humanity be normative for all people everywhere? Balasuriya drives his point home: European Christians, preaching Jesus as the one and only remedy to original sin, led directly to a baneful history of missionary violence and exploitation (see 142–5). In this, Balasuriya is quite correct to a point. European, dogmatic theology has undoubtedly and often unwittingly inflicted an iniquitous and nefarious impact on Asian peoples.

Balasuriya's response to the plight of poor Asians, and especially of Asian women, is to present Mary as a model of human and political liberation: 'The Mary of real life, and even in the scriptures, cannot be encountered without a deep questioning of this original sin of Mariology. This is an important challenge for the liberation of Mary to be Mary the mother of Jesus, and hence one concerned with all our concerns' (145). For 'Is it better for Mary to be immaculate, or to be human as other women and men have been and are?' (150); 'Is it necessarily better to be a virgin mother than an ordinary mother?' (150).

the vatican's rejoinder

On 2 January 1997, the Vatican's Congregation for the Doctrine of the Faith issued a notification declaring that Balasuriya 'has deviated from the integrity of the truth of the Catholic faith and, therefore, cannot be considered a Catholic theologian; moreover, he has incurred excommunication *latae sententiae* (can. 1364, par. 1).'[9] The Latin phrase, *latae sententiae*, means 'by imposed sentence'. It refers in Catholic Church law to a penalty automatically incurred by a person who commits a specified offence. The notification to Balasuriya informing him that he had been excommunicated is signed by Cardinal Joseph Ratzinger and Archbishop Tarcisio Bertone. Significantly, it declares that the Sovereign Pontiff himself, John Paul II, approved its proclamation. The most serious charges against Balasuriya according to the notification were that he relativizes Christological dogma, fails to acknowledge that Jesus Christ wanted a Church to mediate salvation, and denies the dogma of original sin and dogmas defining Mary's Immaculate Conception, Virginity and Bodily Assumption into Heaven. Basically, Balasuriya stood accused of heresy. He denied the charges.[10]

---

heresy, apostasy and schism

'**Heresy**' within traditional Christian theology means 'false teaching'. It comes from a Greek verb meaning 'to choose' or 'to prefer'. A **heretic** is someone who decides to embrace a teaching considered false by others. '**Apostasy**' does not so much refer to a specific teaching, but to a rejection of Christianity. An **apostate** is a baptized person who decides to repudiate Christianity. The word 'apostasy' stems from a Greek term meaning 'to stand apart'. An apostate becomes separated from a Christian community. A **schism**, from the Greek for 'division', is not the same as heresy. The latter is concerned with erroneous beliefs, while a schism is a split between Churches or denominations that arises out of disputes about authority and governance among Christians.

To be guilty of heresy, it does not suffice merely to propagate an erroneous view. All people who attempt to talk about God are guilty of arrogance, presumption, flights of fancy, absurdity and obtuseness, because God is unascertainable, unquantifiable, ineffable and unfathomable. To be a heretic a person needs obstinately to refuse to reconsider contested opinions in order to remain within the Church. Heresy is not a primarily problem of knowledge, but of volition. Estrangement from any community easily follows when individuals doggedly cling to beliefs not shared by the group.

Balasuriya was never allowed to defend himself juridically, with legal counsel, before he received the penalty of excommunication. His accusers acted as his judges and punishers. No third party had been able to arbitrate or defend him. Denying self-defence and competent legal counsel might well have been customary ecclesiastically in the baronial Middle Ages, but it is a repellent to humaneness in cultures moulded by the Enlightenment. Cologne's Cardinal Frings argued in an early debate of Vatican II that the methods of the Vatican's Holy Office (now called the Congregation for the Doctrine of the Faith) are discordant with modern times and constitute a cause of scandal for people in the world. As he said: 'No one ought to be judged and condemned without having been heard, without knowing what he is accused of, and without the opportunity of correcting his views.'[11]

conclusion

The key to evaluating Tissa Balasuriya's fate lies in a choice between doctrinal obduracy or willingness to revise and correct ideas. Balasuriya is not a heretic, for the simple reason that his accusers did not demonstrate that he is *doctrinally contumacious*, or stubborn. His excommunication was rescinded on 15 January 1998, a year after its promulgation. In the 'Preface' of *Mary and Human Liberation*, he says his work is 'open to criticism and correction in a climate and context of a genuine search for the truth' (22). These are not the words of an obdurate person.

Years before he was excommunicated, Balasuriya noted the historical significance of liberation theology:

> Liberation theology is the greatest change in theology that has taken place since the time when the Christian church came to terms with the Roman empire under Constantine. Since that time theology had been done, as it were, from the side of the powerful. This is true particularly of the modern period when the European countries expanded into other continents.
>
> Latin American theology of liberation is the first school of theology that clearly reflected the side of the oppressed.[12]

While Balasuriya has not doggedly declined to submit his work to criticism, he has clearly refused to practise theology from the side of the powerful, and in the mode of a neo-scholastic dogmatism. It is important to recall that the Marian piety of medieval Christendom was salient in Pope John Paul II's theology. Each of his encyclicals ends with a paean of praise to Mary. The Pope's Mary is not interpreted primarily as a social liberator concerned with the plight of impoverished Asians exploited by the armies of European Christendom. Balasuriya's Mary is. He is ever keen to point out that her revolutionary song, the Magnificat, rhapsodizes about a God who unseats the mighty and exalts the downtrodden.

20

Don Cupitt: b.1934

What is truth? said jesting Pilate; and
would not stay for an answer.

Francis Bacon

All the talk of poverty, suffering and human misery in this book cannot occlude a
question that became increasingly irksome for Christian theologians during the
twentieth century: are the time-honoured, orthodox and cherished beliefs of
most Christians true? This question sparks others. Are there two worlds: one
above, ideal and unseen; another below, putrid and everywhere manifest? What
about God? Is God really an Omnipotent Father-Creator, Potentate, Judge,
Lawgiver and Punisher of the wicked? Are all people born into original sin? Was
Mary actually able to give birth to children while always remaining a virgin? Does
the Bishop of Rome, unlike any other human being, enjoy the divine attribute of

being able to pronounce infallibly? Was Jesus the Jew the founder of Christianity? Few theologians of a philosophical bent tangled with such questions so forthrightly during the twentieth century and after as Don Cupitt.

Whatever else he is, Don Cupitt is laudably honest in what he says and writes. He is a priest of the Church of England, and has been so since 1960. While he is still able to communicate *with* his Church, he no longer officiates in the Church. He explains why not: 'Traditionally, a priest has been an institutionally accredited person who purveys a fixed body of knowledge, vocabulary, and set of rituals, and it is no longer in me to be·such a person.'[1]

For such a stance, Cupitt has often been execrated as an atheist, or atheist priest.[2] The charge is inaccurate. He is not an atheist in the sense that he has abandoned talking about and believing in God. What he has renounced is a Greek understanding of God and a Platonic understanding of reality. The former portrays God as other and beyond; the latter sees this world as fleeting and corruptible, unlike an unseen paradise yet to be entered in a higher realm to which human beings ought to aspire. Cupitt says of himself: 'I am a post-dogmatic believer. None of the old dogmas are true any more. The old realistic metaphysics of God is dead, and I certainly do not believe in *that* God any longer.'[3] Since an old metaphysical belief in a God above and out there has disintegrated for Cupitt, he now conceives of God in this way: 'God becomes *an ideal standard of perfection* by which I judge myself and am judged. God is the divinity of *Love*, which above all else makes our life worth living. Commitment to God becomes resolved into commitment to and belief in *life*.'[4] Cupitt latterly thinks that God is a religious ideal and symbol that encapsulates human values and represents to people the goal of a religious life. He regards such an understanding of God as 'the only coherent view of God currently available to us'.[5] In Cupitt's more recent thought, the word 'life' has displaced the word 'God' in everyday speech: people now talk about the meaning and enjoyment of life, in a way former people spoke of God. For Cupitt, 'Life is everything'; 'Life is all there is'; 'Life is God'; 'To love life is to love God'.[6]

a traditional christian beginning

Don Cupitt was born during 1934 in Lancashire, in the industrialized north-west of England. He was initiated into the Church of England as a boy, but lost any enthusiasm for Christian faith as a teenager. He converted back to Christianity when he was 18.[7] By the age of 17 he had become extremely taken by the work of Plato and Charles Darwin.[8]

At 18 he also went to Cambridge and enrolled as an undergraduate to study natural sciences. In his second year of studies he investigated the history and philosophy of science. After completing his degree, he decided to study theology with the aim of becoming a priest. He began his theological pursuits in October 1954. They involved a course on the philosophy of religion. At this stage of his life he was 'a pretty traditional Christian' and 'a metaphysical theist',[9] that is, he believed that God is an objective reality external to human language. Like many of Cupitt's English contemporaries at this point in his life, he was a philosophical realist: he believed that human theories and words about God and the world *refer to realities* exterior to human minds and discourse. Between 1957 and 1958 he studied at Westcott House in Cambridge, an institution devoted to the education of priests and deacons.

In 1959, Cupitt became a Master of Arts in Cambridge, and shortly after was ordained a deacon and then a priest. In 1962 he became the Vice-Principal of Westcott House, and in 1966 he was inducted as a Fellow and Dean of Cambridge's Emmanuel College. The post of Dean required him to preside and preach at religious ceremonies in the College chapel. Coupled with that work were his duties as a lecturer in the philosophy of religion in the University's Divinity Faculty.[10] In that capacity he became a prolific author.

theological non-realism

During the 1970s and 1980s, Cupitt immersed himself in studying and teaching philosophy in Cambridge, especially the philosophy of religion. He began avidly to read French philosophers and cultural theorists such as Michel Foucault, Jacques Derrida and Jean Baudrillard. His studies, and particularly his investigation of avant-garde French thinkers, resulted in five major consequences of his life and thought: first, the formulation of a style of speaking about God that he calls theological non-realism; second, the assertion that Christian orthodoxy has collapsed and is now intellectually bankrupt and incredible; third, a concomitant call for root-and-branch reform in Christian Churches; fourth, the resolute rejection of Platonism coupled with its belief in two worlds – the natural and the supernatural; and fifthly, the articulation of a philosophy and theology focused on daily life in the world. One word serves to explain all these changes in his life – postmodernism. Foucault, Derrida and Baudrillard are all postmodern intellectuals. The topic of the postmodernity will be addressed below. For the moment, more attention is due to Cupitt's later thought.

In 1979, Cupitt described God for the first time as 'non-objective'. In 1980 he spoke of 'theological realism'. Then in 1982 he began to speak of 'non-realism'. Non-realism is a metaphysical world-view which moves beyond the distinction between materialism (reality is only material) and idealism (reality is essentially spirit or ideas). Cupitt was not the first to speak of non-realism. The North American philosopher, Hilary Putnam (b. 1926), began to use the term after 1975.[11]

What does 'metaphysical realism' mean? In Putnam's philosophy it involves two basic theses: first, the assertion that there is a world that is independent of human minds; and second, the view that a single true theory can account for this mind-independent world: it is the goal of science to formulate this theory.[12] In Cupitt's eyes, metaphysical realism is a doctrine about the world which assumes 'that there is a cosmos out there, independent of our minds and yet intelligible to us'.[13]

In opposition, non-realism is the belief that there is no world external to, and independent of, human culture: this-worldly reality is all there is. Transposed to a theological discourse, non-realism means that God is not an objective reality extrinsic to human language. In 1980, Cupitt announced with his book, *Taking Leave of God*, that objective theism had declined. The book is an exercise in negative, or apophatic, theology, but was widely interpreted as an espousal of atheism. With this text, Cupitt concluded that 'For us God is no longer a distinct person over and against us ... .'[14]

His new, inchoate idea of God was tied to a poststructuralist understanding of language. He assimilated this view after reading French postmodernists. For poststructuralists there is no innate framework in language that furnishes words with meaning and referents to a reality external to language. Words are arbitrary signs, and only refer to other words. Such a view is countenanced by Cupitt, beginning notably with his book of 1987, *The Long-Legged*: 'Look up a word in a dictionary. There you find that its origin, its history and its various uses and meanings are all explained in terms of other words'; 'The dictionary's world is self-contained'; 'The dictionary is just print, and never goes outside print.'[15]

It follows for Cupitt and theological non-realists that theology is like a dictionary. Its world is self-contained; its terms only refer to other linguistic signs, and do not designate a reality outside the bubble of language. 'Many people', he says, 'think of the world as being simply there, inertly factual and independent of us. Not so: since our minds, *as* minds, work only in language, nothing is real and nothing is there until it has been formed and produced in and by language.'[16]

The reason Don Cupitt searched for a new comprehension of God was that he diagnosed 'an acute crisis of faith' among his contemporaries.[17] He states: 'Our

structuralism and poststructuralism   Postmodern thought (explored below) is basically the by-product of a twentieth-century fascination with language. In 1916, students of the Swiss linguist, Ferdinand de Saussure, published notes they had taken while attending his lectures on linguistics in Geneva. They published the notes under the title, *Course in General Linguistics*. This book led to the dissemination of the linguistic theory known as structuralism. At the base of Saussure's structural linguistics is an understanding of language that is not to be found among the thinkers of the Enlightenment. For Saussure, 'words, events, ideas and activities don't "mean anything" in themselves – they only made sense when related to other events, ideas and activities.'[18] In other terms, words are only intelligible when considered in a larger structure of other words and ideas. Just as one never understands the Fourth Symphony of Brahms by trying during its performance to listen solely to the leading cellist, one cannot fathom the meaning and truth of words by failing to relate them to other words. Meaning is structured and relational.[19]

Roughly 30 years ago, a group of French intellectuals began challenging Saussure's understanding of language. These intellectuals came to be known as poststructuralists. They included Michel Foucault, Jacques Derrida and Jean Baudrillard. With mention of these three names we encounter the High Priests of postmodernism. The pivotal idea common to them all is the notion that the meaning and truth of statements is unstable, and can never be fixed. For Saussure, the word 'cat' means 'cat' because it is not 'cap' or 'bat'. For poststructuralists, however, the word 'cat' may mean 'a furry four-legged creature, a malicious person, a knotted whip, an American, a horizontal beam for raising a ship's anchor, a six-legged tripod, a short taped stick, and so on.'[20]

great historic belief-systems are now slipping away from us very rapidly';[21] 'The melancholy fact is that today Christian doctrine is dead';[22] for 'by the 1840s the main intellectual claims of ecclesiastical Christianity had finally collapsed'.[23] Perceiving such a crisis, Cupitt set himself the task of 'attempting a reinvention of religious thought as such' partly because 'not one of the major religious traditions can survive in its present form'.[24]

Tied to Cupitt's attempt to reinvent religious thought is his call for Churches to be reformed, especially along the lines of extruding theological realism from their vocabulary: 'Realism', opines Cupitt, 'is spiritual slavery. The realist God of the churches, objective, transcendent, distinct from and in opposition to the believer, is a symbol of religious alienation. The more firmly such a God is believed in ("fundamentalism" being the extreme case) the more demonic and disastrously *ir*religious religion becomes ... .'[25] Cupitt is unsparing in his criticism of long-standing Churches: 'The forms of Christianity that survive longest and have the highest prestige are the least liberal and the most authoritarian, grand, spectacular and cruel.'[26]

Reforming Christianity in Cupitt's scheme involves abandoning Platonism and its adherence to the idea that the world is constituted by two realms. Cupitt often refers to Plato's dualism that involves two domains. His book *Above Us only Sky* is a systematic statement of his thought. Its very title militates against the idea that there is another world above the Earth. It laments the long domination of Platonic thought (roughly 350 BCE to 1800 CE) and posits that the two previously conceived worlds of the supernatural and the natural have merged into one: the everyday life-world of people.[27] Cupitt is clear: the philosophical and religious outlook of medieval theology which was Platonic with its contrast 'between this changing and corruptible material world below and the eternal controllable world above' has collapsed.[28] Announcing its demise is the dominant motif of Cupitt's later thought.[29]

Having declared orthodox, realist theism to be bankrupt, Cupitt has spent the post-1980s part of his career sketching a religion of life: 'Religion must now take a new form. It must become immediate, and fully immanent. It has to be about the way we feel about and relate to life in general, and to our own lives in particular. It is about the principles and values that are to guide our creative, world-building activity.'[30]

postmodernism

One way of describing the recent tradition of humankind with its putative loss of any sense of a higher realm is to call it postmodern. Modern Western cultures formed by the Enlightenment esteem freedom, reason, science, technology, knowledge, tolerance, leisure, wealth, progress and power. In the word's of Philip Toynbee, '"The Modern World" is a phrase which arouses violently different emotions in different members of it, but it might be generally agreed that an apt historical title for it would be *The Age of Analysis*.'[31] The modern mind likes to understand things by analysing their constitutive elements, hence the laborious analytical labours and productive results of modern sciences.

The postmodern mind is very different. It celebrates flux, and venerates impenetrability, chaos, ambiguity, instability and depthlessness. The sense that humanity has emerged from the Age of Analysis into a new phase of its history, clumsily labelled as the Postmodern Era, rose to prominence in the West during the latter half of the twentieth century. The primary consequence for traditional theology that postmodern thought poses is that, unlike the former, the latter denies that meaning and truth can ever be clearly and finally articulated. The truth is, there is no truth. The fact is, there are no facts. All is aimless, rudderless and value-free.

There is no agreement today as to the origin of the term, 'postmodernism'. According to Wolfgang Welsch, it was used as early as the 1870s.[32] Charles Jencks thinks the concept has its origins in the work of the Spanish writer, Frederico de Onis, who uses the term 'postmodernismo' (in Spanish) to describe a literary reaction against modernism in his work of 1934, *Antologia de la poesia espanolae hispanoamericana* ('Anthology of Hispanic and Hispanic-American Poetry').[33]

Despite differences over dating the first appearance of the term 'postmodernism', there is general agreement among commentators that the concept as such became prominent around the 1930s. It became noticeable especially among architects who, reacting against a pragmatic, form-follows-function principle of architectural modernism, developed design styles that were whimsical, playful and ironic. However, it was not until four decades later, during the 1970s, that postmodernism as a philosophy or way of thinking became a topic of major discussion in the academies of the West.

Postmodernism as a posture of thought can be distinguished from *postmodernity*, which refers more to a sociological situation that differs from the modern age and the social arrangements of modernity, and within which postmodernism is a clearly identifiable pattern of thought.[34] Postmodern thought in its most radical guise challenges the key intellectual allegiances of the Enlightenment.

Postmodernism is a hydra-headed monster. It is difficult to define because of its manifold tentacles. At its vaguest, postmodernism is a label that refers to a collective awareness of an epochal termination, and of a transition from one era to another. Writing towards the end of the twentieth century, Albert Borgman puts the point well:

> There is a rising sentiment that we are coming to the close not only of a century
> and a millennium but of an era, too. The sentiment has not quite become universal,
> yet the indications of closure and transition are manifold. One indication is the
> difficulty we have in finding the kind of discourse that would help us chart the
> passage from the present to the future. The idiom we have favoured since the
> beginning of the modern era fails to inspire conviction or yield insight; the language
> of those who are proclaiming a new epoch seems merely deconstructive or endlessly
> prefatory.[35]

As the very word suggests, postmodernism defines itself as a view of the world that stands after and over the modern age. As such, postmodernism falls into two principal categories: (1) destructive or eliminative postmodernism; and (2) constructive postmodernism. The former argues that the intellectual ambitions of the modern project are now bankrupt. So, if modernism stands for reason, destructive postmodernism focuses on illogicality. If modernism champions design and order, postmodernism promotes chance and disarray. If modernism emphasizes determinacy, postmodernism delights in indeterminacy. Destructive postmodernists, like Michel Foucault and Jean Baudrillard, wish to torpedo all-encompassing world-views – like theology. As for the second, more constructive type of postmodernism, it argues that the modern project remains to be developed fully, and that people should not abandon its fidelity to reason and scientific method. In a nutshell, the modern project preached that human beings ought to use their reason and science to produce technologies that would progressively perfect humankind's miserable lot. Eliminative postmodernists insist that the project of modernity went up in a cloud of gas at Hiroshima. Constructive postmodernists, though critical of the dehumanizing consequences of the modern project, hope that it can be improved, rather than abandoned. Jürgen Habermas is a major contemporary German philosopher who is a constructive postmodernist. The North American theologian, David Ray Griffin, stands as an example of a theologian who wishes to elucidate a constructive postmodern theology.

The modern age – postmodernism's foil – that developed with the Enlightenment did not produce what it promised. Enlightened modernity had announced the progressive perfection of humankind's lot by the use of untrammelled reason and natural science. Despite all its success, the Enlightenment engineered world died

> somewhere in the quarter century that began with the allied acceptance of the strategy of obliteration bombing (including using nuclear weapons) in World War II, that continued with the slowly dawning realization of the magnitude of the destruction of European Jewry under Hitler and its manifold significances, that included the revolution of the Second Vatican Council and its remarkable effect on worldwide Catholicism, that saw the emergence of many independent nations in the colonized worlds and the tragic involvement of the super-powers in postcolonial warfare (especially Indochina), that included a profound sexual revolution which provided easy control of human fertility without using aesthetically unappealing means, and that concluded with the variety of cultural revolutions and assassinations which afflicted the NATO world in 1968.[36]

Postmodernism, its champions charge, emerged in the wake of modernity's demise, and is by definition an inherently reactive movement: it rebuffs the major premises of modernity. In other terms, postmodernism is a 'movement of resistance'.[37] It denies, reacts against, vilifies, demytholgizes, attacks and sabotages. It is anti-this and anti-that.

the postmodern condition

If the modern world championed reason, science and technology as the liberators of humanity, it also produced Hiroshima. As some would have it, 'Modernity died on August 6 1945. The postmodern condition we are now living is not merely the result of having been raised on television. As children of Hiroshima, we have always known that modernity is a nightmare from which we must wake.'[38]

Postmodernism, as a late twentieth-century popular notion, was announced eloquently in 1979 by Jean-François Lyotard (b. 1924) in his book *La condition postmoderne: rapport sur le savoir* ('The Postmodern Condition: Report on Knowledge').[39] At the time of writing, Lyotard was the Professor of Philosophy at the University of Paris VIII at Vincennes. He was commissioned to write it by the Council of Universities of the government of Quebec as a report on the state of knowledge in the Western world. In his book he describes how modern cultures try to justify themselves with grand narratives like wealth creation and workers' revolution. He torpedoes these grand narratives by stating that they are simply unreliable because in a highly pluralized world there is no assured and agreed touchstone for guaranteeing indubitable knowledge. All humans enjoy nowadays are particular truths and mere opinion. Hence, in a memorable definition, Lyotard remarks: '... I define postmodern as incredulity toward metanarratives.'[40]

Christian theology is one such metanarrative. It is precisely at this juncture that it becomes evident why postmodernism presents theologians with yet another problem for modern theology. Christian theology, Greek philosophies and the religious discourses and theologies of the world's religions are all metanarratives: they are over-arching, all-encompassing accounts of life's travails and destiny. Even so, eliminative postmodernism denies that any one culture, religion, philosophy or person can articulate an over-arching explanation of reality (a metanarrative). This type of postmodernism seeks to expose the book, the written thesis and the printed page as intellectual arrogances and ideologies. In their place postmodernism locates a new medium of communication, which is a mélange of artificial images, flickering on the TV screen. The postmodern world is a space of pastiche, collage, montage and chiaroscuro.

ten features of postmodernism

Describing and summarizing eliminative postmodernism schematically, it is possible to distinguish at least ten of its principal characteristics.

First, to repeat, it renounces modernism. In its destructive form, it proposes that all that is valid, worthwhile and meaningful in modernity is totally invalid and obsolete in postmodern times. Second, postmodernism is antifoundational. It rejects all forms of truth-claims. It accepts nothing as absolute, and rejoices in total relativism. It is antifoundational in the sense that it 'resolutely refuses to posit any one premise as the privileged and unassailable starting point for establishing claims to truth.'[41] Third, postmodernism entails the denial of reality, in the sense that it insists there is no ultimate reality behind the appearances of things. After the Gulf War of January and February 1991, Jean Baudrillard published a little book called *The Gulf War Did Not Take Place* (French edn, 1991). Therein he argues that the war was not a real war, because it did not involve two adversaries but simply an enemy appearing as a visualized, computerized target.[42] Fourth, postmodernism suggests that people do not perceive a reality but a simulacrum, that is, an image of something. In a postmodern world, all distinction between an image and material reality disappears. Otherwise explained, in the words of Ziauddin Sardar:

> Postmodernism posits the world as a video game: seduced by the allure of the spectacle, we have all become characters in the global video game, zapping our way from here to there, fighting wars in cyberspace, making love to digitised bits of information. All social life is now being regulated not by reality but by simulations, models, pure images and representations. These in turn create new simulations, and the whole process continues in a relentless stream in which the behaviour of individuals and societies bears no relationship to any reality: everything and everyone is drowned in pure simulacrum.[43]

Fifth, postmodernism promotes meaninglessness. For postmodernists, Truth is a lie, and Reason a fiction. The world is a terrain in which no assured knowledge is possible, morality is arbitrary, and reality is indistinguishable in an ocean of tantalizing images. A sixth facet of postmodernism is its generation of radical doubt. Its motto is 'Trust No One', because nobody knows the truth. The secret is, there is no secret. Seventh, postmodernism esteems multiplicities, pluralities and variety. It draws attention to a multitude of perspectives, cultures, reasons, sexualities and genders. It contends that there is no longer one civilization, one religion, or one final truth. Instead, we inhabit a supermarket of competing ethnicities, policies, religions and world-pictures. Eighth, postmodernism is antitotalizing. It concludes that no theory, doctrine or sacred text can explain the fullness of reality: it is incredulity towards metanarratives. Ninth, postmodernism is demystifying, in the sense that it presumes that all attempts to delineate the truth of things are essentially ideological.[44] Finally, and very generally speaking, postmodernists challenge not only the idea that the present is superior to the recently modern past, but also the notion that the modern surpasses the pre-modern.[45] Some postmodernists invest with a renewed importance all that modernity set aside, 'including emotions, feelings, intuition, reflection, speculation, personal experience, custom, violence, metaphysics, tradition, cosmology, magic, myth, religious sentiment, and mystical experience.'[46]

don cupitt's postmodernism

Postmodern principles are amply evident in Cupitt's later writings: 'Everything is contingent; that is, everything is happenstance';[47] 'Contrary to what is even yet widely supposed, our life gets all its moral and religious pathos and dignity precisely from the fact that it's a one-way ticket into nothingness';[48] 'So we see the world as a flux of events-read-as-signs. World-stuff scatters and meanings disseminate unceasingly';[49] 'Much of the popular realistic metaphysics goes when we give up the ideas of substance, matter, mind, pure sense-experience and rational intuition. We are left with a world that is no longer a single cosmos, more a flux of interpretations, theories, perspectives, meanings, signs.'[50]

Don Cupitt is not a destructive postmodernist. He is a priest. He writes endlessly and creatively about God, Christianity, religion and life. The problem with the postmodern tints of his work is that non-realism is not applicable to the majority of human beings who are not sated and wealthy. Their world of grinding unrelenting hunger and destitution is neither a simulacrum nor an arbitrary linguistic illusion. It is a terrain of disease and death.

conclusion

In one of Cupitt's latest books he points out that 'People in the West are about ten times more wealthy than the rest of humanity, have a much longer life-expectancy, and have huge cultural wealth at their fingertips every day. Western society is much kinder to its own weaker members than any previous society ever was.' Cupitt then asks: 'What's wrong with all that?'[51] Not everything, but what about kindness to the gutter-dwellers who are not members of Western society and who are more than ten times poorer than 'People in the West'?

Postmodernists regularly speak in the first person plural: 'we' inhabit a new age of multiple opportunities and in which 'we' must constantly make choices. 'We' are condemned to live by choice in a social supermarket of unlimited possibilities. Problematically, this 'we' does not embrace the downtrodden of the world living in favelas and on putrid streets. They often have no choice, no freedom to change, no means to improve, and no hope for a better future. They are nobodies and nuisances, locked in a numbing nightmare of degrading destitution.

Why are these people absent from postmodern discourses? Because they are too eloquent an indictment of postmodernists' self-absolving strategy of evading social responsibility by declaring that nothing is clearly true, good or morally binding. Ultimately, the postmodern prospectus is not only self-absolving: it is also elegantly self-subverting. It is itself a grand metanarrative. Its argument that no single statement can be recognized as true is thereby by its own canons similarly untrue.

Postmodernism, understood as a collective sense that one age is ending in a period of vertiginous change, while another is tentatively dawning, is a relatively benign affair. Regarded as a valueless celebration of randomness, lack of commitment and apathy with regard to the enfeebled masses of the world, postmodernism is a metanarrative that invites incredulity.

21

Mercy Amba Oduyoye: b.1934

When your hand is in someone's mouth, you do not
hit that person on the head.

Akan Proverb

Theologians born in the same year often produce starkly different discourses.
Disparities between them stem to a very large extent from their biographies and
the settings in which they live. Mary Daly, Gustavo Gutiérrez, Hans Küng,
Wolfhart Pannenberg, Schubert Ogden and Johann Baptist Metz were all born in
1928, and each formed divergent attitudes to God, Jesus Christ, the Church,
politics and economics. Mercy Amba Ewudziwa Oduyoye, the subject of this

chapter, was born in 1934, the same year as Don Cupitt, the preoccupation of the previous chapter. She and Don Cupitt were both students at Cambridge University. Both talk at length about God, Jesus, the Church, culture and the Bible. The way they do so bares hardly any resemblance at all. The primary addressee of Mercy Oduyoye is not the cultivated aesthete troubled by the corrosive effects of postmodern poststructuralism, but impoverished Africans, especially those African women kept under the heel of patriarchy and economically exploited by the results of centuries of colonization.

Hers is a theology of liberation honed for the needs, depredations, sicknesses and crises of Africa. She is Ghanaian, or more specifically an Akan. In her work as a theologian, she has decided that strident confrontation is not a productive way to redress the destructive and demeaning consequences for women wrought by oppressive male social control and economic enfeeblement. Of herself, she tells the story of once becoming piqued by a cabinet drawer that had become stuck. She tried to free the draw with violent pulling, shaking and straining. Without success she became exasperated and opted for the next best solution. She looked for a hammer and an axe. Destruction seemed the only appropriate course. Poised to deliver a blow that would shatter the drawer, she was interrupted by a helper called Richard. He encouraged her to coax the drawer with gentle tapping. He showed her how by gently tapping first the left of the drawer, then to the right. It gave way and opened. She learnt from this experience that gentle coaxing will achieve more than violent, aggressive confrontation.[1]

Instead of belligerence, Mercy Oduyoye has devoted her life and labours to the suppression of oppression, voicing her views with wisdom and wit. She is a virtuoso at formulating unforgettably telling aphorisms, proverbs, sayings and quips. Drawing richly from Akan culture, her pithy prudential observations can convey more comprehension of a seemingly intractable problem than a lengthy dissertation. For instance, when she commented on how and why African women held their peace once they had come to know their oppressors, she disarmingly says, using an Akan proverb, 'When your hand is in someone's mouth, you do not hit that person on the head.' Commenting on the women's liberation movement, she offers the epigram that it was 'trivialized into "women's lib" and articulated by people who cannot distinguish "b" from "p" as "women's lip".'[2] Lamenting people's neglect of their neighbours, she noted: 'We set up neighbourhood watches to ward off crime, but we do not set up neighbourhood watches to look out for the hungry, the homeless, the sick and the housebound.' Ruminating on oppressors and observing that they are only fulfilled if there are people they can suppress, she could remark: 'The tsetse fly must always have blood in its head, or it ceases to be a tsetse fly.'[3] This way of speaking is unlike any other previously encountered in this book. It needs to be, because of the circumstances that bedevilled Africa in the twentieth century and before.

despoiling africa's abundance

Africa is a massive continent, abundant in flora and fauna, minerals, cultures and peoples. It is also a terrain chronically plagued by famine and poverty. As an invaded territory, a substantial contribution to Africa's poverty was European colonization, a result of which is that Africa's national boundaries are arbitrary: the current borders between its countries were fixed by colonial governments and their overlords elsewhere. Poverty is not Africa's only scourge. So too are the human immunodeficiency virus (HIV) and its death-dealing effects, the acquired immune deficiency syndrome (AIDS). HIV/AIDS is not a death sentence in many parts of the West, for people who can afford retroviral drugs. For them, it is an incurable but treatable disease that can be kept in check for many years. Africans are not so fortunate, and are often left to die without the means to pay for the potions of foreign pharmaceutical companies. HIV/AIDS is pandemic, not endemic, in sub-Saharan Africa.

The way colonizers despoiled Africa's abundant riches can be illustrated with reference to one country only – Mozambique. Before Portuguese colonizers took control, Mozambique was a rich source of gold and ivory for Islamic merchants and traders. This trade was destroyed by the Portuguese in the seventeenth century, and replaced by a trade in enslaved people. Enslaved Mozambicans were sent to labour on plantations in Brazil and in the Indian Ocean on the Mascarene Islands. When the Portuguese relinquished control of Mozambique it was one of the most impoverished countries in Africa. So much so, that in 2001 in the Mozambican city of Mascarenha, with a population of more than 500,000, only one ambulance was available to serve the entire population. In that year, 75 per cent of all people – three out of four citizens – lived on less than US40 cents a day.[4]

a life in ghana

Mercy Amba Ewudziwa Oduyoye was born on her paternal grandfather's cocoa farm in Amoana, which lies in the eastern region of Ghana near Asamankese. She was born and baptized on 19 April 1934. Eight days after her birth she was given the name of Amba Ewudziwa. Her four names come from three people: 'Mercy' is the name of her mother; 'Amba Ewudziwa' is taken from her paternal grandfather, Kodwo Ewudzi Yamoah; and Oduyoye is the name of her husband.[5]

The Republic of Ghana used to be a possession of the British Empire known as the Gold Coast. It is officially an English-speaking country. It is a West-African nation on the Gulf of Guinea, and shares its borders with three officially French-speaking countries: Côte d'Ivoire, Togo and Burkina Faso. At the end of the twentieth century its population was about 20,212,000. The peoples in its North are mostly Islamic and speak Gur, while in the South they are predominantly Christian and speak Kwa. Coconuts, coffee and cocoa are the country's principal exports. In 1900, 90 per cent of its population were adherents of traditional African religions, but that figure had fallen to 25.1 per cent by 1995. Catholics arrived in the Gold Coast with the Portuguese in 1471. Protestant missionaries came mostly in the nineteenth century, and the four largest Protestant denominations in Ghana are Methodist, Presbyterian, Evangelical Presbyterian and Seventh-Day Adventist.[6]

After Mercy Oduyoye was born, her placenta and umbilical cord were planted with the seed of yams – an activity among the Akan that links people symbolically with the land from which they survive.[7]

Mercy was born into a matrilineal Akan culture that is unfamiliar to most Westerners. She was the eldest of nine children. Because her culture was mother-centred, her identity and those of all her brothers and sisters depended on who their mother was. Their matrilineally arranged society even determined their political and economic status, which was accorded to them according to the status of their mother.[8]

Mercy Oduyoye's mother was Mercy Yaa Dakwaa Yamoah. Her father was Charles Kwaw Yamoah. Her maternal lineage is linked to a royal family – the Asene, who originated near Kumasi in Amakom, and moved during the Ashanti wars to Akyem. Her maternal grandparents lived in a mission station in Buronikrom, Asamankese, that had been founded by Presbyterians from Basel in Switzerland. When the Presbyterians in charge of the station ruled that only those who had become Christian could live in the compound, Mercy's grandfather moved to another part of the town. He did not want to abandon his attachment to traditional African beliefs. He did later become a Christian, but he never moved back to the Basel mission.

Mercy's paternal ancestors were also considered royal among her people. They came from Apam and Ekwamkrom on the coast in Ghana's central territory. They were Methodists, and worked principally as farmers and traders.[9]

Mercy too is a Methodist. Her father, Charles, became a Methodist minister after having worked as a teacher. She was raised in his Methodist community at

Akyenakrom, and her entire household was involved in the community's ministry. Here father eventually became president of the Methodist Church of Ghana.[10]

---

methodist churches   Methodists, as members of Methodist Churches, take their name from the eighteenth-century religious revival in the Church of England that was led by the brothers John (1703–91) and Charles Wesley (1707–88). The brothers established a Holy Club in Oxford to promote their aim of reinvigorating their religious lives. The members of this club came to be called 'Methodists' because of what others perceived as their 'methodical' routine in worship and daily living.

Most early Methodists were Anglicans who did not intend to secede from the Church of England. They avoided holding their meetings for prayer on Sundays, in order not to be seen to compete with local Anglican parishes.

The Wesley brothers went to Georgia in North America in 1736 to undertake missionary work. The uncoupling of Methodism from the Church of England followed as a result of American Independence.

Theologically, Methodists have been Arminian, believing that Jesus Christ died to save all people, and not just an elect few. They practised infant baptism and celebrated the Lord's Supper, while holding the Bible in high regard. Preaching by lay people was more commonly countenanced than in the Church of England.

Mercy's family lived in various parts of Ghana because her father moved around, teaching in places such as Sunyani, Wenchi, Einneba and Akropong. In the mid-1930s she was educated in Methodist Primary School. Her primary and secondary schooling lasted for ten years. From the Mmofraturo Methodist Boarding School she progressed to Achimota School, where she completed her secondary studies from 1949 to 1952. From there she progressed to the Teachers' Training College in Kumasi College of Technology. She successfully qualified as a teacher and was appointed to teach at Asawase Methodist Girls' School in the region of Kumasi.

While teaching, at the age of 21, Mercy prepared for university studies. She was admitted to the University College of Ghana in 1959. She intended to study geography, but once there she decided to study theology. She undertook further theological studies at Cambridge University, England, where she was taught by theologians such as Alec Vidler and Maurice Wiles. In Cambridge she joined the Student Christian Movement (SCM).

Mercy returned to Ghana after her studies in England and began to teach at Wesley's Girls' School in Cape Coast. Student Christian groups were a major part of her life. She met her Nigerian husband, Modupe Oduyoye, in the SCM, and from 1972 to 1976 she was the president of the World Student Christian

Movement. This led her into a career of mixing academic teaching and writing with ecumenism. She first attended an ecumenical conference in Switzerland in 1966, and in 1988 eventually became a Deputy General Secretary of the World Council of Churches.

Back in Ghana, Oduyoye established the Circle of Concerned African Women in 1989: 'The Circle is a space for women of Africa to do communal theology. ... Circle members are women who are rooted in Islam, Christianity and African traditional religions.'[11] Since 1989, Oduyoye has developed a theology of liberation for Africa in concert with like-minded women concerned by sexism, patriarchy, poverty, political oppression and disease in Africa.[12]

an african theology of liberation

As a Methodist, Mercy Oduyoye holds the Bible in high regard. Her theology has been articulated on the basis of a contentment with the Bible, traditional Christian creeds and the discipline of the Methodist Church.[13] Her publications abound with references to the Bible.

To observe that Oduyoye works and writes from a traditional theological basis is not at all to imply that she is intellectually timorous. She can sting and stimulate with her comments. For example, when once discussing the results of colonization in South America, she observed:

> The spilling over of Europe into the Americas some 500 years ago did not spell peace
> and justice for the indigenous people there. It was in 1992 a real eye-opener for some
> of us that the European descendants of 'Latin America' could think of the word
> 'celebrate' to mark this event and rejoice to name the whole region 'Latin', when it
> is the home of people some of whom are not of Latin descent and do not claim Latin
> as the root of their language. The arrogance of Europe and people of European
> descent knows no bounds![14]

Mercy Oduyoye has published eight books and many articles. Two books in particular, *Beads and Strands* (2004) and *Daughters of Anowa* (1995), are especially useful for glimpsing the main lineaments of her theological thinking. She writes avowedly as a feminist theologian of liberation.[15] As such, she has four principal concerns: first, captivity and oppression as they have been experienced in Afica for centuries; second, the situation and suffering of women in Africa; third, ecumenism; and fourth, theological issues of relevance internationally, discussed from an African vantage point. She strings all of these themes together like beads in a unified necklace, thus forming a comprehensive discourse about God and Jesus and human cravings for liberation and escape from suffering.

In Oduyoye's work, two forms of oppression are specified in Africa: colonial domination of Africans; and the patriarchal subjugation of African women. Struggles to undo colonial and male dominance inspire her theology. She takes the biblical story of the Exodus of Israelites from slavery in Egypt as an apposite paradigm for what God expects of Africans:

> Liberating Israel from slavery in Egypt was a salvific act born out of God's grace (Ex 15: 13). This is what makes the historic exodus so fascinating. It is clear from the political deliverance that the redemption of a community from unjust systems is not outside God's providence, that what God found necessary to do for Israel, God has found necessary to do for the colonised peoples of Africa, and is doing for those held in bondage inside Africa.[16]

As far as Oduyoye is concerned, the colonial period in Africa is not very different from the situation of the enslaved Hebrews in Egypt described in the Book of Exodus. 'White leaders', she points out, were imposed in Africa, '(especially in urban areas), and colonial officers administered the country without involving the people ...'. She regards the Exodus as 'a well-rehearsed event, and in Africa it has not grown stale'.[17] Apart from the colonial domination of Africa she complains of the way a traditional ordering of African societies places burdens on its peoples. According to this ordering, an African woman always needs a suzerain – she needs to be possessed or owned by a man.[18]

women in africa

Helping to liberate women from asymmetrical control exercised by men is a constant aim in Oduyoye's work. She notes that the very concept of a free woman, so prized by feminists in the West, connotes disaster in many Africa societies because an adult female, if she is unmarried, is expected to be obtainable for the satisfaction and pleasure of all males, and will be treated accordingly:

> The single woman who manages her affairs successfully without a man is an affront to patriarchy and a direct challenge to the so-called masculinity of men who want to 'possess' her. Some women are struggling to be free from this compulsory attachment to the male. Women want the right to be fully human, whether or not they choose to be attached to men.[19]

Part of the cultural chaining of women to men in Oduyoye's view is the expectation that women should not resist motherhood and child-bearing, even if fulfilling a duty to give birth to children will result in a woman's death. An expectation such as this can breed 'cultural sexism', in that women are rigidly held in subjugation to the needs of men, while men are free and mobile: 'A woman takes her place and begins to work from the time she takes her first steps until she can no longer move about; then she continues to work with her hands and tongue.'[20]

The influence of Western customs in Africa has only made women's plight worse in Africa, as Oduyoye is at pains to underscore. She charges that Westernization in Africa introduced the idea of a 'maintained' woman: 'house wives who "do nothing", meaning women whose labours in the family are not rewarded with paychecks.' She also observes that an unmarried male, according to Western mores, progresses from the title of 'Master' to 'Mister' on becoming an adult, with no connotation of his marital station. A similar progression for a female involves moving from 'Miss' to 'Mrs', indicating that 'she has passed from the authority of her father to that of her husband'.[21]

Drawing attention to the plight of women in Africa is a constant refrain in the writings of Mercy Odoyuye. She struggles to relate Jesus' gospel (good news) of God's just kingdom in a context in which women are regularly subjugated and their wishes ignored. She notes that among Christians in Africa today, popular theologians are charismatic leaders who preach in mega-churches, mass rallies and through the mass media. People parade Christian slogans on vehicles and store fronts, yet:

> None of this specifically deals with the challenges women have to face, beyond counselling resignation from Satan. What is the good news to a woman accused of being a witch because she could not bear to submit to patriarchy but the institutionalizing agent of the might of men that seeks to control and appropriate the sexuality and reproductive services of women?[22]

In northern Ghana, women often have to seek refuge in Gambaga to flee molestation or death after being accused of witchcraft: 'The gospel for women needs to teach and practice the biblical affirmation that all human beings are made in the image of God and are therefore worthy of honor and *shalom*.'[23]

The women whom Oduyoye speaks about want, she declares, 'the right to be fully human, whether or not they choose to be attached to men', and to decide for themselves for their day and situation 'what constitutes a liberating and liberative life'.[24]

god, jesus and salvation

Oduyoye's description of colonial and partriarchal oppression in Africa is directly linked to her understanding of God, Jesus, and the cravings of subjugated people for deliverance or salvation.

The creation stories in the Book of Genesis were greatly disputed among Christians in the twentieth century. Some saw them as literally descriptive of the world's beginnings, whereas others read them as mythical tales ascribing the origins of everything to God. Oduyoye is dissatisfied with the first of these opposed interpretations: 'In Africa, as elsewhere, a literal reading of the creation narratives has stifled the theological content and buried the chance for real reflection.' She regards the narrative (Gen 1–3) as a challenge to, and a judgement on, the way people run the world. The narrative underscores 'the fact that the universe belongs to God who created it and that there is an interdependence of God's world and God's people. The story is a challenge and a judgement on how we run the world in our day. God speaks to humanity and humanity has the ability to respond to God. Made in God's image, we are expected to be God-like.'[25]

The crucial question in Oduyoye's theology then becomes, 'What is God like?' Unlike uncaring, oppressive colonizers and patriarchs, **'God is the one whose womb becomes agitated at the sight of suffering and meanness.'**[26] No one considered thus far in this book has spoken of God in such a way. As an Akan, Oduyoye concludes that in both Hebrew and Akan perspectives God 'is not the Impassible One of Greek philosophy. God is affected and is not immune to mutability. In fact God is plainly vulnerable.'[27]

She links the suffering of God to that of Jesus regarded as a messiah: 'One of the unique contributions of Christianity to religion is the doctrine that the messiah who suffered is certainly the very image of the suffering God. God's creative and redemptive powers flow out of this suffering love.'[28]

Oduyoye does not present Jesus as a figure who stood apart from practical struggles to free people from oppressors: 'In Jesus God brings us to a style of life that put others first, that saves others, leaving God to bring about the resurrection that will transform one's own wretchedness.' Just as God is said in the Bible to have rescued the Israelites from political bondage, Jesus gives the example of refusing to stand by while others are being hurt, exploited, cheated or left to die. That which constitutes redemption in her work is quite clear: 'Liberated from the principalities and powers of this realm, we continue to work and live before God. That is salvation.'[29]

the unacknowledged neighbour

The implications and usefulness of Mercy Oduyoye's theology are not confined to Africans. They address an ever-present problem in contemporary societies – the neglect of the lonely, insane, decrepit and aged. Some cultures are better than others at tending to old or infirm citizens, but it is easy for anyone to fret as an unacknowledged neighbour in a large metropolitan city. Part of Oduyoye's theology of liberation is a focus on people who remain uncared for and unrecognized in contemporary cultures:

> Absence of community and hospitality develops when we do not acknowledge the existence of the other. The people next door become invisible and inaudible to us. The many isolated and hidden persons whom we simply ignore or actively marginalise, are put beyond the bounds of our neighbourliness. When we pass by on the other side, we cannot even tell who it is we are avoiding. We simply deny their existence. All who are in need of affirmation, survival and healing, tend to exist for us as unacknowledged neighbours or as social problems – never as fellow humans.[30]

Any theology that strives to speak about God from the vantage point of social underdogs is a discourse of liberation. The style and method of liberation theology is now recognized internationally outside South America in mutated forms such as Black, African, Asian, feminist, womanist and political theologies. These are often unpopular with Church leaders, politicians, bankers and military commanders because they encourage suffering people not to accept a stifling social divide between the powerful and disempowered, imposed on them by ecclesiastical hierarchies, international corporations and governments obsessed with acquiring capital by any means. Mercy Amba Oduyoye is undaunted because of her faith in Jesus. Although he was killed by the Prefect, Pontius Pilate, a henchman of the Roman Empire, his world-view ('to bring good news to the poor'; 'to let the oppressed go free' (Lk 4)) survived. It endured long after the fall of Rome, to encourage anyone anywhere today not submissively to accept the imposed status of a victim.

22

The Rainbow Spirit Elders

White man got no Dreaming, him go 'nother way.
Albert Muta

Queensland is the northernmost state on Australia's eastern side. Like the rest of the country, it is sparsely populated. Because of its proximity to the tropics, luxuriant rainforests flourish there. They are home to a vast array of plants. One of them is called the strangler fig. The name is not complimentary, because the plant is a deadly parasite: it survives and grows by choking and killing the trees it uses as hosts. The seeds of strangler figs are secreted by birds as they perch on tree branches. As the seeds drop to the moist forest undergrowth, they are fertilized, and sprout long hair-like roots at the base of their hosts. These embrace their tree-victims, thicken, and slowly climb aloft on the trees' trunks. The roots of the parasite eventually crush those of the host. Queensland is also home to a group of Aborigines, called the Rainbow Spirit Elders – local leaders who began to voice and develop a theology unique to them in the final decade of the twentieth century. Collectively considered, they are the last type of theologian to be explored in this book. They refer to the behaviour of the strangler fig to illustrate what Christian missionaries did to their culture. They record their views in a book called *Rainbow Spirit Theology*. There, they assert that the Christian message was imposed on them from above by missionaries, whose bequest was the same as that of a strangler fig in relation to its hapless host tree. Referring to their people, they lament that an imposed Christian message 'gradually choked the life out of our rich spiritual tradition – and therefore out of our people themselves. How much better it would have been for our people if that message had been planted in Australian soil, and encouraged to take on its own form and find its own place in its new cultural environment.'[1]

Worse than that, the Rainbow Spirit Elders say:

> The rule of the missionaries was supported by the power of the government – and its police force. Our elders had a sacred responsibility as the caretakers of this land and its resources. Because they could no longer exercise this care, they lost their purpose in life. The core beliefs of our people were rejected. The self-esteem of our people was destroyed. And the spirit of our people was crushed.[2]

Australia is the only country on this planet that is simultaneously a continent. It is also the driest continent, and much of it is hostile to the prospect of organisms surviving. Most of its current inhabitants live in cities lying on its coasts, and the largest cities are on the eastern coast. Before the land was declared a British possession by Captain Cook in 1770, its Aborigines could boast of a presence there through a succession of generations beginning as many as 40–60,000 years ago.[3] Aborigines (Latin, *ab origine*, 'from the beginning') were normally nomadic hunter-gatherers who developed a heightened reverence for the land, plants and animals that sustained them.

It is thought-provoking to become aware that Aborigines, over tens of thousands of years, have never known large-scale warfare. Tribes have certainly fought among themselves when their members felt impugned, but sustained warfare over possession of land is alien to their experience. One reason why this might have been the case is that for most of their history it did not occur to them that an individual could own land privately. The land was not anyone's to own. It was to be shared and venerated as a sacred basis of life for people, trees, snakes, kookaburras, goannas and dingoes.[4] A need for armies to fight over land never arose.

When European immigrants and conquerors arrived from Britain in the eighteenth century, there were several hundred aboriginal tribes in Australia (another Latin-formed word), speaking just as many distinct languages, populating the immense terrain in each of what are now eight political provinces – six states and two territories. The arrival of modern immigrants from Europe was calamitous. The colonizers slaughtered Aborigines like vermin. The original tribes in the southernmost state, Tasmania, were hunted and killed to extinction. Those who survived elsewhere often perished after contracting diseases brought from Europe.

By tradition, Aborigines have been, and largely are, communal-loving and respectful of unseen spirits and deities – to use words of Western origin. There is a danger in discussing their ideas about what is most important for humankind, of imposing on their patterns of thought Western categories like 'theology', 'religion' and 'indigenous religion'. European terminology referring to 'indigenous religion' all too easily connotes 'a pagan, godless, unenlightened era redolent of the dim, misty past'.[5] Westerners often fail to recognize the extent to which their own speech and thought were forged in the culture of ancient Greece:

> In all history, no society has aroused the same enthusiasm as ancient Greece. This is a truism, yet it remains incontestable. Greek achievements in literature, art, and architecture set the norms for the Western world for two thousand years. When we think, we still employ the intellectual categories its philosophers and scientists devised. In politics, democracy was a Greek invention. ... Civilization, already millennia old in Egypt, Sumer, India, and China, took a vast leap forward under the stimulus of the Greek experiment.[6]

Almost any word used in English to refer to Aboriginal beliefs about what could be called 'Ultimacy' in abstract terms has a Greek or Latin provenance. The point is: Aborigines – and Torres Straight Islanders – do not think and behave according to patterns devised by Greeks, Romans or modern Europeans. 'Theology', 'mythology', and 'religion' all have Greek roots. Speaking of 'Aboriginal Theology', 'tradition' and 'religion' will therefore of necessity be by way of analogy.

Aborigines over thousands of years did not produce theological texts. What is known about their beliefs has been gleaned from cave and rock paintings, stories cherished by them and passed on to successive generations ('tradition'), and through conversations outsiders have had with them. The book, *Rainbow Spirit Theology*, is a rare and recent phenomenon. It was not penned by Aborigines, but articulated in words by a helper who recorded comments made by the Rainbow Spirit Elders. Theology is well established in Australia, in such institutions as the

Melbourne and Sydney Colleges of Divinity. There are Benedictines, Jesuits, Methodists and Anglicans all writing theologies in Australia. Some of their work is known internationally because it uses the concepts and terminology typical elsewhere – in academies and Churches. The Rainbow Spirit Elders are different: a great deal of their language is entirely original, and they use it to articulate an *Aboriginal* and *Christian* theology in *their own* terms.

Aboriginal art is displayed in museums around the world. It is not unknown for visitors to galleries to comment that the art is the naïve, childish, product of primitive pagans, devoid of devotion to anything remotely resembling a religion.[7] Aborigines certainly speak of myths and legends, but so too do the world's religions, including Judaism, Christianity and Islam.[8] Because Aboriginal myths and stories are different does not imply that they are less sophisticated or primitive than anyone else's myths.

Aboriginal tribes often include a man – called kunki by the Dieri, who establishes contact with Kutchi (spirits) and Mura-muras (divinities). Mura-Muras are the Kutchi of earlier dwellers in the region of the Dieri. Tribes such as the Biamban, Bunjil, Mungangana, Nurelli and Nurrundere, all espouse beliefs in an unsurpassed being.[9] In this, they are just like billions of humans all around the world.

rainbow spirit theology

The process by which *Rainbow Spirit Theology* was aired and recorded began among Aboriginal leaders who met in November of 1994 and 1995. Their meetings took place at Crystal Creek, which is near the city of Townsville in the far north of Queensland. It ought not escape notice that the names of these modest people are not emblazoned on the cover of the book containing their ideas. They are not driven by a craving for recognition, fame or adulation. They are not interested in talking about themselves or producing autobiographies, but in drawing attention to the suffering of others. They do not hanker for university degrees or want to be professors. They are far more driven to uproot and redress the damage caused by the immigrant 'strangler figs' that have stymied their development and muted their voices since the eighteenth century.

The Elders of the Rainbow Spirit are both Christian and Aboriginal. Among them are members of Catholic, Lutheran, Anglican and Uniting Churches (formerly Methodists and Presbyterians). They are thus with a distinction. Their Christianity is secondary to their aboriginality, because their principal goal was to evince a theology that stemmed from their history and experience as

Aborigines. Their interest in and allegiance to Christianity enables them to see similarities between Aboriginal and Christian stories and teachings.

They searched for some time for a suitable name to describe their endeavour, and initially thought of calling it 'Kookaburra Theology', after the kookaburra bird. The kookaburra is a gorgeous animal, and well-known in Queensland. Upon reflection the Elders decided that the kookaburra would work well as a local symbol for their theology, but was without a widespread significance in Australia. After lengthy discussion they set upon the Rainbow Spirit as a religious symbol for their aboriginal theology.[10]

The book published as a result of their talks is significant for them, and others, for three reasons. First, it is a creative and novel expression of their pride in their faith and culture. Second, it attempts to reveal how Christian colonialism is still perpetuated in Australia by Christian priests and pastors, as though Christianity expressed in European idioms is invariable and universally applicable. The Elders regard most of their pastors to have been indoctrinated by a European form of Christianity and they want to help them to free themselves from bondage to relics of colonialism, to discover a new understanding of Christianity so that it might become an authentic Good News for people. Third, the Elders want to communicate to all Australians. They are concerned that economic values are prized above all else in Australia, and they wish to replace the confrontation and competition that faithfully accompanies the acquisition of financial capital with human cooperation. As they conclude: 'In the sixty or more thousand years that our people have been in this continent, we have learned to live in this land. We want to share it with all Australians in a way that will ensure a better future for all our children.'[11]

the rainbow spirit

Who or what is the Rainbow Spirit? For Aborigines, the Rainbow Spirit is what Christians call the Creator. As a theological symbol it represents life and rebirth. Aborigines believe that the Rainbow Spirit gave life to their ancestors, to the land, and to all the creatures of the Spirit – trees, plants and animals. The concept of the Rainbow Spirit in itself evokes a rainbow in the sky: 'The Rainbow Spirit is the symbol of the new day which dawns after the rain sent by the Rainbow Spirit. The rainbow that appears in the sky, is the peace after the storm, the promise of God to care for all creation (Genesis 9). The Rainbow Spirit is also the guardian of the law, the land and the sacred places in the land.'[12]

Aborigines envisage a beginning for the creation of the world, as does the Book of Genesis. Like Genesis, their stories imagine an earth that was originally formless and devoid of any life. Then the Rainbow Spirit, the Creator Spirit, formed the land, with mountains, rivers, seas and trees. The creative activities of the Rainbow Spirit are recounted by Aborigines in ancient narratives about the beginning of creation. In such stories, the Rainbow Spirit swallowed young people, before regurgitating and recreating them as adults. Inside the Rainbow Spirit, the eaten young people were being changed into new beings. They rose as adults having died to youth. Ceremonies among Aborigines that are conducted ritualistically to initiate young people into an adult community often involve a re-enactment of being swallowed and re-formed by the Rainbow Spirit.[13]

The stories just mentioned refer to the most important and easily misunderstood term in Aboriginal discourse – 'the Dreaming'. Stories about the Dreaming are easily mistaken by people who are not Aborigines as quaint and fictitious fables. The Aboriginal idea that the English phrase 'the Dreaming' strives to convey designates an intrinsic, spiritual dimension of reality that has existed since the beginning of the world. This reality is envisaged as a powerful spiritual reality which invests present reality with a spiritual life and which has been active since the creation of the world. Over millennia, Aborigines have told stories about the Dreaming among themselves: 'They expressed a powerful connection with a sacred land and set out goals for human life that was not expressed as an historical narrative, but rather as something given out *all at one go*, so to speak, by their Dreaming ancestors.'[14]

It is virtually unknown for Dreaming stories to be printed, because they are not intended for people who are not able to be present to listen to them as they are told, and they are certainly not meant for people who have no affinity with the ancestors of those who narrate them. Were they to be reproduced in print, Aboriginal sensitivity to tribal secrecy could easily be offended. Even so, some Dreamings have been printed, and secrecy laws most probably would not be offended now if the stories were published decades ago. One Dreaming that can now appear in print is by an Arrente Elder, Albert Namatjira, who is widely admired to this day in Australia as a painter. He retold a Dreaming that was printed in 1966. A mere sampling of it gives a vivid impression of the way two women are gobbled up by a Devil-dog, much in the manner of the Rainbow Spirit who comes forth from the land to devour youths, only later to regurgitate them as adults:

> In the dreaming there was an old man at Ungortarénga with a boomerang and a shield. a) The old man lay down. All the winds blow on him; he is covered with sand. A bird calls from a tree, the old man sits up and looks about, and goes back to sleep. b) A wind blows from the south. He smells the wind. First his nose appears,

then, he crawls in the sand, he shakes the sand off him, he stretches, he sniffs the wind, his ears prick forward, he transforms himself into Erintja the Devil-dog. c) He follows the wind to a water hole. He sees two women, two sisters gathering frogs (Djarra). He follows them, sneaking, holding himself down low like a cat. d) The women are nervous, but make a fire and eat. Fire attracts Erintja, the Devil-dog. The big sister tells younger one to look and see if anyone is there. She looks, No one there, she says. e) The Devil-dog in one bound grabs, eats the bigger sister, the younger one climbs a small tree to escape. The devil-dog pulls the little one from the tree, and swallows her too. He moves on.[15]

It is no doubt not possible for anyone to understand the subtleties of this Dreaming without the interpretative skills of one of the Arrente, but its vivid imagery of sand, wind, fire, frogs, a bird, water hole, tree and the Devil-dog amply reveal how closely Aborigines are tied to the land and love plants and animals. Notice too the present tense of this story. It indicates that the Dreaming is a *current* spiritual dimension of reality and not simply a *past* event.

the sources of rainbow spirit theology

Theology, according to the Rainbow Spirit Elders, is an attempt to make sense of God by relying on a model which functions as a source for organizing thinking about God. The model which informs their theology is a grid of the four compass directions: North, South, East and West. The South stands for truth contained within Aboriginal culture. The North symbolizes wisdom derived from past ancient sources. The East is typified by the Christian Gospel, a direction that helps them find their bearings, while the West stands for strength for Aboriginal people in the future. Each of these four directions is symbolized by an animal that is common in Australia. The South is represented by the emu; the North by the sheep; the East by the kookaburra; and the West by the kangaroo. The animals are depicted in the drawing by Wontulp-Bi-Buya at the beginning of his chapter.[16]

Animals are a prominent feature in Rainbow Spirit Theology. The Rainbow Spirit itself is frequently depicted in Aboriginal art as a powerful snake which comes forth from the land, travels across land leaving a trail of life, and then returns to the land through waterholes, caves or similar sacred sites. This imagery was misunderstood by Christian missionaries when they arrived in Australia. They associated it with the serpent, Satan and the Garden of Eden (Gen 3). The missionaries even convinced some Aborigines that the Rainbow

Spirit is an evil symbol. The Rainbow Spirit Elders are determined to recover its original meaning and identity.[17]

the land

Aborigines have different names for the Spirit who created the world, including Yiirmbal, Biame, Rainbow Spirit, Paayamu, Biiral and Wandjina. All of these names refer to a life-giving Creative Power. For Aborigines, the Rainbow Spirit has been present since the beginning of the world. Crucially, the Rainbow Spirit has always been, and still is, *in* the land. Hence the extraordinarily strong rapport with land experienced by Aboriginies, and the incalculable suffering inflicted on them when they were dispossessed of the lands over which they roamed by colonizers.

For Aborigines, the land is alive and filled with the life-forces of all species. All of these life-forces were brought forth from the land by the Creator Spirit as plants, fish, birds and other animals. Human beings are expected to assume the responsibility of caring for the life-forces within the land. The Creator Spirit is a landowner, while humans are trustees of the land.[18]

Western urbanites have much to learn from Creator Spirit theology. Their nations have so pillaged the land that the ecosystem which enables them to live could itself die under the burden of toxins or pollutants. Aborigines, so often lampooned as primitive savages in the past, have never lost an ancient wisdom which knows that humans live in a web of life sustained by the land. To destroy one part of the web imperils the whole.

The formulation of a theology by the Rainbow Spirit Elders is not regarded by them as 'intellectual game-playing'; 'It is literally a matter of life and death. Behind the tragedy of many Aboriginal communities (poor health, high infant mortality, low life-expectancy, high unemployment, poor housing, alcoholism, malnutrition, deaths in custody – the list goes on) lies a deep spiritual crisis.'[19] At the root of the crisis is the seizing of the land by immigrants who do not have the sense that it has been entrusted to them by the Creator Spirit so that they can care for it.

Despite the massacres and poisonings to which Aborigines were subjected, they have survived and endured. The sufferings they endured as a consequence of being dispossessed from the land are sobering to recount. The following list mentions some of them: the massacre of Aborigines sanctioned by government authorities; the hunting of Aborigines as if they were wild animals; the poisoning of streams and waterholes with the intent of exterminating entire Aboriginal families; the forceful removal of children and women from their families; the humiliation of Aborigines through public punishments; the sexual violation of Aboriginal women by settlers; the desecration of Aboriginal sacred sites; and the denigration of Aboriginal worship as barbaric and evil.[20] The list is incomplete. One historian has noted that in parts of Australia, the toll of Aboriginal deaths outnumbered that of combatants from Australia in overseas wars during the twentieth century:

> About 5,000 Europeans from Australia north of the tropic of Capricorn died in the
> five wars between the outbreak of the Boer War and the end of the Vietnam
> engagement. But in a similar period – say the 70 years between the first settlement
> in North Queensland in 1861 and the early 1930s – as many as 10,000 blacks were
> killed in skirmishes with Europeans in north Australia.[21]

jesus christ as an australian aborigine

The Rainbow Spirit Elders link with ease their baneful history of affliction wrought by dispossession with the life of Jesus Christ. They profess that the power of the Creator Spirit assumed human flesh in Jesus, and in so doing became one of them and part of their culture. It follows for them that 'Christ is revealed not as a German Jesus, an English Jesus, or even a Jewish Jesus, but as an Aboriginal Jesus'.[22] A key phrase here is 'Christ is revealed'. Of course Jesus was inescapably a Galilean Jew, but for the Elders he is manifested *to them* as an Aboriginal Jesus.

It was initially difficult for Aborigines to identity with Jesus because missionaries presented him in language, concepts and images formed in the Northern Hemisphere. What Aborigines could readily understand was that Jesus suffered terribly like them at the hands of imperial powers. As the Elders declare: 'The Christ who suffered on the cross continues to suffer with the land and the people of the land. In the suffering of the land and the people of the land, we see Christ suffering and we hear Christ crying out.'[23]

Suffering is not all that Aborigines share with Jesus. Reading about their attachment to the land, and discovering the way they talk with great regularity about birds, trees, snakes, emus, kangaroos and kookaburras, it soon becomes apparent that their fondness for deferring to the land and all that it supports was shared by Jesus. Scholarly books devoted to investigating him historically in the twentieth century normally ignored the influences on his identity of the geography, topography and ecological environment of lower Galilee, in which he lived as a youth. His place was not altogether unlike the setting of an Aboriginal youth in Queensland. Jesus was clearly antipodean to the concrete and steel jungles of those in the twentieth century who liked to malign Aborigines as barbaric heathens. Eventually, it began to dawn on a few innovative scholars in the early twenty-first century that it is not accidental that the language of Jesus as presented in the Bible is peppered with references to birds in the air, foxes and their holes, fig trees, mustard seeds, vines, lakes, fish, asses, fields, harvests, good soil, thorns, hillsides and ploughs.[24]

While Aborigines can speak of devil-dogs, Jesus is recorded as referring regularly to 'evil spirits' (see Luke's Gospel). Predating Jesus by tens of thousands of years, Aborigines have been nomads, wandering the landscape searching for nourishment. He too was a wanderer, moving from town, to lake, to village, to market place, surviving on what others were prepared to give him. Like Aborigines, he believed in a Creator, whose Spirit is portrayed in Luke's Gospel as having been 'upon him' 'to bring good news to the poor'.

Who could ever know assuredly, and pronounce infallibly, that the divine Spirit with whom Jesus has been linked is not the same Creative Energy envisaged as the Rainbow Spirit?

conclusion

Africans and Aborigines share a common experience of being kept under the boots of colonizers. The experience of some in Africa has led them to liberate their thought from its colonized heritage by formulating a language of terms and concepts peculiar to them.[25] This is precisely what the Rainbow Spirit Elders were striving to do in the far north of Queensland during the final decade of the twentieth century. Ever aware of the strangler fig, the Elders do not accept that their land is an antipodean outpost of Europeans on the world's underbelly. They do not speak of a theology down under like the recent book, *God Down Under: Theology in the Antipodes* (2003).[26] An antipodes is a place diametrically opposite another space. Aborigines are not adept at promoting oppositions and living by stratifications with upper and lower classes, with some countries on top and others down under. They do not want to participate in a frenzy that involves everybody living acquisitively by plundering the earth of irreplaceable resources and killing animals to extinction. They would rather gather in a circle to eat, sing, dance, and chat face-to-face than communicate at great distances with faceless e-mails and text-messages. They are willing to learn from others elsewhere, and recognize that their colonizers have their own prudent traditions. They are also capable of teaching people they need not be alone and adrift in uncaring societies, locked in competition with each other to acquire capital quickly and housed with high-tech gadgets in high-rise apartments, within high-crime suburbs with no sight of loving neighbours or land, and no daily contact with animals.

Many countries of the world might not have changed into the ecologically damaged, war-ravaged, terrified-of-terror places they appeared to have become by the end of the twentieth century, if more of their leaders had behaved like the Rainbow Spirit Elders of Crystal Creek. The Elders' names may not be known far from the forests of Queensland, but their Dreaming has long outlived the far younger and much more aggressive empires of Egypt, Babylon, Rome and Greece.

23

taking stock

The bread of the needy is the life of the poor;
whoever deprives them of it is a murderer.
To take away a neighbour's living is to commit murder;
to deprive an employee of wages is to shed blood.

Sirach 34: 25–7

Jesus, looking at him, loved him, and said, 'You lack one thing;
go, sell what you own, and give the money to the poor,
and you will have treasure in heaven; then come, follow me.'

Mark 10: 21

This book has been a presentation of portraits. It has aired an array of varied voices selected from a cacophony of many more. It has trekked chronologically, geographically and conceptually from the lecture theatres of the University of Berlin in 1900, with Adolf von Harnack explaining the essence of Christianity for note-taking students, to the edges of Crystal Creek in northern Queensland, with the Rainbow Spirit Elders warning of the theological dangers of the strangler fig. The former knew nothing of the latter, but in the twentieth century, both were Christians and theologians.

As a gallery of sketches, the preceding chapters have tried, not so much to recount this or that detail of theologians' publications – although they contain a good deal of talk about texts — but to give an impression of the *kinds* of people who articulated theologies in the twentieth century, and the *historical circumstances* that *determined* the ways they spoke. Why did Evelyn Underhill think pacificism is important for a Christian? What transpired in Alfred Loisy's life to elicit his permanent exclusion from the Catholic Church? The hierarchy of that Church turned its back on him, but the Catholic Mary Daly renounced her Church's leadership and its doctrines before it could denounce her. Why? What led Bonhoeffer to be hanged? How did Congar become emboldened to work tirelessly for the reform of the Church? Who drove John Hick to say that all religions have equal value, and Don Cupitt to assert that there is nothing permanently true to assert? Why did Dorothy Day spend more time with putrid homeless people than Karl Barth or Paul Tillich? What provoked Mercy Oduyoye to think God suffers when people suffer? Was Gutiérrez deranged to conclude that God especially loves the poor, or Gordon Kaufman deluded to think science matters for theology? Texts are always tinctured by their contexts. With theologians of any era, their life-stories and historical circumstances reveal most matters about them — or almost.

It remains a bafflement why so many of the theologians and ecclesiastical leaders of the twentieth century showed few signs of fretting daily about the misery endured by *most* people in their time. Perhaps they were comfortable where they lived, and grateful poverty had not been their lot. They could have been rendered awestruck by the magnificent scientific and technological breakthroughs of their period, which furnished some of them and many of their contemporaries with cars, central heating, TVs, power boats and computers. Over the past 50 years the world's car population grew five times faster than the human population over the same period.[1] The theologians who were forgetful of poverty may have been hopeful, like Jesus, that God's kingdom would soon unseat the overlords of the world and raise up the downtrodden. They might have agreed with the notion that the promotion of justice is the work of politics, not of the Church or theology.

Not only did many theologians of the last century abstain from challenging the international causes of poverty, some fought tirelessly against those theologians who tried to advance the unchaining of people from penury. Wolfhart Pannenberg worked in the Faith and Order Commission of the World Council of Churches to smother liberation theology, and Rudolf Bultmann argued against legislation for socially redressing the plight of impecunious people, on the grounds that the poor ought not be deprived of the virtue of gratitude when the rich exercise the virtue of giving.[2] On balance, fewer theologians of the twentieth century preferred to expend their energies exploring a relation between a Creator-God and the miseries of creatures, than those who favoured dissertating on the Imminent Trinity, the Virginity of Mary, the infallibility of the Bible or Pope, why one religion is better than another, the sanctity of the Church and the divinity of Jesus — all the while comfortably forgetting rigorously to enquire as to why and how Jesus was killed *because of the way he lived*. Benign neighbourly do-gooders are not normally executed. Those who unveil the villainy of extortionists are.

Taking stock of all that has been said thus far in this book about theologians, indigence and human hardship, the following set of hypotheses, and comments on them, attempt to account for Christianity's mutations during the twentieth and early twenty-first centuries:

1. Christianity in the Northern Hemisphere declined steadily as an institution throughout the twentieth century. Christendom is in a state of dissolution. It has lost its cultural hegemony in Europe, and by far the majority of the population in the United Kingdom, as in many other European countries, has nothing to do with Churches on any regular basis.[3]

2. A frequently noticed exception to this diminution was the USA, but clear signs are now emerging there in the wake of the twentieth century that Christianity is losing its grip on people's allegiance. In mid-2006, 6,000 Protestant pastors in the USA were informed, at a series of meetings conducted in 44 cities, that if current rates continue, merely 4 per cent of American teenagers will become Bible-believing Christians, compared with 35 per cent of their parents, and 65 per cent of their grandparents.[4]

3. Christianity increased markedly as an institution in the Southern Hemisphere throughout the twentieth century, particularly in Africa. Pentecostal Protestantism flourished in both South America and Africa.

4. The principal reason why Christianity was incrementally abandoned by Northerners is that most of them have become not only more leisured, learned and financially secure, but far richer in comparison with the majority of Southerners and Asians.

5. This wealth generates at least two deleterious by-products for Christian Churches: (a) people with plenty of money are more able to look after themselves independently of Churches, and less likely to spend the precious time they have when not working attending formal ceremonies in Churches, where the language and customs may strike them as antique, incomprehensible and utterly unrelated to their needs and experiences; (b) it becomes exceptionally difficult for anyone in a wealthy society to discern the purpose and distinctiveness of Christianity if Christian members and leaders of that society are as wealthy as anyone else.

6. In a stinging historical irony, the less inclined Christians and theologians were in the twentieth century to address and redress poverty, and to challenge their governments' policies about finance and war, the more likely it was that others observing them would not be able to see the point of being a Christian.

7. What is the problem with wealth? Nothing in itself, except when it is hoarded by a minority of humankind, and Christians constitute a major component of the minority. Then wealth and a refusal to share it become impediments for anyone wishing to be styled as a Christian, because such a situation is incompatible with what is known of Jesus Christ's life, and what is recorded of his teachings.

8. The majority of human beings today live in Asia. Their population there increased from 1,411 million in 1950 to 3,938 million in 2005.[5] Most of these people are chronically or acutely poor, and Christianity has failed among them to attract large-scale devotion. Christianity is strong in South Korea, but that is a country which mirrors the financial security of the West. India alone has a population of over 1 billion, and only a tiny percentage of the population are not Hindus or Muslims.[6] There is little reason to suppose that impoverished Asians would listen seriously to anyone preaching about a poor Jesus Christ while living in or visiting from satiated Western countries.

9. Throughout the twentieth century, Western ecclesiastical leaders among Catholics and Protestants were not only normally reluctant to challenge governments inspired by capitalism, but expected to receive favours and taxation exemptions from such governments. When these were accorded to them, they were constrained to be mute about the teachings against wealth and violence in the Bible, and unable to speak a liberating word during crises: 'Even if churches inwardly dissociate themselves from a system which makes the rich richer and the poor poorer, institutionally they are so tied up with the system that they have to keep their mouths shut. In order to be able to present their message, they have to keep quiet about this message!'[7]

The muteness of Christian Churches in response to capitalist governments continued in the twenty-first century, with lethal consequences. To illustrate: 2.7 billion people are currently at risk of being adversely affected by armed conflicts. In 1990 alone there were 56 wars on this planet. Between 2003 and 2006 international trade in weapons increased enormously. Countries historically linked with Christianity willingly participated in this trade. In this four-year period, the USA transacted military arms sales worth US$60 billion; the United Kingdom, $14 billion; and France, $14 billion.[8] These are massive amounts of money for armaments that kill and maim, and they only include figures for arms traded to others; not money spent on weapons for the trading countries themselves. Almost nothing in the exporting countries concerned was recorded publicly in that period about bishops, priests and professors of theology vociferously raising collective objections. This silence about military aggression is yet one more possible explanation for Christianity's enfeebled capacity to attract adherents recently, and over the past century. There is no glimpse at all of a poor Jesus Christ in policies of war.

10. Not to be underestimated as a significant catalyst for the renunciation of Christianity in the twentieth century was the sexual revolution of that era, and the traditional devotion of Churches to Plato's body-soul dualism. For most of their history Christians were taught to subdue their bodies and control their passions so that their souls could journey to heaven. When the technology became available in the twentieth century for people to enjoy their bodies sexually, independently of producing children, orthodox body-denying theologies, and Platonism, were shunned on an ever-increasing scale. In 1960, Cardinal Suenens of Belgium advocated a practice for avoiding conception that was labelled in Latin as the *amplexus reservatus* – the reserved embrace.[9] It has been discussed by theologians since the Middle Ages as a way of preventing the emission of semen (thought by medieval thinkers to contain little people), and hence the conception of zygotes. The *amplexus reservatus* involved an obligation placed on married males to stop embracing their wives if they began to become sexually aroused. This practice, and others like it, invited the theologies that informed them to be rejected as humanly repulsive by those enthused by the sexual revolution in the twentieth century.

11. Churches that fought a rearguard action against the Enlightenment, modernity and science in the twentieth century are now paying the price of witnessing more people failing to listen to them in the West. Strident insistence that the Bible is literally true in all its details, that God created the world in six days, that humanly formulated dogmas are legitimated by God, that Jesus established the Church and designed its sacraments, that Darwinian evolutionary theory is nonsense, and that complicated patterns in physical reality prove that God designed them, all unwittingly colluded to spawn an aggressively anti-Christian breed of happy atheists.

12. The hierarchy of the Catholic Church, the largest of all Christian Churches (which is why this point is to be explained at length), has not learnt the lessons it needed to from the single most historically significant event for Christianity in the twentieth century – the Second Vatican Council. The history of Catholicism before that event was deeply seared by the European Enlightenment and the French Revolution – both of which impinged directly

on the papacy based in Rome. Enlightenment Kantian rationalism lionized reason instead of divine revelation, while the French Revolution, when its ideas were transported elsewhere, unseated monarchies. The Catholic Church subsequently found itself profoundly challenged intellectually and politically. Intellectually, because its long-standing assertion of being able to define truth authoritatively on the basis of revelation was undermined by rationalism, and politically because its own monarchical government was questioned to its roots by new, far more egalitarian forms of democracy.

In a countermovement, the Catholic hierarchy resorted to enforcing medieval patterns of thought among its theologians and students of theology as an antidote to modernity. Twentieth-century Catholic theology began with a crisis: a choice between Medievalism and Modernism. The crisis was resolved with a hierarchical condemnation of Modernism and a witch-hunt for Modernists. Neo-scholasticism reigned in Catholic theology throughout the first half of the twentieth century. As it did, the detonators of its intellectual demolition were patiently and painstakingly being laid by like-minded biblical scholars, historians and theologians, including ecclesiologists. Their work triumphed at the Second Vatican Council and was accepted by the majority of its participating bishops. Their success was short-lived. From the end of the Council in 1965 to the end of the twentieth century, the supporting structures of papal monarchy and pre-modern dogmatic certainty were slowly reinforced and entrenched in the Catholic Church.

In 1970, Hans Küng, one of the principal theological architects of the Council's reforms, sounded an alarm by publishing a book called *Infallible?* He called for the dogma of papal infallibility to be reconsidered by theologians. He began it with what he called 'A Candid Foreword'. Candid it was, and prescient too. It could have been written 39 years later in 2009:

> The renewal of the Catholic Church willed by the Second Vatican Council has come to a standstill, and with it ecumenical understanding with other Churches and a new opening out towards the contemporary world. ... In spite of the impulse given by the Council, no significant change, in the spirit of the Christian message, has been brought about in the institutional and personal power-structure of the government of the Church. Notwithstanding the inevitability of change, the Pope, the Curia and many bishops continue to behave in a largely pre-conciliar fashion; little seems to have been learnt from the Council. Both in Rome and elsewhere in the Church the levers of power are now, as before, in the hands of personalities more interested in the maintenance of a comfortable *status quo* than in a serious renewal.[10]

In the second year of his pontificate, John Paul II removed Küng from his professorship, thereby eloquently illustrating what Küng was asserting.

One further vignette confirms that major conclusions of Vatican II have been aborted by subsequent popes. The Second Vatican Council taught that 'the fullness of the sacrament of Orders is conferred by episcopal consecration'.[11] This means that the identity of bishops stems from their ordination as bishops, and not from an act of papal jurisdiction or delegation.[12] They are not papal pawns, and enjoy exactly the same status as the Pope *as* bishops. In January of 1995, John Paul II removed Jacques Gaillot from his bishopric in Évreux (France) for questioning papal teachings on the status of women in the Church, on sexuality, homosexuality, contraception and abortion.[13] Gaillot was treated as a dispensable papal office boy, and the worldwide episcopate could do nothing to constrain a supremely confident Supreme Pontiff. Vatican II's vision of collegial government by bishops and systemic reform was dead.

13. Protestant Churches during the twentieth century educated hordes of astoundingly gifted theologians, especially in German-speaking territories. Many of them have recognized full gender equality between men and women among their worshippers and ministers. And yet, they account for most of the proliferation of Christian denominations last century. Institutional scission within Protestantism has produced tens of thousands of denominations and sects, whose very accumulation rendered it exceedingly difficult for their uncommitted observers last century to discover which if any of them is a legitimate representation of Jesus' religious commitments.[14]

14. Twentieth-century Orthodox Churches were resurgent in the later decades of the century after the collapse of the Berlin Wall, with the repressions and separations it symbolized in Communist Europe. They are normally tied to nationalities, as in the Russian or Greek Orthodox Churches, and have not exposed their doctrines to the same level of post-Enlightenment critical analysis as some other Churches. Their nationalisms have mostly confined their influence to their territories (although some have spread far and wide), and their leaders and theologians, like those among Catholics, Protestants and Anglicans, did not magnetize most inhabitants of the twentieth century.

15. Feminists after the Second World War lucidly exposed a denigration of women among Christians that had been spurred on over many centuries by patriarchal, biblical and ecclesiastical teachings insisting that females are inferior adjuncts to males. A widespread taking flight from Christian Churches in the West during the twentieth century was exacerbated by the persistent reluctance of many Churches to treat women in the same way as men in their communities.

16. Fundamentalism was a pest among Christians last century. It is the belief that Christianity rests on the foundation of a cluster of unambiguous *beliefs* ('fundamentals'), such as the Virgin Birth and the bodily resurrection of Jesus. Its basic flaw is twofold. First, it is unable to recognize that Christianity is not reducible to beliefs, because it involves actions and a way of living, hopefully in a manner not entirely alien to Jesus' way of associating with others; and second, it is blinkered to the subtleties, ambiguities, paradoxes and enigmas tied to any attempt to talk about God. Fundamentalists' literal and ahistorical interpretations of the Bible and dogmas, among Catholics and Protestants alike, their fear of change, and denunciations of anyone inclined to think hermeneutically in a historical-critical way, coalesced to bring Christianity into even more disrepute last century.

The 16 hypotheses and comments enumerated above will neither please nor convince everyone. As thoughts, they are tentative gropes in the dark for possible explanations for the fortunes and fate of Christianity last century. It is for the reader to weigh up whether or not collectively they constitute a plausible account. The crucial hypothesis is the fourth: it links Christianity's institutional sliding in the North during the twentieth century to money – who has it, who is deprived of it, what is done with it, and how lack of it and the resources it can procure plague the penniless paupers of the world.

By and large, twentieth-century theologians struggled as voices crying in a wilderness to make any sense of God for their contemporaries. In the West, they were not even able to convince most members of their own societies, let alone foreigners. That said, the intellectual viability and humanizing worth of any theology is not decided by democratic ballots. Ignoring any theologian's voice might be a symptom of the ignorer's obdurate fickleness and fecklessness.

Despite their failures, the most remarkable occurrence among theologians of the twentieth century was the awakening of many of them to the omnipresence of affliction on this planet for by far the majority of human beings. Their awakening arose in the last 40 years of the century. So too did theologians' unease about ecological destruction, and the relentless killing of animals for fur, hides and flesh. The historical and theological sea-change involved in the movement from Church-obsessed dialogues, to poverty-preoccupied discourse in relation to God, is the greatest accomplishment of theologians in the twentieth century. The work of theologians who realized that it is not possible to declare to people that God loves and saves them, when they are starving or dying, exposes a great deal of modern theology as an introverted, self-satisfied, self-sufficient, self-justifying and cosily clerical sermon that is unable to convince anyone in a world awash with misery.

Why is poverty and the suffering it produces overwhelmingly significant now for Christian theologians? First, because it is numerically and demonstrably worse than it has ever been; and second, because its very severity militates corrosively against the notion that God cares for the world, and that Jesus has rescued the world from perdition.

It has been said that 'A just society must be the achievement of politics, not of the Church'.[15] The following figures reveal clearly that political machinery has failed spectacularly in modern-to-postmodern times to establish justice among the peoples of the planet:

- More than 850 million people *every day* go hungry, and one person in seven is deprived of enough food either to enjoy health or be able to lead an active life.[16]
- Two billion people are currently anaemic. Around 250 million children of pre-school age are deficient in vitamin A, with the result that roughly 500,000 children each year become blind because of this deficiency.[17]
- 16,000 children die *every day* from conditions related to hunger. *Each year* between 5 and 6 million children die from infectious diseases. Were they properly nourished, disease would not kill them. Of these child deaths, 45 per cent occur in sub-Saharan Africa. Every year, 4.8 million children die there before reaching the age of five.[18]
- As many as 150 million children die each year from the combined effects of malnutrition, disease and deprivation of sanitation. 4,500 die *each day* from poor sanitation alone.[19]
- By the late 1990s, around 3 billion people were unable to meet their basic nutritional and other needs, and about 1.4 billion had no option but to subsist in abject poverty on less than a US dollar a day.[20]
- In the poorest countries, at present life expectancy at birth for both males and females is less than 50 years because of chronic shortages of food, disease and lack of access to health care. In rich countries life expectancy can be as high as 80 for females and 75 for males.[21]
- As many as 1 billion people worldwide do not have access to clean water, 1.5 billion have access but do not have enough of it, and 3 billion live without sanitation.[22]
- Human consumption is releasing carbon dioxide, methane, hyrdrofluorocarbons and sulphate aerosol into the atmosphere to such an extent that a depleted ozone layer is making it possible for ultraviolet radiation to kill the krill and phytoplankton that feed many organisms in the sea.[23] Fewer fish in oceans will lead to less food for a massively augmented and ever-hungry human population.

- Atmospheric carbon dioxide has reached its highest level in 650,000 years.[24] While it contributes along with other ozone-diminishing substances to warming the planet's climates, sea levels will rise as arctic zones, glaciers and snowfields melt, thereby endangering the well-being of the 3 billion human beings who inhabit coastal zones.[25]
- Women labour for two-thirds of the world's working hours, cultivate half the world's food, but receive only 10 per cent of the planet's income and own less than 1 per cent of the earth's property.[26]
- Meanwhile, a staggeringly large death-dealing inequality has emerged between wealthy and poor people. 1 per cent of the world's entire population enjoys more income than the poorest 57 per cent. In 2008, the world was home to 1,125 US dollar billionaires. In the USA in the same year, there were 469 billionaires, with more than 51 million of its citizens living in poverty.[27] **The super-rich of the planet, that is, the wealthiest 1 per cent of the richest 1 per cent of all people, control a full 24 per cent of global wealth.**[28]
- As for the wealth of transnational business corporations, in 2006, the gross national income (GNI) of British Airways was $14.25 billion; of Hewlett Packard, $94.08 billion; and of Wal Mart, $348.6 billion. In 2006, revenues from sales in Wal Mart stores were close to Indonesia's GNI. Indonesia is the third most populous country in the world. Wal Mart's GNI exceed that of the *combined* GNI of the world's 49 poorest states.[29]
- All people now live in a world rich in resources, as depleted as they are. The current unequal chasm between wealthy and poor people is death-dealing because the amassing of money, energy and assets by a small minority leaves insufficient resources for a majority to escape a dehumanized life, with millions condemned to die as a result. **A tax of a mere 4 per cent on the richest 1 per cent of the wealthiest 1 per cent of billionaires, or a tax of only 1 per cent on the speculative transactions in the world's capital markets, 'would be more than enough to pay for basic and adequate health care, food, clean water and safe sewers for every person on earth.'**[30]

the story of sonia

John Pilger published a book in the late 1990s called *Hidden Agendas*. It tells the story of a Punjabi girl called Sonia. By the age of 11 she had become blind and struggled to eke out a living. When Pilger was writing, she spent from morning to night stitching footballs for use in the West. Her daily grind of stitching was the cause of her blindness. She remembered the instant she could no longer see: 'It went completely dark in front of my eyes and I was scared.' When Pilger asked Sonia about the fun of being a child she said there was no fun in what she did. 'I have no choice', she remarked. It took her a day to stitch two balls using touch alone, for which she earned the equivalent of 15 pence – not nearly enough to buy a litre of milk in England.[31]

Meanwhile, Eric Cantona retired from England's Manchester United football club in 1997, after being paid £19,000 a week to play with footballs. From 1995 to 1996, Britain imported £8 million worth of sporting equipment from India made by legions of poor people like Sonia.[32] Currently in the United Kingdom, the most esteemed professionals who play with footballs can be paid as much as £70,000–£120,000 a week, if not more. Individuals and corporations who 'prize autonomy as the heart of morality, and who believe that the market makes it possible, do not see that the free market produces lives like Sonia's for most of the world's people, and that this autonomy is parasitic on the unfreedom of the poor.'[33]

To speak in a very general way, politics during the twentieth century, at both national and international levels, not only normally failed to redress worldwide injustices effectively, but in many instances promoted economic policies which fed the ever-widening gap between those who were superabundantly rich and those who were destitute. There is no reason why Churches ought to be quiescent and guilty by association with failed politics because they have too much to lose by biting the hands of governments. There is every reason to suppose that the achievement of a just society could be the achievement of politics, *and* the Church, *as well as* Synagogues, Mosques, Temples, businesses, atheists, agnostics and neighbours.

conclusion

What does any of this have to do with God and the theologians of the twentieth century? Nothing at all if there is no God, and nothing as well if the promotion of life, love, and justice is the enterprise of politics, and is unrelated to theology as well as the purpose of the Church in the world. Obversely, if there is a God, and God is as envisaged by the Hebrew prophets and Jesus as One who despises wealth, expects justice to reign among people, wants human beings to take care of the earth, and who will vindicate the poor when human history has run its course, then those Churches and theologies indifferent to the poor are irrelevant to God as well.

There is a passage in the Bible that refers to the matter of what children should be told when they enquire about the meaning of God's commands: 'When your children ask you in time to come, "What is the meaning of the decrees and the statutes and the ordinances that the LORD your God has commanded you?" then you shall say to your children, "We were Pharaoh's slaves in Egypt, but the LORD brought us out of Egypt with a mighty hand"' (Deut 6: 20–1). Jews have remembered a night of divinely wrought deliverance from oppression for thousands of years. Theirs is a *memoria liberationis* – a memory of liberation. It gave heart to liberation theologians in the latter half of the twentieth century, and is a current hope that what God achieved in the past might reoccur any moment of any day for all who suffer.

glossary

Archbishop

The highest-ranking prelate of a city or province.

BCE

Stands for 'Before the Common Era', an alternative expression for 'BC'/'Before Christ'. It is used as an academic convention to avoid requiring anyone to date the course of human history with reference to Jesus Christ.

Beliefs

Propositions formulating tenets of religious faith.

Bishop

A bishop is a person who exercises a ministry of overseeing the welfare and integrity of groups of Christians. According to Vatican II, a bishop enjoys the fullness of priesthood, while presbyters (priests) participate in that priesthood.

Cardinal

A title in the Catholic Church that is normally conferred by the Pope on a bishop. Cardinals advise popes and participate in the highest levels of administration in the Catholic Church. Many cardinals reside in Rome, but others are scattered in cities internationally. A person who is to exercise the office of cardinal is first so named, and then publicly created as such. Theoretically, a person who is not a deacon, presbyter or bishop could be created a cardinal.

Catholic
A word meaning 'universal' – that which encompasses all Christians. Its opposite is 'sectarian' – that which has separated itself from the worldwide Church. Most Catholics today, also known as Roman Catholics, are Christians who worship according to the Roman or Latin Rite. Other Catholics adopt rites in other languages, as in the case of the Byzantine or Coptic Rites.

CE
Stands for 'The Common Era', an alternative expression for 'AD'/'The Year of the Lord'/'The Year of Our Lord'. It is used as an academic convention that does not compel anyone to refer to Jesus Christ as 'the Lord'. It recognizes that, once Christianity emerged, it joined the course of human history in an era common to people of diverse religious allegiances, and to people with no sympathy for religion.

Church/church
The meaning of the English word 'church' is disputed. Karl Barth liked to teach his students that it derives from the Latin, *circus*, meaning 'ring' or 'circular band'. A church is a circle or group of people involved in a similar activity. Karl Rahner preferred to teach that 'church' comes from the Greek term, *κυριακή*, meaning 'belonging to the Lord'. In Christian circles a church is a community of people who profess faith in Jesus Christ, and worship him, as a manifestation of God in human history. 'Church' is capitalized in this book to refer to a large collection of churches or to an international grouping of them, such as the Catholic Church or the Church of England. When not capitalized, 'church' designates a community or building in a specific location, as in 'the Baptist church in the centre of town'.

Christian
A name, belief or a person that relates to Jesus Christ.

Council
A gathering of bishops that meets to formulate doctrines, or to legislate principles for discipline within the Church.

Deacon
A deacon is a person who is ordained to serve a Christian community.

Denomination
A network of churches that voluntarily align with each other because of doctrinal or liturgical commonalities.

Doctrine
A teaching. 'Doctrine' also serves for some as a synonym for theology.

Dogma
From the Greek, δόγμα, 'what seems right'. A dogma is a proposition regarded by those who assent to it as indispensable to Catholic and Christian faith. In Christian tradition dogmas have normally been formulated by councils of bishops, or popes. The most significant Christian dogma is the teaching of the Council of Chalcedon in 451 CE, according to which the one and the same Jesus Christ is truly God and truly a human being.

Eastern Churches
Christian Churches that do not worship according to the Roman Rite, including those that recognize the jurisdiction of the pope. Historically these Churches formed in the eastern provinces of the Roman Empire. Some split with the papacy around 1054 CE.

Encyclical
A circular letter written by a pope to the world's bishops for the instruction of Catholic Christians.

Exegesis
The process of teasing out meanings of a text. The word comes from the Greek, *exegeomai*, 'to lead out of'. An exegete practises exegesis. Its opposite, eisegesis, is the mistaken reading into a text of meanings that are not feasible.

Faith
A way of living motivated by a decision to hope and trust this-worldly reality is not all there is, and that humans are accountable to God, gods or an unseen Ultimate Reality.

Liturgy/the Liturgy
An act of public and communal worship that is distinguished from an individualistic, private religious practice. The word 'liturgy' is ancient and comes from the Greek, λειτουργία, 'action of the people'. In the Septuagint, a Greek translation

of the Tanakh, the word is used to designate worship. The Second Vatican Council (1962–5) produced a major constitution on the liturgy called 'Sacrosanctum Concilium' ('[This] Sacred Council').

Mass/the Mass

A liturgical action that commemorates the last meal of Jesus before he was executed. Other expressions used to describe this and related rituals are the Lord's Supper, the Eucharist, the Breaking of the Bread, and the Sacred Synaxis. The word 'mass' derives from the Latin phrase 'Ite Missa est' – 'This is the sending' or 'Go the Mass [is ended]'. The phrase is the last uttered by the person presiding at mass in the Roman or Latin Rite. The words 'mass' and 'mission' both derive from the Latin *missio* – 'mission'. At the end of mass the presider sends the assembled worshippers away to live among and serve others as Christians. Since the Second Vatican Council the mass has involved an amalgam of two liturgies: the Liturgy of the Word and the Liturgy of the Eucharist. The former involves readings from the Bible. The latter is a ritual commemoration of, and giving thanks for, the last supper of Jesus. The word 'Eucharist' stems from the Greek, εύχαριστειν, 'to give thanks'.

Ordination

A liturgy or ecclesiastical ceremony which publicly establishes a person as a deacon, priest, bishop, minister or pastor.

Paradenomination

A group of churches that is in the process of forming a new congregation as it distances itself from a more established congregation.

Patristics

The study of the theology of Church Fathers – theologians of the early post-biblical age, who wrote in Greek, Latin, Armenian or Syriac.

Pentecostalism

A movement which first developed in the twentieth century among North American Protestants, from whom it spread to Catholics in the 1960s. The name of the movement stems from a Christian belief in Pentecost (from the Greek, 'the fiftieth day'), described in Acts 2 as an event, 50 days after Jesus' death and professed resurrection, when the Holy Spirit filled the disciples of Jesus emboldening them to preach. Pentecostalism is a non-hierarchical collectivity of churches that celebrates the presence of God's Spirit in worshipping communities.

Pope

This word comes from the Italian, 'papa', *father*. A pope is primarily a bishop, more specifically, the Bishop of Rome. In that role a pope exercises primacy in a college of bishops, that is, a worldwide collectivity of bishops who in turn lead and represent a collectiveness of local churches. This college of local churches forms the Church, a worldwide web of Christians.

Priest

An individual ordained to serve and lead a community by preaching and presiding at liturgies. In the Roman Rite, people who are normally called priests are officially ordained into the Order of Presbyters. A Presbyter is an elder in a community.

Protestantism

One of the three principal international groups of Christians along with Catholicism and Eastern Orthodoxy. It began in the early sixteenth century, most notably with Martin Luther's protest (hence 'Protestant') against the sale of papal indulgences (the granting of remission from divinely wrought punishment after death for the payment of a fee before death). Since the sixteenth century, Protestantism has crystallized into four main types: Lutheranism (inspired by Martin Luther), Calvinism (after John Calvin), Anabaptism (a belief that people who had been baptized as infants needed to be re-baptized as adults because of the invalidity of infant baptism) and Anglicanism. Some Anglicans align them- selves with the Anglo-Catholic Church, a part of the Church of England that ties itself to Catholic tradition, while not submitting to the jurisdiction of the Bishop of Rome.

Sacred Scripture

A term used to designate the Bible when it is regarded as divinely inspired, rather than simply a body of literature.

Synod

The governing body of a Church which is formed by bishops, or by bishops in concert with presbyters (priests), deacons and lay people. The Church of England has synodal government.

Systematic Theology

Any theology that is organized according to an overarching structure may be termed systematic. German philosophers in the eighteenth and nineteenth centuries were keen to articulate philosophical systems: reasoned accounts for all there is. Similarly, theologians have often been motivated to produce syntheses that interrelate all Christian beliefs and teachings into a comprehensive whole. The application of a philosophical or interpretative system to the exposition of theology may also render the latter systematic. A liberation theology that expounds beliefs and teachings regarding God with a consistent reference to God's predilection for the poor is thereby a systematic theology.

Tridentine
That which relates to the Council of Trent (1545–63).

notes

preamble

1 *Global Environment Outlook 2000* (London: Earthscan, 1999), p.6.
2 *Human Development Report 1999* (New York and Oxford: Oxford University Press, 1999), p.22.
3 A dissenting voice here is that of Jack Nelson-Pallmeyer, who is clear that 'God's violence is relentless throughout the Hebrew Scriptures'. See his *Is Religion Killing Us? Violence in the Bible and the Quran* (Harrisburg, PA: Trinity Press International, 2003), p.34.
4 Abraham Heschel, *The Prophets* (Philadelphia: Jewish Publication Society of America, 1962), p.166. See too, Walter Bruggemann, *Revelation and Violence* (Milwaukee, WI: Marquette University Press, 1986). For a more ample discussion of the Bible's gradual disavowal of divine violence, see Daniel C. Maguire, *The Horrors We Bless: Rethinking the Just-War Legacy* (Minneapolis, MN: Fortress Press, 2007), pp.65–8.
5 G.J. Sawyer and Vicktor Deak, *The Last Human: A Guide to Twenty-Two Species of Extinct Humans* (New Haven and London: Yale University Press, 2007).
6 Sam Harris, *Letter to a Christian Nation: A Challenge to Faith* (London: Bantam Press, 2007), p.75.
7 *The Holy Bible: Containing the Old and New Testaments with the Apocryphal/Deuterocanonical Books*, New Revised Standard Version, Anglicized Edition (Oxford: Oxford University Press, 1995).

one

1 See Hugh McLeod, *The Religious Crisis of the 1960s* (Oxford: Oxford University Press, 2007); Steve Bruce, *Religion in the Modern World: From Cathedrals to Cults* (Oxford: Oxford University Press, 1996); and Don Cupitt, *After God: The Future of Religion* (London: Weidenfeld & Nicolson, 1907); *Reforming Christianity* (Santa Rosa, CA: Polebridge Press, 2001); *The Old Creed and the New* (London: SCM Press, 2006); and *Radical Theology* (Santa Rosa, CA: Polebridge Press, 2006).
2 A.C. Crayling, 'Believers are away with the fairies', *The Daily Telegraph* (26 March 2007), pp.20–1 (p.21). See too, A.C. Grayling, *Against All Gods: Six Polemics on Religion and an Essay on Kindness* (London: Oberon Books, 2007). On p.43 the author describes religious

belief as 'an essentially infantile attitude of acceptance of fairy-stories ....'

3 Richard Dawkins, *The God Delusion* (London: Bantam Press, 2006). See too, Christopher Hitchens, *God Is Not Great: The Case Against Religion* (New York, NY: Twelve; and London: Atlantic Books, 2007); Daniel C. Dennett, *Breaking the Spell: Religion as a Natural Phenomenon* (London: Penguin Books, 2006); Sam Harris, *The End of Faith: Religion, Terror, and the Future of Reason* (New York and London: W.W. Norton and Company, 2004); and *Letter to a Christian Nation: A Challenge to Faith* (London: Bantam Press, 2007). For a critical discussion of authors mentioned in this note, see Tina Beattie, *The New Atheists: The Twilight of Reason and the War on Religion* (London: Darton, Longman and Todd, 2007); Richard Grigg, *Beyond the God Delusion: How Radical Theology Harmonizes Science and Religion* (Minneapolis, MN: Fortress Press, 2008); Alister E. McGrath, *Dawkins' God: Genes, Memes, and the Meaning of Life* (Oxford: Blackwell Publishing, 2004); and Keith Ward, *Why There Almost Certainly Is a God: Doubting Dawkins* (Oxford: Lion, 2008).

4 Jeremy Morris, *The Church in the Modern Age* (London and New York: I.B. Tauris, 2007), p.xvii.

5 Michael Howard and Wm. Roger Louis, eds, *The Oxford History of the Twentieth Century* (Oxford and New York: Oxford University Press, 2000), 'Forward', pp.xix–xxii (pp.xx–xxi).

6 See Noam Chomsky, *Profit Over People: Neoliberalism and Global Order* (New York: Seven Stories Press, 1999).

7 Victoria de Grazia, *Irresistible Empire: America's Advance through 20th-Century Europe* (Cambridge, MA and London: The Belknap Press of Harvard University Press, 2005), pp.3 and 5.

8 Achin Vanaik, ed., *Selling US Wars* (Adlestrop: Arris Books, 2007), p.1.

9 See Daniel C. Maguire, *The Horrors We Bless: Rethinking the Just War Legacy* (Minneapolis, MN: Fortress Press, 2007), pp.16–17.

10 Eric Fromm, *The Anatomy of Human Destructiveness* (New York: Holt, Rinehart and Winston, 1973), p.105.

11 Loring Wirbel, *Star Wars: US Tools of Space Supremacy* (London: Pluto Press, 2004), p.xv.

12 Joerg Rieger, *Christ and Empire: From Paul to Postcolonial Times* (Minneapolis, MN: Fortress Press, 2007), p.3.

13 On new forms of imperialism, see David Harvey, *The New Imperialism* (Oxford: Oxford University Press, 2003); Ziauddin Sardar and Merryl Wyn Davies, *American Dream Global Nightmare* (Cambridge: Icon Books 2004); L. Panitch, 'The New Imperial State', *New Left Review*, II: 1 (2000), pp.5–20; R. Went, 'Globalization in the Perspective of Imperialism', *Science and Society*, 66: 4 (2003–4), pp.473–97; and Zillah Eisenstein, *Against Empire: Feminisms, Racism, and the West* (London and New York: Zed Books, 2004).

14 Maguire, *The Horrors We Bless*, p.73.

15 Jane Chrispin and Francis Jegede, *Population, Resources and Development*, 2nd edn (London: HarperCollins, 2000), p.39, Figure 3.5.

16 See Jan Aart Scholte, *Globalization: A Critical Introduction* (Houndmills and New York, NY: Palgrave, 2000); Alex MacGillivray, *A Brief History of Globalization: The Untold Story of Our Incredible Shrinking Planet* (London: Robinson, 2006); Anthony Giddens, *Runaway World: How Globalisation is Reshaping Our Lives* (London: Profile Books, 1999); David Held, Anthony McGrew, David Goldblatt and Jonathan Perraton, *Global Transformations: Politics, Economics and Culture* (Cambridge: Polity Press, 1999); and Zygmunt Bauman, *Globalization: The Human Consequences* (Cambridge: Polity Press, 1998).

17 Callum G. Brown, *Religion and Society in Twentieth-Century Britain* (Harlow: Pearson/Longman, 1996), p.2.

18 Useful chronologies and overviews of political events, scientific discoveries, cultural transformations and artistic activity during the twentieth century can be found in Richard Overy, *Collins Atlas of the 20th Century* (London: Collins Books, 2005); Terry Burrows, ed., *The Visual History of the Modern World* (London: Sevenoaks, 2005); Robert Tignor and others, *Worlds Together, Worlds Apart: A History of the Modern World from the Mongol Empire to the Present* (New York and London: W.W. Norton & Company, 2002);

and H.E.L. Mellersh, R.L. Storey, Neville Williams and Philip Waller, *Chronology of World History*, Compact edn (Oxford: Helicon, 1995).

19 For a similar list, see Douglas John Hall, 'Christianity and Canadian Contexts: Then and Now', in Don Schweitzer and Derek Simon, eds, *Critical Theologies in a Land of Diversity* (Ottawa: Novalis, 2004), pp.18–32 (p.19).

20 Mark Kurlansky, *1968: The Year That Rocked the World* (London: Vintage, 2005), p.xv.

21 Paul VI, *Humanae Vitae, Acta Apostolicae Sedis*, 60 (1968), pp.481–503. Consult as well Charles Curran, *History and Contemporary Issues: Studies in Moral Theology* (New York, NY: Continuum, 1996), pp.106–12; and Richard P. McBrien, *Report on the Church, Catholicism After Vatican II* (New York, NY: HarperSanFrancisco, 1992), pp.36–8.

22 Elise Boulding, *Cultures of Peace: The Hidden Side of History* (Syracuse, NY: Syracuse University Press, 2000), p.233.

23 Jack Nelson-Pallmeyer, *Is Religion Killing Us?: Violence in the Bible and Quran* (Harrisburg, PA: Trinity Press International, 2003), p.5.

24 Maguire, *The Horrors We Bless*, p.58.

25 Gordon D. Kaufman, *Theology for a Nuclear Age* (Manchester: Manchester University Press and Philadephia, PA: The Westminster Press, 1985), p.16.

26 On German imperial anti-Semitism and the genocide of Jews commanded by Hitler, see Victor Karady, *The Jews of Europe in the Modern Europe: A Socio-historical Outline* (Budapest and New York: Central European University Press, 2004), pp.367–86.

27 For overviews of the entire history of Christian theologies and ways of living, consult Adrian Hastings, Alistair Mason and Hugh Pyper, eds, *The Oxford Companion to Christian Thought: Intellectual, Spiritual, and Moral Horizons of Christianity* (Oxford and New York: Oxford University Press, 2000); Leslie Houlden, ed., *Jesus in History, Thought, and Culture: An Encyclopedia*, 2 vols (Santa Barbara, CA: ABC-CLIO, 2003); John Bowden, ed., *Encyclopedia of Christianity* (Oxford and New York: Oxford University Press, 2005); Richard McBrien, *Catholicism*,

3rd edn (London: Geoffrey Chapman, 1994); Alister E. McGrath, *Christian Theology: An Introduction*, 4th edn (Oxford: Blackwell Publishers, 2007); and Richard Harries and Henry Mayr-Harting, eds, *Christianity: Two Thousand Years* (Oxford and New York: Oxford University Press, 2001).

28 Enrique Dussel, *Beyond Philosophy: Ethics, History, Marxism, and Liberation Theology* (Lanham: Rowman & Litterfield, 2003), pp.30–1.

29 For a detailed discussion of this passage and its possible consequences for Christians today, see Antonio González, *The Gospel of Faith and Justice* (Maryknoll, NY: Orbis Books, 2005), pp.41–69.

30 See the *Human Development Report 2006. Beyond Scarcity: Power, Poverty and the Global Water Crisis* (New York, NY: United Nations Development Programme, 2006), pp.1–21, esp. p.7; and Larbi Bouguerra, *Water under Threat* (London and New York: Zed Books, 2006).

31 John McDade, 'Catholic Theology in the Post-Conciliar Period', in Adrian Hastings ed., *Modern Catholicism: Vatican II and After* (London: SPCK; and New York: Oxford University Press, 1991), pp.422–43, (p.425).

32 Paul Spicker, Sonia Alvarez Leguizamó, and David Gordon, eds, *Poverty: An International Glossary*, 2nd edn (London and New York: Zed Books, 2007), p.91. See too the *World Health Report 1995: Bridging the Gaps* (Geneva: World Health Organization, 1995).

33 The image comes from Bob Sutcliffe, *100 Ways of Seeing an Unequal World* (London and New York: Zed Books, 2005), Section 17. The height of the vertical bars represents levels of income. In Section 17 of his book, Sutcliffe explains his three-dimensional image in these terms: 'From the left to the right we move from the poorer to the richer countries; from the back to the front we move from the richer to the poorer groups (tenths) within each national population. Each country has a number of these back-to-front rows of bars equivalent to its population (one row for every 10 million people). The result is an image of the distribution of income among the population of the whole

world.' There is no pagination in Sutcliffe's text. It is divided into a series of 123 images, each of which is accompanied by an explanatory note.

34 Vincent A. Gallagher, *The True Cost of Low Prices: The Violence of Globalization* (Maryknoll, NY: Orbis Books, 2006), p.20. Consult as well Paul Collier, *The Bottom Billion: Why the Poorest Countries Are Failing and What Can Be Done About It* (Oxford: Oxford University Press, 2007).

35 Andrew Glyn, *Capitalism Unleashed: Finance, Globalization, and Welfare* (Oxford: Oxford University Press, 2007), p.189.

36 Jonathan Schell, *The Unfinished Twentieth Century* (London and New York: Verso, 2001), pp.xi–xii.

37 Schell, *Unfinished*, p.xi.

two

1 According to David B. Barrett, George T. Kurian and Todd M. Johnson, *World Christian Encyclopedia: A Comparative Survey of Churches and Religions in the Modern World*, 2 vols, Vol. I: *The World by Countries: Religionists, Churches, Ministries* (Oxford and New York: Oxford University Press, 2001), p.10.

2 On attempts to specify Christianity's essence during and since the nineteenth century, consult W.A. Brown, *The Essence of Christianity: A Study in the History of Definition* (New York, NY: Scribner, 1902); Hans Wagenhammer, *Das Wesen des Christentums: Eine begriffsgeschichtliche Untersuchung* (Mainz: Matthias Grünewald Verlag, 1973); Stephen Sykes, *The Identity of Christianity: Theologians and the Essence of Christianity from Schleiermacher to Barth* (London: SPCK, 1984); and Hans Küng, *Christianity*, trans. John Bowden (London: SCM Press, 1995).

3 Pater McEnhill and George Newlands, *Fifty Key Christian Thinkers* (London and New York: Routledge, 2004), p.132.

4 Eric W. Gritsch and Robert W. Jenson, *Lutheranism: The Theological Movement and Its Confessional Writings* (Philadelphia, PN: Fortress Press, 1976), pp.5–6.

5 On the far-reaching transformation of Europe during modernity, see Larry

Krasnoff, *Hegel's 'Phenomenology of Spirit': An Introduction* (Cambridge: Cambridge University Press, 2008), pp.1–3.

6 H. Richard Niebuhr, *The Meaning of Revelation* (Louisville, KY: Westminster John Knox Press, 2006; first published by the Macmillan Company in 1941), p.4.

7 Klaus Scholder, *The Birth of Modern Critical Theology: Origins and Problems of Biblical Criticism in the Seventeenth Century*, trans. John Bowden (London: SCM Press, 1990), pp.10–11.

8 Ludwig Feuerbach, *The Essence of Christianity*, trans. George Eliot (New York, NY: Prometheus Books, 1989).

9 Feuerbach, *Essence*, pp.83, 159 and 271.

10 Feuerbach, *Essence*, p.63.

11 Feuerbach, *Essence*, p.14. Feuerbach mentions the process of projection by which humans transfer human attributes to God on pp.29–30.

12 Feuerbach, *Essence*, p.123.

13 Feuerbach, *Essence*, p.140.

14 Friedrich Smend, *Adolf von Harnack: Verzeichnis seiner Schriften* (Munich: K.G. Saur Verlag, 1990; originally published in Leipzig between 1927 and 1931).

15 Cited in Eberhard Busch, *Karl Barth: His Life from Letters and Autobiographical Texts* (Philadelphia, PA: Fortress Press, 1976), p.39.

16 H.E.L. Mellersh et al., *Chronology of World History*, Compact edn (Oxford: Helicon, 1995), p.267.

17 For the details of Harnack's life and thought, see W.H.C. Frend, 'Church Historians of the Early Twentieth Century: Adolf von Harnack (1851–1930)', *Journal of Ecclesiastical History*, 52: 1 (January 2001), pp.83–102; and Agnes von Zahn-Harnack, *Adolf von Harnack*, 2nd edn (Berlin: de Gruyter, 1951).

18 Frend, 'Church Historians', p.85.

19 See Zahn-Harnack, *Harnack*, pp.65–75 and 70–1; and Frend, 'Church Historians', pp.86–7.

20 Frend, 'Church Historians', p.85.

21 Adolf Harnack, *What Is Christianity? Sixteen Lectures delivered in the University of Berlin during the Winter-Term 1899–1900*, trans. Thomas Bailey Saunders (London, Edinburgh and Oxford: Williams and Norgate; and New York: G.P. Putnam's Sons, 1901). For the

manner in which the lectures were delivered and recorded, see the 'Translator's Preface'.

22 Bernard M.G. Reardon, *Liberal Protestantism* (London: Adam and Charles Black, 1968), p.45.

23 Reardon, *Liberal Protestantism*, pp.51–77, esp. p.51.

24 Reardon, *Liberal Protestantism*, p.56.

25 Reardon, *Liberal Protestantism*, p.68.

26 John E. Wilson, *Introduction to Modern Theology: Trajectories in the German Tradition* (Louisville, KY; and London: Wesminster John Knox Press, 2007), p.135.

27 Adolf Harnack, *History of Dogma*, vol. 1 (New York: Russell and Russell, 1958), p.11. See too, pp.127–8.

28 Adolf Harnack, *History of Dogma*, vol. 7 (New York: Russell and Russell, 1958), p.272.

29 Friedrich Schleiermacher, *The Christian Faith* (Edinburgh: T&T Clark, 1994), p.387.

30 On the meaning of 'liberal', see Peter C. Hodgson, *Liberal Theology: A Radical Vision* (Minneapolis, MN: Fortress Press, 2007), pp.13–14.

31 James Byrne, *Glory, Jest and Riddle: Religious Thought in the Enlightenment* (London: SCM Press, 1996), p.32.

32 Harnack, *History of Dogma*, vol. 7, p.274.

three

1 (Paris: Émile Nourry, 1930–31). Subsequent references to this work will refer to its three volumes as either I, II or III.

2 Loisy, II, pp.642–3.

3 Marvin R. O'Connell, *Critics on Trial: An Introduction to the Catholic Modernist Crisis* (Washington, DC: The Catholic University Press of America Press, 1994), pp.24–5.

4 Loisy, I, pp.9–19.

5 Loisy, p.21.

6 Loisy, I, pp.30–1.

7 O'Connell, *Critics*, p.9.

8 Loisy, I, p.33.

9 O'Connell, *Critics*, p.13.

10 Loisy, I, p.59.

11 O'Connell, *Critics*, p.15.

12 Albert Loisy, *Choses passées* (Paris: Émile Nourry, 1913), p.46.

13 For the history and a fuller description of the historical-critical method, see Joseph A. Fitzmeyer, *The Interpretation of Scripture: In Defence of the Historical-Critical Method* (New York, NY: Paulist Press, 2008).

14 See Alice L. Laffey, 'Biblical Scholarship: Past, Present, and Future', in Dermot A. Lane, ed., *Catholic Theology Facing the Future: Historical Perspectives* (Dublin: The Columba Press, 2003), pp.24–45 (p.26).

15 For a complete list of Loisy's publications, consult Albert Houtin and Félix Sartiaux, *Alfred Loisy, sa vie et son oeuvre* (Paris: CNRS, 1960), pp.304–24.

16 O'Connell, *Critics*, p.69.

17 Loisy, I, p.306.

18 See T.M. Schoof, *A Survey of Catholic Theology: 1800–1970* (Paramus, NJ: Paulist Newman Press, 1970), p.60.

19 See Loisy, *L'Évangile*, pp.22–3 and 37–42.

20 Loisy, *L'Évangile*, p.111.

21 See Hans Küng, *The Church* (Wellwood: Burns & Oates, 1968), p.43.

22 Albert Loisy, *Autour d'un petit livre* (Paris: Picard et Fils, 1903), p.254.

23 See O'Connelll, *Critics*, p.270. The five books were *L'Évangile et l'Église*, *Autour d'un petit livre*, *La religion d'Israel* (1901), *Études évangéliques* ('Evangelical Studies', 1902) and *Le quatrième Évangile*.

24 Loisy, II, p.493.

25 Rosemary Haughton, *The Catholic Thing* (Springfield, IL: Templegate, 1979), pp.21–2.

26 Marcel Clément, *Vie du Cardinal Ricard* (Paris: De Gigord, 1928), p.408.

27 Richard P. McBrien, *Catholicism*, 3rd edn (London: Geoffrey Chapman, 1994), pp.49–50.

28 Quoted in O'Connell, *Critics*, p.33. For the original Latin text, see Pius X, *Pascendi Dominici Gregis*, 8 September 1907, in *Acta Sanctae Sedis* (Rome: Vatican, 1907): 40: 593–650 (p.33).

29 Timothy G. McCarthy, *The Catholic Tradition: The Church in the Twentieth Century*, 2nd edn (Chicago, IL: Loyala Press, 1998), pp.47–8. See too, Michael, 'A New Modernist Crisis? Hardly', *America*, 129 (6 October), pp.239–42.

30 Gabriel Daly, 'Forward', in George Tyrrell, *Medievalism: A Reply to Cardinal Mercier* (Wellwood: Burns & Oates, 1994; original, 1908), pp.7–18 (p.10).

31 George Tyrrell, *Medievalism: A Reply to Cardinal Mercier* (London: Longman, Green and Co., 1908).

32 (Paris: Ceffonds, 1908).

33 Loisy, II, p.645.

34 Loisy, III, p.36.

35 Loisy, II, p.651. The original text reads: 'Je ne sais si je comprends les signes des temps, mais je crois que, pour le protestantisme comme le catholicisme, l'idéal, ce de disparaître pour céder la place à quelque chose qui vaudra mieux que catholicisme et protestantisme.'

four

1 Cited in Margaret Cropper, *Evelyn Underhill* (London: Longmans, 1958), p.5.

2 Hence Dana Greene, ed., *Evelyn Underhill: Modern Guide to the Ancient Quest for the Holy* (Albany, NY: State University of New York Press, 1988), p.2: 'She was not a theologian, but a student of human achievement and potentiality.'

3 John Macquarrie, *Twentieth Century Religious Thought* (London: SCM, 1981), pp.408–9. John Macquarrie was an Anglican Scottish theologian and, before his retirement, was the Lady Margaret Professor of Divinity in Oxford.

4 A complete bibliography of Underhill's published works is contained in Greene, *Underhill*, pp.224–56. For anthologies of the writings, see T.S. Kepler, ed., *The Evelyn Underhill Reader* (Nashville, TN: Abingdon Press, 1962); and John Stobbart, ed., *The Wisdom of Evelyn Underhill: An Anthology of Her Writings* (London: A.R. Mowbray, 1951).

5 See Evelyn Underhill, *The Grey World* (London: William Heinemann, 1904); *The Lost Word* (London: Heinemann, 1907); and *Column of Dust* (London: Metheun and Company, 1909).

6 For additional reading on mysticism, see Jess Byron Hollenback, *Mysticism: Experience, Response, and Empowerment* (University Park, PA: The Pennsylvannia State University Press, 1996); Richard Woods, ed., *Understanding Mysticism* (London: The Athlone Press, 1980); and Denise Lardner Carmody and John Tully Carmody,

Mysticism: Holiness East and West (New York and Oxford: Oxford University Press, 1998).

7 Hans Küng, *Great Christian Thinkers* (New York, NY: Continuum, 1995).

8 Pater McEnhill and George Newlands, *Fifty Key Christian Thinkers* (London and New York: Routledge, 2004).

9 *New Catholic Encyclopedia*, Vol. IV (New York, NY: McGraw-Hill Book Company, 1967), p.939.

10 See Greene, *Underhill*, pp.7–8.

11 Susan Rakoczy, *Great Mystics and Social Justice: Walking on Two Feet of Love* (Mahwah, NJ: Paulist Press, 2006), p.100.

12 Chris Cook, *Britain in the Nineteenth Century: 1915–1914* (London and New York: Longman, 1999), p.111.

13 Jean Bottéro, *The Birth of God: The Bible and the Historian* (University Park, PA: The Pennsylvania State University Press, 2000), pp.3–4; and Rene Labat et al., *Les religions du Proche-Orient asiatique* (Paris: Fayard-Denoël, 1970), pp.145–226 and 26–36.

14 Evelyn Underhill, *A Bar Lamb's Ballad Book* (London: Kegan, Paul, Trench, Trubner, and Co., 1902).

15 Dana Greene, *Evelyn Underhill: Artist of the Infinite Life* (London: Darton, Longman & Todd, 1991), p.25.

16 Friedrich Schleiermacher, *The Christian Faith* (Edinburgh: T&T Clark, 1989; German original: *Glaubenslehre*, 1821–2), p.12.

17 Evelyn Underhill, *Mysticism*, 12th edn (London: Methuen & Co., 1960; which contains the Preface to the first edn), p.xiv.

18 Underhill, *Mysticism*, p.iv.

19 Evelyn Underhill, *Practical Mysticism* (Columbus, OH: Ariel, 1914/1992), p.28.

20 Underhill, *Practical Mysticism*, p.72.

21 Underhill, *Practical Mysticism*, p.81. All subsequent quotations in this paragraph are from the same page.

22 Underhill, *Practical Mysticism*, p.81.

23 See Rakoczy, *Great Mystics*, p.101.

24 Evelyn Underhill, *Essentials of Mysticism and Other Essays* (London: J.M. Dent, 1920), pp.6–7.

25 Greene, *Underhill*, p.20.

26 Evelyn Underhill, *The Church and War* (London: Anglican Pacifist Fellowship,

1940), reproduced in Greene, *Underhill*, pp.213–17 (p.216).

27 Underhill, in Greene, *Underhill*, p.213.

28 See John Bowden, *A Chronology of World Christianity* (London and New York: Continuum, 2007), p.392.

five

1 Consult George Seaver, *Albert Schweitzer: The Man and His Mind*, 5th edn (London: Adam and Charles Black, 1955), pp.37–52.

2 Albert Schweitzer, *Out of My Life and Thought*, trans. Anje Bultmann Lemke (Baltimore and London: The Johns Hopkins University Press, 1998). This book was first published in English in London (by Allen & Unwin) and New York (by Henry Bolt) in 1933. Further references are to the 1998 edition, and are placed between parentheses in the body of this chapter's text.

3 For detailed studies of Schweitzer's life and thought, consult Norman Cousins, *Albert Schweitzer's Mission: Healing and Peace* (New York and London: Norton, 1985); and *Doctor Schweitzer of Lambaréné* (London: Black; and New York: Harper and Row, 1960); James Brabazon, *Albert Schweitzer: A Biography* (New York: Putman, 1975); George Marshall and David Poling, *Schweitzer: A Biography* (London: Bles; and New York: Doubleday, 1971); George Seaver, *Albert Schweitzer: The Man and His Mind* (London: Black, 1947); and Werner Picht, *The Life and Thought of Albert Schweitzer* (London: Allen and Unwin, 1964). See too, Albert Schweitzer, *The Forrest Hospital at Lambaréné* (New York: Henry Holt, 1931); and *From My African Notebook* (London: Allen and Unwin, 1938).

4 Oskar Kraus, *Albert Schweitzer: His Work and His Philosophy* (London: Adam & Charles Black, 1955), pp.18–19.

5 H.J. Holtzmann, *Die synoptischen Evangelien. Ihr Ursprung und geschichtliche Character* (Leibzig: Wilhelm Engelmann, 1863).

6 See Raymond, *The Elusive Messiah: A Philosophical Overview of the Quest for the Historical Jesus* (Boulder, CO: Westview, 1999), pp.14–17; and Stephen J. Patterson, 'Sources for a Life of Jesus', in Herschel Schanks and others, *The Search for Jesus: Modern Scholarship Looks at the Gospels* (Washington, DC: Biblical Archaeology Society, 1994).

7 Friedrich Schleiermacher, *The Christian Faith* (Edinburgh: T&T Clark, 1994; originally published in German in 1821–2), p.643.

8 Hermann Samuel Reimarus, *Reimarus: Fragments*, ed. Charles H. Talbert, and trans. Ralph S. Fraser (Philadelphia, PA: Fortress Press, 1970), p.248.

9 William Wrede, *The Messianic Secret*, trans. J.C.G. Greig (London: James Clark & Co., 1971).

10 Albert Schweitzer, *Von Reimarus zu Wrede: Eine Geschichte der Leben-Jesu-Forschung* (Tübingen: Mohr [Siebeck], 1906).

11 These editions were not incorporated into English translations until 2000. See Albert Schweitzer, *The Quest of the Historical Jesus*, First Complete Edition, ed. John Bowden (London: SCM, 2000). This is a translation of Schweitzer's second German edition, *Geschichte der Leben-Jesu-Forschung* (Tübingen: J.C.B. Mohr, 1913).

12 David Friedrich Strauss, *The Life of Jesus Critically Examined*, trans. George Eliot (Ramsey, NJ: Sigler Press, 1994).

13 Don Cupitt, *The Sea of Faith: Christianity in Change* (London: BBC, 1984), p.104.

14 Johannes Weiss, *Die Predigt Jesu vom Reiche Gottes* (Göttingen: Vandenhoech & Ruprecht, 1892). This book is available in English as *Jesus' Proclamation of the Kingdom of God*, ed. L.E. Keck, Lives of Jesus Series (Philadelphia, PA: Fortress Press, 1971); Schweitzer, *The Quest of the Historical Jesus*, p.198.

15 Albert Schweitzer, *The Mystery of the Kingdom of God: The Secret of Jesus' Messiahship and Passion* (London: Black; and New York: Dodd and Mead, 1914).

16 A useful extract from this lengthy work is contained in Gregory W. Dawes, *The Historical Jesus Quest: Landmarks in the Search for the Jesus of History* (Louisville, KY: Westminster John Know Press, 2000), pp.187–204.

17 See Schweitzer, *The Quest*, pp.482 and 485.

18 Albert Schweitzer, *Die psychiatrische Beurteilung Jesus* (Tübingen: J.C.B. Mohr,

1913). This thesis appeared in English as *The Psychiatric Study of Jesus: Exposition and Criticism*, trans. Charles R. Roy (Boston: Beacon, 1948).

19 Consult John W. Miller, *Jesus at Thirty: A Psychological and Historical Portrait* (Minneapolis, MN: Fortress Press, 1997), p.104.

20 Similar ideas are voiced in Schweitzer's *The Quest*, pp.483–4.

21 Albert Schweitzer, *The Decay and the Restoration of Civilization*, Part 1 of *The Philosophy of Civilization* (London: Black 1923); and *Civilization and Ethics*, Part 2 of *The Philosophy of Civilization* (London: Black, 1923).

22 Albert Schweitzer, *Reverence for Life: Sermons 1900–1919* (New York: Harper and Row, 1969).

23 Consult D.E. Nineham, 'Schweitzer, Albert (1875–1965)', in Leslie Houlden, ed., *Jesus in History, Thought, and Culture: An Encyclopedia*, 2 vols (Santa Barbara, CA; and Oxford: ABC-CLIO, 2003), vol. 2, pp.764–9 (p.767).

24 See Max H. Charlesworth, ed., *Jesus and Archaeology* (Grand Rapids, MI; and Cambridge, UK: Eerdmans, 2006), p.46.

six

1 See Gary Dorian, *The Barthian Revolt in Modern Theology* (Louisville, KY: Westminster John Knox Press, 2000), p.7.

2 Quoted in Eberhard Busch, *Karl Barth: His Life from Letters and Autobiographical Texts*, trans. John Bowden (London: SCM Press; and Philadelphia, PA: Fortress Press, 1976), p.46.

3 Consult John Webster, *Barth* (London and New York: Continuum, 2000), p.4.

4 Eberhard Busch, *Barth*, trans. Richard and Martha Burnett (Nashville, TN: Abingdon Press, 2008), pp.2–3.

5 Friedrich von Bernhardi, *Vom heutigen Kriege*, 2 vols (Berlin: Mittler, 1912); and *Deutschland und der Nächste Krieg* (Stuttgart: Cotta, 1912).

6 See Friedrich von Bernhardi, *Germany and the Next War* (New York: Longman, Green & Company, 1914), pp.16–20, 85–105, 114 and 167–82.

7 Robert Tignor et al., *Worlds Together, Worlds Apart: A History of the Modern World from the Mogal Empire to the Present* (New York and London: W.W. Norton, 2002), pp.349–51, esp. p.351.

8 Karl Barth, 'Concluding Unscientific Postscript on Schleiermacher', in *The Theology of Schleiermacher* (Edinburgh: T&T Clark, 1982), pp.261–79 (p.264).

9 H. Richard Niebuhr, *The Kingdom of God in America* (Chicago: Willet, Clark & Co., 1937), p.193.

10 Karl Barth, *Der Römerbrief*, 2nd edn (München: Christian Kaiser Verlag, 1922; 12th edn, 1978); *The Epistle to the Romans*, trans. Edwyn C. Hoskyns from the 6th German edn (London, Oxford and New York: Oxford University Press, 1933). The English version is variously referred to as either 'the Letter' or 'Epistle' to the Romans.

11 Consult Busch, *Barth*, p.4.

12 Barth, *Romans*, p.44.

13 William Stacy Johnson, *The Mystery of God: Karl Barth and the Postmodern Foundations of Theology* (Louisville, KY: Westminster John Knox Press, 1997), p.20.

14 Karl Barth, *God, Grace and Gospel*, trans. James Strathearn McNab (Edinburgh: Oliver and Boyd, 1959), p.34.

15 Karl Barth, *Fides Quaerens Intellectum*, 2nd edn (Zürich: Evangelischer Verlag, 1958); trans. I.W. Robertson, *Faith Seeking Understanding* (London: SCM, 1960).

16 Karl Barth, *How I Changed My Mind*, ed. by J. Godsey (Richmond, VA: John Knox Press, 1966), p.42.

17 See Alister I.C. Heron, *A Century of Protestant Theology* (Cambridge: The Lutterworth Press, 1980), pp.74–5.

18 See Busch, *Barth*, p.10.

19 Karl Barth, 'Reformationstag 1933', in *Dokumente der Begegnung Karl Barths mit dem Pfarrernotbund in Berlin*, ed. Eberhard Busch (Zürich: Theologischer Verlag Zürich, 1998), p.106; and Busch, *Barth*, p.12.

20 Timothy J. Gorringe, *Karl Barth: Against Hegemony* (Oxford and New York: Oxford University Press, 1999), pp.121 and 297.

21 Emil Brunner, *Natur und Gnade: Zum Gespräch mit Karl Barth* (Tübingen: J.C.B. Mohr, 1934).

22 Brunner, *Natur und Gnade*, pp.18–19.

23 Karl Barth, *Nein! Antwort an Emil Brunner* (Munich: Chr. Kaiser Verlag, 1934). The texts by both Brunner and Barth were translated into a single volume by Peter Fraenkel as *Natural Theology* (London: Geoffrey Bles, 1946). Brunner published a second edition of his pamphlet in 1935. The debate between Barth and Brunner is examined by Trevor Hart in his *Regarding Karl Barth: Essays Toward a Reading of His Theology* (Carlisle: Paternoster Press, 1999), ch. 7.

24 Karl Barth, *Kirchliche Dogmatik* (Zollikon: Evangelischer Verlag, 1932–67); trans. G.M. Bromiley, *Church Dogmatics* (Edinburgh: T&T Clark, 1956–75).

25 Karl Barth, *Church Dogmatics*, trans. G.M. Bromiley, 2nd edn (Edinburgh: T&T Clark, 1975), I/1, p.17.

26 Karl Barth, *Dogmatik im Grundriss* (Munich: Christian Kaiser Verlag, 1947); trans. G.T. Thompson, *Dogmatics in Outline* (London: SCM Press, 1949).

27 Karl Barth, *Church Dogmatics*, I/1, p.3.

28 Barth, *Dogmatics in Outline*, p.9.

29 Consult Garrett Green, *Theology, Hermeneutics, and Imagination: The Crisis of Interpretation at the End of Modernity* (Cambridge: Cambridge University Press, 2000), pp.5–8.

30 Barth, *Church Dogmatics*, I/1, p.III.

31 Barth, *Church Dogmatics*, I/1, p.28.

32 See Barth, *Church Dogmatics*, I/1, § 4: 'The Word of God in Its Threefold Form', pp.88–124.

33 Barth, *Church Dogmatics*, I/1, p.55.

34 Cited in Busch, *Karl Barth: His Life from Letters and Autobiographical Texts*, pp.379–80.

35 See Barth, *Dogmatics in Outline*, p.68.

36 See Barth, *Church Dogmatics*, I/2, pp.105–6.

37 Busch, *Barth*, p.35.

38 See Barth, *Church Dogmatics*, I/1, pp.375–83.

39 David Tracy, *The Analogical Imagination: Christian Theology and the Culture of Pluralism* (London: SCM Press, 1981), ch. 1.

seven

1 Renate Wind, *A Spoke in the Wheel: The Life of Dietrich Bonhoeffer*, trans. John Bowden (London: SCM Press, 1991), p.124.

2 Eberhard Bethge, *Dietrich Bonhoeffer: A Biography* (London: Collins, 1970), p.827.

3 F. Burton Nelson, 'The life of Dietrich Bonhoeffer', in John W. de Gruchy, ed., *The Cambridge Companion to Dietrich Bonhoeffer* (Cambridge: Cambridge University Press, 1999), pp.22–49 (p.27); and Eberhard Bethge, *Dietrich Bonhoeffer: Theologe, Christ, Zeitgenosse* (Munich: Chr. Kaiser Verlag, 1967), pp.13–14.

4 Bethge, *Bonhoeffer*, p.3.

5 John de Gruchy, ed., *Dietrich Bonhoeffer: Witness to Jesus Christ* (Minneapolis, MN: Fortress Press, 1991), p.2.

6 Nelson, 'The life of Dietrich Bonhoeffer', p.24.

7 Bethge, *Bonhoeffer*, pp.5–8.

8 Recorded in Bethge, *Bonhoeffer*, p.22.

9 G. Leibholz, 'Memoir', in *Dietrich Bonhoeffer, The Cost of Discipleship*, trans. R.H. Fuller (London: SCM Press, 1959/1994), pp.9–27 (p.9).

10 Cited in Renate Bethge and Christian Gremmels, eds, *Dietrich Bonhoeffer: A Life in Pictures*, trans. Brian McNeil (Minneapolis, MN: Fortress Press, 2006), p.36. This book was published to mark the centenary of Bonhoeffer's birth.

11 Dietrich Bonhoeffer, *'Sanctorum Communio': A Dogmatic Enquiry into the Sociology of the Church* (London: Collins, 1963). See too, Bethge, *Bonhoeffer*, pp.55–60, esp. pp.59–60.

12 Dietrich Bonhoeffer, in Geffrey B. Kelly and F.Burton Nelson, eds, *A Testament to Freedom: The Essential Writings of Dietrich Bonhoeffer* (New York, NY: Harper Collins, 1990), p.380.

13 Dietrich Bonhoeffer, *Habitilationsschrift, Akt und Sein: Transzendentalphilosophie und Ontologie in der systematicschen Theologie*, ed., Hans-Richard Reuter (Munich: Chr. Kaiser Verlag, 1988); trans. H. Martin Rumscheidt, *Act and Being: Transcendental Philosophy and Ontology in Systematic Theology* (Minneapolis, MN: Fortress Press, 1996); and Bethge, *Bonhoeffer*, p.97.

14 Dietrich Bonhoeffer, 'Report on a Period of Study at the Union Theological Seminary in New York, 1930–31', in *No Rusty Swords: Letters, Lectures, and Notes, 1928–1936, Collected Works of Dietrich Bonhoeffer*, vol. 1 (New York,

NY: Harper & Row, 1965), p.91. 'De Servo Arbitrio' means 'On the Bondage of the Will'.

15 Quoted in Nelson, 'The life of Dietrich Bonhoeffer', p.26; and Renate Bethge, 'Bonhoeffer and the Role of Women', *Church and Society* (July/August, 1995), p.36.

16 Robert Tignor et al., *Worlds Together, Worlds Apart: A History of the Modern World from the Mongol Empire to the Present* (New York, NY: W.W. Norton & Company, 2002), pp.388–9.

17 'Pastoral Constitution on the Church in the Modern World', in *Vatican Council II: Constitutions, Decrees, Declarations*, ed. Austin Flannery (North Port, NY: Costello Publishing Company; and Dublin: Dominican Publications, 1996), Section 80, p.267.

18 Gerhard Leibholz, 'Memoir', p.23.

19 J. Noakes and G. Pridham, eds, *Documents on Nazism, 1919–1945* (New York: Viking Press, 1975), pp.229–30.

20 Dietrich Bonhoeffer, *Die Mündige Welt V: Dokumente zur BonhoefferForschung, 1928–1945*, ed. J. Glenthøj (Munich: Chr. Kaiser Verlag, 1969), p.104; and John de Gruchy, *Dietrich Bonhoeffer*, p.19.

21 See Bonhoeffer, *No Rusty Swords*, p.235.

22 Dietrich Bonhoeffer, *Discipleship*, *Dietrich Bonhoeffer Works*, Vol. 4, trans. Martin Kuske and Ilse Tödt (Minneapolis, MN: Fortress Press, 2001).

23 Nelson, 'The life of Dietrich Bonhoeffer', p.35.

24 Dietrich Bonhoeffer, *Gemeinsames Leben*, 5th edn (Munich: Chr. Kaiser Verlag, 1949), trans. John W. Doberstein as *Life Together* (London: SCM Press, 1954).

25 Nelson, 'The life of Dietrich Bonhoeffer', p.38.

26 Cited in Nelson, 'The life of Dietrich Bonhoeffer', pp.38–9.

27 See Bethge, *Dietrich Bonhoeffer*, p.644; and Nelson, 'The life of Dietrich Bonhoeffer', p.40.

28 Bethge, *Dietrich Bonhoeller*, p.840; and Ruth Zerner, 'Church, state, and the "Jewish Question!"', in De Gruchy, ed., *The Cambridge Companion*, pp.190–205 (p.191).

29 Dietrich Bonhoeffer, *Letters and Papers from Prison*, ed. Eberhard Bethge, Enlarged edn (London: SCM Press/Folio Society, 2000), p.27.

30 P.S. Best, *The Venlo Incident* (London: Hutchinson, 1950), p.200.

31 Cited in Bethge, *Dietrich Bonhoeffer*, p.830; and Best, *The Venlo Incident*, p.200.

32 Bonhoeffer, *Letters and Papers*, p.50.

33 See Stanley J. Grenz and Roger E. Olson, *20th-Century Theology: God & the World in a Transitional Age* (Downers Groves, IL: InterVarsity Press and Carlisle: The Paternoster Press, 1992), p.149.

34 Bonhoeffer, *Letters and Papers*, p.347.

35 Bonhoeffer, *Letters and Papers*, p.348.

36 Bonhoeffer, *Letters and Papers*, p.322. The Latin expression, 'deus ex machina', means 'God from the machinery'. It refers to the mechanisms by which gods were suspended above the stage in ancient Greek theatre. It alludes to an unexpected divine intervention to correct a seemingly hopeless human situation.

37 Bonhoeffer, *Letters and Papers*, p.289.

38 Bonhoeffer, *Letters and Papers*, pp.247–8.

39 Bonhoeffer, *Letters and Papers*, p.247.

40 Bonhoeffer, *Letters and Papers*, p.248.

41 Bonhoeffer, *Letters and Papers*, p.247.

42 Dietrich Bonhoeffer, *Ethics*, ed. by Eberhard Bethge and trans. Neville Horton Smith (New York: Macmillan, 1965), pp.196–7.

43 Bonhoeffer, *Discipleship*, p.37.

44 Bonhoeffer, *Discipleship*, pp.37–8.

45 Bonhoeffer, *Discipleship*, p.253.

46 Bonhoeffer, *Discipleship*, p.87.

47 Bonhoeffer, *Discipleship*, p.89.

48 Bonhoeffer, *Discipleship*, pp.87–8.

49 Bonhoeffer, *Discipleship*, pp.43–4.

50 Renate Bethge, *Dietrich Bonhoeffer: A Brief Life*, trans. K.C. Hanson (Minneapolis, MN: Fortress Press, 2004), pp.80–1.

eight

1 On divergent views as to what constitutes the centre of theology, see John McDade, 'Catholllic Theology in the Post-Conciliar Period', in Adrian Hastings, ed., *Modern Catholicism: Vatican II and After* (London: SPCK; and New York, NY: Oxford University Press, 1991), pp.422–43 (p.440).

2 For detailed accounts of Tillich's life and thought, see James Luther Adams, *Paul Tillich's Philosophy of Culture, Science and Religion* (New York, NY: Harper & Row, 1965); James Heywood Thomas, *Paul Tillich: An Appraisal* (London: SCM Press, 1963); David Kelsey, *The Fabric of Paul Tillich's Theology* (New Haven: Yale University Press, 1957); and Charles Kegley and Robert W. Bretall, eds, *The Theology of Paul Tillich* (New York, NY: Macmillan, 1952).

3 Paul Tillich, *On the Boundary: An Autobiographical Sketch* (New York, NY: Charles Schribner's Sons, 1966), p.14.

4 John Heywood Thomas, *Tillich* (London and New York: Continuum, 2000), p.2.

5 Thomas, *Tillich*, pp.2–3.

6 See Wilhelm and Marion Pauck, *Paul Tillich: His Life and Thought*, Vol. 1: *Life* (New York: Harper & Row, 1976), p.14; and John P. Newport, *Paul Tillich* (Waco, TX: Word Books, 1984), pp.197–205.

7 Thomas, *Tillich*, p.3.

8 Martin Kähler, *The So-Called Historical Jesus and the Historic, Biblical Christ*, trans. Carl E. Braaten (Philadelphia, PA: Fortress Press, 1964 [1896]), pp.66–7.

9 See Raymond Martin, *The Elusive Messiah: A Philosophical Overview of the Quest for the Historical Jesus* (Boulder, CO; and Oxford: Westview Press, 1999), p.42.

10 Published as *Die religionsgeschichtliche Konstruktion in Schellings positiver Philosophie, ihre Voraussetzungen und Prinzipien* (Breslau: H. Fleischmann, 1910).

11 Published as *Der Begriff des Übernatürlichen, sein dialektischer Charakter und das Prinzip der Identität, dargestellt an der supra-naturalistischen Theologie vor Schliermacher* (Königsberg: H. Madrasch, 1915).

12 Mark Kline Taylor, ed., *Paul Tillich: Theologian of the Boundaries* (Minneapolis, MN: Fortress Press), p.16.

13 Hans Schwarz, *Theology in a Global Context: The Last Two Hundred Years* (Grand Rapids, MI; and Cambridge, UK: Eerdmans, 2005), p.355.

14 Taylor, *Paul Tillich*, p.16.

15 Taylor, *Paul Tillich*, p.14.

16 See Wilhelm and Marrion Pauck, *Paul Tillich*, p.36; and Taylor, *Paul Tillich*, p.14.

17 On theologies of mediation, consult Claude Welch, *Protestant Thought in the Nineteenth Century*, vol. 1: *1799–1870* (New Haven, CT: Yale University Press, 1972), pp.269–73.

18 Paul Tillich, *Die Religiöe Lage der Gegenwart* (Berlin: Ullstein, 1926), trans. as *The Religious Situation* (New York: Henry Holt, 1932); and *Die Socialistische Entscheidung* (Potsdam: Protte, 1933), rendered in English as *The Socialist Decision* (New York: Harper & Row, 1977).

19 Langdon Gilkey, *Gilkey on Tillich* (New York, NY: Crossroad, 1990), p.3.

20 Schwarz, *Theology*, p.356.

21 See Warren A. Kay, 'Paul Tillich: 1886–1965', in Donald W. Musser and Joseph L. Price, eds, *A New Handbook of Christian Theologians* (Nashville, TN: Abingdon Press, 1996), pp.449–59 (p.451).

22 See Jack Mouw and Robert P. Scharlemann, 'Bibliography of the Publications of Paul Tillich', in *The Theology of Paul Tillich: A Revised and Updated Classic*, ed. Charles W. Kegley (New York: The Pilgrim Press, 1982), pp.395–423.

23 Paul Tillich, *Systematic Theology*, 3 vols (London: SCM Xprints, 1997). All three volumes were initially published by the University of Chicago Press: Vol. 1 (1951), Vol. 2 (1957), and Vol. 3 (1963). Subsequent references to the work will be designated as *ST* and will be to the 1997 London edition and placed in the body of the text of this chapter.

24 Tillich's method is examined carefully in John P. Clayton, *The Concept of Correlation: Paul Tillich and the Possibility of a Mediating Theology* (Berlin and New York: De Gruyter, 1980).

25 Kay, 'Paul Tillich', p.453.

26 Consult Adrian Thatcher, *The Ontology of Paul Tillich* (Oxford: Oxford University Press, 1978); and Ian E. Thompson, *Being and Meaning: Paul Tillich's Theory of Meaning, Truth and Logic* (Edinburgh: Edinburgh University Press, 1981).

27 On Avicenna's discussion of essence and existence, see Amélie-Marie Goichon, *La distinction de l'essence et l'existence d'après Ibn Sina* (Paris : Desclée de Brower, 1937). For a

commentary in English on Avicenna and Aquinas, see Steven E. Baldner and William E. Carroll, translators, *Aquinas on Creation* (Toronto: Pontifical Institute of Mediaeval Studies, 1997), pp.12–34.

28 Paul Tillich, *The Courage to Be* (New Haven, CT: Yale University Press, 1952).

29 See John E. Wilson, *Introduction to Modern Theology: Trajectories in the German Tradition* (Louisville, KY; and London: Westminster John Knox Press, 2007), p.224.

30 Schwarz, *Theology*, p.358.

31 Maurice Wiles, *Reason to Believe* (London: SCM Press, 1999), p.50.

32 John Dillinger, 'Paul Tillich (1886–1965)', in Mark G. Toulouse and James O. Duke, eds, *Makers of Christian Theology in America* (Nashville, TN: Abingdon Press, 1997), pp.420–6 (p.425).

33 Paul Tillich, *A History of Christian Thought: From Its Judaic and Hellenistic Origins to Existentialism*, ed. Carl E. Braaten (New York, NY: Simon and Schuster, 1968), p.227. This book was originally published in two separate volumes: *A History of Christian Thought*; and *Perspectives on 19th and 20th Century Protestant Theology*.

34 See Raymond F. Bulman and Frederick J. Parrella, eds, *Religion in the New Millennium: Theology in the Spirit of Paul Tillich* (Macon, GA: Mercer University Press, 2001).

35 David Tracy, *The Analogical Imagination: Christian Theology and the Culture of Pluralism* (London: SCM Press, 1981); Sallie McFague, *Metaphorical Theology: Models of God in Religious Language* (Philadelphia, PA Fortress Press, 1982); Langdon Gilkey, *Religion and Scientific Future: Reflections on Myth, Science and Theology* (New York, NY: Harper & Row, 1970); John B. Cobb, Jr, *Christ in a Pluralistic Age* (Philadelphia, PA: Westminster, 1975); Gregory Baum, *Religion and Alienation: A Theological Reading of Sociology* (New York, NY: Paulist Press, 1975); and Gordon Kaufman, *In Face of Mystery: A Constructive Theology* (Cambridge, MA: Harvard University Press, 1993).

nine

1 Quoted in William D. Miller, *Dorothy Day: A Biography* (New York, NY: Doubleday, 1982), p.311.

2 David O'Brien, 'Pilgrimage of Dorothy Day', *Commonweal*, 107 (19 December 1980), pp.711–15.

3 Robert Ellsberg, ed., *The Duty of Delight: The Diaries of Dorothy Day* (Milwaukee, WI: Marquette University Press, 2008). Hereafter referred to as Day, *The Duty of Delight*.

4 Robert Ellsberg, ed., 'Introduction', in *Dorothy Day: Selected Writings* (Maryknoll, NY: Orbis Books; and London: Darton, Longman & Todd, 2005), p.xvii.

5 Dorothy Day, *The Long Loneliness* (New York, NY; HarperCollins, 1997; originally published in 1952), pp.40–1.

6 Jim Forest, *Love Is the Measure: A Biography of Dorothy Day* (Maryknoll, NY: Orbis Books, 2006; originally 1986). p.3.

7 Elaine Murray Stone, *Dorothy Day: Champion of the Poor* (New York/Mahwah, NJ: Paulist Press, 2004), p.4.

8 Forest, *Love Is the Measure*, p.6.

9 Day, *The Long Loneliness*, p.45.

10 Forest, *Love Is the Measure*, p.13.

11 Stone, *Dorothy Day*, pp.12–16.

12 Forest, *Love is the Measure*, p.17.

13 Stone, *Dorothy Day*, pp.18–19.

14 Stone, *Dorothy Day*, pp.29–30.

15 Robert Coles, *Dorothy Day: A Radical Devotion* (Cambridge, MA: Da Capo Press, 1987), p.3.

16 Stone, *Dorothy Day*, 31.

17 Rosalie G. Riegle, *Dorothy Day: Portraits by Those Who Knew Her* (Maryknoll, NY: Orbis Books, 2003), p.5.

18 Day, *The Long Loneliness*, p.17.

19 Coles, *Dorothy Day*, p.3; Forest, *Love Is the Measure*, pp.35–7; Stone, *Dorothy Day*, pp.32–3.

20 Coles, *Dorothy Day*, p.3.

21 Forest, *Love Is the Measure*, p.38.

22 Day, *The Long Loneliness*, p.94.

23 Coles, *Dorothy Day*, p.3; Stone, *Dorothy Day*, p.34.

24 Ellsberg, in *Dorothy Day: Selected Writings*, p.xxiii.

25 Day, *The Long Loneliness*, p.113.

26 Day, *The Long Loneliness*, pp.136–7.

27 Forest, *Love Is the Measure*, p.51; Stone, *Dorothy Day*, p.45.

28 Forest, *Love is the Measure*, p.54.

29 Coles, *Dorothy Day*, pp.11–12; Stone, *Dorothy Day*, pp.49–50; Forest, *Love Is the Measure*, p.54.

30 Day, *The Long Loneliness*, p.166.

31 See Charles P. Kindelberger, *The World in Depression, 1929–1939* (Berkeley and Los Angeles, CA: University of California Press, 1986); and John Kenneth Galbraith, *The Great Crash: 1929* (Boston: Houghton Mifflin Company, 1954).

32 Day, *The Long Loneliness*, p.169.

33 Forest, *Love Is the Measure*, pp.56–7; Stone, *Dorothy Day*, p.51; Coles, *Dorothy Day*, p.12.

34 Pope Leo XIII, *Rerum Novarum* (1891), re-published in David J. O'Brien and Thomas A. Shannon, eds, *Catholic Social Thought: A Documentary Heritage* (Maryknoll, New York, NY: Orbis Press, 1992), pp.14–39 (p.30).

35 Forest, *Love Is the Measure*, p.57.

36 Ellsberg, ed., in *Dorothy Day: Selected Writings*, p.xxix. See p.xxviii as well.

37 Forest, *Love Is the Measure*, p.65.

38 Day, *The Duty of Delight*, p.66.

39 Day, *The Long Loneliness*, p.215.

40 Day, *The Duty of Delight*, p.71.

41 Day, *The Duty of Delight*, p.459.

42 Day, *The Duty of Delight*, p.310.

43 Day, *The Duty of Delight*, p.90.

44 Day, *The Duty of Delight*, p.9.

45 Day, *The Duty of Delight*, p.29.

46 Day, *The Duty of Delight*, p.15.

47 Day, *The Duty of Delight*, pp.38–9.

48 Day, *The Duty of Delight*, p.185.

49 Day, *The Duty of Delight*, p.29.

50 Day, *The Duty of Delight*, pp.33–4.

51 See Ellsberg, ed., *Dorothy Day: Selected Writings*, p.xvii.

52 Day, *The Duty of Delight*, pp.64–5.

53 Day, *The Duty of Delight*, p.95.

54 A similar reading of Day's aversion to being called   a saint is recorded by Sallie McFague in her book, *A New Climate for Theology: God,* the World, and Global Warming (Minneapolis, MN: Fortress Press, 2008), p.157: "'Don't dismiss me so easily" – meaning, *Don't let yourself off the book so fast.*'

ten

1 See Harvey D. Egan, *Karl Rahner: Mystic of Everyday Life* (New York, NY: The Crossroad, 1998), p.19. Bibliographies of Rahner's writings include Roman Bleistein, *Bibliographie Karl Rahner, 1969–1974* (Freiburg: Herder, 1974); Herbert Vorgrimler, *Wagnis Theologie* (Freiburg: Herder, 1979); James Bacik, *Apologetics and the Eclipse of Mystery: Mystagogy according to Karl Rahner* (Notre Dame, IN: University of Notre Dame Press, 1980), pp.143–9; M. Dudley, 'On Reading Rahner', *Scottish Journal of Theology*, 37: 1 (1984), pp.81–96; C.J. Pedley, 'An English Bibliographical Aid to Karl Rahner', *The Heythrop Journal*, 25: 3 (July, 1984), pp.319–65; and also by C.J. Pedley, 'An English Biographical Aid to Karl Rahner: Supplement', *The Heythrop Journal*, 26: 3 (July, 1985), p.310.

2 John Macquarrie, 'The Anthropological Approach to Theology', *The Heythrop Journal*, 25 (1984), pp.272–87.

3 This episode is recounted by Philip Endean, ed., in *Karl Rahner: Spiritual Writings* (Maryknoll, NY: Orbis Books, 2004), p.9.

4 Karl Rahner, *I Remember: An Autobiographical Interview with Meinhold Krauss* (New York, NY: Crossroad; and London: SCM Press, 1985), pp.24–5.

5 Rahner, *I Remember*, pp.24–5.

6 These are, *I Remember*, already cited, together with Karl Rahner, *Karl Rahner in Dialogue: Conversations and Interviews, 1965–1982*, ed. by Harvey D. Egan (New York, NY: Crossroad, 1986); and Karl Rahner, *Faith in a Wintry Season: Conversations with Karl Rahner in the Last Years of His Life*, ed. Paul Imhof and Hubert Biallowons (New York, NY: Crossroad, 1990).

7 Egan, *Karl Rahner*, p.20.

8 Herbert Vorgrimler, *Understanding Karl Rahner: An Introduction to His Life and Thought* (London: SCM Press, 1986), pp.48–50.

9 See Pierre Rousselot, 'Les yeux de la foi', *Reserches de Science Religieuse*, 1 (1910), pp.241–59 and 444–75; On Rousselot's life and thought, see Georges Van Riet, *L'Epistemologie Thomiste: Rescherches sur le problème de la connaissance dans l'école thomiste contemporaine* (Louvain: Éditions de l'Insitut Supérieur de Philosophie, 1946), pp.301–13.

10 Karl Rahner, *Sehnsucht nach dem geheimnisvollen Gott: Profil – Bilder-Texte*, ed. Herbert Vorgrimmer (Freiburg: Herder, 1984), pp.78–80. The translation quoted here is by Philip Endean, ed., in *Karl Rahner*, p.32.

11 Edward Schillebeeckx, *Jesus in Our Western Culture: Mysticism, Ethics and Politics*, trans. John Bowden (London: SCM Press, 1987), p.66.

12 Geffrey B. Kelly, ed., *Karl Rahner: Theologian of the Graced Search for Meaning* (Edinburgh: T&T Clark, 1993), p.3.

13 Rahner, *I Remember*, pp.39–40.

14 Pius X, 'The Oath Against Modernism', reprinted in Anthony Mioni, ed., *The Popes Against Modern Errors* (Rockford IL: TAN Books and Publishers, 1999), pp.270–2, (p.271).

15 Rahner, *Faith in a Wintry Season*, p.16.

16 Thomas Aquinas, *Summa Theologiae*, Part I, Question 84, Article 7.

17 Karl Rahner, *Geist in Welt. Zur Metaphysik der endlichen Eerkenntnis bei Thomas von Aquino* (Innsbruck: Rauch, 1939), trans. William Duch as *Spirit in the World* (New York: Herder and Herder, 1968).

18 Thomas Sheehan, *Karl Rahner: The Philosophical Foundations* (Athens: Ohio University Press, 1987), p.1.

19 See Kelly, *Karl Rahner*, p.7.

20 Rahner, *I Remember*, p.40.

21 Rahner, *Faith in a Wintry Season*, p.16.

22 Karl Rahner, *Hearers of the Word*, trans. Michael Richards (London: Sheed and Ward; and New York, NY: Herder and Herder/Seabury Press, 1986).

23 Karl Rahner, 'Selbstporträt', *Forscher und Gelehrte*, ed. W. Ernst Böhm (Stuttgart: Battenberg, 1966), p.21. See too, Egan, *Karl Rahner*, pp.19 and 24.

24 Karl Rahner, *The Eternal Year*, trans. by John Shea (Baltimore: Helicon, 1964); *Encounters with Silence*, trans. James Demske

(Westminster, MD: Newman, 1966); *On Prayer* (New York, NY: Paulist Press, 1968); and *Spiritual Exercises*, trans. Kenneth Baker (New York, NY: Herder and Herder, 1965).

25 Rahner, *Faith in a Wintry Season*, p.19.

26 Rahner, *Faith in a Wintry Season*, p.39.

27 Karl Rahner, *Grundkurs des Glaubens: Einführung in den Begriff des Christentums* (Freiburg im Breisgau: Herder, 1976), trans. William Dych, *Foundations of Christian Faith: An Introduction to the Idea of Christianity* (New York, NY: Crossroad, 1978).

28 Karl Rahner, *Faith in a Wintry Season*, p.21.

29 Rahner, *Faith in a Wintry Season*, p.48.

30 Rahner, *Faith in a Wintry Season*, pp.48–9.

31 Rahner, *Faith in a Wintry Season*, p.21.

32 Karl Rahner, *The Trinity*, trans. Joseph Donceel (New York, NY: Herder and Herder, 1970).

33 Rahner, *Faith in a Wintry Season*, p.29.

34 Rahner, *Faith in a Wintry Season*, p.17.

35 Rahner, *Faith in a Wintry Season*, p.19.

36 Thomas P. O'Meara, *God in the World: A Guide to Rahner's Theology* (Collegeville, MN: The Liturgical Press, 2007), p.3.

eleven

1 See Rainer Liedtke and Stephan Wendehorst, eds, *The Emancipation of Catholic, Jews and Protestantss: Minorities and the Nation State in Nineteenth-Century Europe* (Manchester and New York: Manchester University Press, 1999).

2 Nicholas Atkin and Frank Tallett, *Priests, Prelates and People: A History of the Catholic Church since 1750* (London and New York: I.B. Tauris, 2003), p.291.

3 Melissa J. Wilde, *Vatican II: A Sociological Analysis of Religious Change* (Princeton, NJ; and Oxford: Princeton University Press, 2007), p.1. To say that Vatican II 'eliminated the Latin mass' does not mean that Mass could no longer be celebrated in Latin, but that it was no longer compulsory for Catholics to conduct this rite in Latin.

4 Yves M.-J. Congar, *The Mystery of the Temple or The Manner of God's Presence to his Creatures from Genesis to the Apocalypse*, trans. Reginald

F. Trevett (London: Burns & Oates, 1962), p.177; originally published as *Le Mystère du Temple* (Paris: Les Éditions du Cerf, 1958).

5 See Yves Congar, 'The Church: The People of God', *Concilium*, I: I (January 1965), pp.7–19; 'The People of God', in *Vatican II: An Interfaith Appraisal*, ed. by John H. Miller (Notre Dame, IN: Notre Dame University Press, 1966), pp.197–207; *Le concile de Vatican II: son Église people de Dieu et corps du Christ*, Théologie Historique, 71 (Paris: Beauchesne, 1984); and Flynn, *Gongar's Vision of the Church*, p.100.

6 Richard P. McBrien, *Report on the Church: Catholicism After Vatican II* (New York, NY: HarperCollins, 1992), p.212.

7 Yves Congar, *Divided Christendom: A Catholic Study of the Problem of Reunion*, trans. M.A. Bousfield (London: Geoffrey Bles, 1939), p.275.

8 On Congar's published anticipations of the ecclesiology of Vatican II, see Richard P. McBrien, *Catholicism*, 3rd edn (London, Geoffrey Chapman, 2000), p.660.

9 In Jean Puyo, *Jean Puyo interroge le Père Congar. 'Une Vie pour la vérité'* (Paris: Éd. du Centurion, 1975), p.6. Hereafter referred to as 'Une Vie'.

10 Joseph Famerée and Gilles Routhier, *Yves Congar* (Paris: Les Éditions du Cerf, 2008), p.17; and 'Une Vie', pp.23 and 76.

11 Marie-Dominique Chenu, *Une école de théologie: le Saulchoir* (Paris: Les Éditions du Cerf, 1985; originally published in 1937).

12 T.M. Schoof, *A Survey of Catholic Theology: 1800–1970* (Paramus, NJ: Paulist Newman Press, 1970), p.103.

13 Maime Allard, 'Yves Congar', in Jean Genest, ed., *Penseurs et apôtres du vingtième siècle* (Québec: Éditions Fides, 2001), pp.469–95 (p.471); and Flynn, *Congar's Vision of the Church*, p.10.

14 Quoted in Giuseppe Alberigo and Joseph A. Komanchack, eds, *History of Vatican II*, Vol. 1: *Announcing and Preparing Vatican Council II. Toward a New Era in Catholicism* (Maryknoll, NY: Orbis Books; and Leuven: Peters, 1995), p.1.

15 Hans Küng, *The Catholic Church: A Short History*, trans. John Bowden (London: Weidenfeld and Nicolson, 2001), p.190.

16 John W. O'Malley, *What Happened at Vatican II* (Cambridge, MA: The Belknap Press of Harvard University Press, 2–8), p.292.

17 Yves Congar, *Mon Journal du Concile*, Vol. 1 (Paris: Les Éditions du Cerf, 2002), p.7.

18 Congar, *Mon Journal*, p.6.

19 Congar, *Mon Journal*, p.9.

20 Congar, *Mon Journal*, p.464.

21 Giuseppe Alberigo and Joseph A. Komonchak, *History of Vatican II*, Vol. 2: *The Formation of the Council's Identity. First Period and Intersession. October 1962-September 1963* (Maryknoll, NY: Orbis Books; and Leuven: Peters, 1997), pp.227–32.

22 *Sacrosanctum Concilium* ('This Sacred Council'), 4 December 1963.

23 Wilde, *Vatican II*, p.1.

24 On the People of God, see Yves Congar, *This Church that I Love*, trans. Lucien Delafuente (Denville, NJ: Dimension Books, 1969), ch. 2.

25 Wilde, *Vatican II*, p.61.

26 Vatican II, 'Dogmatic Constitution on Divine Revelation' (*Dei Verbum*), nos. 23–4, in Austin Flannery, ed., *Vatican Council II: Constitutions, Decrees, Declarations* (Northport, NY: Costello Publishing Company; and Dublin: Dominican Publications, 1996), pp.112–13.

27 Yves Congar, *The Meaning of Tradition* (San Francisco, CA: Ignatius Press, 2004; originally published in French in 1963). The commentator referred to by Congar is R. Rouquette, 'Bilan du Concile', *Études* (January 1963), p.104.

28 Congar, *The Meaning of Tradition*, p.37.

29 Congar, *The Meaning of Tradition*, pp.9–10.

30 Yves Congar, *Je crois en l'Esprit Saint* (Paris: Éditions du Cerf, 1979 [Vols 1 and 2], and 1980 [Vol. 3]).

31 J.P. Jossua, *Le père Congar: la théologie au service du people de Dieu* (Paris: Éditions du Cerf, 1967), pp.43–4.

32 Yves Congar, *Diversity and Communion*, trans. by John Bowden (London: SCM, 1984; originally published in 1982), p.161.

33 Congar, *Diversity and Communion*, p.161.

34 Yves Congar, 'The Place of Poverty in Christian Life in an Affluent Society', *Concilium*, 5 (1966), pp.29–39 (p.38).

twelve

1 Edward Schillebeeckx, *Christ the Sacrament of the Encounter with God*, trans. Paul Barrett (London: Sheed & Ward, 1963), pp.13–14.

2 Schillebeeckx, *Christ the Sacrament*, p.15.

3 Schillebeeckx, *Christ the Sacrament*, p.15.

4 Edward Schillebeeckx, *For the Sake of the Gospel*, trans. John Bowden (London: SCM Press, 1989), p.107.

5 Schillebeeckx, *For the Sake of the Gospel*, pp.43–4.

6 Edward Schillebeeckx, *Jesus in Our Western Culture: Mysticism, Ethics and Politics*, trans. John Bowden (London: SCM Press, 1987), p.63.

7 Schillebeeckx, *For the Sake of the Gospel*, p.66.

8 For a detailed account of Schillebeeckx's upbringing and education, see Erik Borgman, *Edward Schillebeeckx: A Theologian in His History*, trans. John Bowden (London and New York, NY: Continuum, 2003).

9 Edward Schillebeeckx, in conversation with Huub Oosterhuis and Piet Hoogeveen, *God is New Each Moment* (Edinburgh: T & T Clark, 1983), p.2.

10 Schillebeeckx, *God is New Each Moment*, p.2.

11 See Schillebeeckx, *God is New Each Moment*, p.13.

12 Edward Schillebeeckx, *Church: The Human Story*, trans. John Bowden (London: SCM Press, 1990), p.98.

13 Edward Schillebeeckx, 'La Théologie', in *Les Catholiques Hollondais*, in conversation with H. Hillenaar and H. Peters (Brugge and Utrecht: Desclée de Brouwer, 1969), p.3.

14 On Chenu's involvement with the priest-workers, see François LePrieur, *Quand Rome Condamme: Dominicains et Prêtres-Ouvriers* (Paris: Éditions du Cerf, 1989).

15 Edward Schillebeeckx, *De Sacramentele heilsec-onomie: Theologische bezinning op St. Thomas' sacramentenleer in het light van de traditie de henendaagse sacramentsproblematik* (Antwerp: 't Groeit/Bilthoven: H. Nelissen, 1952).

16 Schillebeeckx, *Maria, Christus' mooiste wonder-schepping* (Antwerp: Apostolaat van de Rosenkrans, 1954); and *Maria, Moeder van de verlossing* (Antwerp/Haarlem: Apostolaat van de Rosenkrans, 1955).

17 Edward Schillebeeckx, *Mary, Mother of the Redemption* (London: Sheed and Ward, 1964), p.136.

18 Edward Schillebeeckx and Catharina Halkes, *Mary: Yesterday, Today, Tomorrow*, trans. John Bowden (New York, NY: Crossroad, 1993), pp.32–3; originally published as *Maria, Gisteren, Vandaag, Morgen* (Baarn: Uitgeverij H. Nelissen, 1992).

19 Schillebeeckx, *God is New Each Moment*, p.15.

20 Patrick Vandermeersch, 'Twee manieren van Geloven: een historische Belichting van het Vlammse en het Nederlandse katholicisme', *Kultuurleven*, 56 (1989), pp.32–9 (p.37).

21 See John A. Coleman, *The Evolution of Dutch Catholicism, 1958–1974* (Berkeley, CA: University of California Press, 1978).

22 See Paul Collins, ed., *From Inquisition to Freedom* (New York, NY: Continuum, 2001); *God's New Man: The Election of Benedict XVI and the Legacy of John Paul II* (London: Continuum, 2005); and *Papal Power: A Proposal for Change in Catholicism's Third Millennium* (London: Fount, 1997).

23 Edward Schillebeeckx, *Het huwelijk: aardse wekelijkheid en heilsmysterie* (Bilthoven: H. Nelissen, 1963, trans. as *Marriage, Secular Reality and Saving Mystery* (London and Melbourne: Sheed and Ward, 1966)); and *Christus' tegenwoordigheid in de eucharistie* (Bilthoven: H. Nelissen, 1967, trans. as *The Eucharist* (New, London, and Sydney: Sheen and Ward, 1968)).

24 Edward Schillebeeckx, 'Het nieuwe Godsbeeld, secularisatie en politiek', *Tijdschrift voor Theologie*, 8 (1968), pp.44–66 (p.44).

25 Schillebeeckx, 'Het nieuwe Godsbeeld', p.52.

26 Edward Schillebeeckx, 'Zwijgen en spreken over God in een geseculariseerde wereld', *Tijdschrift voor Theologie*, 7 (1967), 337–359 p.337).

27 Schillebeeckx, 'La Théologie', p.15.

28 Edward Schillebeeckx, 'De kerk op drift?', *Tijdschrift voor Geestelijk Leven*, 22 (1966), pp.533–54 (p.554).

29 Edward Schillebeeckx, 'Forward', in Daniel Speed Thompson, *The Language of Dissent: Edward Schillebeeckx on the Crisis of Authority in the Catholic Church* (Notre Dame, IN: University of Notre Dame Press, 2003), pp.ix–xiv (p.ix).

30 Edward Schillebeeckx, *Jezus, het verhaal van een levende* [*Jesus, the Story of a Living One*, or *Jesus, the Story of One Alive*] (Brugge and Bloemandaal: H. Nelissen, 1974); *Jesus: An Experiment in Christology* (New York: Seabury, 1979; London: Collins, 1979; New York: Crossroad, 1981).

31 Edward Schillebeeckx, *Gerechtigheid en liefde: Genade en bevrijding* [*Justice and Love: Grace and Liberation*], 2nd edn (Baarn: H. Nelissen, 1977); *Christ: The Christian Experience in the Modern World* (London: SCM, 1980); USA edn: *Christ: The Experience of Jesus as Lord* (New York, NY: Crossroad, 1981).

32 Edward Schillebeeckx, *Mensen als verhaal van God* [*Humans as the Story of God*], 1st edn (Baarn: H. Nelissen, 1989); 2nd edn (Baarn, 1990); *Church: The Human Story of God*, trans. John Bowden (London: SCM, 1990).

33 The prominence of the theme of suffering in Schillebeeckx's theology has now been carefully studied. See Aloysius Rego, *Suffering and Salvation: The Salvific Meaning of Suffering in the Later Theology of Edward Schillebeeckx* (Leuven: Peeters Press, 2006); and Kathleen Anne McManus, *Unbroken Communion: The Place and Meaning of Suffering in the Theology of Edward Schillebeeckx* (Lanham, MD: Rowman & Littlefield Publishers, 2003).

34 John P. Galvin, 'The Story of Jesus As the Story of God', in Mary Catherine Hilkert and Robert J. Schreiter, eds, *The Praxis of the Reign of God: An Introduction to the Theology of Edward Schillebeeckx* (New York: Fordham University Press, 2002), pp.79–95 (p.81).

35 Edward Schillebeeckx, *Jesus: An Experiment in Christology* (New York: The Seabury Press, 1979), p.620.

36 Edward Schillebeeckx, *For the Sake of the Gospel*, trans. John Bowden (London: SCM Press, 1989), p.117.

37 Schillebeeckx, *For the Sake of the Gospel*, pp.106–7.

thirteen

1 Maurice Merleau-Ponty, *Humanisme et Terreur: Essai sur le problème communiste* (Paris: Éditions Gallimard, 1947/1980), p.94.

2 Gavin I. Langmuir, *History, Religion, and Antisemitism* (Berkeley, Los Angeles; and Oxford: University of California Press, 1990), p.257.

3 Mary Daly, *The Problem of Speculative Theology* (Washington, DC: The Thomist Press, 1965), p.36.

4 Mary Daly, *Gyn/Ecology: The Metaethics of Radical Feminism* (London: The Women's Press, 1999; originally published in 1978), p.38.

5 Katherine Keller, 'Mary Daly: 1928–', in David W. Musser and Joseph L. Price, eds, *A New Handbook of Christian Theologians* (Nashville, TN: Abingdon Press, 1996), pp.127–34 (p.127).

6 Mary Daly, *Outercourse: The Be-Dazzling Voyage* (New York, NY: HarperSanFrancisco, 1992), p.33. This book contains a great deal of autobiographical information.

7 Daly, *Outercourse*, p.51.

8 Daly, *Outercourse*, p.51.

9 Daly, *Outercourse*, p.55.

10 Daly, *Outercourse*, p.74.

11 Daly, *Outercourse*, pp.76–7.

12 Mary F. Daly, 'Catholic Women and the Modern Era', in *Wir schweigen nicht länger! – We Won't Keep Silence Any Long!*, ed. Gertrud Heinzelmann (Zurich: Inter-feminas Verlag, 1965), pp.106–10; and 'A Built-In Bias', *Commonweal*, LXXXI (15 January 1965), pp.508–11.

13 Gertrude Heinzelman, *We are No Longer Silent: Women Express Themselves about the Second Vatican Council* (Zurich: Inter-feminas Verlag, 1964); and Catharina Halkes, *Storm na de stilte* (Utrecht: Ambo, 1964).

14 Daly, *Outercourse*, p.79.

15 Mary Daly, *The Church and the Second Sex* (Boston, MA: Beacon Press, 1985; originally published in 1968), p.10. Hereafter referred to as *The Church*.

16 Daly, *Outercourse*, p.79.

17 Daly, *The Church*, pp.9 and 11.

18 Simone de Beauvoir, *Le dieuxième sexe*, 2 vols (Paris: Gallimard, 1949); *The Second Sex* (London: Jonathan Cape; New York: Alfred A. Knopf, 1953). Subsequent references to this book are to the Knopf edition.

19 Daly, *The Church*, p.56.

20 De Beauvoir, *The Second Sex*, p.98.

21 See Daly, *The Church*, p.58.

22 De Beauvoir, *The Second Sex*, p.171.

23 De Beauvoir, *The Second Sex*, p.167.

24 De Beauvoir, *The Second Sex*, p.290.

25 See De Beauvoir, *The Second Sex*, pp.130 and 714 ; and Daly, *The Church*, pp.66–9.

26 See Daly, *The Church*, pp.180–1.

27 Daly, *The Church*, p.223.

28 Cited in Daly, *Outercourse*, p.138.

29 See Daly, *Outercourse*, pp.144 and 396–9.

30 Daly, *Outercourse*, p.300.

31 Mary Daly, *Beyond God the Father: Toward a Philosophy of Women's Liberation* (Boston: Beacon Press, 1973/1985), p.13.

32 Daly, *Beyond God the Father*, p.19.

33 Daly, *Beyond God the Father*, p.19.

34 Daly, *Beyond God the Father*, p.198.

35 Mary Daly, *Quintessence … Realizing the Archaic Future: A Radical Manifesto* (Boston: Beacon Press, 1998), p.201.

36 Back cover of Mary Daly, *Amazon Grace: Re-Calling the Courage to Sin Big* (New York, NY: Palgrave Macmillan, 1996).

37 Mary Daly, *Quintessence*, p.207.

fourteen

1 See Jürgen Moltmann, *A Broad Place: An Autobiography*, trans. Margaret Kohl (London: SCM Press, 2007), pp.16–17.

2 Moltmann, *A Broad Place*, p.17.

3 Jürgen Moltmann, *Theologie der Hoffnung* (Munich: Chr. Kaiser Verlag, 1965); *Theology of Hope: On the Ground and Implications of a Christian Eschatology* (London: SCM Press, 1967). This English translation is of the fifth German edition.

4 Jürgen Moltmann, *Experiences in Theology: Ways and Forms of Christian Theology*, trans. Margaret Kohl (Minneapoliis, MN: Fortress Press, 2000), p.xviii.

5 Moltmann, *A Broad Place*, p.4. See too, pp.3–9.

6 Moltmann, *A Broad Place*, p.14.

7 Moltmann, *A Broad Place*, p.26.

8 Moltmann, *A Broad Place*, p.30.

9 Moltmann, *A Broad Place*, p.33.

10 Moltmann, *A Broad Place*, p.52.

11 Geiko Müller-Fahrenholz, *The Kingdom and the Power: The Theology of Jürgen Moltmann,*

trans. John Bowden (London: SCM Press, 2000), pp.22–23.

12 Moltmann, *A Broad Place*, p.61.

13 See Wayne Hudson, *The Marxist Philosophy of Ernst Bloch* (London: Macmillan, 1982).

14 Ernst Bloch, 'Topos Utopia', in *Abschied von der Utopie?* (Frankfurt: Suhrkamp, 1980), p.43. The suggestion that this quotation is the motto of Bloch's philosophy comes from David Brown, *Continental Philosophy and Modern Theology* (Oxford: Basil Blackwell, 1987), p.192.

15 Ernst Bloch, *The Principle of Hope*, Vol. 1 (Oxford, Basil Blackwell, 1986), p.24.

16 See Hans-Dieter Bahr, 'Bloch', in Simon Critchley and William R. Schroeder, eds, *A Companion to Continental Philosophy* (Malden, MA; and Oxford: Blackwell Publishers, 1998), pp.382–8 (pp.383–4).

17 David McLellan, *Marxism and Religion* (Houndmills: Macmillan Press, 1987), p.131.

18 Ernst Bloch, *Atheismus im Christentum: Zur Religion des Exodus und des Reichs* (Frankfurt: Suhrkamp Verlag KG, 1985), pp.90–2; and Brown, *Continental Philosophy*, p.193.

19 Jürgen Moltmann, *Theologie Hoffnung* (Munich: Christian Kaiser, 1964). See too, Moltmann, *A Broad Place*, pp.78–79.

20 Jürgen Moltmann, *Theology of Hope: On the Ground and Implications of a Christian Eschatology*, trans. James W. Leitch (London: SCM Press, 1967), p.16.

21 Moltmann, *Theology of Hope*, p.165.

22 Richard Bauckham, *Moltmann: Messianic Theology in the Making* (Basingstoke: Marshall Pickering, 1987), p.23.

23 Moltmann, *Theology of Hope*, p.17.

24 Moltmann, *A Broad Place*, p.147.

25 Moltmann, *A Broad Place*, p.156.

26 Moltmann, *A Broad Place*, p.136.

27 Moltmann, *A Broad Place*, pp.143–4.

28 Jürgen Moltmann, *Der gekreuzigte Gott* (Munich: Christian Kaiser Verlag, 1972); *The Crucified God: The Cross of Christ as the Foundation and Criticism of Christian Theology*, trans. R.A. Wilson and John Bowden (London: SCM Press, 1974).

29 See Müller-Fahrenholz, *The Kingdom*, p.71.

30 Moltmann, *The Crucified God*, p.227.

31 Moltmann, *The Crucified God*, p.190.

32 Moltmann, *The Crucified God*, p.192. Emphasis added.

33 Moltmann, *The Crucified God*, p, 243.

34 Moltmann, *The Crucified God*, pp.243–4. See too, Jürgen Moltmann, *The Spirit of Life: A Universal Affirmation* (Minneapolis, MN: Fortress Press, 2001), p.299.

35 Moltmann, *The Crucified God*, p.327, for this and the preceding quotation.

36 Moltmann, *The Crucified God*, p.4.

fifteen

1 For a clear overview of twentieth-century scientific innovations, see Lisa Rosner, ed., *The Hutchinson Chronology of Science* (Oxford: Helicon, 2002), pp.197–351.

2 Gordon D. Kaufman, *In the Beginning … Creativity* (Minneapolis, MN: Fortress Press, 2004), pp.108–9.

3 Kaufman, *In the Beginning*, p.109.

4 Kenneth Nordgren, *God as Problem and Possibility: A Critical Study of Gordon Kaufman's Thought Toward a Spacious Theology* (Uppsala: Uppsala Universitet, 2003), p.22.

5 Kaufman, *In the Beginning*, pp.109–10.

6 See Kaufman, *In the Beginning*, pp.110–11.

7 See Gordon D. Kaufman, *Relativism, Knowledge and Faith* (Chicago: The University of Chicago Press, 1960); and Nordgren, *God as Problem and Possibility*, pp.23–4.

8 See M. Thomas Thangaraj, 'Gordon D. Kaufman 1925–', in Donald W. Musser and Joseph L. Price, eds, *A New Handbook of Christian Theologians* (Nashville, TN: Abingdon Press, 1996), pp.253–9 (pp.253–4).

9 Gordon D. Kaufman, *God the Problem* (Cambridge, MA: Harvard University Press, 1972), p.xi.

10 Kaufman, *God the Problem*, p.xviii.

11 Kaufman, *God the Problem*, p.xix.

12 Kaufman, *God the Problem*, p.148.

13 Kaufman, *God the Problem*, p.7.

14 See Kaufman, *God the Problem*, p.160.

15 Gordon Kaufman, *An Essay on Theological Method*, 3rd edn (Atlanta, GA: Scholars Press, 1995).

16 Kaufman, *Essay*, p.2.

17 Kaufman, *Essay*, p.2.

18 Kaufman, *Essay*, p.2.

19 Kaufman, *Essay*, p.2.

20 Kaufman, *Essay*, p.3.

21 Consult Gordon D. Kaufman, 'Critical Theology as a University Discipline', in David Ray Griffin and Joseph C. Hough, Jr, eds, *Theology and The University: Essays in Honor of John B. Cobb, Jr* (Albany, NY: State University of New York Press, 1991), pp.35–50.

22 Kaufman, *Essay*, p.4.

23 Gordon D. Kaufman, *The Theological Imagination: Constructing the Concept of God* (Philadelphia, PA: The Westminster Press, 1981).

24 Kaufman, *The Theological Imagination*, p.12.

25 Kaufman, *The Theological Imagination*, p.22.

26 Kaufman, *The Theological Imagination*, p.22.

27 Gordon D. Kaufman, *Theology for a Nuclear Age* (Manchester: Manchester University Press; and Philadelphia, PA: The Westminster Press, 1985), p.55.

28 Kaufman, *In the Beginning*, pp.75–6.

29 Gordon D. Kaufman, *In Face of Mystery: A Constructive Theology* (Cambridge, MA; and London: Harvard University Press, 1993), p.4.

30 Kaufman, *In Face of Mystery*, p.15.

31 Kaufman, *In Face of Mystery*, p.15.

32 Kaufman, *In Face of Mystery*, p.15.

33 See Nordgren, *God as Problem and Possibility*, pp.26–7.

34 Kaufman, *In the Beginning*, p.2.

35 Gordon D. Kaufman, *God – Mystery – Diversity: Christian Theology in a Pluralistic World* (Minneapolis, MN: Fortress Press, 1996), p.99.

36 See Kaufman, *In the Beginning*, p.5.

37 Consult Ralph A. Alpher and Robert Herman, *Genesis of the Big Bang* (Oxford and New York: Oxford University Press, 2001).

38 See Kaufman, *In Face of Mystery*, pp.330–1.

39 See Kaufman, *In Face of Mystery*, pp.107 and 325–8.

40 See Kaufman, *In Face of Mystery*, p.xii.

41 See Kaufman, *In Face of Mystery*, pp.394–5.

42 Kaufman, *In Face of Mystery*, p.375.

43 Kaufman, *In Face of Mystery*, p.396.

44 Gordon D. Kaufman, *Jesus and Creativity* (Minneapolis, MN: Fortress Press, 2006), p.7. See p.6 as well.

45 Kaufman, *Jesus and Creativity*, p.15.

46 Consult Kaufman, *Theology for a Nuclear Age*, p.18.

sixteen

1 Padre J. Guadalupe Carney, *To Be a Revolutionary: An Autobiography* (San Francisco: Harper & Row, 1985), p.xv. The publication of this autobiography was arranged by friends after its author went missing.

2 Carney, *To Be a Revolutionary*, p.109. See too, pp.238–9.

3 Joseph and Eileen Connelly in an Epilogue to Carney's *To Be a Revolutionary*, p.446. The North Americans mentioned in the quotation are two CIA agents and a Honduran military officer whose names have been passed to the House Intelligence Committee of the United States Congress.

4 Gustavo Gutiérrez, 'Toward a Theology of Liberation' (July 1968), in Alfred T. Hennelly, ed., *Liberation Theology: A Documentary History* (Maryknoll, NY: Orbis Books, 1990/1997), pp.62–76 (pp.62–3). Henceforth, 'Liberation'.

5 Gutiérrez, 'Liberation', p.64. See the preceding page as well.

6 Gutiérrez, 'Liberation', p.64. Emphasis added.

7 Gutiérrez, 'Liberation', p.65.

8 Gutiérrez, 'Liberation', p.65.

9 Gutiérrez, 'Liberation', p.73.

10 Gutiérrez, 'Liberation', p.72.

11 Gutiérrez, 'Liberation', pp.72–3.

12 Johann Baptist Metz, *Glaube in Geschichte und Gesellschaft* (Mainz: Matthais-Grünewald-Verlag, 1977); trans. David Smith as *Faith in History and Society: Toward a Practical Fundamental Theology* (New York, NY: The Seabury Press, 1980). Consult the 'Excursus: Theology as biography', pp.219–28; and Johann Baptist Metz, *A Passion for God: The Mystical Dimension of Christianity*, trans. J. Matthew Ashley (Mahwah, NJ: Paulist Press, 1998), pp.1–5.

13 The biographical details which follow are taken for the most part from Robert McAfee Brown, *Gustavo Gutiérrez: An Introduction to Liberation Theology* (Maryknoll, NY: Orbis Books, 1990), p.26.

14 Deane William Ferm, *Profiles in Liberation: 36 Portraits of Third World Theologians* (Mystic, CT: Twenty-Third Publications, 1988), p.155.

15 Consult Gaspar Martinez, *Confronting the Mystery of God: Political, Liberation, and Public Theologies* (New York, NY; and London: Continuum, 2001), pp.89–91. See too the *World Development Report: 1999/2000* (New York, NY: Oxford University Press, 2000), pp.230–1 and 251.

16 Martinez, *Confronting*, p.98. See too, pp.92–6.

17 See Gustavo Gutiérrez, *The Density of the Present: Selected Writings* (Maryknoll, NY: Orbis Books, 1999), p.84.

18 David Batstone, Eduardo Mendieta, Lois Ann Lorentzen and Dwight N. Hopkins, eds, *Liberation Theologies, Postmodernity, and the Americas* (London and New York: Routledge, 1997), p.13.

19 See Gutiérrez, *The Density of the Present*, p.86.

20 Second General Conference of Latin American Bishops, 'The Church in the Present-Day Transformation of Latin America in the Light of the Council (August 26–September 6, 1968)', in Alfred T. Hennelly, ed., *Liberation Theology: A Documentary History* (Maryknoll, NY: Orbis Books, 1990/1997), pp.89–119 (p.116). Emphasis added. Hereafter, 'Medellín'.

21 Third General Conference of the Latin American Bishops, 'Evangelization in Latin America's Present and Future', in Hennelly, publication details provided in the previous note, pp.225–68 (p.254). Emphasis added.

22 'Medellín', reprinted in Hennelly, p.116.

23 Gustavo Gutiérrez, *A Theology of Liberation: History, Politics, and Salvation*, 2nd edn, trans. Caridad Inda and John Eagleson (Maryknoll, NY: Orbis Books, 1998), p.xx. Hereafter, *A Theology*.

24 Edward Schillebeeckx, 'La teología', in *Los católicos holandeses* (Bilbao: Desclée de Brower, 1970), quoted in Gutiérrez, *A Theology of Liberation*, p.8.

25 Gutiérrez, *A Theology*, p.4.

26 Consult, Gustavo Gutiérrez, *The Power of the Poor in History: Selected Writings* (Maryknoll,

NY: Orbis Books, 1983), p.vii; and *A Theology*, p.11.

27 Nicholas Lobkowicz, *Theory and Practice: History of a Concept from Aristotle to Marx* (New York, NY; and London: University Press of America, 1967), p.9.

28 Gutiérrez, *A Theology*, p.xxvii.

29 Gustavo Gutiérrez, *The God of Life*, trans. Matthew J. O'Connell (Maryknoll, NY: Orbis Books, 1991), p.1.

30 See Gutiérrez, *A Theology*, pp.xxv–xxvi.

31 Consult Gutiérrez, *A Theology*, pp.xxvv and 24.

32 D. Piachaud, 'Problems in the definition and measurement of poverty', *Journal of Social Policy*, 16 (1987), pp.147–64 (p.161). See too, Ruth Lester, *Poverty* (Cambridge: Polity, 2005), pp.1–2.

33 Hennelly, *Theology for a Liberating Church*, p.69.

34 Paul Freire, *Pedagogy of the Oppressed*, trans. Myra Bergman Ramos (London: Penguin Books, 1970), p.5.

35 Freire, *Pedagogy*, p.68.

36 Gutiérrez, *The Power of the Poor in History*, p.103.

37 Freire, *Pedagogy*, p.158.

38 See Hennelly, *Theology for a Liberating Church*, p.69.

39 Gustavo Gutiérrez, *Las Casas: In Search of the Poor Jesus Christ*, trans. Robert R. Barr (Maryknoll, NY: Orbis Books, 1993), p.47.

40 Alfred Hennelly, *Theology for a Liberating Church: The New Praxis of Freedom* (Washington, DC: Georgetown University Press, 1989), pp.28–9.

41 Clodovis Boff, *Theology and Praxis: Epistemological Foundations*, trans. Robert R. Carr (Maryknoll, NY: Orbis Books, 1987).

42 Leonardo Boff, *Church: Charism and Power*, trans. John W. Diercksmeier (New York, NY: Crossroad, 1992), p.47.

43 Boff, *Church*, p.22.

44 See Harvey Cox, *The Silencing of Leonardo Boff: The Vatican and the Future of Christianity* (London: Collins, 1989), pp.3–4.

45 Benedict XVI, *Deus Caritas Est* (London: Catholic Truth Society, 2006), pp.31–2.

46 James R. Brockman, *Romero: A Life* (Maryknoll, NY: Orbis Books, 2005), pp.244–55.

seventeen

1 Jean Genest, 'Uta Ranke-Heinemann', in Jean Genest, ed., *Penseurs et Apôtres du XXe Siècle* (Québec: Fides, 2001), pp.63–76 (p.63).

2 Uta Ranke-Heinemann, *Eunuchs for Heaven: The Catholic Church and Sexuality*, trans. John Brownjohn (London: André Deutsch, 1990), p.302.

3 Genest, 'Uta', p.63.

4 Uta Ranke-Heinemann, *Putting Away Childish Things: The Virgin Birth, the Empty Tomb, and Other Fairy Tales You Don't Need to Believe to Have a Living Faith*, trans. Peter Heinegg (New York: HarperSanFrancisco, 1994), p.ix.

5 Ranke-Heinemann, *Childish Things*, p.ix.

6 Ranke-Heinemann, *Childish Things*, pp.ix–x.

7 Rudolf Bultmann, *New Testament and Mythology: And Other Basic Writings*, ed. and trans. Schubert M. Ogden (Philadelphia, PA: Fortress Press, 1984), pp.39–40. The original German version was published in 1941. See too, David Fergusson, *Rudolf Bultmann* (London and New York: Continuum, 1992), p.112.

8 Ranke-Heinemann, *Childish Things*, p.x.

9 Ranke-Heinemann, *Eunuchs for Heaven*, p.23.

10 Phil Zuckerman and Christel Manning, 'Sex and Religion: An Introduction', in Christel Manning and Phil Zuckerman, eds, *Sex and Religion* (Belmont, CA: Thompson Wordsworth, 2005), pp.1–17 (pp.2–3).

11 Anthony F. LoPresti, 'Christianity', in Manning and Zucherman, *Sex and Religion*, pp.117–41 (p.122).

12 Ranke-Heinemann, *Eunuchs for Heaven*, pp.vii–x.

13 John Paul II, *Letter of the Supreme Pontiff to All the Bishops of the Church on the Occasion of Holy Thursday 1979* (London: Catholic Truth Society, 1979).

14 Quoted in Ranke-Heinemann, *Eunuchs for Heaven*, p.viii.

15 Thomas Aquinas, *Summa Theologiae*, I, q. 98, a. 2; Josef Fuchs, *Die Sexualethik des heiligen Thomas von Aquin* (Köln: J.P. Bachem, 1949);

Ranke-Heinemann, *Eunuchs for Heaven*, pp.170–1.

16 Ranke-Heinemann, *Eunuchs for Heaven*, p.208; Aquinas, *Summa Theologiae*, I, q. 51, a. 3 and 6.

17 Christine Gudorf, 'Sexuality: Profane or Sacred', in Maureen Fiedler and Linda Rabben, eds, *Rome Has Spoken: A Guide to Forgotten Papal Statements and How They Have Changed Through the Centuries* (New York: The Crossroad Publishing Company, 1998), pp.144–8 (pp.145–6).

18 Eugene C. Kennedy, 'The Problem That Has No Name', in Hans Küng and Leonard Swidler, eds, *The Church in Anguish: Has the Vatican Betrayed Vatican II* (San Francisco: Harper & Row, 1987), pp.300–5 (p.303); Rudolf Bell, *Holy Anorexia* (Chicago: The University of Chicago Press, 1985).

19 John Knox, 'Introduction' to the Acts of the Apostles and the Epistle to the Romans, *The Interpreter's Bible*, Vol. 9 (New York: Abingdon, 1954), p.355.

20 Louis Crompton, *Homosexuality and Civilization* (Cambridge, MA; and London: The Belknap Press of Harvard University Press, 2003), p.115.

21 Merry E. Wiesner-Hanks, *Christianity and Sexuality in the Early Modern World: Regulating Desire, Reforming Practice* (London: Routledge, 2000), p.31.

22 Wiesner-Hanks, *Christianity*, p.31; and Ranke-Heinemann, *Eunuchs for Heaven*, p.62.

23 Ranke-Heinemann, *Eunuchs for Heaven*, p.62.

24 Hera Cook, *The Long Sexual Revolution: English Women, Sex, and Contraception 1800–1975* (Oxford: Oxford University Press, 2004), p.11.

25 Cook, *The Long Sexual Revolution*, p.53.

26 Cook, *The Long Sexual Revolution*, pp.42, 137 and 268.

27 Charles E. Curran, *History and Contemporary Issues: Studies in Moral Theology* (New York: Continuum, 1996), p.124. See as well, Angus McClaren, *A History of Contraception from Antiquity to the Present Day* (Oxford: Basil Blackwell, 1990).

28 LoPresti, 'Sex and Christianity', p.122.

29 Bruce Bagemihl, *Biological Exuberance: Animal Homosexuality and Natural Diversity* (London: Profile Books, 1999), p.12.

30 See Augustine's *De Trinitate*, XII, VII, 12.

eighteen

1 John Hick, *An Autobiography* (Oxford: Oneworld, 2002/2005), pp.147–8.

2 Chester Gillis, 'John Harwood Hick: 1922-', in Donald W. Musser and Joseph L. Price, eds, *A New Handbook of Christian Theologians* (Nashville, TN: Abingdon Press, 1996), pp.221–8 (p.226). Gillis thinks it is 'likely' that Hick will be remembered in this way.

3 See Ninian Smart, *The World's Religions*, 2nd edn (Cambridge: Cambridge University Press, 1998); *Dimensions of the Sacred: An Anatomy of the World's Beliefs* (Berkeley, CA: University of California Press, 1999); and Keith Ward, *Why There Almost Certainly Is a God: Doubting Dawkins* (Oxford: Lion, 2008), p.6.

4 See in particular, Ninian Smart and Keith Ward, *Religion and Revelation* (Oxford: Clarendon Press, 1994); *Religion and Creation* (Oxford: Clarendon Press, 1996); *Religion and Human Nature* (Oxford: Clarendon Press, 1998); *Religion and Community* (Oxford: Clarendon Press, 2000); and *The Case for Religion* (Oxford: Oneworld, 2004).

5 Gillis, 'John Hick', p.221.

6 Hick, *Autobiography*, p.19.

7 Hick, *Autobiography*, p.19.

8 Hick, *Autobiography*, p.27. For details of Hick's primary and secondary education, see pp.14–18.

9 Hick, *Autobiography*, pp.34 and 78.

10 Hick, *Autobiography*, pp.36–65, 70–1, 83 and 88.

11 Hick, *Autobiography*, pp.100–1.

12 Hick, *Autobiography*, pp.124–9; esp. p.125.

13 Gillis, 'John Hick', p.221.

14 Hick, *An Autobiography*, pp.160–1.

15 John Hick, *An Interpretation of Religion: Human Responses to the Transcendent* (London: Macmillan Press, 1989), pp.233–51.

16 John Hick, *The Rainbow of Faiths: Critical Dialogues on Religious Pluralism* (London: SDCM Press, 1995); and *The Fifth Dimension: An Exploration of the Spiritual Realm* (Oxford: Oneworld, 1999). See too, John Hick, *God Has Many Names* (Philadelphia, PA: The

Westminster Press, 1980), ch. 6: 'Toward a Philosophy of Religious Pluralism'.

17 Maurice Wiles, in John Hick, ed., *The Myth of God Incarnate* (London: SCM Press, 1977), p.150. See pp.148–9 as well.

18 Hick, *Autobiography*, p.227.

19 John Hick, *The Metaphor of God Incarnate* (London: SCM Press, 1993), p.ix.

20 Quoted in Hick, *Autobiography*, p.228.

21 See Hick, *The Metaphor of God Incarnate*, p.ix.

nineteen

1 Tissa Balasuriya, *Mary and Human Liberation* (London: Mowbray, 1997). This work was originally published in 1990 in two issues of the journal *Logos* (Vol. 29: numbers 1 and 2, March/July, 1990).

2 Edmund Hill, 'Introductiory essay: The Balasuriya file', in Balasuriya, *Mary and Human Liberation*, pp.1–11 (p.2).

3 For a fuller account of Balasuriya's life and work, see Deane William Ferm, *Profiles in Liberation: 36 Portraits of Third World Theologians* (Mystic, Connecticut: Twenty-Third Publications, 1988), pp.81–6.

4 David B. Barrett, George T. Kurian and Todd M. Johnson, eds, *World Christian Encyclopedia: A Comparative Survey of Churches and Religions in the Modern World*, 2nd edn, Vol. 1 (Oxford and New York: Oxford University Press, 2001), pp.694–5.

5 Aloysius Pieris, *An Asian Theology of Liberation* (Edinburgh: T&T Clark, 1988).

6 See James Byrne, *Glory, Jest and Riddle: Religious Thought in the Enlightenment* (London: SCM, 1996), pp.11–12 and 129–30.

7 One should note that Balasuriya speaks anachronistically in saying that the patriarchal, Colonialist, First World of Christendom was 'capitalist'. Christendom before the eighteenth century was economically feudalistic, not capitalistic.

8 Ernst Cassier, *The Philosophy of the Enlightenment* (Princeton: Princeton University Press, 1951), p.141.

9 Congregation for the Doctrine of the Faith, 'Notification concerning the Text *Mary and Human Redemption* by Father Tissa Balasuriya, OMI' (Rome, 1997), p.5.

10 See Balasuriya, *Mary and Human Liberation*, pp.256–62, which reprints a letter Balasuriya wrote in self-defence to Cardinal Ratzinger on February 1997.

11 Quoted in Henri Fesquet, *The Drama of Vatican II: The Ecumenical Council June 1962–December 1965* (New York: Random House, 1967), p.215.

12 Tissa Balasuriya, 'Christ and the World Religions: An Asian Perspective', in Marc H. Ellis and Otto Maduro, eds, *The Future of Liberation Theology: Essays in Honour of Gustavo Gutiérrez* (Maryknoll, NY: Orbis Books, 1989), pp.337–45 (p.337).

twenty

1 Don Cupitt, *Is Nothing Sacred? The Non-Realist Philosophy of Religion, Selected Essays* (New York: Fordham University Press, 2002), p.98.

2 See Scott Cowdell, *Atheist Priest? Don Cupitt and Christianity* (London: SCM Press, 1988); and Stephen Ross White, *Don Cupitt and the Future of Christian Doctrine* (London: SCM Press, 1994).

3 Cupitt, *Is Nothing Sacred?*, p.101.

4 Cupitt, *Is Nothing Sacred?*, p.101.

5 Don Cupitt, *The Last Philosophy* (London: SCM Press, 1995), p.145.

6 Don Cupitt, *Above Us Only Sky: The Religion of Ordinary Life* (Santa Rosa, CA: Polebridge Press, 2008), p.4; *Life, Life* (Santa Rosa, CA: Polebridge Press, 2003); *The Way to Happiness* (Santa Rosa, CA: Polebridge Press, 2005), pp.2–3; *The New Religion of Life in Everyday Speech* (London: SCM Press, 1999); *The Meaning of It All in Everyday Speech* (London: SCM Press, 1999); *Kingdom Come in Everyday Speech* (London: SCM Press, 2000); and *Only Human* (London: SCM Press, 1985), p.xi.

7 Scott Cowdell, *Atheist Priest? Don Cupitt and Christianity* (London: SCM Press, 1988), p.xv.

8 Cupitt, *Is Nothing Sacred?*, p.x.

9 Cupitt, *Is Nothing Sacred?*, pp.x–xi.

10 See Cowdell, *Atheist Priest?*, pp.xvi–xviii.

11 Cupitt, *Is Nothing Sacred?*, pp.48–9.

12 Denis Pollard, 'Putnam, Hilary', in Stuart Brown Diané Collinson and Robert Wilkinson, eds, *Biographical Dictionary of*

Twentieth-Century Philosophers (London: Routledge, 1996), pp.638–9 (p.639).

13 Don Cupitt, *Life Lines* (London: SCM Press, 1986), p.58.

14 Don Cupitt, *Taking Leave of God* (London: SCM Press, 1980/1993), p.85.

15 Don Cupitt, *The Long-Legged Fly: A Theology of Language and Desire* (London: SCM Press, 1987/1995), p.13.

16 Don Cupitt, *Creation Out of Nothing* (London: SCM Press, 1990), p.194.

17 Don Cupitt, *Radical Theology* (Santa Rosa, CA: Polebridge, 2006), p.3. Consult too, Don Cupitt, *The Sea of Faith: Christianity in Change* (London: British Broadcasting Corporation, 1984).

18 Geoff Danaher, Tony Schirato and Jen Webb, *Understanding Foucault* (London: Sage Publications, 2000), p.7.

19 See Thomas Pavel, *The Feud of Language: A History of Structuralist Thought* (Oxford: Basil Blackwell, 1989); and Yishai Tobin, *Semiotics and Linguistics* (London and New York: Longman, 1990), ch. 1.

20 Terry Eagleton, *Literary Theory: An Introduction* (Oxford: Blackwell Publishers, 1996), p.112.

21 Don Cupitt, *Mysticism After Modernity* (Malden, MA; and Oxford: Blackwell Publishers, 1998), p.46.

22 Don Cupitt, *The Great Questions of Life* (Santa Rosa, CA: Polebridge Press, 2005), p.22. See too, Don Cupitt, *The Old Creeds and the New* (London: SCM Press, 2006).

23 Don Cupitt, *After All: Religion without Alienation* (London: SCM Press, 1994), p.16.

24 Don Cupitt, *Impossible Loves* (Santa Rosa, CA: Polebridge Press, 2007), p.ix.

25 Don Cupitt, *Solar Ethics* (London: SCM Press, 1995), p.50.

26 Don Cupitt, *Radicals and the Future of the Church* (London: SCM Press, 1989), p.23. Consult as well, Don Cupitt, *Reforming Christianity* (Santa Rosa, CA: Polebridge Press, 2001).

27 Cupitt, *Above Us Only Sky*, pp.1–2, 33 and 131.

28 Cupitt, *Is Nothing Sacred?*, p.37. See p.29 as well.

29 Don Cupitt, *The New Christian Ethics* (London: SCM Press, 1988), ch. 2; and

Philosophy's Own Religion (London: SCM Press, 2000), p.16.

30 Cupitt, *The Great Questions of Life*, p.40.

31 Philip Toynbee, *Part of a Journey: An Autobiographical Journal 1977–1979* (London: Collins, 1981), p.279.

32 Claude Welsch, *Unsere postmoderne Moderne* (Weinheim: Acta Humaniora, 1987), p.12.

33 Charles Jencks, *What is Post-Modernism?* (London: Academy/New York: St Martin's Press, 1986), p.8.

34 For the distinction between postmodernism and postmodernity, see David Lyon, *Postmodernity* (Buckingham: Open University Press, 1995), p.7.

35 Albert Borgman, *Crossing the Postmodern Divide* (Chicago and London: University of Chicago Press, 1992), p.2.

36 Terrence W. Tilley and others, *Postmodern Theologies: The Challenge of Religious Diversity* (Maryknoll, NY: Orbis Books, 1995), p.x.

37 A.K.M. Adam, *What Is Postmodern Biblical Criticism?* (Minneapolis, MN: Fortress Press, 1995), p.1.

38 Marck C. Taylor and Esa Saarinen, *Imagologies: Media Philosophy* (New York: Routledge, 1994), Telepolitics, p.2 (no conventional pagination).

39 Jean-François Lyotard, *La Condition Postmoderne* (Paris: Les Éditions de Minuit, 1979).

40 Jean-François Lyotard, *The Postmodern Condition: A Report on Knowledge* (Minneapolis: University of Minnesota Press, 1993), p.24.

41 Adam, *What Is Postmodern Biblical Criticism?*, p.5.

42 Jean Baudrillard, *The Gulf War Did Not Take Place* (Sydney: Power Publications, 1995), p.62.

43 Ziauddin Sardar, *Postmodernism and the Other: The New Imperialism of Western Culture* (London: Pluto Press, 1998), p.10.

44 Adam, *What Is Postmodern Biblical Criticism?*, p.5.

45 See Gianni Vattimo, *The End of Modernity: Nihilism and Hermeneutics in Post-Modern Culture* (London: Polity Press, 1988).

46 Pauline Marie Rosenau, *Post-Modernism and the Social Sciences: Insights, Inroads, and*

Intrusions (Princeton, New Jersey: Princeton University Press, 1992), p.6. See too, Gerald Graff, *Literature Against Itself* (Chicago: The University of Chicago Press, 1979), pp.32–3.

47 Don Cupitt, *Emptiness and Brightness* (Santa Rosa, CA: Polebridge Press, 2001), p.117.

48 Don Cupitt, *What is a Story?* (London: SCM Press, 1991), p.30.

49 Don Cupitt, *After God: The Future of Religion* (London: Weidenfeld & Nicolson, 1997), p.89.

50 Don Cupitt, *The Time Being* (London: SCM Press, 1992), p.109.

51 Don Cupitt, *The Meaning of the West: An Apologia for Secular Christianity* (London: SCM Press, 2008), pp.3–4.

twenty-one

1 This story is recounted by Isabel Apawo Phiri and Sarojini Nadar in '"Treading Softly but Firmly": African Women, Religion, Religion, and Health', in Phiri and Nadar, eds, *African Women, Religion, and Health: Essays in Honour of Mercy Amba Ewudziwa Oduyoye* (Maryknoll, New York: Orbis Books, 2006), pp.1–16 (p.1).

2 Mercy Amba Oduyoye, *Daughters of Anowa: African Patriarchy* (Maryknoll, New York: Orbis Books, 1995), p.3.

3 Mercy Amba Oduyoye, *Beads and Strands, Reflections of an African Woman on Christianity in Africa* (Maryknoll, New York: Orbis Books, 2004), pp.54–5 and 7.

4 For the details on Mozambique in this chapter, see Steven M. Beaudoin, *Poverty in World History* (London and New York: Routledge, 2007), pp.1 and 113.

5 Oduyoye, *Beads and Stands*, p.xi; and Elizabeth Amoah, 'Preface', in Phiri and Nadar, *African Women*, pp.xvii–xxii (p.xviii).

6 David B. Barrett, George T. Kurian and Todd M. Johnson, eds, *World Christian Encyclopedia: A Comparative Survey of Churches and Religion in the Modern World*, 2nd edn, Vol. 1 (Oxford and New York: Oxford University Press, 2001), pp.307–8.

7 Amoah, 'Preface', p.xviii.

8 Oduyoye, *Deads*, p.57.

9 Amoah, 'Preface', pp.xviii–xix.

10 Amoah, 'Preface', p.xix.

11 Musimbi R.A. Kanyoro, 'Beads and Strands: Threading More Beads in the Story of the Circle', in Phiri and Nadar, *African Women*, pp.19–42 (p.20).

12 For the biographical details in the previous four paragraphs, see Oduyoye, *Beads and Strands*, pp.xii–xiii and Amoah, 'Preface', pp.xx–xi.

13 See Oduyoye, *Beads*, p.xii.

14 Oduyoye, *Beads*, p.39.

15 Mercy A. Oduyoye, 'Reflections from a Third World Woman's Perspective: Women's Experience in Liberation Theologies', in Ursula King, ed., *Feminist Theology from the Third World: A Reader* (London and Maryknoll, NY: SPCK and Orbis Books, 1994), pp.23–4.

16 Oduyoye, *Beads*, p.22.

17 Oduyoye, *Beads*, p.5.

18 Oduyoye, *Daughters*, p.4.

19 Oduyoye, *Daughters*, p.5.

20 Oduyoye, *Daughters*, p.159.

21 Oduyoye, *Daughters*, p.159.

22 Mercy Amba Oduyoye, 'Three Cardinal Issues in Africa', in Robert J. Schreiter, ed., *Mission in the Third Millennium* (Maryknoll, New York: Orbis Books, 2001), pp.40–52 (p.48).

23 Oduyoye, 'Three Cardinal Issues', p.48.

24 Oduyoye, *Daughters*, p.5.

25 Oduyoye, *Beads*, pp.14–15.

26 Oduyoye, *Beads*, p.55. Emphasis added.

27 Oduyoye, *Beads*, p.13.

28 Oduyoye, *Beads*, p.13.

29 All quotations in this paragraph are from Oduyoye, *Beads and Strands*, pp.24–5.

30 Oduyoye, *Beads*, p.54.

twenty-two

1 The Rainbow Spirit Elders, *Rainbow Spirit Theology: Towards an Australian Aboriginal Theology*, 2nd edn (Hindmarsh, ATF Press, 2007; 1st edn, 1997), p.3. Hereafter, The Elders, *Rainbow Spirit*.

2 The Elders, *Rainbow Spirit*, p.3.

3 Rod Horsfield, 'Upside Down Theology: A Trinitarian Theology for the Antipodes', in Winifred Wing Han Lamb and Ian Barns, eds,

God Down Under: Theology in the Antipodes (Adelaide: ATF Press, 2003), pp.xvii–xxvii (p.xvii).

4 See Deborah Bird Rose, *Dingo Make Us Human: Life and Land in an Aboriginal Australian Culture* (London: Cambridge University Press, 1992), p.125.

5 Christian Nichols, 'God and Country: An Analysis of Gali Yalkirriwuy's Three Wise Men', in Rebecca Pannell and Wes Campbell, eds, *Beyond Idols and Icons: The Search for a Christian Imagination in Australia* (Hindmarsh: Australian Theological Forum, 2002), pp.84–94 (pp.84–5).

6 Louis Crompton, *Homosexuality and Civilization* (Cambridge, MA; and London: The Belknap Press of Harvard University Press, 2003), p.1.

7 John Hilary Martin discusses such visits in his chapter, 'Aboriginal Dreaming as a Text', in *Wisdom for Life*, ed. Michael A. Kelly and Mark A. O'Brien (Adelaide: ATF Press, 2005), pp.189–207 (p.189).

8 Consult David Leeming, *Myth: A Biography of Belief* (Oxford and New York: Oxford University Press, 2002).

9 David B. Barrett, George T. Kurian and Todd M. Johnson, eds, *World Christian Encyclopedia: A Comparative Survey of Churches and Religions in the Modern World*, 2nd edn, Vol. 1 (Oxford and New York: Oxford University Press), pp.694–5.

10 The Elders, *Rainbow Spirit*, pp.vii and ix.

11 The Elders, *Rainbow Spirit*, p.6. See pp.4–5 as well.

12 The Elders, *Rainbow Spirit*, p.14.

13 The Elders, *Rainbow Spirit*, pp.14 and 29.

14 John Hilary Martin, 'Aboriginal Dreaming as Text', pp.195–6. See too, The Elders, *Rainbow Spirit*, pp.xi–xii; and W.E.H. Stanner, *White Man Got No Dreaming* (Canberra: Australian University Press, 1979), esp. pp.24–5.

15 The longer version of this Dreaming is reproduced by John Hilary Martin, 'Aboriginal Dreaming as a Text', pp.196–8.

16 The Elders, *Rainbow Spirit*, pp.15–28.

17 The Elders, *Rainbow Spirit*, p.13.

18 The Elders, *Rainbow Spirit*, pp.29–41.

19 The Elders, *Rainbow Spirit*, p.4.

20 See The Elders, *Rainbow Spirit*, p.48.

21 Henry Reynolds, *Dispossession* (Sydney: Allen & Unwin, 1989), p.22.

22 The Elders, *Rainbow Spirit*, p.61. See pp.58–9 as well.

23 The Elders, *Rainbow Spirit*, p.67.

24 Consult in particular Sean Freyne, *Jesus, A Galilean Jew: A New Reading of the Jesus-Story* (London and New York: T&T Clark International, 2004), ch. 2: 'Jesus and the Ecology of Galilee'; and Halvor Moxnes, *Putting Jesus in His Place: A Radical Vision of Household and Kingdom* (Louisville, KY; and London: Westminster John Knox Press, 2003).

25 Mirimba Ani, *Yurugu: An African Centred Critique of European Cultural Thought and Behavior* (Trenton, NJ: Africa World Press, 1994), pp.10–11.

26 Winifred Wing Han Lamb and Ian Barns, eds (Adelaide, ATF Press, 2003).

twenty-three

1 Dan Smith, *The State of the World Atlas* (Brighton: Earthscan, 2008), p.114.

2 Jürgen Moltmann, *A Broad Place: An Autobiography*, trans. Margaret Kohl (London: SCM Press, 2007), pp.50 and 107.

3 Peter Hünermann, 'Evangelization of Europe? Observations on a Church in Peril', in Robert J. Schreiter, *Mission in the Third Millennium* (Maryknoll, New York: Orbis Books, 2001), pp.157–80 (pp.158–60); Jan Kerkhofs, ed., *Europe without Priests* (London: SCM Press, 1995); Callum G. Brown, *The Death of Christian Britain* (London and New York: Routledge, 2001); *Religion and Society in Twentieth-Century Britain* (Edinburgh: Pearson, 2006); Hugh McLeod and Werner Ustorf, *The Decline of Christendom in Western Europe, 1750–2000* (Cambridge: Cambridge University Press, 2003); and Hugh McLeod, *The Religious Crisis of the 1960s* (Oxford: Oxford University Press, 2007).

4 Julia Duin, *Quitting Church: Why the Faithful Are Fleeing and What to Do about It* (Grand Rapids, MI: BakerBooks, 2008), p.37. See too, Steve Bruce, *God is Dead: Secularization in the West* (Oxford and Malden, MA: Blackwell Publishers, 2002), ch. 11.

5 Diarmuid O'Donovan, *The Atlas of World Health: Mapping the Challenges and Causes of Disease* (Brighton: Earthscan, 2008), p.15.

6 See V.T. Rajshekar, *Development Redefined* (Bangalore: Dalit Sahitya Akademy, 2006), p.3.

7 Edward Schillebeeckx, *Christ: The Experience of Jesus as Lord*, trans. John Bowden (New York, NY: Crossroad, 1981), pp.788–9.

8 Smith, *State of the World*, pp.116, 159 and 165.

9 Uta Ranke-Heinemann, *Eunuchs for Heaven: The Catholic Church and Sexuality*, trans. John Brownjohn (London: André Deutsch, 1990), pp.151–5.

10 Hans Küng. *Infallible : An Enquiry*, trans. Eric Mosbacker (London: Collins, 1971; German original, *Unfehlbar?*, 1970), pp.1–2.

11 'The Dogmatic Constitution on the Church', section 21, published in Austin Flannery, *Vatican Council II: Constitutions, Decrees, Declarations* (Northport, New York: Costello Publishing Company; and Dublin, Dominican Publications, 1996), pp.28–9.

12 Consult Richard P. McBrien, *Report on the Church: Catholicism After Vatican II* (New York: HarperSanFrancisco, 1992), p.22.

13 Pierre Pierrard, *Jacques Gaillot* (Paris: Desclée de Brower, 2002); and Jacques Gaillot, *Liberté et Exclusion: suivi d'une interview avec Daniel Laprès* (Québec: Éditions Fides, 1996).

14 For an impression of the proliferation of denominations, see Peter Day, *A Dictionary of Christian Denominations* (London and New York: Continuum, 2003).

15 Benedict XVI, *Deus Caritas Est* (London: Catholic Truth Society, 2006), pp.31–2.

16 Diarmuid, *The Atlas of Health*, p.29.

17 Erik Millstone and Tim Lang, *The Atlas of Food: Who Eats What, Where, and Why*, 2nd edn (Brighton: Earthscan, 2008), p.26.

18 United Nations World Food Programme, *World Hunger Series 2007: Hunger and Health* (London: Earthscan, 2007), pp.19, 44 and 47.

19 Henry Veltmeyer, *Illusion or Opportunity: Civil Society and the Quest for Social Change* (Halifax, Fernwood Publishing, 2007), p.29.

20 Veltmeyer, *Illusion or Opportunity*, p.13.

21 *World Hungers Series 2007*, pp.12 and 21.

22 Smith, *State of the World*, p.11; and *Human Development Report 2007/2008: Fighting Climate Change: Human Solidarity in a Divided World* (Houndmills and New York, NY: Palgrave Macmillan, 2007), p.25.

23 See Patrick Hossay, *Unsustainable: A Primer for Global Environmental and Social Justice* (London and New York: Zed Books, 2006), pp.14–19.

24 Gary Gardner and Thomas Prugh, 'Seeing the Sustainable Economy', in Worldwatch Institute, *State of the World 2008: Ideas and Opportunities for Sustainable Economies*, 25th edn (London: Earthscan, 2008), pp.3–17 (p.3).

25 See Hossay, *Unsustainable*, p.13.

26 Jeremy Seabrook, *The No-Nonsense Guide to World Poverty*, 2nd edn (Oxford: New Internationalist Publications, 2007), p.27.

27 Smith, *State of the World*, p.38.

28 Veltmeyer, *Illusion or Opportunity*, p.28.

29 Smith, *State of the World*, p.43.

30 Veltmeyer, *Illusion or Opportunity*, p.28.

31 John Pilger, *Hidden Agendas* (London: Vintage, 1999), p.59–6.

32 See Pilger, *Hidden Agendas*, p.60.

33 Timothy Gorringe, *Fair Shares: Ethics and the Global Economy* (London: Thames and Hudson, 1999), pp.40–1.

a guide to further reading

Baum, Gregory, ed., *The Twentieth Century: A Theological Overview* (Maryknoll, NY: Orbis Books, 1999).

Beeson, Trevor, *Rebels and Reformers: Christian Renewal in the Twentieth Century* (London: SCM Press, 1999).

Braaten, Carl E., and Robert W. Jenson, eds, *A Map of Twentieth-Century Theology: Readings from Karl Barth to Religious Pluralism* (Minneapolis, MN: Fortress Press, 1995).

Brown, Callum G., *Religion and Society in Twentieth-Century Britain* (Harlow: Pearson Longman, 2006).

Clifford, Anne M., *Introducing Feminist Theology* (Maryknoll, NY: Orbis Books, 2001).

Espin, Orlando O., and James B. Nickoloff, eds, *An Introductory Dictionary of Theology and Religious Studies* (Dublin: The Columba Press, 2007).

Hennelly, Alfred T., *Liberation Theologies: The Global Pursuit of Justice* (Mystic, CT: Twenty-Third Publications, 1997).

Herzog II, William R., *Prophet and Teacher: An Introduction to the Historical Jesus* (Louisville, KY: Westminster John Knox Press, 2005).

Hodgson, Peter C., *Liberal Theology: A Radical Vision* (Minneapolis, MN: Fortress Press, 2007).

Howard, Michael, and Wm. Roger Louis, eds, *The Oxford History of the Twentieth Century* (Oxford: Oxford University Press, 2002).

Kerr, Fergus, *Twentieth-Century Catholic Theologians: From Neoscholasticism to Nuptual Mysticism* (Malden, MA/Oxford, UK: Blackwell Publishing, 2007).

Larsen, Timothy, and Daniel J. Treier, eds, *The Cambridge Companion to Evangelical Theology* (Cambridge: Cambridge University Press, 2007).

Livingston, James C., and Francis Schüssler, with Sarah Coakley and James H. Evans, Jr, *Modern Christian Thought: The Twentieth Century*, 2nd edn (Minneapolis, MN: Fortress Press, 2006).

McBrien, Richard P., *The Church: The Evolution of Catholicism* (New York, NY: HarperOne, 2008).

McCarthy, Timothy G., *The Catholic Tradition: The Church in the Twentieth Century*, 2nd edn (Chicago, IL: Loyola Press, 1998).

McLeod, Hugh, *The Religious Crisis of the 1960s* (Oxford and New York: Oxford University Press, 1997).

Morris, Jeremy, *The Church in the Modern Age* (London and New York: I.B. Tauris, 2007).

Musser, Donald W., and Joseph L. Price, eds, *A New Handbook of Christian Theologians* (Nashville: Abingdon Press, 1996).

O'Malley, John W., *What Happened at Vatican II* (Cambridge, MA; and London: The Belknap Press of Harvard University Press, 2008).

Overy, Richard, *Collins Atlas of 20th Century History* (London: Collins Books, 2005).

Rieger, Joerg, ed., *Opting for the Margins: Postmodernity and Liberation in Christian Theology* (Oxford and New York: Oxford University Press, 2003).

Schoof, T.M., *A Survey of Catholic Theology: 1800–1970* (Paramus, NJ; and New York, NY: Paulist Newman Press, 1970).

Schwarz, Hans, *Theology in a Global Context: The Last Two Hundred Years* (Grand Rapids, MI/Cambridge, UK: William B. Eerdmans Publishing Co., 2005).

Sell, Alan P.F., *Nonconformist Theology in the Twentieth Century* (Milton Keynes: Paternoster Press, 2006).

Sobrino, Jon, *The Eye of the Needle: No Salvation Outside the Poor: A Utopian-Prophetic Essay*, trans. Dinah Livingston (London: Darton, Longman and Todd, 2008).

Taylor, Mark C., *After God* (Chicago and London: The University of Chicago Press, 2007).

Thomas, Linda E., ed., *Living Stones in the Household of God: The Legacy and Future of Black Theology* (Minneapolis, MN: Fortress Press, 2004).

Tilley, Terrence W., *History, Theology and Faith: Dissolving the Modern Problematic* (Maryknoll, NY: Orbis Books, 2004).

Ward, Keith, *Re-Thinking Christianity* (Oxford: Oneworld, 2007).

Weber, Günter, *I Believe, I Doubt: Notes on Christian Experience*, trans. John Bowden (London: SCM Press, 1998).

Wilson, John E., *Introduction to Modern Theology: Trajectories in the German Tradition* (Louisville, KY; and London: Westminster John Knox Press, 2007).

index